"A PROSE VOICE OF RARE TIMBRE . . . A BOOK WORTH DEVOURING."
—*Washington Post*

Joan Baez's autobiography is more than a wonderfully written portrait of one of the most celebrated performers and political activists of our time; it is a magnificent inside view of our turbulent recent history by a gifted woman who has survived and grown with the times. Her emotions are frankly revealed as she describes falling for the then undiscovered Bob Dylan, and her marriage and divorce from war-resister David Harris, with whom she had a son. On every page she makes us feel that we are there—at the center of the burgeoning folk music scene in the 1960s; in the South fighting for civil rights with Martin Luther King, Jr.; visiting the killing fields of Cambodia; in Poland feeling the inspiration of Solidarity. Whether she is reliving the instant stardom that made her a *Time* cover story when she was just 21, or discussing her militant activism for causes like human rights and disarmament, the openness and vulnerability that have touched us in her music, and the passion and integrity that have marked her politics, radiate from every page. Joan Baez is an extraordinary woman who has led an eventful and fascinating life, and this intimate and fascinating book—illustrated with photos and drawings—lets us share it.

"What sustains and brightens is a compelling bluntness and candor."
—*The Wall Street Journal*

"Clear, precise, lovely and honest as her voice . . . chronicles Baez's life with intense immediacy . . . wonderfully appealing. She spares no one in her acid observations, least of all herself."
—*The Minnesota Daily*

# AND A VOICE TO SING WITH

A MEMOIR

## JOAN BAEZ

A PLUME BOOK

**NEW AMERICAN LIBRARY**

NEW YORK AND SCARBOROUGH, ONTARIO

PLUME TRADEMARK REG. U.S. PAT. OFF. AND FOREIGN COUNTRIES
REGISTERED TRADEMARK—MARCA REGISTRADA
HECHO EN CHICAGO, U.S.A.

SIGNET, SIGNET CLASSIC, MENTOR, ONYX, PLUME, MERIDIAN
and NAL BOOKS are published *in the United States* by NAL PENGUIN INC.,
1633 Broadway, New York, New York 10019,
*ini Canada* by The New American Library of Canada Limited,
81 Mack Avenue, Scarborough, Ontario M1L 1M8

Library of Congress Cataloging-in-Publication Data

Baez, Joan.
    And a voice to sing with.

    1. Baez, Joan.   2. Singers—United States—Biography.
I. Title.
[ML420.B114A3   1988]     784.4'924   [B]     88-5201
ISBN 0-452-26094-9 (pbk.)

First Plume Printing, July, 1988

1  2  3  4  5  6  7  8  9

PRINTED IN THE UNITED STATES OF AMERICA

*FOR GABE*

# CONTENTS

CONTENTS

While you and i have lips and voices which
are for kissing and to sing with
who cares if some oneeyed son of a bitch
invents an instrument to measure Spring with?

e.e. cummings

# AND A VOICE
# TO SING WITH

# PREFACE

*God respects me when I work. He loves me when I sing.*

Tagore

I was born gifted. I can speak of my gifts with little or no modesty, but with tremendous gratitude, precisely because they are gifts, and not things which I created, or actions about which I might be proud.

My greatest gift, given to me by forces which confound genetics, environment, race, or ambition, is a singing voice. My second greatest gift, without which I would be an entirely different person with an entirely different story to tell, is a desire to share that voice, and the bounties it has heaped upon me, with others. From that combination of gifts has developed an immeasurable wealth—a wealth of adventures, of friendships, and of plain joys.

Over a period of nearly three decades I have sung from hundreds of concert stages, all over the world: Eastern and Western Europe, Japan, Australia, Northern Africa, South, Central, and North America, Canada, the Middle East, the Far East. I sang in the bomb shelters of Hanoi during the Vietnam War; in the Laotian refugee camps in Thailand; in the makeshift settlements of the boat people in Malaysia. I have had the privilege of meeting some extraordinary citizens of the world, both renowned and unsung: Andrei Sakharov and Elena Bonner; The Mothers of the Disappeared in Argentina,

Mairead Corrigan in Belfast, Bertrand Russell, Cezar Chavez, Orlando Letelier; Bishop Tutu, Lech Walesa; Presidents Corazon Aquino, François Mitterrand, Jimmy Carter, and Giscard d'Estaing; the King of Sweden. Through Amnesty International I have met political prisoners who have endured repression and tortures under both right- and left-wing governments and who have astounded me with their humor, good cheer, and courage. And, of course, Martin Luther King, Jr., more than any other public figure helped to solidify my ideas and inspired me to act upon them.

The music business has brought me into contact with some of the most creative artists of our time, from Bob Dylan and the Beatles to Luciano Pavarotti. But the last six or seven years have been difficult for me musically, though I enjoy a distant respect from the music industry. But distant respect does not pay the bills. My music has suffered more of an identity crisis in the United States than in the other countries where I am known, and as a result I have often felt something of a dissident in my own land.

My personal life has also been complicated—and public—though I am beginning to find more of a sense of peace and self-acceptance than I ever thought possible. Once I wanted to be married and have heaps of kids scrambling around me, licking cake mix off eggbeaters and riding Saint Bernards through the kitchen while I cooked stew over an open fire. Alas, those images bore no relation to my areas of competence, and since my marriage to David Harris dissolved in January of 1974 I have lived mainly alone, with occasional romantic interludes, the best of which are magical and splendidly impractical. The last was with a Frenchman half my age who entered my life on horseback one misty afternoon and kept my spirit aglow for four years. My art, work, family and friends, my son Gabe, and a curious relationship with God remain the sustaining forces in my life.

Through all these changes my social and political views have remained astoundingly steadfast. I have been true to the principles of nonviolence, developing a stronger and stronger aversion to the ideologies of both the far right and the far left and a deeper sense of rage and sorrow over the suffering they continue to produce all over the world. Here at home the current trends toward "new patriotism," Ramboism, and narcissism, and the emphasis on feeling good about oneself threaten our cultural, spiritual, moral, and artistic values and preclude any honest perception of or caring about the world beyond our borders. I have long worked for Amnesty International and am currently president of a human rights organization called Humanitas, which attempts to initiate projects on both human rights and disarmament. And, oddly enough, my own business, the music business, has taken some of the first steps—Live Aid and some of its follow-ups—out of what I call the "ashes and silence" of the 1980s.

I am writing this book in the kitchen of my home in California. Gabe is living with me for his last year of high school. I have loved writing, especially in the winter, early in the morning, sitting with my back to the fireplace at a card table bearing my word processor, the only sign of the space age present in this rustic room, or this rustic house, for that matter. As I put the finishing touches on this work, I'm also preparing to go into the studio and make a record for the first time in six years. The roses outside the window have at least one last bloom to come before winter. It has taken me two years to trace these threads of my personal, political, spiritual, and musical lives—how they came together and how they fell apart, depending on the times and the circumstances. I've told about the people I've loved. I've told all as I have remembered it, knowing full well that, like everybody else, I am blessed with a selective memory and, perhaps more so than some, a vivid imagination. I have recorded these facts, first of all, because I have led an extraordinary life and want to tell people about it; and second, because I am only forty-five years old, active, creative, in vocal prime, and do not wish to be relegated to obscurity, antiquity, or somebody else's dewy-eyed nostalgia about days gone by. Third, and most important, I am recording them for myself, to take a hard look back before facing forward in these most bizarre of times.

___ *PART*
*ONE*

# "THE KINGDOM
OF CHILDHOOD"

# 1

# "MY MEMORY'S EYE"

We learned everything from her, little by little, year by year, long before washing machines, dryers, dishwashers, Quik ovens, new improved vacuum cleaners, and drip-dry clothes. My mother was the hen; my father was the rooster. We were little chicks, we were little helpers. When we came to supper at six o'clock in the evening, my mother would take off her apron and hang it over a chair. She would wipe her hands dry on a kitchen towel, push her hair back a little, sit down at her end of the table, take a long breath in and let out a sigh. She was very beautiful.

My mother, Joan Bridge, was born in Edinburgh, Scotland, the second of two sisters, and raised in the United States. Her mother died when she was only two. Her father was a kindhearted, liberal, intellectual Episcopalian minister who fell in love with domineering women. Mother's sister Pauline, older by two years, was physically abused by the two women their father married after her mother died. But somehow Pauline grew up looking like a Renoir painting. She was fair-haired, fair-skinned, and full-bosomed, with dreamy but infinitely sad eyes. She would never condemn the mistreatment she had endured, but was endlessly forgiving, paying for her Christian ethics with years of pain and a deep and lifelong melancholy. Mother didn't get battered so much as she got neglected. She resisted the ferocity of the stepmothers to the point of defending herself physically. Mother was a dark beauty, thin, angular, vampy. She did not know she was beautiful.

Pauline took refuge in books, nature, dance, poetry, and intellectual companionship with her father. Mother took refuge in summer theater, in the woods, at the houses of friends where she would run to hide, and later in Oakwood School, which appears for a short while like a soothing balm in the dark pages of her childhood. And the sisters took refuge in each other.

At eighteen Pauline married a handsome, wavy-haired artist and settled in an artists' community in Maine. Their father, leaving two more children, was dying of a liver ailment. Mother was living with a succession of foster mothers who cared for her, bought her nice clothes, and tried to bring some normality into her shipwrecked childhood. Mother talks of those days as of a foggily recalled dream. She had no idea of what she would do with her life. She was a leaf in the wind, floating this way and that. With no driving ambition or encouragement from the foster mothers, she did not pursue the idea of becoming an actress. She was catching her breath, wondering what would befall her next, when she met my father.

She was attending a dance at Drew University, on the arm of a young suitor, when (gazing off from the punch bowl, I have always imagined) she spotted a terribly handsome young man—dark-skinned, with thick wavy black hair and perfectly white flashing teeth. He was sitting on the school steps amidst a gaggle of attentive and twittering girls, making airplane noises and dive-bombing motions with his hands. Spotting my mother beyond his ring of admirers, he winked at her. She was overcome with shyness and hurried off to control a boiling hot blush.

This young man who was to become my father came to this country at the age of two from Puebla, Mexico. His father had left the Catholic faith to become a Methodist minister and now chose to work with the underprivileged in the States. Albert developed into a bright, conscientious, attractive, inventive, hardworking kid with a deep respect for his parents and for God, and an insatiable curiosity about everything, especially the construction of crystal set radios. He lived in Brooklyn, and when he was nineteen, preached in his father's church there. I remember visiting his parents in the same dark and spooky brownstone where he grew up. The temperature dropped fifteen degrees as you walked from the front doorstep into the pitch black corridor, which smelled damp and mysterious and strangely like oatmeal. His father smelled of Palmolive soap and had a cozy chuckle, and his mother frightened us considerably because she was very stern. My father started off intending to become a minister, too, but he changed his mind in favor of mathematics and finally physics.

Albert Baez was working his way through school when he met my mother. He drove a Model-T which he had personally rebuilt into a race car.

It was a year after the airplane noises and the wink before Al Baez actually took Joan Bridge out on a date, but the foster mothers had long since been picking out wedding dresses. It must have been like a fairy tale to my mother, the idea of getting married and having a place of her own. Most of all she wanted to have children. I know that she wanted girls. She got three of them: Pauline Thalia, born October 4, 1939, in Orange, New Jersey; Joan Chandos, born January 9, 1941, in Staten Island, New York; and Mimi Margharita, born April 30, 1945, in Stanford, California. Before Mimi came we had moved to Stanford so my father could work on his master's degree in mathematics. We lived in a beautiful little house across from an open field of hay which was piled into small hills after it was cut. There is a picture of my mother and father straddling their bicycles in front of that field, young and smiling, the sun in their eyes, the wind blowing wisps of hair from my mother's braids, and across my father's forehead.

Mother grew sweet peas in our backyard on strings that stretched from the tops of the fence slats down to sticks placed firmly in the earth. I see the neighbor's mulberry tree whose branches hung down so low you could duck right under them and hide against the trunk, peeking out and staining your mouth and cheeks and hands with mulberry juice. I see our rabbit in his cage over the lettuce rows in the vegetable garden, and the clothesline filled with sheets and tiny dresses, all stuck on the line with wooden clothespins. I see the trees lining the sidewalk in the front yard which bloomed in masses of deep pink in the spring. I would pin clumps of blossoms to my dresses and put them in my hair. I recall one evening when my mother and father were making a fuss over me, holding me up to the stairwell window, exclaiming at the night with its sliver of a moon and scattered twinkling stars. I didn't know which of them to love the most, and so I hugged my father, and then my mother, and then leaned back over to my father again. Springtime in my chest, and a lucky star on my forehead. That's what I had in our first California house.

After Mimi's birth the place was too small, so my mother and father got a job as house parents at the progressive Peninsula School in the same town.

I didn't want to go to kindergarten because the boys pulled up my skirt, so I began to wear overalls. I behaved badly in class and was put into the cloakroom during milk and graham crackers for clowning and being disruptive. My only real goal was to get home by midmorning and be with my mother.

Since she lived on the property, my escapes were easy enough, and back in her room I comforted myself listening to Uncle Don's Nursery Rhymes, having lovely tea parties with my dollies, scribbling in my Three Little Piggies book, or helping Mother with chores. Outside I played alone, climbing oak trees, picking and eating the Miner's lettuce which grew in abundance at the base of the redwood trees, taking my Raggedy Ann for walks.

A short time later Tia (our favorite aunt, Pauline) left her husband and moved out West with her two children. She and my parents bought a huge house on Glenwood Avenue where we could rent out rooms to boarders—as many as five at a time—while my father student-taught and continued to work toward his Ph.D. We had college kids, Chinese scholars, sailors, writers, bus drivers, wanderers, and a cellist who played so beautifully that Mother would click off the vacuum cleaner and stand in the hallway to listen, and I would sit outside his door trying to decide whether to become a cellist in the symphony or to grow long dainty nails.

By age five I was vaguely aware that little children in other parts of the world went to bed hungry every night. I also knew that ants ran around in circles dragging their broken legs if you stepped on one by mistake. I assumed that they were in pain. I imagined that my baby sister, Mimi, hurt when she screamed, but I didn't care about her the way I cared about the ants and bugs. I was in the practice of pinching the neighbor's baby. I'd wait till the other kids were out of sight and then move in on the fat little diapered thing sitting in his stroller smelling of baby powder, pablum, and throw-up. I'd pat his chubby arm as he flailed it happily up and down, banging his chin and drooling saliva down to the stroller beads. Nervous and excited, I'd give his arm a horrible tweak, then watch his face crumple up and his mouth turn down and his legs stop wagging while he prepared to let out a heartbreaking scream. Immediately I would begin to feel terrible, and would pick him up in my arms and try to comfort him, out of fear that I'd been spotted and because I suddenly felt sorry for him. And I'd lug him into the kitchen saying, "Oh, Missiz Robinson, Luke is crying about something and I'm trying to make him feel better." She would scoop him up and bustle off, not particularly concerned about his racket because Luke was the eighth child and she was used to noise. She would certainly never bother snooping around to find the pinch mark on his arm.

Everyone in the boardinghouse gathered for dinner on Sundays. Mother and Tia would prepare roast beef, popovers, mashed potatoes, and vegetables grown in our own garden. My sister Pauline and I would set the table or do the dishes, jobs which we alternated with Tia's children: fifteen-year-old, boy-crazy Mary, who had a photographic memory and an unchartable I.Q. and could play classical music by ear on the piano; and her son, Skipper, at thirteen badly in need of a father's strong hand, who lit fires in his basement bedroom, smoked, was flunking out of school, and generally raised hell with his delinquent friends. He was my favorite cousin. After we'd all held hands and sung "Thank You for the World So Sweet" my father would put Bach or Brahms or Beethoven on the phonograph and my mother would carve the roast, and while the boarders would try to carry on a conversation, Pauline and I would pinch and swat each other under the table. Mimi, who had learned to dance almost before she learned to walk, would pirouette around the floor with her toes curled under, changing the records on the phono— her latest trick, which everyone except Pauline and me thought was terribly cute. With her black hair and blue eyes, Mimi, "the littlest one," was beautiful. Pauline and I were united against her.

In one of my mother's albums there's a photograph of me sitting all alone at the big oak table with its extra leaves and knife scars rubbed smooth and shiny. I am wearing my navy blue corduroy dress with the gold buttons and the white eyelet smock tied over it, and I'm staring through the heavy tiresome minutes that follow an afternoon nap. I remember the stony feeling, as though weights hung from my shoulders and my eyelids were made of clay. I longed to be awake and lively, dashing and playing. But whatever demons would haunt me for the rest of my life were busy at work even then.

The scrape of a new school lunch pail filled me with terror. Because overalls were not allowed in the new school, I wore sweaters tied in giant knots around my waist. I had attacks of nausea, and one teacher or another would hold my head while I hung over the toilet, but nothing was ever forthcoming—from the age of five, I had developed a fear of vomiting that remains with me (to a much lesser extent) today. What cataclysmic event shook my sunny world so that it was shadowed with unmentionable and unfathomable fright? I don't know. I never will know. Every year, with the first golden chill of fall or the first sudden darkness at suppertime, I am stricken with a deadly melancholy, a sense of hopelessness and doom. I become weighed down, paralyzed, and frozen; the hairs on my arms and legs rise up and my bones chill to the marrow. Nothing can warm me. In the eye of this icy turbulence I see, with diamond clarity, that small shining person in the photograph, with slept-on braids and a groggy pout, and a ribbon of worry troubling her black eyes as she sits down with all her small might on the memories of a recurring dream: *I am in the house and something comes in the night and its presence is deathly . . . I scream and run away, but it comes back at my nap time and gets into my bed. Then a voice says angrily, "Don't look at me!" as I peer at the face on the pillow next to me, and I feel very ashamed.*

That's all I have ever remembered—just that much and no more.

The boardinghouse lasted a chaotic two years until my father finished his degree. At that time most of the bright young Stanford scientists went off to Los Alamos, New Mexico, where the atomic bomb was being developed. My father recognized the potential destructive power of the unleashed atom even in those early days. So he took a job as a research physicist at Cornell University in Ithaca, New York. We settled into a two-story house on a street lined with maple trees, in a tiny town of eight hundred called Clarence Center, an hour's drive from Buffalo. Suddenly life was calm. Pauline and I took piano lessons. While Mother cooked supper she would hum and I would sit and listen to the evening serials "Sergeant Preston of the Yukon" and "Jack Armstrong" on the big kitchen radio. The new school was small: I didn't leave class and run home; I stayed and got straight A's. I also acquired my first best friend, a girl named Lily who lived on a real farm, where I discovered piglets and slept overnight in the hayloft.

Soon my father was invited to become head of Operations Research at Cornell. Exactly what the job entailed was classified information, but he was offered a three-week cruise on an aircraft carrier as an introduction to the project and promised a huge salary. As it turned out, he would be overseeing Operation Portrex, a vast amphibious exercise which among other things involved testing fighter jets, then a relatively new phenomenon. Millions of dollars would be poured into the project, about which he was to know little and say less. Mother showed us the letter he wrote from "sea" with little hand-drawn cartoons of his feet tilting back and forth in his bunk during a week-long storm. He had been very, very seasick.

By now my father had begun to ask himself whether, with the

overwhelming capacity of the A-bomb to wreak total ruin, there was any such thing as "defense." As he struggled with the question—and with the lucrative offers that would assure him and his family comforts thus far unknown to us, my mother suggested we change churches. Though she personally did not like organized religion, for my father's sake we had joined the Presbyterian church out west. I, for one, had enjoyed dressing up, polishing my patent leather shoes with Vaseline, and sitting next to my mother during the service, smelling her perfume and face powder. When the congregation stood up to sing, her voice rose up more sharply and prettily than all the others, at least to my ears, and I loved the cozy sound of purses clicking open, of the little paper envelopes slipping into the collection plate, and the rustling of the ushers. But now my mother shepherded us, innocents, to the Quaker meetinghouse in Buffalo, hoping to help my father find some spiritual guidance and direction.

Quaker Meeting—what a horror! A room full of drab grown-ups who sat like ramrods with their eyes closed, or gazed blissfully at the ceiling. No one dressed up and there was an overabundance of old people. The few other children were no consolation because we didn't like them. Their parents were "permissive," a term we came to understand by way of a horrible little redheaded boy who slithered off his chair and crawled the entire length of the floor every Sunday. One day he caught Pauline scowling at him, and he bit her leg and scuttled off, leaving her clutching her wound and fighting back tears. His mother chose that meeting to rise and speak on the godliness of children, while Pauline and I tried to scorch her flesh with our eyes.

It seems extraordinary that we sat in that room for only twenty minutes each Sunday, so vivid is my memory of the weight of time upon our young souls, the depressing tedium of silence broken only by tummy-rumbling, throat-clearing, and an occasional message from someone whom "the spirit" had moved to speak. The grown-ups stayed there, by choice, for a full hour, but after twenty minutes we would be herded out to First Day School (Quaker Sunday school) and left in the charge of a dear old white-haired lady whom we were determined to dislike, though she had only goodness in her soul and love for us, and a determination to teach us the wonders of the Lord. One Sunday she announced to her squad of five- to ten-year olds, "Today we are going to witness a miracle." Pauline and I looked at each other and then heavenward.

"A meer-a-cul. P.U.," I said. "How stupid," said Pauline.

The old lady was poking around in a big cardboard box, mixing fertilizer with rich dark earth. Her wrinkled hands lovingly crumbled the earthen chunks with such care and pleasure and efficiency that I salivate now as I see it. She had us fill tin cans with earth and then, from her garden apron pocket, she produced a palmful of whitish green-bean seedlings. Each of us planted one, watered it, stuck it on the windowsill and promptly forgot about it.

Returning the following Sunday, we peered into our tin cans and saw the shiny bump of a spear poking its way out of the earth. The old lady looked delighted, standing in the winter sunshine pouring in from the window, her face, fringed by the tufts of her white hair escaping the bun in back, radiating a childlike joy. "This wondrous sprout growing up from its shell is seeking the sunlight," she explained. "And that is what we all must do daily with our lives."

I must say we were not impressed with the miracle. Certainly the lesson was lost on me then, and I quit attending Meetings when I was eighteen, as soon as I left home. I did not return for more than two decades, until, in my forties, I encountered one of those tedious mid-life crises. One morning, just before waking from a long and mystifying dream, I clearly saw that dear old white-haired lady from the Buffalo Quaker Meeting, still standing in the sunlight and smiling down upon a two-inch-high bean sprout. I wanted to apologize for having been such a brat, but she dissolved into a mist and I woke up in tears. I decided to go back to Meeting, which I have been attending irregularly ever since, rather belatedly coming to appreciate the miracle of the bean.

As for my father, whose struggles of conscience had drawn us to Quaker Meetings in the first place, in that austere silence he became a pacifist. Rather than get rich in defense work, he would become a professor. We would never have all the fine and useless things little girls want when they are growing up. Instead we would have a father with a clear conscience. Decency would be his legacy to us.

Shortly after Mr. Everette, our cross-eyed piano teacher, had assisted me in conquering the three-note "Ann, Ann, Sister Ann," and had explained all about sharps and flats, I went home and took a book from the piano bench and, making sure I was alone, placed it on our little upright. I searched the pages for the shortest song, with the least number of sharps and flats, and taught myself, note by note, Beethoven's Sonata in G (opus 42). The glorious calm that resulted inside me lasted for our whole stay in Clarence Center.

Soon we were on the move again. My fifth grade was spent in southern California, where Popsy (as we called my father) taught physics at the University of Redlands. In my dreams, our tiny one-story white house in Redlands is the one I return to most often. It had a front lawn lined on one side with huge, many-colored roses which my mother tended. Another house much like it stood on our right side, and an empty lot full of stickers lay like a desert on the left, bordered by Mrs. Fisher's row of pomegranate trees, behind which she lived a dank existence with her aging spaniel, Sunny. Ivy grew all around our front porch. My father had paid eleven thousand dollars for the house. I felt that my mother and father had the most sophisticated taste of anyone on the block. I'm sure they did. In fifth grade the three outstanding people in my life were my collie dog, Woolie, Mr. Macintosh, my wonderful teacher, and Judy Jones, a girlfriend.

After one year Popsy took a job with UNESCO, to teach and build a physics lab at the University of Baghdad. Perhaps that was where my passion for social justice was born. The day we landed, in the heat and the strange new smells, we were horrified to see an old beggar being driven out of the airport gates by policemen using sticks and shouting in a crude and guttural language. In Baghdad, I saw animals beaten to death, people rooting for food in our family garbage pails, and legless children dragging themselves along the streets on cardboard, covered with flies feasting on open sores, begging for money.

We all got sick with "Baghdad tummy." Pauline and Mimi recovered, but had already passed on to me a case of infectious hepatitis they'd just gotten over. Mother says that the first time she took me to the hospital, I staggered over and gave my two sugar candies to an Arab woman who was wrapped in her filthy black *chador*, hunched on the tile floor, moaning in pain. I wanted everyone to feel better. It would be a long time before I felt better.

I was in bed for months, and for all that time my mother was always near, her strong hands tilting my head up for rice water and glucose powder, and later, mashed black bananas. The life line in my right hand split and disappeared. Even when I stretched the skin across it, hard, it wouldn't come back. I thought I would surely die in that strange land, where the sweet smell of oranges filtered through the thick odor of diesel exhaust. But as I slowly regained my strength, the illness became a wonderful excuse to spend a year at home drawing, knitting, cooking, playing with ants, collecting bugs, and, when I was better, rescuing dogs.

Pauline and Mimi, by contrast, had a miserable time of it at the Catholic convent school. Mimi swears she never recuperated after Sister Rose displayed her math paper to the class as an example of poor work, then wadded it up and threw it at her, over the ducking heads of the diplomats' sons and daughters who constituted the English-speaking classroom. Pauline, more for-

tunate, discovered that she was an able seamstress and spent her school year buying cloth with Mother at the open bazaars and making her own wardrobe.

All in all, Baghdad was a melancholy place. The sky turned red at sunset, the birds flying in zigzagging clouds, singing in a thousand voices. Despite my illness I began to feel a part of Baghdad, as though its sufferings were also mine. I certainly felt closer to the beggars in the streets than I did to the people who sat around the British country club talking about punting on the Cam and how difficult it was to get these bloody natives to do anything. I felt sorry for the bloody natives.

More than twenty years later, in 1974, I returned to the Middle East on a concert tour. On a stopover in Lebanon, I met an Arab woman in designer sunglasses out by the hotel pool. "I read your book *Daybreak*," she said to me. "Why you deen't say something nice about Bach-dad? It is a beautiful ceety."

I should have told her that, driving across Tunisia, I had been flooded with memories of Baghdad. How when the winter was over, we kids moved our beds out to the roof, and through the musty-smelling mosquito net I spoke to the stars, telling the Big Dipper things I could never tell any person. How I sat in the sun and ate Haifa oranges and browned my skin, dreaming that the King of Iraq, at the time only a prince of twelve, would pick me out of the crowd of onlookers as he pranced down Al Rashid Street on a white horse, and tell me how beautiful I was. (I had learned enough Arabic to carry on an imaginary dialogue with him which would lead to my being a chosen visitor at the palace, and eventually an Arabian princess.) And how during the dust storms which would enshroud us in a fierce brown wind for days at a time I inhaled the desert into my lungs and absorbed it into every pore of my body, and understood the hardships of my brothers and sisters who inhabited that arid land.

It was not till Tunisia that I understood the magic and sorrow of the Middle East—in an ocean village where magenta blossoms drooped over white walls and I danced through the streets in a purple dress bought for fifty cents in an open store front. I rode a small Arab horse beside the sea and learned the popular song "Jaria Hamouda" from the five daughters of an innkeeper, all perched like fat crows on the same note as they sang into my tape recorder.

At the end of our year in Baghdad—1951—we returned to Redlands, California, where I faced junior high school with the same enthusiasm with which I'd faced all new schools. I averaged about three days a week in class, and the rest at home with the excuse that I was still feeling sick. Mother began a round-robin of taking me to clinics for testing, but there was in fact nothing physically wrong with me. My real problems were the fears that continued to plague and sometimes incapacitate me, now compounded by the rigors of adolescence.

One of the first problems I had to confront in junior high school was my ethnic background. Redlands is in southern California and had a large Mexican population, consisting mainly of immigrants and illegal aliens who came up from Mexico to pick fruit. At school, they banded together, speaking Spanish—the girls with mountains of black hair, frizzed from sleeping all night long on masses of pin-curls, wearing gobs of violet lipstick, tight skirts and nylons, and blouses with the collars turned up in back. The boys were *pachucos*, tough guys, who slicked back their gorgeous hair with Three Roses Vaseline tonic and wore their pegged pants so low on the hip that walking without losing them had become an art. Few Mexicans were interested in school and they were ostracized by the whites. So there I was, with a Mexican name, skin, and hair: the Anglos couldn't accept me because of all three, and the Mexicans couldn't accept me because I didn't speak Spanish.

My "race" wasn't the only factor that kept me isolated. The 1950s were the heart of the Cold War, and if anyone at Redlands High School talked about anything other than football and the choice of pom-pom girls, it was about the Russians. I had heard that the Communists had rioted at the University of Baghdad when my father taught there, and that some of them always warned him to keep away when there was going to be trouble. But in America during the overheated McCarthy years, *communism* was a dirty word and the arms race a jingoistic crusade. In my ninth-grade class I was almost alone in my fear of and opposition to armaments (to me they made the world seem even more fragile) and was already considered an expert on anything political.

It wasn't that I knew so much but rather that I was involved, largely because of the discussions taking place in my own home. And the family attended Quaker work camps where I heard about alternatives to violence on personal, political, national, and international levels. Many of my fellow classmates held me in great disdain, and some had been warned by their frightened parents not to talk to me.

I don't know how Pauline felt about politics in those days. She was an excellent student but suffered terribly from shyness. I idol-ized her because she got good grades, never carried a wrinkled lunch bag, wore a ponytail which didn't make her ears stick out, and smelled of violets. Also because she was white. She never said a word about social issues. And Mimi—well, my own pacifism did not yet extend to Mimi, who was avoiding me in public because I was brown.

It was the sense of isolation, of being "different," that initially led me to develop my voice. I was in the school choir and sang alto, second soprano, soprano, and even tenor, depending on what was most needed. Mine was a plain, little girl's voice, sweet and true, but stringy as cheap cotton thread, and as thin and straight as the blue line on a piece of binder paper. There was a pair of twins in my class who had vibratos in their voices and sang in every talent show, standing side by side, each with an arm around the other, angora sweaters outlining their developing bosoms, crinoline slips flaring. They swayed to and fro and snapped their fingers, "Oh, we ain't got a barrel of money . . ." I heard a teacher comment that their voices were very "mature." I tried out for the girls' glee club, and when I wasn't accepted, figured it was because (1) I was not a member of the in crowd and (2) I had no vibrato so my voice wasn't mature. Powerless to change my social standing, I decided to change my voice. I dropped tightrope walking to work full time on a vibrato.

First I tried, while standing in the shower, to stay on one note and force my voice up and down slowly. It was tedious and unrewarding work. My natural voice came out straight as an arrow. Then, I tried bobbling my finger up and down on my Adam's apple, and, to my delight, found I could create the sound I wanted. For a few brief seconds, I would imitate the sound without using my hand, achieving a few "mature"-sounding notes. This was terrific! This is how I would train!

The time it took to form a shaky but honest vibrato was surprisingly short. By the end of the summer I was a singer.

At the same time I was giving myself a new voice, I was also under the tutelage of my father's much-loved physics professor, Paul Kirkpatric, P.K. for short, conquering the ukulele. I knew the four basic chords used in ninety percent of the country and western and rhythm and blues songs then dominating the record market, and I was learning a few extra chords to use if I needed to sing in a key other than G. Some of my favorites were "You're in the Jailhouse Now," "Your Cheatin' Heart," "Earth Angel," "Pledging My Love," "Never Let Me Go," and the "Annie" series—"Annie Had a Baby," "Work With Me Annie," "Annie's Aunt Fanny" (I was disgusted

with the watered-down "white version," "Roll With Me Henry")—
as well as "Over the Mountain," and "Young Blood." These songs
all could be played with five chords, most with only four. All were
either melodic and sweet, upbeat and slightly dirty, or comic. I even
did a vile racist version of "Yes Sir, That's My Baby" called "Yes Sir,
Zat-a My Baby," and Liberace's inane "Cement Mixer, Putty Putty."
And this list is only a bare beginning of what I listened to on my
little grey plastic bedside radio. I cannot describe the satisfaction I
got from memorizing tunes by ear and scribbling down words anytime day or night, finding the right key (the choices were C or G)
and making the song my own.

At school, I had gained a reputation as a talented "artist." I could
sketch cartoons as well as likenesses of movie stars, Bambi and the
other Disney characters, and any student who was willing to sit still
for ten minutes. I also painted campaign posters, once even for two
of my classmates who were running against each other.

I did have a few friends. Bunny Cabral was a Mexican girl who
wouldn't speak Spanish, and we ended up pretending to be sisters.
She had four brothers and a television set, and I loved to stay at her
house. We'd listen to the rhythm and blues station late into the
night, and I'd break into a sweat when her oldest brother, Joe, came
home. He never noticed me, but another brother, Alex, did, and
later was the first person I ever dated. He gave me a record of *The
Flowering Peach* for Christmas when I was fourteen. And there was
Judy Jones, who continually risked her status as a "popular" kid to
befriend me. She was like my sister Pauline: beautiful, with her hair
curled and pulled back in a flawless ponytail, eyebrows plucked, the
colors of her sweater, collar, and scarf perfectly coordinated, her
skirt even at her ankles, her saddle shoes fastidiously polished. Her
lunch bag was new, and her books and binder were in impeccable
order. She wore "natural" lipstick. By contrast, I was Joanie Boney,
an awkward stringbean, fifteen pounds underweight, my hair a
bunch of black straw whacked off just below my ears, the hated
cowlick on my hairline forcing a lock of bangs straight up over my
right eye, my collar cockeyed, my scarf unmatched and wrinkled,
my blouse too big, my socks belled, my shoes scuffed, my lunch
bag many times used and crumpled, lines under my eyes, and no
lipstick. My best feature was what my parents referred to as my
"million-dollar smile."

The rest of my world was just as disordered as my person. I kept
the bedroom which I shared with Mimi looking like a cross between
a garbage dump and a remnants sale. It was strewn with T-shirts,

dirty socks and gym clothes; old lunch bags filled with peanut butter sandwich crusts, banana peels, and dried-up orange sections; crinoline slips and wrinkled nylon scarves; my collections of porcelain animals and bones; and my drawing equipment—pencils from B to H, pens of every existing quill size, bottles of india ink, chalk pastels, charcoal, oil and watercolor paints and brushes. Examples of my artwork were pinned and pasted from one end of the room to the other. My textbooks languished unused amid the clutter on my unused desk. In this chaotic section of my family's tidy house, I would pick up my ukulele, flop onto my lower bunk of our bunk bed, hook my toes around the springs of the upper bunk, and play my four chords and practice my new voice. One song I distinctly remember singing from that heap of rubble (one of the first non-r&b songs I learned) went:

> When you climb the highest mountain
> When you think you can't find a friend
> Suddenly there's a valley
> Where the earth knows peace with men
> And life and love begin.

It is not a coincidence that this popular song was a favorite of mine when I was fourteen, or that I remember it so clearly now. In the chaos of my teenage life it held out hope for the end of my mystifying problems, and also for the end of the troubles of the earth.

Before long an exhibitionist impulse overcame me. I took my ukulele to school. At noontime I hung around the area where the popular kids ate lunch and waited for them to ask me to play, which they did soon enough. I sang "Suddenly There's a Valley" and when they applauded and asked for more, I sang the current hits of the day: "Earth Angel," "Pledging My Love," and "Honey Love." I was a big hit, and came back the next day for a command performance. This time I did imitations of Elvis Presley, Della Reese, Eartha Kitt, and Johnny Ace. Before the week was out I had gone from being a gawky, self-conscious outsider to being something of a jesterlike star.

Someone suggested that I try out for the school talent show. At the tryouts, while standing at the microphone, I rested my foot on the rung of a stool to feign calm, and discovered that my knee was shaking. Afraid I would rattle the stool, with seeming nonchalance I raised my foot off the rung and held my knee suspended in the air, foot dangling, my entire leg trembling. The rest of my body was impressively composed, and I sang "Earth Angel" all the way from start to finish with a "mature" vibrato. Nobody noticed my shaky knee, and I discovered that I had an innate poise and a talent for bluffing. Clearly I would "make" the talent show. I hoped to win the prize.

For my first stage performance I wore my favorite black jumper, polished my white flats, and even dabbed on some lipstick. I was terrified, but was told later that I had been "cool as a cucumber." As the crowd clapped and cheered I grew so nervous and thrilled I thought I would faint. They wanted me back for an encore, so, knees watery, I went back out and sang "Honey Love."

There had been nothing showy about my performance. I had walked out and sung exactly the way I would in my room or on the back porch. The actual time in front of an audience was both frightening and exhilarating, and afterwards I was euphoric.

I did not win the prize. It went to David Bullard, the only black in the show. The judges had picked the only horse darker than me. David had befriended and defended me in the fifth grade and I loved him. He was tall and smoky black, had perfect teeth, and may have been the only person in that school who smiled as readily as I did. He also had a good voice. The fact that I didn't win the prize I'd been expecting dampened that day only a little. For all the anxiety, I knew I'd been really good and that, in some strange way, my peers loved me and were proudly claiming me as one of their own, as someone who truly *belonged* to Redlands High School. My sense of having arrived was almost as heady as my satisfaction with the performance.

I started "going out" with a very attractive senior named Johnnie Dahlberg, a Mexican who used his stepfather's Swedish name. He was cute and drove a Mercury. I would lie in bed at night and conjure up Johnnie's face as it looked in the reflection of the flickering movie lights, and I would dream of kissing. I had lain in his imaginary arms for so many sweaty hours that I was almost sick of his face when I saw him on campus Monday mornings. Then, on the third date, Johnnie tried to kiss me good-night, Hollywood style, and in spite of all the romance magazines I'd seen at Bunny's, I was caught unawares. After I'd run, traumatized, into the house and stared in the mirror for twenty minutes to see if I was still my parents' little Joanie, I wrote him a three-page letter about how wicked he'd been, and then spent the next three months wishing he'd try again.

I would have only one more year to enjoy my new stature at

Redlands, for the following summer we'd be moving back to Stanford University, where my father had accepted a teaching job. During that final year I wrote and illustrated an essay, which I rediscovered thirty years later when preparing to write this book. I'm reproducing part of it here with some of the original drawings because it so perfectly reflects the youthful self I remember—though of course its wistful earnestness and painful bravado are somewhat embarrassing to me now. But I'm struck by its prescience—not only how well it anticipates some of my life's events but also how consistent some of its sentiments are with my beliefs today.

## What I Believe (1955)

*ME*

I am not a saint. I am a noise. I spend a good deal of my time making wise cracks, singing, dancing, acting, and in the long run, making a nuisance of myself. I love to be the center of attention, and pardon the conceit, I usually am. I like to show off, and if you know me at all, I needn't elaborate on the subject.

Showing off, in a far distant way, coincides with my philosophy. Because for every five or six people who get disgusted and sore at me for getting so much attention, there is at least one who is getting some fun out of it. I am making somebody get a little joy out of life.

I am a very moody person. For although I am all the things that I have mentioned so far, I also do a little thinking once in a while. I sit sometimes and just think; about whether I'm turning out to be what my parents want, or whether I'm letting them down, about life, death, and religion, then I wind up thinking about boys and that's what really makes me moody.

Another point in me is that I am friendly. I always like to stick up for the underdog. I don't like to snub anybody. Why should I? "There is that of God in every man." Even the cheapest of us. It's annoying to society when I am talking with them and I stop in the middle of a sentence to say high to some degenerate looking dilinquent with an I.Q. zero. I prefer middle and low class people to snob hill when it comes to friends.

Many things interest me. (This is not according to some personality test I took in ninth grade. That told me I had no interests and great withdrawel tendencies.)

I love to draw. I am taking a correspondence art course and maybe someday I'll end up doing it professionally. Mother said I have been drawing since I was too young to rember. She said we always had the beds, bureaus, and walls repainted frequently. She got tired of seeing roosters, Indian tee-pees and cows with big udders crayoned all over the house.

As you see, my art often runs along the gruesome lines. I get inspired by various people to create these lovely ditties.

With art I guess I can help fulfill my philosophy by creating for others.

I like to act as well as to draw. In acting I can make a lot of people enjoy themselves at one time (or visa-versa). I like to play all sorts of rolls; negro maids, fairy queens, and even the mother of John the Baptist.

Please don't think that I do all this for the sake of others only. I live on glory.

I enjoy singing also. I sing most of the time, performance or otherwise. My geometry teacher doesn't appreciate it much when he is trying to explain how to bisect a quadrilateral and I start singing "You're All Wrong".

I find that singing is a good outlet. When I get depressed I sing songs to prove to me that life isn't really so bad and when I am bursting with goodwill I pick up a guitar and bellow it out of me. I sing for the family and for company alot, but I have found it wiser not to sing for my contemporaries anymore.

I have been told by an authority on the subject that I don't know how to dance. But for some reason, I was bop queen in

9th grade. I do not pretend to know how to dance because I don't. I have found, however, that if you look and act enough as if you know what your doing, it deceives about 99/00% of the people watching.

I love to dance (even if I can't) and I have fooled enough people into thinking I can that I am considered quite superior on the subject of bopping.

## MY MALE

I always worry about what my male will be like, because I want him to be as wonderful as my father, but I don't think it's possible.

Popsy is hard working, good looking, fun-loving, faithful, and he likes music. Besides he's smart. If I expect all that I will end up an old maid. (Maybe I oudda just settle for good looks.)

I want to be a good wife someday, but not for awhile yet. I am going to do the rounds first, and then pick one out and set-

tle down peacefully for the rest of my life. Sounds nice, doesn't it? Well it won't work out that way. Because I won't want to "settle down peacefully." I will want to travel and he will probably be a pauper anyway so, you see, it won't work out.

I don't speak seriously on this subject because I think I am too young to *really* know what I want yet.

Right now I am at the stage where I am in love with the whole opposite sex. I get chills everytime I see certain people and it's been going on like this since I was ten.

I can say this though. I do want my man to be faithful and hard-working, and I shall try to please him as best I can.

## RACE EQUALITY

Our family is all race prejudice. We are always on the side of the black, brown, yellow, or red. Whenever there is an argument going on between a negro and an anglo, I immediately take the side of the negro. It isn't a good habit, I suppose, but it is better than the other way around.

I think one of the saddest and stupidest things in our world is the segregation and discrimination of different races. A man is what he makes himself and fortunately the "minority" races are getting more and more of a chance to prove their worth. The negro, for instance, has proved his talents in singing, dancing, and most of all, sports. Robinson, Louis, and, at one time, Robeson, show what the race is capable of doing.

I have run into a few problems myself because of the fact that I am 1/2 mexican. I turn pretty dark in the summer.

Once when we moved to a very small, narrow-minded town in New York, somebody yelled out of a window at me, "Hey! Watcha doin, nigger?" I wasn't the least bit hurt, my reply was, "Wait till you see me this summer when I get my tan!"

That concludes my little section on race.

## ME AND RELIGION

I am now entering my most touchy subject.

I don't know what to believe. I

would like to be able to believe everything straight out of the Bible, fact for fact, in the manner of a devout catholic. But common sense, or perhaps disbelief tells me no.

My parents are Quakers. I like the idea the Quakers have of silent meditation, but I hate the meeting here in town. Perhaps if I had not been brought up by Quakers, who do *not* believe in taking what the Bible says literally, I might believe.

I do believe this. There is a supreme power that makes us do the good we do, that makes our concience tick. Some supreme power supplies all the everyday miricles that take place.

Scientists can prove facts about the beginning of man and animals that seem to contradict the Bible stories. But these proofs can go back just so far. They go back to say that the earth was once a big round blob floating around in nothingness. But no one can ever prove how that blob got put there. Some power got it started. That same power, I think, is the power that rules men's spirits today. That, I think, is God.

Sometimes I see God as an old man with a great white beard and a flowing robe. I love this old man and he loves me. Right now he is sad about the condition his little world is in now. He shakes his head and wrinkles his brow when he sees the mushroom cloud of the A Bomb blast. I think this God is going to leave everything up to us. He is going to see what we do to ourselves. He will not warn us before we make a fatal move, but he will be sad and disappointed when he sees our world destructed by wars.

I want to do things to make this old man pleased. I don't want to be selfish. When I think of God, I think of the earth as a very small thing. Then I think of myself as hardly a speck. Then I see there is no use for this tiny dot to spend its small life doing things for itself. It might as well spend its tiny amount of time making the less fortunate specks in the world enjoy themselves.

That is what I believe.

I began the eleventh grade at Palo Alto High School, which did not have a Mexican problem because all the Mexicans lived in nearby San Jose. Aside from the expected bouts of nausea and anxiety that were simply part of my life, I fit in surprisingly well. I was finding friends through a more unlikely source, too—the Quakers, or more specifically, their social action wing, the American Friends Service Committee. That year, along with three hundred other students, I attended a three-day conference on world issues held at Asilomar, a beautiful spot on the pine-speckled, foggy beaches of Monterey. Not only did I fall in love with ten or twelve boys at once, but I was galvanized by the discussions, inspired in a way I had never been before. I found that I spoke forcefully in groups both large and small, and was regarded as a leader.

There was great excitement about our main speaker, a twenty-seven-year-old black preacher from Alabama named Martin Luther King, Jr. He was a brilliant orator. Everyone in the room was mesmerized. He talked about injustice and suffering, and about fighting with the weapons of love, saying that when someone does evil to us, we can hate the evil deed but not the doer of the deed, who is to be pitied. He talked specifically about boycotting busses and walking to freedom in the South, and about organizing a nonviolent revolution. When he finished his speech, I was on my feet, cheering and crying: King was giving a shape and a name to my passionate but ill-articulated beliefs. Perhaps it was the fact of an actual movement taking place, as opposed to the scantily attended demonstrations I had known to date, which gave me the exhilarating sense of "going somewhere" with my pacifism.

It was also through the Quakers that I met Ira Sandperl the following year. One sunny day at Meeting, in place of the usual sinking Sunday boredom, there was a conversation with a funny, brilliant, cantankerous, bearded, shaven-headed Jewish man in his early forties with immense, and immensely expressive, eyes. I couldn't know when I first met him that he would end up being my political/spiritual mentor for the next few decades.

Ira read to the teenage First Day School from Tolstoy, the Bhagavad-Gita, Lao-tse, Aldous Huxley, the Bible and other texts we had never discussed in high school. For the first time in my life I looked forward to going to Meeting. Ira was a Mahatma Gandhi scholar, an advocate of radical nonviolent change. Like Gandhi, he felt that the most important tool of the twentieth century was organized nonviolence. Gandhi had taken the concept of Western pacifism, which is basically personal, and extended it into a political force, insisting that we stand up to conflict and fight against evil, but do so with the weapons of nonviolence. I had heard the Quakers argue that the ends did not justify the means. Now I was hearing that the means would determine the ends. It made sense to me, huge and ultimate sense.

Ira adhered to nonviolence with a kind of ferocity which would eventually come to me as well. People would accuse us of being naive and impractical, and I was soon telling them that it was they who were naive and impractical to think that the human race could continue on forever with a buildup of armies, nation states, and nuclear weapons. My foundations in nonviolence were both moral and pragmatic.

One day it was announced at school that we were to have an air-raid drill: three bells would ring in sharp succession, and we would all get up quietly from our seats and calmly find our ways home. We could call our parents, or hitch rides, or whatever we pleased, but the point was to get home and sit in our cellars and pretend we were surviving an atomic blast. The idea, of course, was as ludicrous then as it is now—despite the fact that in the atomic fever of the 1950s even some fairly sensible people were stocking their cellars with drums of water, saltines, and Tang.

I went home and hunted through my father's physics books to confirm what I already knew—that the time it took a missile to get from Moscow to Paly High was not enough time to call our parents or walk home. I decided to stay in school as a protest against misleading propaganda.

I was in French class when the three bells rang, and with pounding heart, I remained seated and reading. The teacher, a kindly foreign exchange teacher from Italy, waved me toward the door.

"I'm not going," I said.

"*Now* what ees eet."

"I'm protesting this stupid air raid drill because it is false and misleading. I'm staying here, in my seat."

"I don't theek I understand," he said.

"That's OK. Neither will anybody else."

"*Comme vous êtes un enfant terrible!*" he mumbled as he left the room, shaking his head and tucking his multitude of disorganized notes higher under one arm.

The next day I was on the front page of the local paper, photograph and all, and for many days thereafter letters to the editor streamed in, some warning that Palo Alto had communist infiltrators in its school system.

Having opposed it before, my father now seemed pleased with my bold public action: I may have proven to him that I was serious about something aside from boys. My mother thought it was wonderful.

The action delighted Ira and cemented our relationship, to the great unhappiness of his wife. We'd walk for hours around the Stanford campus, talking and laughing until we were in tears at the folly of humankind, then we'd plan future actions to organize a nonviolent revolution and create a better world. I was enormously happy. My father was nervous about Ira and thought I should be paying more attention to school and studies.

"Doesn't this man have a wife?" he asked Mom. But Ira and I have such a unique and special relationship that neither of us has ever adequately defined it: a platonic, deeply spiritual relationship, bound by the commitment to nonviolence and tempered with loud and frequent laughter and a healthy cynicism about the state of the world.

Ira and politics didn't diminish the excitement I found in music. For fifty dollars of my own money I had acquired an old Gibson guitar. I don't know now how I ever got my fingers wrapped far enough around the neck to press down on the strings. When I stood up the belly of the guitar reached almost to my knees, and I had to hunch over to get a grip. (Not knowing much about guitars I never thought to shorten the shoulder strap.) There's an old photo of me singing at a college prom, dressed in a white evening gown with black straps that Pauline had sewn for herself the year before, topped with a silver lamé bolero my mother made especially for me. I have bare feet. My hair is in a pageboy, cowlick poking up gaily, sabotaging my attempts to look sultry. My mouth is a gob of lipstick and my eyebrow pencil is carefully sculpted for the Liz Taylor look. The guitar is hanging down on one hip, which is appropriately cocked to balance it. I look sort of funny and sort of sweet. On the one hand I thought I was pretty hot stuff, but on the other, I was still terribly self-conscious about my extremely flat chest and dark skin.

I was offered my first out-of-town job by a teacher from Paradise High School who'd heard me sing at the Asilomar conference. Although I wasn't paid, my air fare was taken care of, and bumping through the clouds toward Paradise on a small aircraft (somewhere near Sacramento, California) I felt both very proud and very afraid. I was truly fawned over on this trip. Senior girls battled over whose house I should stay in and teachers wanted me to visit their classes. The father of one of the girls was a Shriner who dragged me off to sing at a dance hosted by members of his club. After three songs I sat down to have a Shirley Temple and a red-eyed old Shriner teetered over, put his arm around me and said in a kindly way, but with breath that could have withered a young oak, "You've got a helluva voice, kid. Don't sign cheap." I was far from thinking of signing anything, but I was blossoming in the attention.

I discovered the magnificent voice of Harry Belafonte. Tia told me about a man named Pete Seeger who was the daddy of folk music and I went to see him when he came to town, and soon after that heard the music of the queen of folk music, Odetta. I was slowly drifting from "Annie Had a Baby" and "Young Blood" to Belafonte's "Scarlet Ribbons," Pete Seeger's "Ain't Gonna Study War No More" and Odetta's "Lowlands," all of which I attacked with deadly seriousness.

My mother and father loved me to sing at gatherings of friends and students in our living room, and I was happy to oblige. I had no idea what Pauline thought of my new role, but Mimi liked it, and was herself soon to take up the guitar, which she would eventually play much better than I.

I was performing all the time. I sang at lunchtime and in the All Girls' Talent Show. I sang at other high schools' proms and in smoky dives for the parents of friends. And I was developing stage fright. Sometimes I was convinced that I had the flu—easy to believe with a headache, sore throat, nausea, stomach cramps, dizziness, and sweating fits. Once, at age sixteen, I had a terrible attack that turned my insides to water and had me crouching on the floor of the ladies' room in a dance hall where I was scheduled to sing a couple of songs. A kindly woman felt my forehead and proclaimed a fever, called my parents, and sent me home. As soon as I was safely in the living room, in front of the fire with a cup of tea, all my symptoms vanished, and I stayed up and plunked and sang happily into the night. That, to my memory, is the only time I didn't make it onto the stage.

Once I reached the stage, my voice usually functioned on cue, although occasionally the demons would strike during the concert: I would get short of breath, feel faint, or develop double vision; the words of the song would lose their meaning, or sound like a foreign language, and my terror would mount until I thought I would burst and evaporate into a dust cloud. By screaming silently to myself that I would be okay, I could usually overcome the sensations.

Still, singing helped me cope with the inevitable, overwhelming sexual tensions and excitement of adolescence. I flirted furiously from behind my guitar, sometimes staring into the eyes of one un-suspecting boy for an entire song. If he was tough, he'd look back the whole time. If he was with a girlfriend, the game was even more exhilarating. If the gaze really lasted, I'd feel myself go red and prickly from my toes to my scalp. There was no way to follow up on those forbidden stares, which was no doubt why I indulged in them so often. I flirted and sang, and developed a reputation for both.

By the time I reached my senior year, I had boyfriends: Sammy Leong, the only one my mother ever wanted me to marry (she wanted a Chinese Mexican grandchild); a football-playing born-again Christian with whom I tore around on motorcycles, squinting against the wind to see the speedometer top 110 while he shouted scripture over his shoulder; a millionaire Stanford student who bought me dresses and watches, and who would frown and pout when he was ticketed for speeding in his Ferrari, wait until the policeman had walked back to his car, then peel out from the curb with a great "HAH!" and race furiously into the next county, grind-ing his teeth and cursing to the accompaniment of screaming sirens. Through Ira I met Vance, whose name I thought was wonderful and who was an "intellectual"; I soon threw him over for Richard, who sat up all night necking with me on some streetlit steps where the air smelled of orange blossoms and gardenias. I didn't have friend-ships or affairs; I had escapades. I remained a virgin and kept myself in a psychic frenzy of unfulfilled crushes. My demons staged a pow-erful comeback, and finally, after a winter of seven colds and mount-

ing attacks of nausea and despair, Mother packed me off to a
psychiatrist.

I took a Rorschach test, identifying myriads of pelvises and skulls,
and waited expectantly for the results so that I could be cured and
feel better. To my great disappointment (I remember hot tears building up behind my downcast eyes), Dr. Heenen suggested that he
did not have a crystal ball, and all the inkblot test could do was help
find a starting place. I was with him only a short while before we
moved, but I shall never forget that one day, when I was so
frightened and anxious that I had curled up on the floor of his office,
he reached out and took my hand, and I felt as if someone had saved
me from drowning. I didn't know then that my demons would never
vanish, but I would have taken heart if I had known to what extent
they could be placated, tricked, cajoled, and bargained with. The
other day I gave a concert celebrating the twenty-seventh anniversary of my singing career. I looked out at a sparkling crowd of six
thousand relaxed fans and marveled at how many years I had been
walking out on stage. At that moment my stomach cramped up. I
shook my head, laughed, and had a beer.

_PART_
TWO

# "RIDER, PLEASE
PASS BY"

# 1

# "FILL THEE UP MY LOVING CUP"

After high school we moved to Boston. My father had a new job at M.I.T. and I had been rejected at every school except Boston University's School of Drama.

Traveling across country with my mother and sisters, we heard the commercial songs of the budding folk music boom for the first time, the Kingston Trio's "Tom Dooley" and "Scotch and Soda." Before I turned into a snob and learned to look down upon all commercial folk music as bastardized and unholy, I loved the Kingston Trio. When I became one of the leading practitioners of "pure folk," I still loved them, but kept their albums stuffed at the back of the rack.

Shortly after we'd arrived at our new house in Belmont, Massachusetts, not far from Boston and Harvard Square, my father took us to see a new phenomenon, the "coffee houses," where you could order a cup of coffee or tea, no alcohol, and sit around in a stimulating intellectual atmosphere. The Harvard students brought in their books to study, and people played guitars and banjos and sang.

We went into a tiny, smoky, jam-packed coffee house called Tulla's Coffee Grinder. My father saw young minds interlocked in Socratic dialogues, expanding their horizons of knowledge and understanding, or simply reading books and playing chess. I saw the guy under the tiny orange lamp, leaning over his classical guitar, his hair a soft yellow in the diffused light, playing "Plaisir d'Amour." I was entranced. I wanted a classical guitar, I wanted to learn that beautiful, sweet, haunting melody, and I wanted to move into Harvard Square and fall in love with every guitar player and singer I met, and never think about going to college or studying or taking exams or being normal.

My first day at Boston University I made friends with Debbie and Margie, who looked like the only other nonconformists in the freshman class. They, along with myself, refused to wear beanies to the freshman class picnic, a horrible affair held in a smelly old lodge in the country in a rainstorm. The three of us fell in love that very day with a sort of psychotic, James Dean-y-looking youth (also beanieless), who fell in love with all of us, one at a time, starting with me because I was the most aggressive and had cornered him under a tree in the rain and hurled a series of homemade Zen puzzles at him. We three maidens all loved folk music, and as he switched from flower to flower, we became closer, and when he finally quit school and went home to his wife, we soothed and mended our broken hearts with song.

Although I officially lived at home, I would drive my ninety-nine-dollar blue-green Studebaker to school, stay for a class or two, and then go to Margie's. The three of us spent hours in her tiny apartment on Plympton Street in Harvard Square. Margie baked bread (after letting the dough rise twice on the radiator); Debbie taught me new songs and how to really play the guitar. And we practiced duets, "Fair and Tender Maidens" appropriately being our finest offering. She also taught me "All My Trials," a song which would be one of my "most requested" over the years to come. Debbie and Margie, to my constant envy and frustration, had waist-length hair. I had cut mine short just before leaving California, and now waited impatiently for it to grow out into tresses so that I could be like them, and like all the fair and tender maidens in all of the long and tragic ballads. The melodic, repetitive songs of love forsaken spoke to my young and fragile heart, and I would sometimes get so carried away with a song that I wept while trying to learn it.

> Cold blows the wind o'er my true love
> And gently drops the rain
> I've never had but one true love
> And in Greenwood he lies slain.

And poor young Geordie . . .

> Geordie will be hanged in a golden chain
> Tis not the chain of many
> He stole sixteen of the king's wild deer
> And sold them in Boheny.

And Geordie's lover . . .

> Two pretty babies have I born
> A third lies in my body
> I'd gladly give you them, every one
> If you'll spare the life of Geordie.

And our theme song, "Fair and Tender Maidens" . . .

> Come all ye fair and tender maidens
> Take warning how you court young men
> They're like a star of a summer's morning
> First they appear, and then they're gone.

I met blues singers, the most famous in the area being Eric Von Schmidt. He looked like a grizzly bear with granny glasses, and his best-known song was about a grizzly bear. At Margie's, I listened to all of her Huddie Ledbetter (Leadbelly) records. I loved Eric's white blues and Ledbetter's black, but I could not sing the blues. A blues song had to be belted low, mean, chesty and soulful. I sang high and pure (and very white), and it was for what Bob Shelton later referred to as an "achingly pure soprano" that I was becoming known. Debbie and I began going out to coffee houses and singing our duets. We scanned the smoky room for our respective princes, inevitably discovered the same adorable boy at the same time, sang our hearts out, or got the giggles. Or both. Jesus, I was only seventeen! I bought a Goya classical guitar with gut strings. I learned "Plaisir d'Amour." And I wanted to fall in love.

I did not understand then that in my tender narcissism I was reaching out for what someone recently described to me as a "tattered remnant of my own self." An outlaw, a savage, someone who understood what it was to be "different" and could enter my secret garden and leave the blemished and terrifying world of adults and reality outside.

Many years later I wrote a song made up of titles and characters
from the folk songs I had learned in Harvard Square.

> Ah, the time spent in the foggy dew
> With the raven and the dove
> Barefoot she walked the winter streets
> In search of her own true love.
>
> For she was Mary Hamilton
> Lover of John Riley
> And a maid of constant sorrow
> And the mother of the doomed Geordie.
>
> One day by the banks of the river
> Midst tears and gossamer
> Sweet Michael rowed his boat ashore
> And came to rescue her.

Sweet Michael was perfection. Aside from the compulsory mop of
tousled hair, he was handsome, bright, intense, sexy, and talented,
but also troubled and preoccupied, with a hint of a wounded look in
his lovely blue eyes. It seems to me that I knew all that in the first
glance when he rowed over to where I was sitting wistfully plunking
my new Goya and singing on the banks of the Charles. We exchanged looks and shy hellos, and then the song was over and he
was gone. I heard later that he was expelled from the Harvard row-
ing team for loafing.

I was smitten. I began haunting the streets late at night, peering
into the busy hangouts and bookstores, and, of course, my already
familiar coffee houses. In a matter of days I spotted him in Hayes
Bickford's cafe, a fluorescent-lit cafeteria which sold awful food and
attracted droves of students because it was cheap and open twenty-
four hours a day. I stood barefoot on the pavement and stared at
him through the big dirty windowpane. He stared back and neither
of us made a move. I walked around the block with heart and mind
in a dither, and when I came back his chair was empty, but his friend
was still there. I charged into the busy room which smelled of cigarette butts and Franco-American spaghetti, sat myself down in the
empty chair and pumped his friend for information.

Michael studied Greek. Perfect. He was from the West Indies.
Dazzling. He spoke French, did not have a girlfriend, and, yes, had
noticed me, in my bohemian knitted and tasseled garb and bare feet,

gaping at him from the sidewalk. What a fortuitous beginning. Our meeting was arranged. We fell in love and became inseparable.

I told my mother I needed some birth control. "Do you love him?" she asked, and then sent me off to a doctor, who reluctantly fit me for a diaphragm. Birth control was illegal in Massachusetts in 1958.

Margie loaned us her apartment and at long last, after years of telling myself I would go to hell if I did "it" (and Michael agonizing because he was sure I had already done "it" plenty of times and was lying to him), I finally knew that my body was making more sense than my Spanish demons. "It" was marvelous, and for quite some time after, Michael and I spent most of our energy figuring out where we could go to do "it" next.

And so, in the winter of 1958 my eighteenth birthday found me deeply in love, as in love as I would ever be in my life. I had found my fellow savage, rebel, soul mate, a nineteen-year-old West Indian would-be poet, actor, writer, sailor, philosopher, wonderboy. Michael went to classes occasionally, and I dropped out of school completely. We were together every possible moment. When I first saw snowflakes on Michael's hair, they looked so beautiful that I wanted to be one of them and melt down through to the roots and then under his skin and just live there, because that was where I belonged.

In the middle of all of this, I was offered a job singing at Club Mt. Auburn 47, a jazz club in the middle of the square whose owner wanted to convert it, on Tuesdays and Fridays, into a folk club to accommodate the changing times. I was to be paid ten dollars.

For my first performance I was accompanied by my mother and father, Mimi, and two friends. Another friend of the family showed up, and there were the proprietress and her partner. That made eight. Aside from that, there was no one. I was clammy and nauseated and my mouth was dry as dust. With my heart lodged down in my winter boots, I began the first set. It was a ridiculous situation, friends and family all trying to look like an audience, trying not to peer hopefully over at the door every time they heard footsteps. In the middle of "Black Is the Color of My True Love's Hair," Michael breezed in, his tan duffel coat flapping open and snow in his hair, and my throat swallowed all by itself right in the middle of a note, and I began to blush, a long and merciless blush from my toes to my scalp, and didn't look up from the floor until both the blush and the song were finished. A few stragglers wandered in for the second set. When I returned the following Tuesday, word had gotten around and we had a half-filled house. I took a job at another coffee shop, the Ballad Room, one night a week. A schoolmate from B.U. passed me on the street one day, and asked if I had picked up my report card. B.U. seemed a thousand years in the past but I drove across the river out of curiosity and asked for my grades. I didn't know there were so many ways to flunk: X's, F's, zeros and incompletes. That was the official end of my college career. I never gave a second thought to what I would "do with my life."

I would finish at Club 47 around midnight and run, sometimes barefoot in the snow, over to Adams House, where Michael officially lived with three other freshmen. Carrying a cup of coffee (through the gates forbidden to "girls" in the daytime, not to mention the middle of the night), I'd burst into his apartment, past his flustered roommates, and find him slouched languorously on a floor cushion in his tiny room, reading Greek history, or Blake, or Camus in French. He'd accept the coffee, and we would nestle down together and talk about his dream of building a boat and sailing "away" to an island. It didn't matter which island, as long as the climate was warm.

We understood each other. What I did *not* understand was what I would do with myself on an island, and if I could be happy singing to parrots and monkeys, and perhaps an occasional non-English-speaking islander, and eating coconuts and bananas and lighting fires without matches. I was also terrified of boats, because sailing naturally meant you threw up in bad weather, so I was secretly hoping that Michael would find a way to remain true to himself and never have to leave the United States (which he said he hated). But I thought it was a noble idea that if you truly loved someone, you didn't need anything else in the world except that person. We would crawl into his tiny bed and have our dreams, both private and shared, and have each other, like two small woodland animals hidden in a dry stump, safe in the night from dangers both real and imagined.

Sometimes when he slept I'd sneak over to the window and watch the snowflakes go past in a ghostly cavalcade to cover the streets in silent blankets of white for the morning. I'd listen for the chiming of the Harvard bells in their tower and sit with a blanket wrapped around me, smiling like a bohemian Mona Lisa, at one with the snowflakes, with the tiny room, with Michael and myself.

And then, of course, there was morning, and stark realities edged in, jagged and imperfect against the new-fallen snow. My car wouldn't start. My parents thought I was at Margie's, and I worried they might have called. Adams House security had seen me racing up the stairs in the middle of the night, and Michael would no doubt have to see some awful disciplinary committee about rule-breaking, and if he was kicked out of school, we might be in serious jeopardy of having to realize his dream of sailing away, when in my heart all I wanted to do was stay in my beloved Harvard Square with him as a rebel student and me as a troubadour.

While I was generally subservient to Michael, I was a tyrant on stage. If some innocent student wandered into the coffee house thinking it was like all the others, namely a place to relax and read, he was mistaken. I'd stop in the middle of a song and tell him that if he wanted to study he could use the library. My growing collection of utterly pure, nearly sacrosanct folk songs was not something to be paid only partial attention to, and neither, apparently, was I.

As my repertoire expanded, my rigidity stayed the same. Each new song was as desperately serious as the last. One evening two young men got the giggles while I was singing, and I realized, to my embarrassment, that it was because the songs had been unrelenting in their plots of death, misery, and heartbreak: "Don't sing love songs/You'll wake my mother/She's sleeping here right by my side/ And in her right hand a silver dagger/She says that I can't be your bride." "All of my days I have seen trouble/And now I know it's common run/I'll hang my head and weep in sorrow/Just to think on what you done." "I leaned my back against an oak/Thinking it was a mighty tree/But first it bent and then it broke/So did my love prove false to me." "Oh mother, oh mother, go dig my grave/Make it both long and narrow/Sweet William died of love for me/And I will die of sorrow." I groped around in my mind for one single cheery song with a happy ending, and finished the set with "John Riley," because John Riley lives through a war to come back and claim his own true love after seven years, and she is actually alive to be claimed. But it sounded exactly like all the rest, and the giggling persisted. After that night, I made it a point to add some "humorous" numbers to the repertoire, my first concession to commerciality.

I began to frequent another club called The Golden Vanity. One night we had a double-bill show featuring Joan Baez in concert and a screening of Marlon Brando's *The Wild One*. My Harvard motorcycle friends had dreamed up the idea. Just as I was getting up to sing, there was a great roar out on the street, and the Hell's Angels pulled up. They were loud, tough, hairy, and obviously not coming to hear me. I was scared as hell, because I wanted to be a big hit and was sure the Angels would think me ridiculous in my madras curtain dress and bare feet, singing quaint unrequited love songs. But they decided I was okay, and even listened and clapped, and then I let them know, modestly, that I rode bikes, too, small ones, of course, but that I had learned on the largest Harley, which was true, and all in all the evening was a grand success.

Trouble nudged its way into Michael's and my dream existence by way of his jealousy of my popularity, his general incapacity to face the "real world," and soon after that, the awakening of new and more fierce demons in me, making my behavior more neurotic than it had been since my early teens. I was torn between my total infatuation with Michael and the fun of being a "well-known person." Michael halfway convinced me that if I pursued a career in music, I would inevitably become lost in the filthy world of show business, and so lost to him. I had a support system of boys who were going about their business and waiting for Michael to drop dead, and when he and I fought I would flirt wildly with all of them and sleep with none of them. And Margie would look wistfully at us as she gave me the key to her apartment and left for the evening to waitress. Her hair was sweet and fell like cornsilk to her waist, and she was crazy and tilted her head and smiled like a hexed cat. Margie was waiting for me to drop dead.

Michael and I shared one friend whom we both loved equally. He was one of those uncatagorizable souls, rare and therefore treasured, a celestial junkie madman named Geno Foreman. He was eighteen, like us, but seemed to have lived several lifetimes. He was a hustler and a schemer and a dreamer, the original fuck-up, but such a stylish one that he was impossible not to admire. No school had been able to contain him. He had no normal sense of fear, and would drive a motorcycle the wrong direction down a one-way street in the snow. He was six feet tall and beautiful, with pale white skin; fierce, mad black eyes under an artistic sweep of eyebrows; and a mane of black hair. He played the guitar and piano, both with natural brilliance. Geno ate yogurt, wheat germ and vitamin C and was hooked on heroin. None of us ever understood why Geno was the way he was. His parents, Clark and Mairi, were the first couple I'd ever met who appeared to love one another deeply, run their lives in an intelligent way, and relate totally to the younger generation. They had two normal daughters and Geno. The first time Michael and I went to New York we stayed at the Foreman apartment on Ninety-seventh Street and Riverside Drive. We slept together in Geno's tiny cavern of a room, and when I emerged, guilt-stricken in the morning, Mairi put her arm around me and said, "Oh, darling, we don't consider you and Michael sharing Geno's room wrong! As long as you love each other, and Clark and I feel that you do!" And in the evenings when Clark came home from work, the two of them would lie side by side on the thin divan talking to us and watching the sun set over the Hudson River.

Geno died in England at age twenty-six. He was standing up waiting for the ambulance when his appendix burst. His last words were "Don't worry . . ."

Peter, a friend of my family, offered to manage me and set up a recording date in the cellar of another friend's house. I went there with Bill Wood and Ted Alevizos to make an album. Bill was an engineering major at Harvard who hosted a folk show on the campus radio station. I harbored a wild crush on him, first because he was cute, second because the family thought he'd be a good date for my sister Pauline, and third because of how he played the guitar between the verses on "John Henry." Ted Alevizos sang Greek songs and had a gorgeous timbre to his voice, had had vocal training and was a conservative. Gossip had it that Ted had tried this new drug called LSD and gone completely out of his mind and had taken weeks to realize that he was back on planet earth. We sang some solos, some duets, and, for the finale, our own unique and special version of "When I'm Dead and Buried, Don't You Weep After Me." Peter designed the record cover in red and black with a big circle and a big square, and a shot of the three of us superimposed over them both. It was called *Folksingers 'Round Harvard Square*. I had bare feet, bangs, and at long last, tresses. Many years later a producer took it upon himself to repackage it with a new cover and call it *The Best of Joan Baez*. He also magically turned monaural into stereo, advertised it as by "America's Most Exciting Folk Singer," and released it just when my yearly record was due. We had to go to court to stop its continuing production and distribution.

Under Peter's guidance and inspiration I decided, in spite of Michael, to give my first concert. It would be with Bill and Ted, and it would be held at Club 47. I don't remember what we charged; I do remember the crisis over the poster design when I couldn't make up my mind whether to change my name. The choices were Rachel Sandperl—Rachel sounded biblical and mysterious, and Sandperl was the last name of my political and spiritual mentor, Ira. Or it could be Mariah—after the song that the Kingston Trio had made popular, "They Call the Wind Mariah." At the last minute, I opted to keep my real name, as people might think I had changed it because it was Mexican.

It was a funny sensation seeing our poster around the Square. I liked it; Michael hated it. Somehow I was managing to hold on to both Michael and my mini-career, though not without the help of a psychiatrist because the contradictions were literally driving me crazy. Michael was my God, and I didn't question him because I didn't want to lose him. But when I was showered with compliments and praise, he became wretched, blaming me for the disintegration of our relationship. In between fights, we made love at Margie's, and I forgot all about singing until we went back out on the street and heard someone say, "Look, it's her!" and the cycle would repeat itself. I drank in compliments like a thirsty sapling after a drought to brace myself for the next siege of self-hatred brought on by the doubts of my own true love.

Spring came, and feeling guilty for having flunked out of school, I found a "real" job at the Boston Vespa Company, teaching people how to drive the scooter and then taking them to get their license. Summer came, and Michael went home to Trinidad to see his parents. I was still living at home and earned enough money to buy my father a brand-new four-speed Vespa and then quit. I went on singing, learning songs, riding motorcycles with the elite Harvard bikers, seeing Debbie and Margie and my psychiatrist, and pining over Michael and flirting with all the lovely boys who were still waiting for Michael to drop dead.

Big management approached me in the form of Albert Grossman, a sly, furtive, nervous, soft-spoken, funny, generous, and bizarre man with a round form, round face, round eyes, and round glasses. Above his round eyes arched black eyebrows, like smudges of charcoal, rose in an expression of surprise. He terrified me by saying things like, "You can have anything you want. You can have any-*body* you want. Who do you want? I'll get him for you." I wanted Marlon Brando, but wanted more for Albert to quit talking that way.

My father was impressed by the kind of money Albert was talking, but I didn't trust him. Neither did my mother. He wanted me to sing in his nightclub in Chicago, and offered me two hundred dollars a week, a lot of money. I said no. He told my mother I was very young and naturally frightened of leaving home for the first time. I said yes. He was right, of course: I was frightened of flying alone, of staying alone, of a club where people drank and might not listen, of everything, and that's why I went. The money sounded terrific, but I couldn't have cared less.

Albert's club was one of the finest in the country, The Gate of Horn, and featured Bob Gibson, at that time a very popular singer who played twelve-string guitar and banjo. I got a crush on Bob, of course, and was terrified of him because he was at home in a den of sin called a nightclub, was marvelously sarcastic and funny, drank too much, sang both serious and silly songs, and cracked jokes in between them: he actually "entertained" people. I lived in the Y.W.C.A.; it was July and I spent my days on the beach playing with black slum kids, my evenings at the club, and my nights writing frantic letters to Michael about how nothing could ever come between us, and reading letters from him about how he doubted me every minute of the day. I began to wonder why I was spending so much energy staying out of bed with attractive musicians. The time left over was spent sitting in the metal stairwell of the Y where the acoustics were positively liquid, practicing the songs I'd learned from Bob.

One night the Queen of Folk, Odetta, came to the club. I was a nervous wreck waiting to see her and was at the bar when I realized that she had arrived. I watched her for a minute from across the room. She was big as a mountain and black as night. Her skin looked like velvet. She wore massive earrings that dangled and swung and flashed, and her dress looked like a flowing embroidered tent. She had a split between her front teeth which showed all the time because her face, between expressions of worry, surprise, concern, and mock anger, would shift back into a smile big enough to match the rest of her. Her chin jutted out round and full of dimples when she laughed, and I thought she was the most dignified person I'd ever seen. To overcome the panic welling up in my chest, I went up to her and flat out did an imitation of her singing, "Another Man Done Gone." She looked surprised and then pleased, and then she enveloped me in her great velvet arms. I felt about six years old, and my heart didn't get back to normal for a week.

I spent two weeks at The Gate of Horn baffled, flattered and terrified by what appeared to be dazzling success just within reach. Within me the demons engaged in a riotous dance, coaxing me with the soft light, the maleness around me, the overt sexuality that erupted as inhibitions were anesthetized by alcohol. I knew only that at age eighteen, I was not cut out for the cocktail crowd. I needed my academic, rebellious coffee-drinking admirers who listened single-mindedly to their madonna, and dared not touch her.

Bob Gibson invited me to appear as his guest at the first Newport Folk Festival. I have only patches of memories of that historic occasion. It was August. I went to Newport with Odetta and her bass player. It rained every day. Bob Gibson had a very rich girlfriend named Penny, who was nice to me. I looked like the Original Bohemian, wearing knit tops from Latin America or India, nondescript skirts or blue jeans, dangling earrings like my heroine, Odetta, and sandals with thongs that laced up to just below the knee. There were tents full of folksingers, banjo pickers, fiddle players, and gospel groups, and streets full of hitchhikers. The kids who flocked to the festival were trim and had short hair: the sixties had not begun yet. Pete Seeger was there, my second living idol. (Martin Luther King, Jr., was the first.) There were black blues singers with broken-down guitars, and white kids trying to sound like them. There were big dinners where fiddle bands played long into the night. People put dishes of food into my lap and then asked me to sing. I was like a tiny star in the middle of an as yet unnamed firmament.

On the second night there were thirteen thousand people sitting out in the Rhode Island mist. After other performers (I don't remember who), Bob went on to delight the audience with his ballads and jokes while I stood in gladiator sandals down in the mud, stage left, gripping the handrail that led upstairs to the stage. I was wearing a bright orange knit and crocheted rebozo made in Mexico. It was lined in silk and was the fanciest bit of clothing I'd ever worn on-stage. My other sweaty hand was clutching a guitar.

Finally, I heard Bob Gibson announce a guest and say a few words about me. I have no idea what they were, but I knew that in a minute I would be singing before what seemed to me to be the biggest crowd ever assembled in the history of the world. In that moment there was only the speeding of my heart; all movement was a silent film, and all sound was surface noise. There were nods of encouragement and thumbs up all around. It is my style when I am let out of the chute to walk swiftly and steadily, and I did so up the soggy stairs to my doom or glory. Bob was giving me a bright and cheery smile, and his cocky look which meant that life was only one big joke anyway, so not to worry. We sang, "Virgin Mary Had One Son." He played the twelve-string, and with eighteen strings and two voices we sounded pretty impressive. I had a solo part next, and my voice came out just fine. We made it to the end and there was tumultuous applause. So we sang our "other" song, an upbeat number (thanks to Bob) called "Jordan River." The two songs were religious, and I looked and sounded like purity itself in long tresses, no makeup, and Bible sandals. No wonder the press labeled me "the Madonna" and "the Virgin Mary" the next day.

An exorbitant amount of fuss was made over me when we descended from the stage. Into one tent and out of another. Newspapers, student press, foreign correspondents, and, of course, *Time*

magazine. I gave *Time* a long-winded explanation of the pronuncia-
tion of my name which came out wrong, was printed wrong in *Time*
magazine, and has been pronounced wrong ever since. It's not
"Buy-ezz"; it's more like "Bize," but never mind. The French pro-
nounce it "Bayz," which (phonetically speaking) is the present tense
of the verb *baiser*, which in slang means "to fornicate."

Bob asked me if I'd like to make an easy hundred dollars the next
day singing at a party for wealthy Newport types. He was to be paid
five hundred, and if I helped him out, he'd give me one fifth. Making a hundred dollars in twenty minutes impressed me more than
anything else that year at Newport, aside from realizing in the back
of my mind and the center of my heart that in the book of my destiny
the first page had been turned, and that this book could no longer
be exchanged for any other.

Back home in Harvard Square, I went to sing my usual Tuesday
night stint at Club 47, and there was a line of people going right
down the block and around two corners. Albert Grossman was back
and wanted to talk about making records.

I had already been in touch with one half of Vanguard Records,
twenty-nine-year-old Maynard Solomon, a music scholar who, with
his brother Seymour, operated a first-rate classical music recording
company. They were low-key and interested in making a quality
recording of me.

Al Grossman wanted me to go to New York with him and meet
John Hammond, president of Columbia Records. John was a well-
known and gifted talent scout who had the power to push what he
liked and push it well. In my mind, the difference between the two
companies was that one was commercial and had mostly to do with
money, and the other was not so commercial and had mostly to do
with music. But I went to New York, convinced that I should do so
in order to be "fair to myself."

I will never forget my first impression of Columbia. All I could see
was gold. The walls were decorated with gold records and everything seemed to shine and glitter. And the air-conditioning was icy.
I was led directly into John Hammond's office, no waiting. He was
very nice, but the first thing he said was, "D'you want to meet
Mitch?" I didn't know who Mitch was, but I said "Sure!," and he
poked some buttons on a box on his desk and talked to his secretary,
who quickly ushered in a man whose face was only vaguely familiar.
He had a coiffured mustache and a goatee and I thought maybe he
was Colonel Sanders. But I shook his hand and looked duly impressed. He was, of course, Mitch Miller, known in all the millions

of living rooms in the country which had a television set. We still didn't have one, so all I knew about "Mitch" were some unkind jokes made by my music purist friends to whom his name was anathema, as he epitomized the kind of music and presentation against which we were, knowingly or otherwise, in rebellion. That episode over, a discussion commenced about recording contracts. At one point, a contract was slipped across John Hammond's big desk. They would have had me sign right then and there what I believe was an eight-year contract. I was developing a head cold, partly from the air-conditioning and partly from stress. I told Al that I wanted to go across town and talk to Maynard at Vanguard. Albert hated Maynard, and vice versa. My nose was stuffing up and I had chills. Grudgingly, he packed us into a cab to "go see Maynard, because I told him I would."

When we walked into Vanguard, the first thing I noticed was that there were no gold records on the wall. Maynard came out from behind his desk briskly and shook hands with us. Then he went back around and sat down again. He had pale blue intellectual eyes, one of which drifted off toward the periphery every so often and seemed to snap back on command. He wore tennis shoes and a brown sweater his wife had knit him, and he was going not grey, but white, and was so intense that he seemed a little goofy. I liked him. Perhaps it was my being a primitive classicist—I couldn't tell a sonata from a concerto from a suite, but I could hum ninety percent of the music played twenty-four hours a day on the classical music station. I knew that Maynard had made a career of recording the classics, and I was fascinated and felt at home. We talked.

After we left I told Albert, who wanted me to tie the knot with Columbia that afternoon, that I needed two days before making this very big decision. If I had not been tempted by the gloss and flattery and shining gold of the "major company," I would not have been so afraid. And as for Albert, he was right in his own way. Before the end of the sixties he would be managing Bob Dylan, Peter, Paul and Mary, Janis Joplin, and Jimi Hendrix, to name just a few. If I wanted to go "big-time," Albert was the best and so was Columbia. Over the next forty-eight hours I had to figure out if the big time was something I could stomach.

The next night was a Friday, and I went to sing in Greenwich Village. Both Maynard and John Hammond came to see me. I talked with my parents on the phone and with my friends in New York. In the end, of course, I discussed it with myself and resolved to go with Vanguard. Albert faded out of my life for the time being except as a show business shadow who persisted, whenever he saw me, in reminding me that no matter how well I was doing, I could do a lot better if I teamed up with him.

The leaves turned, Michael came back from Trinidad, and I went to work as a housemother at Perkins Institute for the Blind, and continued at Club 47 Tuesdays and Fridays. My pay had been upped to twenty-five dollars a night. I met Manny Greenhill, a local Boston impresario who presented performers when they came to the area and also was personal manager to some famous blues acts. Manny worked out of a dingy old office overlooking Boston's South Station. He prided himself in his egalitarian behavior, and like a certain brand of good old Marxists who consider themselves working-class no matter how much money they make, always looked as if he had just stepped off a bread line, in his golf cap of nondescript color and wrinkled ancient raincoat. He was proud of his boxer's nose which had no septum and made him look like George C. Scott. He loved to tell stories about his old blues singers and the difficulties that arose because they couldn't read or write. Half of Manny's time was spent banging on doors of orphanages in the deep South hunting down birth certificates for blind guitar players so they could meet the rising demand for performances in Europe, for which they needed something called a passport.

Manny, too, wanted me to be heard by the largest number of people, but he also understood that I was a political being, and though I did not share his leftist ideology (which was the cause of many minor battles between us), he accepted my nonviolence and shared with me the understanding that speaking up for peace and justice involved risks which would inevitably interfere with commercial success.

We decided not to sign a formal written contract, but for a certain percentage Manny would work with me for a year. If at the end of the year the arrangement was mutually satisfactory, we would shake hands and continue it for another year. This agreement continued for eight years before we ever had a written contract.

To start, Manny got me jobs opening the second half of concerts with established artists. The first was in the Summer Series of 1959 at the University of Massachusetts, with John Jacob Niles, the well-known traditionalist and old crank, a singer-songwriter who sang in a high falsetto and played the dulcimer. As we had gone with my family in Manny's old rattletrap and as it had run out of gas, we were late to the performance and sat down in the back of the brightly lit auditorium. Someone else came in late and chose to sit up front.

Mr. Niles stopped in the middle of a note, waited in deathly silence until they were seated, and then announced that "Attention follows motion, not sound." I was mortified and intimidated, but after intermission, when I sang my two songs, I was given an enthusiastic encore, which didn't do much to improve Mr. Niles's mood.

Manny also arranged for my first concert with Pete Seeger. I was late as always, and Pete was already finishing his first set when I got there. It was a tiny hall; too tiny, I thought, but Pete was wailing away on the banjo and everything looked to be in order. He came off the stage and greeted me. I went onstage and was utterly baffled: there were only a couple hundred students sitting around on the floor. I bowed and turned around to see if anyone was seated in the rear of the stage and discovered that I had been facing the wrong direction. Apparently Pete had sung his last song of the set to the overflow crowd seated up on the stage. I was thrown off balance, and as my heart began to slam in my poncho-covered chest, I launched into my first song. In the middle of the first sustained note I swallowed a large gulp of air and went on strumming while trying to gather a little spit with which to swallow and coat my bone-dry throat. As the note had been cut off, most ingloriously, I decided to say something—an event rare enough in my performances, but I had to see if I had a voice at all, or if it had vanished with the gulp of air. I said something like, "Oh! What a lot of people!" and then managed to collect myself and continue the song.

The first snows came. I was fired from Perkins Institute for going barefoot and looking like a bohemian. Soon after, I sang a concert with my Harvard Square blues buddy, Eric Von Schmidt, and went to a hootenanny in New York City.

By winter of 1959, neither Michael nor I could imagine our lives separate from each other. But I was sick with demons. Sometimes I needed to be held like a lost and trembling waif, and other times to flirt and conquer. I was the perfect example of the common high school expression "P.T." (prick teaser), and in refusing to consummate my seductions could tell myself that I had been and was still "good." The Madonna was in the Village; she didn't drink, take drugs, or make love, and yet somehow she was like a whore, and her demons were running wild. Many years later, Michael told me that that was why he fell in love with me. The "virgin" he worshiped and the "whore" he wanted to save.

Back in Boston, one day I sat in the psychiatrist's office, exhausted and crazy after a fight with Michael. The doctor asked what I thought would happen if I left Michael. I shut my eyes and saw the earth explode and a tiny figure tumble into blackness.

One night I found myself on a street corner in Greenwich Village, alone, with a suitcase and a guitar. Someone took me in; I have never remembered who. I walked down MacDougal Street and hung out in cafes. I didn't eat or sleep. I met people who smoked marijuana and talked about drugs.

For a few nights I followed my giddy beckoning demons, staying up until dawn, feeling sick, taking Miltown (which preceded Librium, which preceded Valium). I was sickest at the first morning light, tasting the metallic tang of *guilt* sliding to the back of my throat, running down my spine and emptying into my stomach.

It was safer back in Harvard Square. I had grown close to Mimi, who played duets with me, and I had "all my lovely Harvard boys." They were in love with Mimi and me, and we were in love with them collectively. We were both like Guy de Maupassant's whimsical character Mouche, only Mouche slept with all her lovely boys, and they loved her none the less for the sharing. Our boys seemed satisfied to love us as they would two Mexican virgins who would eventually be given in marriage to the boy proven to be the truest and purest. Dear Goodie, Stein, Todd. Dear Piper, Cooke, Billy B. Dear Geno.

Once I was driving through the Square to Adams House and I saw Michael out in front of a bookstore, leaning forward to kiss a beautiful woman on the lips. Her hair was pulled back into a sophisticated bun, and she looked like a grown-up. I parked down the street in a nauseated daze and waited long enough to see Michael flash into the dorm late for our meeting. He yawned and put his book down when I walked in, and I watched him lie for the first time.

School let out and the summer of 1960 arrived. Michael went home again to Trinidad, and I went to New York to make my first Vanguard album.

We worked in the Manhattan Towers Hotel on a dingy block of Broadway. The ballroom was available every day of the week except Wednesday, when it was transformed into a bingo parlor for the local residents and their guests. I stood on the dirtiest rug in New York City in my bare feet, dwarfed by the huge, musty room, and sang into three microphones, two on the outside for stereo, and one in the center for monaural. Freddy Hellerman of the Weavers used a fourth microphone for six songs after I had decided, under great pressure, that a second instrument, tastefully played, was not "commercial," but rather enhanced the music. The beautiful ballad "Mary Hamilton" was secured in one take, without a run-through. I would work for a few hours, and then Maynard and the engineer and I would go down the street for roast beef sandwiches. In three days we recorded nineteen songs, thirteen of which made up my first legitimate solo album.

My parents were moving back out west; I was staying east. We had a mother-father-Joanie-and-Manny meeting at the house. I was tight-lipped and distracted as Manny asked questions which I let my parents answer. The only thing I kept bringing up was that I didn't want to sing in nightclubs, but wanted to give regular concerts. Manny said he was willing to work on it, provided there was a big enough audience for me. The meeting was terribly tense. I was paralyzed by the fact that my parents were leaving, and I would actually be on my own. I suddenly felt so tiny, not at all like a star of any size or import. For the first time in my life my mother would not be waiting by the fire with a cup of tea for me and some violin or cello or piano on the phonograph. But I couldn't think about it. I just clammed up and stared out the window and let everybody else discuss my future. I thawed a little when Tia arrived with a glass of wine in her hand and cheer in her heart and a wonderful understanding of the child she had always referred to as her "little songbird." Somehow she made me feel that I could take the next step in my life and not die from it. It was decided that Manny would try to set up concerts for me, I would continue my two nights at Club 47 and weekends at the Ballad Room, and I would not do nightclubs.

My parents left. Margie disappeared. Debbie was in love. McDoo, a good high school friend, moved east to live with me. We found a fourth-floor apartment, no elevator, with one bedroom, a living room, kitchen, and bath, a few blocks from Harvard Square. What we had in common was that we were both professor's daughters. What we didn't was that she was blond, very pretty, exactly as I had known her when we had graduated together and had made a vow, along with Muff Calloway, that we would all remain virgins until we were married.

I was fascinated by McDoo's magnificent breasts. Even when she lay on her back daydreaming, they pointed skyward, with or without a bra. She curled her hair at night in huge plastic rollers, was hygienically squeaky-clean, pink-and-white complected, sweet-tempered, and wanted to be a beatnik. So she bought black panty hose and stopped wearing lipstick. For a while, we had a wonderful time,

fixing up the apartment, making a lot of salads, and feeling independent.

Michael and I hung out in the living room, drawing, talking, making love, and fighting. McDoo would poke her head out of the bedroom door, curlers abounding and towel wrapped around her
gorgeous body, say " 'Scuse me" in a high-pitched voice, and fly
across the hall to the bathroom with a little wave.

One night Michael and I had been to the movies. The last scene
had left Joanne Woodward standing on a street corner yelling at her
husband, who was driving away with his lovely young mistress. On
the way home I had a nausea attack, and by the time we reached the
fourth floor, I collapsed on my bed. Michael was telling me that I
was like Joanne Woodward, and I had thought I was like the lovely
young mistress. I asked Michael to change the subject or, better yet,
just tell me I wouldn't throw up. Michael went into the kitchen and
made an avocado and banana sandwich and sauntered back into the
bedroom chewing noisily.

Suddenly, very suddenly, the nausea vanished and I found myself
flexing my toes around the upright lamp we'd bought at the flea
market, and in dreamlike slow motion, lifting it with my leg and
hurling it across the room. It landed directly on Michael's head. His
mouth froze open over the avocado and banana sandwich and the
whole scene vanished into darkness.

I got up feeling like Godzilla and headed toward the living room.
The first thing to catch my eye was the wine bottle with a candle in
it and a year's supply of wax dripping down in multicolored lumps.
I grabbed it by the neck and threw it against the wall with all my
might and was rewarded by the sound and sight of shattering glass
and wax chips in flight. But I was already on my way to the kitchen.
First the coffee pot went, but it was metal and suffered only a small
dent while spewing the cup or two of stale coffee and grounds into
splotches against the wall. I headed for the plates in the cupboard.
Michael stepped up behind me, saying, "You stupid . . . Are you
crazy, or what?" and grabbed my arms at the elbows. Empowered
with the strength of rage, I turned myself around, and in a quiet and
determined frenzy, grabbed his hair and pulled, kicking furiously at
his ankles. He hopped up and down to get out of the way of my
feet, squeezing my wrists to unlock the grip I had on his curly locks,
and cursing and hissing in shock and anger. I finally gave up and
collapsed in tears.

Michael left, smoothing back his hair but clearly shaken. I sat on the floor in pools of damp coffee grounds and sobbed my heart out. McDoo came home and helped me up and listened to the whole story. By the time the story was over, I was resolved never to see Michael again. McDoo helped me pack all his things into boxes, put them out in the hall and double-bolt the door. I pinned a note to one box saying something original like "I never want to see you again." Drained and exhausted, I went to bed. Awakened by the first morning rustlings, I heard McDoo tiptoe past me into the bathroom. There was a brick lodged between my eyes in back of my nose. Then I heard a scream and by the time I could prop myself up, she was in the doorway next to my bed with her beautiful blue eyes wide above the night's mascara blotches.

"Michael's trying to climb in the bathroom window!" He had picked the screen off, opened the window, and hoisted himself over the tub with the still-steaming one inch of water and three inches of bubbles that was supposed to have been McDoo's bath.

Wherever you are, McDoo, I apologize. And you needn't have cried when you told me that you just weren't cut out to be a beatnik and were going home. I hope your wild ride in Harvard Square afforded you some laughter in memories.

Michael and I groped for a way to make a fresh start. He was stifling in New England. Even I felt it might be time to move on. We began talking about moving to California.

# 2
# "BLUE JEANS AND NECKLACES"

In the fall of 1960 I gave a series of concerts with various folk and country groups, mostly in colleges—Radcliffe, Trinity, Wheaton, Yale—in halls seating two to five hundred. On the fifth of November I gave my first solo concert, in New York City at the 92nd Street Y, and filled the eight hundred seats without a problem. After a concert at Bennington College, Michael and I packed our hi-fi into a new Corvair and left Harvard Square, his school, and my music career. Manny cried when I explained to him that we needed to live on the West Coast for a while. I was staving back a flood of my own tears and got annoyed with him for nagging me about my career. We still had our handshake agreement, I reminded him brusquely, and I would come back to do concerts, and he could see if there was anything on the West Coast for me. I didn't tell my parents about the move. The plan was to write them from halfway across the country, giving time to adjust to the fact that Joanie was officially living in sin (the part that concerned my father) with an unemployed college dropout (the part that concerned my mother and father) on Joanie's money (the part that concerned everybody except me).

My record came out in time for Christmas, just as Michael and I arrived in California. I watched in amazement as *Joan Baez* soared to number three on the top 100 best-selling albums in the country.

Michael watched with a jaundiced eye but held his tongue, as my music was our bread and butter.

We settled in a one-room house just off the highway in Carmel Highlands, just south of Carmel, California. Michael began to write a book; I kept house. We collected dogs and cats and a totally unique community of new friends whom we met through one of Michael's Harvard schoolmates and who took us in and looked after us with a warmth we both relished. The Williams household, which included their own children as well as wandering souls of the early sixties like ourselves, was directly across the street. The old man of the mountain and his wife, Don and Rosa Doner, legendary Russian Jewish immigrants, lived just above us in the highlands. Don tried to teach me how to cook. I kept a two-burner hot plate illegally in a cubbyhole we called a kitchen. Cynthia Williams, the mom and Realtor Extraordinaire, found jobs for Michael working on houses. We were accepted by our marvelous new friends as a young, offbeat couple, our neediness no doubt appealing to their own battered vulnerability, kindness, and generosity.

Our living situation was hardly a nurturing one for my music, but I really had no choice. I felt a part of Michael the same way Cathy feels in *Wuthering Heights* when she realizes that Heathcliff, the stable boy, is running off in a storm, and in a great clap of thunder her eyes grow big with realization, and in answer to the question "Do you *love* Heathcliff?" she says, "I *am* Heathcliff!" We were inseparable and couldn't imagine each other with anybody else. Michael was my poet, my suffering artist whose genius lay undiscovered. He played Ping-Pong and discussed books and philosophy in French with Don Doner, who found him lazy but delightful. He danced to steel-drum music and my Brazilian carnival records, his eyes continued to sparkle like no one else's, and we made love often. When he didn't despise me he adored me, and he was tender toward my insecurities, and I remained his virgin whore for four ambiguous years.

While at home in the highlands, my social-political conscience and my music were obscured by my chaotic lifestyle and determination to stay with Michael. He had little regard for social action of any kind, especially if it was something which involved me, and looked upon my infatuation with nonviolence as airy-fairy and unrealistic. The only overt public action I'd been involved in since I'd known him was a forum on nuclear disarmament sponsored by SANE in the Boston Arena where Erich Fromm was hit in the face by two flying eggs.

Almost as soon as we had settled into our house in the highlands I was off to the East Coast for concerts. For that entire year I Ping-Ponged back and forth from home to the road. In the summer I made another album, and in the late fall did a much anticipated solo concert in New York's Town Hall. I remember reading a clip from *Billboard* or *Variety* which said, "JOAN BAEZ S.R.O. TOWN HALL NYC." I pondered over the "S.R.O." and finally figured it must mean Sold Right Out, because that's exactly what had happened. (I learned later that it meant Standing Room Only, but it was the same general idea.) I gave twenty concerts in 1961, and could have done two hundred, or so Manny told me. I made heaps of money, which was fun, I suppose, but confusing. I could have made heaps more, but was not interested. I was offered fifty thousand dollars to do a Coca-Cola ad ("Come all ye fair and tender ladies, drink Coca Cola, it's the best . . . !") and I know Manny was torn as to how to counsel me, but there was no issue anyway, because, "Manny," I said, "I don't even *drink* Coke." (In 1965 when I was traveling with the Beatles, someone brought a vending machine into their dressing room because they couldn't go out into the hall, the security was so tight. The machine had been rigged so it didn't need any coins; you just pushed a button and got a free soft drink. By that time, the Beatles must have been millionaires several times over, but in their minds they were still working-class Liverpudlians, and couldn't get over the thrill of having free drinks.)

I had a mini-version of that same identity confusion when Michael and I moved to Big Sur later that year. For thirty-five dollars a month, we rented a cabin consisting of one bedroom (doubling as a living-dining room), a tiny bathroom, no closets, and a kitchen. We had four dogs and many cats. One afternoon in Monterey we went to buy a flashlight, and finding the hardware store closed for lunch, wandered around the corner to look at the British Motors display window. We ended up writing out a check for six thousand dollars and driving back to Big Sur in a silver Jaguar XKE. I lived in blue jeans when I got dressed, and a granny gown when I didn't, and the house was a pigsty. We owned one pair of sheets and when they were dirty, I washed them out by hand and hung them on the porch railing until they dried in sunburst designs from hand scrubbing. There was no phone in our house, so when Manny called to try to schedule concerts, I had to run down to the lodge in the rain, sleet, mud, and ocean mist. I bought condensed milk that you mix with two parts water to save money, and at the same time thought nothing of buying silk blouses and cars for friends. When my mother said, "Gosh, honey, what can we get for Christmas for the girl who has everything?" I said, "How 'bout some sheets and pillowcases and a frying pan?"

In the East, I gave concerts with Lester Flatt and Earl Scruggs, at the time the best-known bluegrass performers to come up from the South. Our collaboration was unprecedented, and caused a slightly humorous reaction among the urban hillbillies and college intellectuals who made up the audience. Flatt and Scruggs and I took the contrast of our mutual publics good-naturedly and chalked it up as one more phenomenon in the rapidly expanding and changing folk scene. One reporter said that I sang to "troubled intellectuals." I saw the review and said to Manny, "But I'm not an intellectual." My mere existence as a rebellious, barefooted, antiestablishment young girl functioning almost totally out of the context of commercial music and attaining such widespread notoriety designated me a counterculture heroine, whether or not I understood the full import of the position.

Back home I doubled up on psychiatry sessions, sometimes driving into Carmel four times a week to try to sort out the mounting pressures. Was I really a devoted wife-out-of-wedlock, darning socks for my beloved who was building a boat on my money so that we could float off to the island where no one worked? By now I knew that I would not go with him if he sailed.

It was autumn. One evening someone called us to come outside. The sky was a blazing orange-reddening-to-crimson blanket far up over our heads, and the ocean reflected it back like a mirror. Two tiny boats were approaching each other on the horizon, and on the shore we joined our neighbors and shook our heads in amazement at the closing of this day, the burning of the sky aglow in each other's faces, the boats seeming to merge into one and stop moving for a few minutes.

Christmas came; the new year came, and from our porch we could see the whales heading south, spouting glorious geysers into the air. Somewhere within me a resolution began to form that I could not express, but with it came moments of calm. I was able to tell Michael that I needed to stay in the States for my concerts, and that if the boat ever sailed I would not be on it. Michael saw that I was growing more and more independent, and reacted by tightening his hold on me. My doctor suggested that Michael "get some help." Michael was outraged: I was the sick one; not he.

But now, when I went on the road, I was an established "star," a little less afraid of my profession as I gained control in it. I preached a tiny bit more in each concert, and in the dressing room afterwards was treated as a kind of sage, usually speaking of nonviolence and Gandhi. When Michael accompanied me, I spoke less freely or not at all.

We decided to take a trip to Mexico in the summer, something which I dreaded for the same reason I dreaded sailing. If you went to Mexico, you eventually ate the wrong combination of persistent little bacteria and had to throw them up. In July we packed up the XKE and headed south. My only time in Mexico not fraught with fear was when we stayed on the beach, two hundred yards from the most expensive and vulgar hotels in Acapulco. For $1.50 a day, we had hammocks, a blanket, and all the fresh shrimp, homemade tortillas, and Coca-Cola we could consume. I watched the shrimp come in from the boat and go into the pan, and watched the tortillas being pounded, then cooked until there was no way any germ could have survived, and I ate them and drank the Coke (which I supposedly never touched) in peace. The rest of the trip was a kind of nightmare, and I lost a lot of weight. I discovered that my records were known to the art circles and upper-middle-class intellectuals of Mexico.

Upon our return to the United States I became very ill. During a concert somewhere in a tent, during a storm, I thought the sky would split with the sound of the thunder, and I wished it would, and that an angel in white robes would come and gather me up and bathe my forehead in cool water and sing me to sleep. I was feverish, my stomach was in spasms, and I seemed to be living on a diminishing reserve of raw nerves. At that exact moment, with my second record out and doing better than the first, *Time* decided to do a cover story on me. Between dizzy spells I posed for a portrait in oil; I felt like death and was depicted accurately. Back home trying to finish interviews with *Time*, I ended up in the hospital diagnosed as malnourished, dehydrated, and hosting a variety of viruses in my ears, nose, throat, lungs, and stomach. The nurse left me standing in my hospital gown, so I weighed myself, made a note of 102 pounds, and crawled between the embracing cool sheets, shoving the kidney-shaped basin under the bed and out of sight.

Michael, along with everyone else, was forbidden to see me, and after a visit and instructions from my doctor, I was blissfully alone, bathed and asleep. The bed was the angel in robes I had so longed for. Michael's phone call got past the nurses' desk and his voice broke into my indescribable peace, nervous and agitated and demanding to know what was going on. I truly wished he was dead.

When I felt better, I went around visiting people. I met an extraordinary little girl named Raylene. She had black hair and black eyes with long lashes, was very pale, and smiled at me as though she and I had been sisters in a previous life. She was in critical condition with a kidney problem, and her mother thought she was going to die. She didn't behave like a little girl at all, but rather like a wise old woman. She told me she had heard the doctors whispering and that she didn't have much of a chance, and then she shrugged her shoulders and blinked sleepily and smiled an indescribable smile. She seemed all-knowing, and she was apparently not afraid of death. (She did not die, and I remained friends with her and her family for years. Recently, she found my address from someone and stopped by with her two kids. She was more beautiful than ever, hair to her waist now, no makeup. While her kids played with Gabe's long-forgotten mountain of Legos, we discussed marriage and divorce and children and how life then goes on, and she shrugged, and blinked and smiled exactly the same way she had twenty-five years ago . . . or was it a hundred?)

One day a nurse handed me a bizarre note and explained that it was from a very odd girl dressed in ripped cutoffs and a T-shirt and a strange hat. The note requested permission to wash my car. I supposed it was from a fan. The next day there was another note, and the nurse said the odd girl was out in the hall. I said I'd be happy to see her.

A girl blew in, fresh, tan, skittery, ragged, shy, rebellious. She had superb cheekbones, a fine nose, and managed to hide her eyes under spikes of blond hair mashed down on her forehead by a grey, pillbox-shaped knitted hat. Occasionally, her eyes darted a glance from behind the scraggly hair spikes, but she was terrifically shy and laughed nervously and blushed, trying to cover her discomfort by waving her hands in the air and telling me stories. All I gathered from that first visit was that she was not happy at home, adored her father, rode horses, slept on the beach, stole steaks and toilet paper and other basic necessities, and could surf for hours without a break. She was seventeen and her name was Kim.

I felt a cheerful lightness after she left, and when Michael came by and put his feet up on the bed in a confrontational manner, it barely fazed me. After two weeks, when I got out of the hospital, I went to group therapy and told everyone that I was scared I would lose Michael. My own words put me into a panic. Instead of practicing guitar and singing, I wept and watched Michael furtively and anxiously, working myself into such a state that all the healing done in the hospital was nearly undone.

The pilot for the "Hootenanny Show" was being filmed in Rochester and Manny wanted me nearby in case ABC gave in and invited Pete Seeger, who had been banned for his political beliefs. Relieved to get on the road, I packed up to go on tour. My mom joined me and we went east.

Unlike mine, Pete Seeger's music, lifestyle, social concerns, and personality were well integrated. I found the blacklisting of the daddy of folk music ludicrous and refused to appear unless he, too, was invited. Pete and I sang in Hartford, where we were picketed by the Veterans of Foreign Wars. Unfortunately, I arrived in a limousine, and felt very out of place and embarrassed when the old men drew up to the windows in a fury, yelling and waving their fists. I got out and tried to talk to them, but Manny was afraid, and ushered me to a dressing room. After the show, the local police offered me an escort, which I declined (the limousine was bad enough), but they ignored me, and raced us through and out of town with motorcycles fore and aft, sirens blaring. I felt flattered by all the attention, though I knew that the police simply had instructions to make sure that if I was hurt, it was not to be on city property.

I ran into an old boyfriend who looked terrific. He listened to my story of the tumultuous four years since last I'd seen him and took me to dinner and bought me a lovely little jewel hanging on a gold chain.

Back at the Foremans' house on Riverside Drive, in the middle of the tour, I sat on Clark and Mairi's grey couch and looked out across the Hudson at the SPRY sign. As though on a whim I took some of Mairi's stationery and sat down to write a letter to Michael. I felt nothing except that after four years a goodbye should really take up more than a page, but I couldn't conjure up much more than "Put the dogs in the kennel, give the cats away, pay so-and-so to clean the place up, and pay the rent. I'm not coming back," though I added a P.S. about his lovely eyes and how wonderful the first three months had been. When I had finished I felt light as silk, and I wrote a letter to Kim. Something about her eyes, too, I think.

I felt as if I'd been hit on the forehead with a big stick called "brand-new." I met the old boyfriend who had given me the necklace, and we walked around New York in the freezing cold, looking for a nice place to eat dinner, and ended up in the 21 Club.

We spent the night in his apartment. Sometime in the night I moved over to the couch. There was something about a new maleness that I found unbearable. New arms, new legs, new hairs on a new chest. Being courted was like drinking from a well after a long drought. Instant intimacy was like being pushed into the well. I needed air, and went home to the Foremans' and wrote another letter to Kim.

Soon after, I was in a hotel in Champaign, Illinois, with my mom, brushing my hair at the bathroom mirror, watching how the little necklace jewel sparkled on its chain, and how nicely it rested on the lace yoke of my dress. In fact, I was having a good indulgent stare at the whole picture. All those little muscles just under the surface of the skin which had been tied up in angry little knots for so long had undone themselves like so many pretty ribbons. I was even a little bit pleased with the brown serious face in the mirror, which, if I tilted it back and got the lighting just right, was actually quite romantic and . . . well, not exactly pretty, but "attractive," and the new word I'd heard so much recently, "charismatic" . . . There was a knock at the door. I opened it and looked smack into the face of a very sickly Michael. I was shocked at his appearance and at how little I felt for him. My response to "We have to talk" was "After the concert," and "You're telling me that three thousand people you've never met are more important than me?" got a simple "Yes." I had an attack of nerves just before going onstage, and had to shoo everyone out of the ladies' room and curl up on the floor. Mom and I ended up laughing, because I *knew* I was sick from the shock of seeing Michael, and I *still* couldn't stop it. After the concert I spent the night with Michael, in his room, trying to say goodbye. He, contrite and apologetic and full of promises and shaky and overtired and smelling of stale cigarettes; me sitting up in bed in my slip, trying to keep my thoughts from flying out the window, fingering my pretty necklace and thinking that it would somehow hurt him less if I just stayed a few more hours.

Back home in California I had no place to live, so I checked into a hotel called the Carmel River Inn, which had cottages. I rounded up my stereo and records, some cooking utensils and clothes.

Kim burst back into my life like a sun ray. I offered her the tiny room in the back of the cabin, and she holed up there like a wild animal, handling her psychiatrist appointments by sleeping through them in her new hideout with her goofy hat down over her eyes. We listened to Fauré's *Requiem*, E. Power Biggs playing Bach, Glenn Gould's recordings of the *Goldberg Variations*, and my collection of rock and roll hits from the mid-fifties to the present.

"You know what?" I said to my psychiatrist.

"No, what?"

"I'm having daydreams about this girl, Kim."

"Well, quit having them."

"Okay."

And three days later:

" 'Member those daydreams I told you about? Well, I stopped them, and now I'm having night dreams."

"Yeah, well you better stop them, too."

And a week later:

"Well, I stopped the daydreams, and then I stopped the night dreams, and now I think I'm gonna have an affair."

This was 1962.

"Well," he said after a while, "don't hold hands in public."

There are pools which run deep, bathing pools for ladies only. In those cool and private places we can go undefended. In the quiet and nonresistant waters and on the warm shores beside them we can go and let out a lifelong sigh of relief and know that we are understood at last. We have white underbellies of softness which we expose only to the gentlest touch. Along the shores is an unspoken alliance of "us against the world" which purges resentments innate in us, resentments we have inherited from centuries of myth.

I tried to watch Kim and me from a distance, but distance became harder and harder to maintain when I thought of, or watched, the divine softness of Kim. I was not confused about what I was feeling, which seemed very clear to me, but rather about what to do about what I was feeling. What I wanted to do was lie down with her in a field of daisies and hold her and let her hold me, and then probably kiss. That was as far as my fantasies went. My confusion came mainly from what everybody else would think.

Kim coped with her own confusion by calling up her surfing boyfriend and challenging him to down a six-pack of beer with her when he came to pick her up. She would put on a stack of 45's and turn up the volume to an unbearable pitch, and bolt back and forth in front of him in our tiny cottage like a colt in a training paddock, forcing him into conversation over the sound of rock and roll, guzzling bottles of beer, and becoming generally hysterical. When she was thoroughly buzzed, she'd say "Okay, c'mon," and lead the poor, submissive young fellow, who was infatuated with her, out to his car. I was amazed at my agitation when she was with him. They would no doubt have a roll in the hay. I couldn't understand why she wasted her time with him.

In the afternoon we would lie on the bed barely touching hands, listening to music. Once, while she slept, I lay there next to her, and at the end of Fauré's *Requiem*, when it sounds like angels ascending into the heavens, I felt as if raindrops of pure gold were falling all around us, and I cried tears of gratitude.

We bought bottles of Aqua Velva and Bay Rum and drenched ourselves in them. She took long showers behind a locked bathroom door and came out in a huge cloud of steam, clean and sweet and fresh in T-shirt and cutoffs. Inspired by her wardrobe, I began to dress more and more outrageously. One day I showed up in group therapy wearing hiking boots, knee-high socks, cutoffs, several layers of T-shirts under a pair of rainbow-colored suspenders, and a headband. The doctor asked everyone what they thought I looked like. One of them said "artistic," one said "happy," one said "like a hippie," and he said "I think she looks like a crazy person." They were all right.

One night we kissed, ever so lightly and briefly in the privacy of our little motel cottage. All my puritanical lineage loomed up in my face, wagging a finger of disapproval. I looked into Kim's eyes.

"Um. Do you know what we're doing?" I said softly.

"What are you talking about!?"

"Well, I mean, you're so young and sometimes I feel as if I'm leading you into something over your head—"

"*Leading me into what?*" She bolted up, and cramming her hat halfway over her eyes, charged toward the door crying out in a heartbreaking voice, "That's filthy! *You're* filthy! I don't *get* this, I just don't *get* it."

For the next fifteen minutes she stormed up and down the wooded driveways of the cottages, furiously brushing tears from her eyes and sniffing and shaking her head in disbelief and terror. After two or three "Don't touch me"s, she consented to be driven to the beach, where we walked up and down in the healing salt air—or rather, she charged and I walked. I would talk to her, and she would bolt away from me, but never farther than a few yards, and by dawn, like the child that she was, she had put the wound out of her mind. In a matter of hours she managed to block it out as if it had never happened, and I knew that if I never referred to it again, neither would she. It took me longer than that to stop feeling like a dirty old lech, but that was entirely my problem.

When Kimmie and I did finally make love, it was superb and utterly natural. It made me wonder what all the fuss was about, both society's and my own.

I hired an architect to build me a home in the hills of Carmel Valley, and he drew up plans. Kim went everywhere with me, and in public, we still tried to pass as buddies. I bought Kimmie a motorcycle, and we each got a Doberman pinscher. Mine was puny and needed constant care, and I carried her around in a wastebasket on a heating pad, which I would plug in wherever we went. Kim's was a stud.

When a good friend of mine was killed in a car accident, Kimmie and I hung out at the hospital wondering how his wife, whom we both loved, was really feeling, with a broken clavicle, broken ribs, numerous fractures, and a broken heart. A nurse said she wanted to see me, and we spent the next two weeks going to and from the hospital. Kimmie would dart in and out of the room, and Colleen would laugh at us. I think she was the only friend I could be honest with, even if all the others knew anyway.

Kimmie and I decided to do something special for Colleen, so we started by going to I. Magnin's to look for a pretty bathrobe, because her hospital gown was depressing. Dressed in our usual costume of cutoffs, T-shirts, headbands, and bare feet, we began plowing through the intimate apparel racks and, at the same moment, spotted a mannequin draped in a turquoise-blue Indian silk floor-length robe embroidered with gold thread.

"That one is two hundred dollars," said a whiskey tenor from under a seven-inch-high platinum beehive. "Perhaps you'd like to have a look at this rack over here. These are in a little bit more accessible price range."

"But ma'am, they are all ugly," I said, "and we like the pretty one that costs two hundred dollars." And before she gift-wrapped it, I asked her to remove the Magnin's label because it was too pretentious.

Colleen loved the robe, and she sat up in bed like a queen, talking about how insane everything was, and how she had no idea what to do with her life, and now didn't even have a car. Kimmie and I glanced at each other, and when we left the hospital, tore off to find a blue car. It was not the most intelligent way to shop, but it was certainly the most fun, and we bought a bright blue Falcon, cash on the line. Letting her three kids in on the secret, we all met at the hospital, urged our heartbroken queen out of bed to take a walk, something the hospital staff had not yet been able to accomplish, and lured her toward the stairs. I remember her floating along in her regal silk, wondering why we had all lost our minds at the same time.

At the top of the stairs, we said, "Okay, now go over to the main door," and her son folded the keys of the Falcon into her hand. She figured it out looking through the glass entranceway to where the shiny blue thing was parked illegally at the curb. We grabbed her hands and dragged her out and danced around her like jesters and puppies, pointing out the car's extra features, all of us babbling at once. She hadn't worn any makeup since her husband had died, and she was so ghostly and quiet and beautiful, laughing at us and crying and shaking her head and thinking, I assumed, as she would for the rest of her life, "I wish Dick were here."

Two months went by and Kimmie and I rented a house in the Carmel highlands. It was made of glass and owned by Brett Weston, of the family of brilliant photographers, and one of the world's oldest living teenagers. My house in the valley was being built. Mimi and her writer husband, Richard Farina, moved in close by, and we saw a lot of each other. Kimmie's motorcycle fell apart and I bought her another one. We had a closet full of T-shirts, cutoffs, sandals, tennis shoes, and boots. My sister argued with Dick that Kimmie and I were just friends. My father and mother weren't around much, and when they were my father didn't seem to notice, and my mother couldn't have cared less. We threw dinner parties, and I took a couple of courses at Monterey Junior College to try to overcome a recurring nightmare I had of being late to class, flunking an important test, and forgetting the combination to my locker.

I bought her an Austin Healey; we became a two-car family. When it came time to tour again, we decided that she would come with me and take a correspondence course to get her high school diploma, and keep my records and receipts. This was during the time period when I wouldn't fly, and we had marvelous romantic sojourns on long-distance Pullmans, and long wild rides through deserts in rented cars. We would insist on a room with two beds, sleep in one, and then jump up and down on the other to muss it up. I'm sure we fooled no one.

That summer I gave a series of concerts at black colleges in the South. Somewhere on that tour things began to fall apart with Kimmie. When we were home for a break, I was easily distracted by one male or another, especially by a six-foot blond loner who appeared each day at our favorite outdoor breakfast spot, driving a black motorcycle with a sidecar. In the sidecar rode a ferocious-looking Doberman pinscher and a black cat. The very attractive blond never glanced my way, which intrigued me no end, and so one morning as he was putting on his black gloves, preparing to leave, I sauntered up and said it was a gorgeous Doberman he had there, and could I pat him? He mumbled an instruction to the dog, whose name was

Satan. Satan, having been instructed to be nice—that is to say, not to kill me—bowed his head sheepishly and allowed me to pat him.

"And the cat?" I inquired.

"That's Satin. I'm Zack, and I know who you are."

It was decided that he would take me for a ride and to dinner, and Kimmie responded to the good news by breaking everything in the bedroom.

"And don't get pregnant!" she spat out en route to the front door, stopping for a moment to lean toward me and deliver the words.

"I won't, Kim," I said, feeling the sinking in my chest which signified the beginning of the end of our wild and good times together. She stormed back in the house and said she wanted to drive the Jag. I said no, that I thought the Healey was quite adequate. I heard her shifting gears furiously as she rode up and down the hills, never venturing far from home, and I knew how vulnerable she was, and how careful I wanted to be. And I went to dinner with the mysterious stranger, and shelved any further involvement.

Back on the road we had a fight about her driver's license. It had been revoked for the final time, for a series of minor traffic violations, and now she wanted me to sign something illegal to get her a New York license, and I said no. She accused me of never doing anything for her, and in response to a slew of insults, I gave her a stinging slap across the face. When she left the room (somewhat triumphant at having made me lose my temper), I thought for a long time. Then I went to her and told her straight out that it was time to end the affair because it had run its course, and if we didn't do too much damage to each other we could be friends later on. Kim was magnificent: she had great pride, and preferring to take her heartbreak with dignity she packed her things and left at once. I'm not sure where she was headed, but she said to friends, and I gave her some money. We embraced for a long moment in the cold gusty wind on the corner of Ninety-seventh Street and Riverside Drive. I remember her, in a big coat, leaning over the dirty New York sidewalk to retrieve something . . . just a little piece of paper or a ticket that kept escaping a few inches at a time in the wind, until she trapped it under her boot, snatched it up, swiped her nose with her cuff, and was gone.

In 1972 I was talking with a young reporter from a Berkeley paper. He asked me if I was heterosexual. I said simply that if the affair I'd had ten years ago counted, then I was bisexual. I didn't realize what a catch he had when he left my house and tore back up the coast to print his story. To give him credit, he printed the other matters we'd discussed, and put the sexuality issue in context.

The next morning, Gail, a good friend who had helped me at Gabe's birth and was staying with me at the time, helping with Gabe after David and I had split up, poked her head into the bedroom and said, "There's a guy here from the press. Did you tell someone you were a lesbian?"

"Tell him to bugger off," was my response.

Half an hour later Gail reappeared and said, "There's one of them in the living room and another one in the hedge."

I sighed and got dressed. Just my luck to have a woman greet them at the door in her nightgown.

What I said to them then, and what I would say now if asked the same questions, is the following:

I had an affair with a girl when I was twenty-two. It was wonderful. It happened, I assume, after an overdose of unhappiness at the end of an affair with a man, when I had a need for softness and understanding. I assume that the homosexuality within me, which people love to say is in all of us, made itself felt at that time, and saved me from becoming cold and bitter toward everyone. I slowly mended, and since the affair with Kimmie have not had another affair with a woman nor the conscious desire to.

But what of my daydreams? Someone who can dance a waltz, the samba, the swing, and the tango picks me up in a limo and takes me to a great old-fashioned tea dance. I am dressed in my black velvet V-neck evening dress, wearing clip-on rhinestone earrings, a rhinestone choke necklace and my silver dancing shoes. We make intelligent conversation about world affairs, speaking half French and half English (though English will do). Then we dance splendidly for many dances, breaking in between for sips of tea. When the dance is over, he takes me home, and while he tells me about his wife in Paris, I amuse myself looking at the white gloves on the steering wheel and dark eyes of the limousine driver in the rearview mirror.

# 3
# "WINDS OF THE OLD DAYS"

This morning, in spite of a darkening sky, I took the wash out to hang with bright-colored clothespins on the circular clothesline. The big German shepherd and pint-size Sheltie danced around my feet in hopes that I would throw the ball for them. As I was reaching up to grab a yellow clothespin to tuck into my mouth, the dogs knocked over the basket. I started to scold them softly and leaned down to scoop up the towels and socks. My hand came back in a startled reflex. It was filled with uncut gems. And as I hunched over the tipped basket, yanking my blue jean skirt out of the dew, my throat clutched painfully at a long-forgotten memory and tears spilled rapidly down my face, landing in the emeralds, which sparkled in their own light. There were garnets and sapphires, too, and rubies. And there were diamonds.

> Ten years ago I bought you some cufflinks
> You brought me something
> We both know what memories can bring
> They bring Diamonds and Rust.

Only it was twenty years ago, not ten. I wiped my nose, stood up, and hung out the wash.

I first saw Bob Dylan in 1961 at Gerde's Folk City in Greenwich Village. He was not overly impressive. He looked like an urban hillbilly, with hair short around the ears and curly on top. Bouncing from foot to foot as he played, he seemed dwarfed by the guitar. His jacket was a rusty leather and two sizes too small. His cheeks were still softened with an undignified amount of baby fat. But his mouth was a killer: soft, sensuous, childish, nervous, and reticent. He spat out the words to his own songs. They were original and refreshing, if blunt and jagged. He was absurd, new, and grubby beyond words. When his set was over, he was ushered to my table and the historic event of our meeting was under way. He stood there nervously, mumbling politely, smiling and looking amused. I sipped my Shirley Temple, feeling like the old dowager of the folk scene, and wished Michael would evaporate. I wanted the freedom to gush over Bobby, and couldn't under Michael's suspicious and critical eye. There was no question that this boy was exceptional and that he touched people, but he had only just begun to touch me.

The next image I have of him is in the doorway of Gerde's, on another night, his round face white under his corduroy railroad hat, asking where my sister Mimi was. I was quietly jealous of his interest in her but managed to laugh and tease him. He seemed very small and very young. I was older by six months, and I felt like his mother.

Back home in Big Sur, some of my East Coast friends told me that Big Albert (Grossman) had approached Bob and the talk of the music scene was that Bob was going to make it "Big." I was dubious. "Bigger than Elvis Presley," they told me. "You're nuts," was my response, remembering the unglamorous scruffball who had mumbled and blurted his nasal-toned songs. "Yeah," one of them continued, "and you know the first thing Dylan did when they started talking about how much money he could make? He went over in a corner by himself, and started scribbling down a list of who his friends were, because if he was gonna be rich, he'd have to know." I smiled, but couldn't quite imagine that rebellious-looking hayseed in the undersized jacket caring about money.

> Now I see you standing with brown leaves falling all around
> and snow in your hair
> Now we're smiling out the window of that crummy hotel
> over Washington Square . . .

The crummy hotel over Washington Square was twelve dollars a night. It had no room service, and a regular clientele of junkies, pushers, transsexuals in transition, young alcoholics, and other dubious New York street riffraff. It made me feel "beat" and made Bob

feel quite at home. I bought Bob a big black suit jacket which almost
fit. He had been wary, but had also succumbed to a white shirt and
—the crowning glory—a pair of cuff links made out of lumpy,
opaque, violet rocks. I was falling in love.

We sat in our room being interviewed about our respective ca-
reers. Maybe that afternoon was the closest I ever felt to Bob: his
eyes were as old as God, and he was fragile as a winter leaf. He was
a Sunday child, fidgeting there on the couch in an oversized jacket
and new cuff links, and I was Mom. But I was also sister mystic and
fellow outlaw, queen to his jack, and a twin underground star. We
were living out a myth, slumming it together in the Village. We
walked around the windy streets and had afternoon breakfast on
MacDougal Street. *Our breath came out white clouds, mingled, and hung
in the air . . . and speaking strictly for me, we both could have died then
and there.*

Bob spoke bad English in quick startling images, and most of what
he saw was for his eyes only. The thoughts he shared were usually
unfinished. Years before, when walking in the woods in Massachusetts, I came upon a woman perched on a stool, drawing furiously
on a big art pad which she clutched with her other hand in her lap.
She looked up occasionally and scrutinized the trees. I greeted her,
and peered for a while at her creation. The page was filled with
goblins, monsters, snakes, Goya-esque eyes shaped like nooses. Unable to restrain myself, I asked the idiotic question, "What are you
drawing?" She glanced up and said pleasantly, indicating the trees
with a wave of her hand, "Oh, just what I see." I imagined Bob's
most moderate fantasies to be a lunatic psychedelia, racing at astro-
speed.

He was rarely tender, and seldom reached out to anticipate another's needs, though occasionally he would exhibit a sudden concern
for another outlaw, hitchhiker, or bum, and go out of his way to see
them looked after. He was touching and infinitely fragile. His indescribably white hands moved constantly: putting a cigarette almost
to his mouth, then tugging relentlessly at a tuft of hair at his neck,
inadvertently dumping the cigarette ashes in dusty cavalcades down
his jacket. He would stand thinking, his mouth working, his knees
flexing one at a time, right, left, right, left. He seemed to function
from the center of his own thoughts and images, and like a madman
he was swallowed up by them.

His humor was dry, private, and splendid. Sometimes he would
start to chuckle. A little at a time, his lips would move from a genuine smile to a pucker. Then, instantly, he would tighten them back

in, until a tiny convulsion of laughter would bring them back to the smile, and sometimes, a full grin followed by laughter. I was always flattered when he would share one of his bizarre images with me, or ask me what a line in a song meant. If I guessed right, he would say, "How the fuck did you know?" Once, at his request and for his amusement, I told him my interpretation of a whole song. He seemed impressed. Then he said, "You know, when I drop dead, people are gonna interpret the shit outta my songs. They're gonna interpret every fuckin' comma. They don't know what the songs mean. Shit, I don't know what they mean."

There were times to come when we would sing together, laugh and horse around, get crazy, talk, go to movies, ride motorcycles, sleep. But never again, after that day in the Village, would I feel the naturalness of just being with him, and understanding, for a while, that nothing we did or said to each other had to be second-guessed or guarded. From that day forward, it was as though we moved slowly out of the eye of the hurricane into the turbulence, the wind knocking his hand away from mine at the first step.

Bobby invited me, Mimi, and her husband, Dick Farina, to house-sit Albert Grossman's, in Woodstock, New York. Dick and Bob were writing, Mimi was singing and being a wife, and I was hanging out between tours. Bob had a 350 Triumph motorcycle which I rode around in the woods and on the back roads, sometimes with him on the back. Most of the month or so we were there, Bob stood at the typewriter in the corner of his room, drinking red wine and smoking and tapping away relentlessly for hours. And in the dead of night, he would wake up, grunt, grab a cigarette, and stumble over to the typewriter again. He was turning out songs like ticker tape, and I was stealing them as fast as he wrote them.

In the coolness of selective recall I never would have betrayed my gushing enthusiasm for the time spent with Bobby in Woodstock. I found it here in a letter home, along with an interesting addendum.

Summer, 1964

Dear Mummy—

Better not let the old man see this—Bobby Dylan wrote it. I've gotten very close to Bobby in the last month. We have such FUN! Wow and he takes baths and everything. Anyway I said "I think I'll write Mummy today" and he jumped up in the air and said he wanted to write it as though it was from me and made me promise I'd sign it. It's a little lewd—he giggled over it for an hour. He is beautiful to me. He bought me a beautiful coat and a dress and earrings, and he's just a joy to be with. We understand each other's need for freedom and there are no chains, just good feelings and giggles and a lot of love. And I enjoy his genius.

The record is done, and should be out in a month, and so should the book. I'm going home alone. It's been fun all this trip, most of the time has been spent with Bobby, but I want to be alone again for a while, and start spending time with Ira. My house is supposed to be finished when I get home. I'm gonna meet the Beatles in Denver. I just adore them, then home on a train. It will be good to be alone. Bobby is a very good business man, and he's given me the name of a business advisor in L.A. to help me out with all my damned lawyers, managers, etc. They need to be pushed. Bobby has his things amazingly well taken care of. You'd never guess it. He's just smart. Everything is cool. Mimi and Dick aren't too cool, but it comes and goes. I think Bobby will come out and stay with me for a while if my house is done, but he has a tour starting Sept. 8. You would be pleased to see what fun we have together. I really love him.

Love

Love

Love—Joanie

on the 21st
sometime

dear mummy

it's me here. i'm up in woodstock at uncle alby's. nice house you oughta be here. swimming pool. all that stuff. i'm with you-know who. dick an mimi're also round the place but i've hardly seen them sinse you-know-who got a hold on me. mummy you must believe me. i was gonna stay at the foremans as planned i mean i was all set to an everything. anyway when me an mimi got t town right away first thing we did was t go there. an you know me i was tired and it was already past noon an well i fuigureed like t get t sleep you know an well i got in t bed y'know an jesus i pulled back the blankets an who do you think was hiding under the quilt? yeah him. i mean like i dont know if you'll believe me or not but i swear t gawd he was rolled up like a ball inside the pillow. mummy, i shit. the first thing i did was t call for mimi.

mimi came running down the hall but do you think it did anygood? you-know-who just slowly stood up an jumped on the floor. mummy, his hair had grown down past his waist. he was wearing this monster sweater that stank like he hadn't taken a bath for a year. mummy, he was terrible. i mean like even alfredo the cuban was heard t comment later, "ay tairdbil" (aye, que terrible) anyway, mimi saw him there an she turned an ran. mummy, she just turned an ran. you*know-who didnt waste any time let me tell yuh. he threw me on the bed like some kind of caveman. (he hadnt shaved for about four days mummy. honest t gawd. four days!) an you know how tired i get. i mean like i was in no position t fight. an he wa sayin something. he was sayin like i never heard before. i mean like i never heard it in any movie. i mean like he was sayin "hey c'mon hey c'mon" over an over again. hey an you know me like i just fall like an anvil. clunge. when it comes t new things that i aint never heard before. i mean like i dont want you t think he's (you-know who) influenced me or nuthin mummy i just fall into all these traps. maybe that second shrink was right. maybe i DONT know myself as i should know myself. maybe he was right when he said "Joannie darling, you just dont know your-self" anyway, you*know-who, for lack of better word, just about seized me. it wasnt like any captain kid came swirling down from the masttype thing but still it was kind of wierd. i mean he really did sort of take me by surprise. i mean like what would you do? i mean i fought an everythin. mummy i fought him no end. i bit the shit out of his nose. kicked him where it really hurts. clawed the back of his neck till blood came out a his bellybutton. mummy, i blew so hard in his ear, i thought his eyes would pop out. but then he did this dumb thing. i mean like he was still sayin "hey c'mon, c'mon" but then also too now he started reciting poetry. like it was about the time i was scratching an trying t bend his elbow off he started calling me ramona. i swear at first i thought it was some game. he kept sayin things like "no use tryin" an words like "exist" an mummy i swear he even mentioned something about crack country lips. mummy, i couldnt fight. i mean like i just couldnt fight. yeah like so i passed out. yeah an i woke up here. aint played a concert for a month. manny is calling perpetually. vic-tor keeps answering the phone an says "no, she's not here" in a funny voice an you*know-who doesnt say nothin excpt "everything's all right" an "nuthin matters" yeah well i gotta

go. you-know who's making this movie an he wants me t rub
his head while he gets ready. all in all everything i guess is ok.
house is coming along. oh, i signed over my car t you-know-
who. yeah, he said it'd take a lot of worry off my mind about
owning things an well . . . it has a little i guess. i wouldn't mind
that too much but well . . . you-know-who sold the car. he says
that's better that way cause now i wont be pesterin him t let me
drive it. mummy, he's the worst driver in the world. i swear i
nearly have a bird everytime he takes me t the shrink. my shrink
hates him but that's another story an i'll write you later about it.
    ok then faretheewell


manard solomon says hello
an keeps asking when you're
coming back
    ok 'bye
an dont worry bout me none

oh, p.p.s
    i gave that little tiny picture of me
    t you-know-who an he posted it on top
    of his ford station wagon interior

    mummy, i'm fine.
    dont worry about me please
    everything passes everything changes
        oh, mummy mummy I love you so much
    oh mummy
give regards t brice an pauline

        oh oh! here comes you-know-who
        i dont want him t catch me writing
          t you
          gotta go
                luv yuh


                Joanie


Bob had the kind of charisma which never really allowed him
privacy. Everyone wanted to be the one to get under his skin, to say
the clever thing which would make him laugh, to somehow score a
point so later on they could think back to that moment and feel

special. Even though I had a proximity to him, and had a coveted position in the growing world of Dylan fans, I felt the same way. He held us all at a distance except for rare moments, which we all sought.

Although I wished to be the one person who wouldn't clutch at Bob, I was ferocious in my possessiveness. One evening at the restaurant with Mimi and Dick, some other friends, and me, Bob caught the eye of a recently arrived pilgrim sitting across the room staring imploringly at our table. As Bob returned her stare, Mimi and I began to cluck like two angry old hens, commenting snidely on the poor girl's pallor, miserable and slightly crazed expression, and stereotypical rags and tatters. I knew that Bob gorged when he got drunk, so I filled his glass over and over until his wandering eyes were red and bleary, and then offered him dessert. As soon as he had finished one dessert, I would shove another one under his chin, and he would poke at it, looking kind of forlorn, as though he wished it would go away, and then he'd eat it, washing it down with more wine and coffee. Finally, the girl, responding to Bob's more and more frequent stares, floated across the room and landed unceremoniously at the table, sinking clumsily into a chair, her eyes riveted upon him. He was drunk, flattered, disgusting, and rude.

My fury was twofold. Fifty percent was jealousy of Bob's attention to the girl, the other of her attention to him: the outrage of seeing a look of adoration which was usually reserved for me, now bestowed upon the drunken sot sitting next to me. I went to the ladies' room and fumed, Mimi blew up at Bob, and the next thing I remember was waiting out in the alley for Bob to come find me and say something wonderful like, "I'm sorry. I don't know what came over me. How could I have been such an idiot when all I really want to do is be with you." Instead, he just kept repeating that his stomach was killing him, and what-all had he eaten, for Chrissake. I told him what he'd eaten, and then began to feel sorry for him, he looked so miserable with his stomach hard as a rock and bulging under his T-shirt. So finally I drove him home, certain at every curb that he would throw up two custard pies and a pecan fudge cake before we could get to a tree. But instead, he fell asleep and snored, and I had to wake him up and practically carry him to bed, where he fell immediately back into what looked very much like a guiltless slumber.

In August of 1963 I went out on tour and invited Bobby to sing in my concerts, following the example set for me by Bob Gibson four years before. I was getting audiences of up to ten thousand at that point, and dragging my little vagabond out onto the stage was a grand experiment and a gamble which I knew he and I would eventually win. The people who had not heard of Bob were often infuriated and sometimes even booed him when he would interrupt the lilting melodies of the world's most nubile songstress with his tunes of raw images, outrage and humor. I would respond by wagging my finger at the offenders like a schoolmarm, advising them to listen to the words, because this young man was a genius. They listened.

One afternoon on tour I drove us into a hotel parking lot and asked Bob if he would go and check us in. When I got to the desk, I was greeted warmly, but the management was eyeing Bob most unenthusiastically.

"And do you have a room for my friend?" I asked. No, they did not.

Bob was nosing around a stand-up ashtray on the other side of the lobby, looking, to the artistic eye, like a poet, but to the untrained eye, more like a bum. I was in an impetuous protective rage by the time the management rustled up a room, which they did only after I told them I would go elsewhere if they didn't find a "really nice room" for Mister Dylan. I apologized to Bob, who said it didn't bother him none. But that evening, by the time the concert was over, he had written an entire song called, "When Your Ship Comes In." It was outraged, vengeful, strong, and lyrical.

I've never experienced charisma like that which Bob displayed in his reverse-showmanship performances. There was a strange out-of-place forlornness about his appearance on stage. Even now, though he has been a seasoned rock and roller for more than twenty years, and single-handedly controls his management, crowd, security, and stage personnel with only a word or a scowl, when the lights come on and the crowd roars in anticipation, he manages to find his way onto the stage with his back to the audience, fidgeting with a harmonica or two. When he faces the crowd, he looks as though he'd rather be in a dark parlor playing chess. Perhaps in a sense he is.

Once in a while (as much later on the Rolling Thunder Revue in 1975), he seemed terribly happy. Happy to put on a hat bedecked with bright flowers, happy to walk jauntily out on the stage, happy to see the crowd. (I don't think he sees very far. One of the last times I talked to him was at a swimming pool in Berlin during a tour. He was squinting at where he thought I was sitting. "I'm over here, Bob," I said, pointing to some chairs at my left. He squinted over to where I was pointing. "How far *can* you see?" I asked as he stood there in a floor-length bathrobe with a pointed hood. "Oh, the eye

doctor says my eyes are gettin' better." "How far *can* you see, Bob?")
For a while, he wore bright-colored scarves and white-face, and
would grin at the band, and smile to himself behind the makeup,
and say ridiculous things to the audience, which would try to decipher his words as if they had just sprung from the holy tablets up
on the mountain. I think he was enjoying his big joke on everybody,
but it didn't matter. The songs were powerful, the musicians capti-
vating, and the stage a mad circus. On the Rolling Thunder tour, I
never missed a night of hearing him. It was the intensity, I guess,
and the words.

Before Bob "went electric," there was just him and the guitar, and
his disjointed, magnificent, mystical words.

Those words, which Bob would drop onto an empty page like so
many gold nuggets shaken from somewhere up his sleeve, were the
words which would move me out of the ethereal but archaic ballads
of yore and into the contemporary music scene of the 1960s. More
than once I had stood on stage and said, even stopping in the middle
of a song, so strong was the feeling, "I have something to say, but I
don't know what it is . . . It has to do with this poor old world of
ours." And I'd go back into the song, a ballad which relayed compassion, depths of human struggle, and caring, but in a way so
personalized that I felt it was divorced from the more-and-more
pressing issues of the day. Bob was with me the first time I sang
"With God on Our Side" in concert. I had barely finished memorizing it and the auditorium was very hot. There was perspiration running down the small of my back and behind my knees. I was
nervous, excited, and exhilarated.

Up until then, the songs which integrated my music and my deep
social concerns were "Last Night I Had the Strangest Dream," "We
Shall Overcome," and some black spirituals. Bob's songs seemed to
update the concepts of justice and injustice. And if the songs were
not about justice, he made you think they were, because of his
image, his rejection of the status quo, set against the mounting turbulence in the country.

Nothing could have spoken better for our generation than "The
Times They Are A-Changin'." The civil rights movement was in full
bloom, and the war which would tear this nation asunder, divide,
wound, and irreparably scar millions upon millions of people was
moving toward us like a mighty storm. When that war began, I,
along with thousands of others, would go to battle against it. We
would lose Bob to other things, but before the first official bullet was
fired, he had filled our arsenals with song: "Hard Rain," "Masters

of War," "The Times They Are A-Changin'," "With God on Our Side," and finally, "Blowin' in the Wind," which endured the sixties to become everything from a fireside camp song for German Boy Scouts to Hyatt House Muzak to the best-known anthem of social conscience throughout the world. Bob Dylan's name would be so associated with the radical movements of the sixties that he, more than all the others who followed with guitars on their backs and rainbow words scribbled in their notepads, would go down forever in the history books as a leader of dissent and social change, whether he liked it or not, and I gather he doesn't much care one way or the other.

Even now, in the 1980s, "Farewell, Angelina," a beautiful little love song laced with cockeyed imagery, is enough to transport a festival audience of forty thousand people in France back to the meaningful days of the sixties, and to give them a sense of empowerment, because for a few minutes they can become a part of a dream from the years when "everything was happening," life seemed to have a purpose, and everyone made a difference. And that, dear Bob, is not fuckin' bad.

I left Woodstock and went home to Carmel Valley, where you planned to come and stay after a while. You and Mimi and Dick saw me off, and I'm told you went directly from the train to a phone booth and called up Sara. Ignorant that there even was a Sara, I left happily with memories, songs, some disillusionment, and a blue nightgown I'd found in a closet in Albert's house, which you had said I could keep. Twelve years later, when I finally met and became friends with Sara, we talked for hours about those days when the Original Vagabond was two-timing us. I told Sara that I'd never found Bob to be much at giving gifts, but that he had once bought me a green corduroy coat, and had told me to keep a lovely blue nightgown from the Woodstock house. "Oh!" said Sara, "that's where it went!"

When you came to stay in Carmel Valley, we went to coffee houses on Cannery Row, drove up and down the Big Sur coast, and bought an upright piano for two hundred dollars. You stood at the big kitchen windows with your typewriter perched on top of a waist-high adobe structure and faced the hills. You wrote "Love Is Just a Four-Letter Word" and "The Lonesome Death of Hattie Carroll," among other things, and one evening, while you were talking, you picked all the meat out of a stew I'd made, and ate it, leaving only vegetables and potatoes for anyone else.

You and I talked in a playful way over that summer month about "our futures." We even named a baby. I think the name was Shannon. As I remember it, you called me one day after you'd returned to Woodstock and, with what sounded like a party in the background, mumbled something about marriage. I do remember that I said "no." It had not been a proposal; it had been a noncommittal continuation of our fun and games which might very well have led to a noncommittal joining of two lives in a noncommittal marriage. That is my memory. I'm sure you remember it differently, if at all.

In spite of what did or did not happen that summer, we made plans to sing together in a short concert tour of the States in March and April of 1965. Manny was in charge of the poster, which we both had to okay. The billing was to be exactly equal, and a design by Eric Von Schmidt was finally agreed upon which had Bob's head a little higher than mine, and my name a little higher than his, and somehow, especially at first glance, gave no deference to either one of us.

We were something of a phenomenon, packing houses and getting rave reviews. The show was divided exactly in half. We opened together, I sang for forty minutes, there was an intermission, Bob sang for forty minutes, and we closed together. We had fun; we traveled a lot by car, we were a big deal, and we were taken to meet the Beatles.

(A letter home)

Dear Everyone—
Sometimes I'm so lucky it's just ridiculous. There were at least 10,000 people who would gladly have given their right arm and leg to touch, talk to, or just be in the same room with any one of the Beautiful Beatles. I must say I felt pretty much the same way. As it turned out, I was taken by the press to their press conference. *They* found out I was there and asked to see me and I ended up watching their "performance" from the stage after having fixed their ties, cufflinks, hair, etc. and leaving with them in their limousine with police sirens, motorcycles, etc. all the way to the hotel, going up to their suite for what I imagined would be a horrible noisy party, but they got rid of *everyone* and the five of us just sat around and giggled and acted goofy and sang songs until 3:00 a.m.

I loved the fame, attention, and association with Bob, but soon our real differences surfaced and began to dominate our relationship. Once I asked him how he came to write "Masters of War." His reply was that he knew it would sell; I didn't buy his answer then and I don't now. I think his active commitment to social change was limited to songwriting. To my knowledge, he never went on a march. He certainly never did any civil disobedience, at least that I knew about. I've always felt that he just didn't want the responsibility. Once he commented to me about the kids in the audience calling out for "Masters of War": "They think I'm something I ain't." And then he joked about it and told me to take care of them and "all that stuff." I told him I'd do my best.

We were outside somewhere; I was yanking up blades of grass, troubled that our paths were splitting and going in very different directions. I asked him what made us different, and he said it was simple, that I thought I could change things, and he knew that no one could. I was upset by his remark. Perhaps he would end up Rock and Roll King to my Peace Queen.

One day we went to get something to eat before the show. Bob had left what I referred to as his vomit jacket hanging on a coat rack in the dressing room. I had been trying (one of my sterling qualities) to get him to wear something other than that revolting, undersized, beat-up, unflattering English orphan jacket, which he loved with all his heart. I must have temporarily won, because when we went for hamburgers he was wearing something else, and when we got back the jacket was gone. I felt terrible, and Bob screamed, red-faced, at the six-and-a-half-foot-tall black security guard to "Get the fuck outta here!" The guard slunk out. Bob turned to me and continued screaming. His face was distorted and the veins were popping out and his eyes were brimmed with red. I got ahold of myself and told him never to talk like that to me or anyone else in the world, and said that when he was ready to rehearse I'd be in my dressing room. I exited, a pillar of strength to any onlooker and a mass of jelly within. Bob was fine when we rehearsed, and his part of the concert was stupendous. I made the brilliant remark after the show that he ought to get mad more often because his performance had been even better than usual, and he blew up all over again, saying that he wasn't mad, and hadn't never bin mad. So we knew something about each other by the time we left for Europe. Bob had invited me on his tour of England, and I was thrilled.

Sometimes I think that you pulled away from all reality on that English tour of spring 1965. You were mantled with praise, sought after by hysterical fans, appealed to by liberals, intellectuals, politicians, the press, and genuinely adored by fools like me, and I don't think you ever really recuperated. You had invited me to come, and I assumed you'd invite me up to sing with you. Did you know how wonderful that would have been for me? I had introduced you in the States, and to have returned the favor not only would have been natural, but would have given me the perfect leg up I needed before my own tour, which followed directly after yours. Apparently it was not in the cards.

When we landed at Heathrow Airport I decided to stay out of your way, as this was clearly your moment. You gave a typical Dylan press conference, playing with a giant light bulb and confounding the press with your nonanswers, some of which were hilariously funny. In a crush of people you headed for the door, and for a split second you looked around, saw me, and reached out your hand. Did I imagine that fleeting moment and imploring gesture? You looked vulnerable and wild. You were about to be gobbled up by fans, but I thought it would be out of place to grab your hand at that moment, so I stayed back, shaking my head and smiling encouragingly as you were swallowed up by tweed jackets and raincoats. I thought we would talk sometime later, after it all calmed down, when you just wanted a quiet cup of tea.

It never calmed down. And why the hell would you want a quiet cup of tea with me, ever again? They thought you were God. I thought you were my friend, and I wanted to be on the stage with you and share in the success and excitement. You wanted that tour all to yourself, and if I had not been so devastated that I lost all reason, I would have flown home after a quiet visit to the London Bridge, which was still in England at that time.

It was not love that made me such a nuisance for that entire tour, Bob (though I am sure you were completely unaware that I was unhappy); it was desperation. For the first time in my short but monumentally successful career someone had stolen all my thunder from under my nose. I simply hung around and got sick. If it hadn't been for Neuwirth, our mutual friend, acting as your traveling companion and my suicide-control center, I would have had a total collapse. One night I went to Neuwirth's room crying. He put his arms around me and mopped a pint of tears off my cheeks and chin, and begged me to pack up my bags and leave the tour.

"But Bob *asked* me to come. He *asked* me," I protested.

"I know, but he don't know what's happening anymore, can't you see? He's just out there spinnin' and he wants to do it by himself."

One morning, Bob's large entourage was piling into limousines to head off to Liverpool. No one ever knew where to sit, and Bob never invited anyone. I was concerned about some new guest he'd asked along, and ventured to Bob, "Don't you think so-and-so ought to sit with you today?"

Bob's face clouded over in instant annoyance.

"*Ought* to sit here?! *Ought* to sit here?! I don't give a fuck where they sit. Let 'em take care of themselves." And he plowed head first into the limousine, leaving the hordes to muddle things out for themselves. I climbed in after him. He picked up the stack of daily newspapers and began reading about himself. He came across a quote from me. I had been asked, at an inopportune moment, what the *real* Bob Dylan was like.

I had toyed for a fleeting second with giving an honest answer, but had decided against it, and said, simply, "Bob is a genius."

"What the fuck is this?" Bob's mood was blackening.

"What the fuck is what?"

"Quotes you as saying that I'm a genius. What the fuck is that all about?" I was deceivingly calm.

"It's what you say when you can't think of anything else, Robert."

"Where do you get off calling me a genius?"

"Would you rather I told them what I really think?"

Sometimes I thought I was the only one who saw what was really happening to him. Bob was being spoiled to death on his first tour. He was tacking pictures up on the Savoy walls, ordering heaps of food and letting it pile up around him. Albert was footing the bill, and the room was filled with sycophants who praised each new line that he peeled off the typewriter.

It didn't occur to me that I was also a sycophant. I was still desperately hanging on to the hope that I would be asked to sing. But despite petitions to Bob from English kids to hear me sing (which were probably never delivered to him by his protective staff), I was never asked. I was a wounded but still impetuous queen, long since dethroned but hanging on by the teeth to dreams of power. The tour ended up with Bob sick in bed after a spur-of-the-moment trip to some exotic restaurant for dinner.

I gave my own concert in London. It was a sold-out success, but I was too sick to enjoy it, especially since almost all of the remaining entourage stayed in the hotel with Bob. That sold-out concert was the first of many to come, but I couldn't know that at the time. I'd forgotten that I had a career, a huge following, a voice of my own. It never occurred to me that many English and European fans had followed me for five years already and didn't care about the original vagabond, the unwashed phenomenon, at all.

I had not been asked to his room, but went out to find him a present anyway. My mother and father, in London to see my debut at the Royal Albert Hall, went with me. Having bought him a dark blue Vyella shirt, with great trepidation, I went unannounced and uninvited to knock at his door. It was answered by Sara, whom I'd never seen before and who had been flown in to look after Bob. Everyone had carefully avoided telling me she was there. She took the package from me with a patient and quizzical look on her lovely face, blinked her massive black eyes, thanked me softly, and shut the door.

## PART THREE

# "SHOW ME THE HORIZON"

# 1

# "THE BLACK ANGEL OF MEMPHIS"

*"Somebody gotta wake up Martin."*

*"Ain't gonna be me, no suh!" [Laughter]*

*"Folks bin waitin mos' two hours at the church. Somebody gotta wake him up. He cain't sleep through this one."*

*"Well, he the mos' tired out ole nigger ever throwed his body down on a bed, and I ain't wakin' him up."*

*"How 'bout you, Joan? Y'all go sing him a li'l song, wake him up real nice."*

*"Me? I don't want to wake him up!"*

I was ushered into the bedroom of the modest home in the black section of Grenada, Mississippi, where Dr. Martin Luther King, Jr., and some of his aides were staying, and where Ira and I had joined them all for breakfast. It was the fall of 1966. The door closed quietly behind me. I waited a few seconds and then walked around to the side of the bed he was facing. He was dead to the world. He looked so peaceful I didn't want to make a sound. His black head made a cozy dent in the clean white pillowcase, and he looked like a big chocolate angel. I leaned over for a closer look. His Aida eyes were slanted upward and closed, and the lashes were downright kinky. His eyebrows were thick and well defined on the smooth brown skin. No lines. The famous little moustache jutted out over the huge, handsome lips of possibly the finest orator this country has ever produced. Those lips were drooping into the gravity of a daytime slumber.

I went back around to the other side of the bed and sat down on a well-worn stuffed chair with starched white doilies covering the arms. I started to sing softly.

> I am a poor pilgrim of sorrow
> I travel this wide world alone . . .

I sang it the way I'd learned it from a soprano in a Birmingham church, using long, sustained, free-form notes and no particular rhythm.

> No hope have I for tomorrow
> I'm trying to make heaven my home.

The chocolate mound didn't move.

> Sometimes I'm tossed and I'm driven, Ohhh.

The notes soared upwards.

> Sometimes I don't know where to roam, Mmmmm,
> But I know that there must be King Jesus, Ohhhh,
> And I'm trying to make heaven my home.

The lump rolled slowly, in shifts, all the way around to face my chair, uttering a big delicious groan all the while.

"B'lieve I hear the sound of an angel. Sing me 'nother one, Joan . . . Mmmm, thaz beautiful." He was smiling sleepily, and had faded out completely by the time I started the next line. I was worried about all the people waiting for him in the church, but I just went on singing until Andy Young poked his head in the door and smiled his half smile and said, "Shoulda known," and together we woke up God's darkest messenger and got him on his feet and full of coffee to go and preach the word to another town's flock.

Oh, how I loved to hear him speak. Sometimes I think he spoke more fervently about nonviolence when I was there, because he mentioned one time that all he had to do was say, "Non-VAH-olence!" and I'd turn into one of his folk. It seemed a miracle that I would meet, and have the blessing to know and work with, one of the two saints of the phenomenon which had won my heart when I was barely sixteen years old: the concept of radical nonviolence, introduced to the world as a revolutionary political tool by Mahatma Gandhi in India, and reintroduced now by Martin Luther King, Jr., in the United States of America.

Gandhi had said that the job of India was to free the Indians from being in front of the British guns, and free the British from being behind them. The same rule was applying in the South, largely because King truly believed that white men were his brothers, and because his followers loved him enough to at least take his word for it and hold tenaciously to the tactics of nonviolence.

I was in Washington in 1963 when King gave his most famous speech: "I have a dream." It was a mighty day, which has been described many times. I will only say that one of the medals which hangs over my own heart I awarded to myself for having been asked to sing that day. In the blistering sun, facing the original rainbow coalition, I led 350,000 people in "We Shall Overcome," and I was near my beloved Dr. King when he put aside his prepared speech and let the breath of God thunder through him, and up over my head I saw freedom, and all around me I heard it ring.

The first time I was in the South was in 1961. I was on a regular concert tour, and was barely aware of the civil rights movement, probably because I hadn't yet made the transition from Michael to the real world. I did discover, however, that no blacks were at any of my concerts, and would not have been allowed in if they had come. The following summer I wrote into the contract that I wouldn't sing unless blacks were admitted into the hall. The movement was beginning to swell in ranks and spirit, and I returned to the South and discovered that no blacks came to my concerts anyway, because they'd never heard of me. We had to call up the local NAACP for volunteers to integrate an audience for someone they'd never heard of. By then I was singing "Oh, Freedom" and "We Shall Overcome," and aligning myself entirely with the struggle. Not satisfied with the level of my own commitment, I decided that the next time down I would sing in black schools. Even if I was unknown to the black population, the students would come to hear me simply out of curiosity and boredom. With a little negotiating, in '62 Manny set up a tour which included four black colleges deep in the heart of the South and he and Kimmie and I went. The most memorable of those would be Miles College in Birmingham, Alabama.

We had arrived a couple of days early to be with Dr. King and his entourage and stayed with them at the Gadston Motel, the only

place which took both blacks and whites. Birmingham was organized to the teeth for demonstrations and civil disobedience, and we
were wild with anticipation about the next few days.

We went to a Baptist church meeting on Sunday morning. The
young preacher had a packed house. His sermon was called "Singing at Midnight." People got up to testify, and instead of talking
about pie in the sky, they were talking about going to jail for their
freedom. A woman stood up and testified that she and the other
mothers must not be afraid to let their children go to jail because,
she said, "Jail be the only thang leff t'do, an it ain't a disgrace lahk
Ah always bin taught, no *suh* (PRAISE THE LORD!), it is a *honuh*
t'go t'jail in the footsteps of ow-uh great leaduh, Dr. Mawtin Luthuh
King!" At the sound of King's name, a great response of "YES,
WELL . . . YES, UH-HUH!" and nods of affirmation and weeping
and humming struck up and resounded throughout the room, and
the choir burst into song, and an old man across the aisle "got
happy" and went stiff and was carried out by four women in rustling
white who fanned him and continued right on with the song. I was
unashamedly drenched in tears, and next to me Kimmie began to
shake. A lovely big black lady came and unbuttoned the top of Kim's
blouse and fanned her, and smiled sweetly at the innocent white
folks from "up North."

Then I heard the preacher saying, "An we lucky enough to have
with us t'day a frien' o' *all* of us, come down from the North to be
with us in ow-uh struggle . . ." Oh, Christ, not now, I thought. "An
we gone ask her up heah to sing a li'l sumthin' f'us," he went on,
". . . Miss Jo-ann . . . Jo-ann Bah-ezz." Folks mumbled and shifted
around and wondered what else could possibly happen at their congregation in these strange times, and I went up to the pulpit. I
started in singing "Let Us Break Bread Together on Our Knees," and
folks joined in. I sang in a voice very different from the pure white
one which is on all my records. I sang with the soul I was adopting
right there in that room, and heads began to nod in approval, and
wrinkled old faces smiled in confusion and pleasure. Then I sang
"Swing Low," and folks started to get happy. Handkerchiefs came
out and fans doubled their speed. A couple of folks yelled out "UH-
HUH, LAWD!" and then one old lady in a magenta hat went stiff
and had to be carried out, and I was scared but I kept on singing,
because, I suppose you might say, I had gotten the spirit.

The next day was the first day of mass arrests. The police chief,
Bull Connor, known for riding around town in a baby blue tank,

was giving orders to prepare for the fire hoses, tear gas, attack dogs, and arrests. I was furious because I had to give a concert and couldn't be arrested with my brothers and sisters. I promised Manny I'd be back at the hotel in time to leave for the concert, and went off with Kimmie in a movement car, me hiding face down on the back seat, Kim on the floor, to a church where children from all over Birmingham were gathering.

The church was already packed with kids marching up and down the aisles, filling the pews, clapping, singing, chanting, talking, and laughing. Periodically, over the din, a new group would start up the most popular tune of the day, which was simply the word "Freedom," sung over and over again to the tune of "Amen," substituting different opening lines like "Everybody needs . . ." or "All the children need . . ." and even "Bull Connor needs . . . freedom, freedom, free-*dom*, free-*dom*!"

There was one other white in the room aside from Kimmie and me, brave Barbara Deming, who did march that day, committed civil disobedience, and spent time in the Birmingham jail, from where she wrote her well-known *Prison Notes*.

An organizer took the microphone and told the crowd that when Bull Connor realized that all the jails in Birmingham wouldn't be enough to contain all the folks who were planning to pay 'em a visit, he let the word out, and some rich white folks donated their tennis courts. Cheers and laughter went up all around, and whispers of anticipation by some children who had never seen a tennis court.

I made friends with some teenage girls, who laughed and talked and sang with me. When it came time for me to leave, I covered my hair with a scarf and held their hands and strutted right out the front door, jabbering and giggling, past the huge policemen who were swinging their billy clubs like pendulums. The billy clubs stopped swinging and hung still as Spanish moss in a breezeless swamp as we walked past. I was as dark as the lightest of the girls, and sounded pretty black when I wanted to. I guess I confused the police a little. Kimmie stayed in the church, promising not to get arrested, and I trudged reluctantly back to the Gadston to meet Manny and wait for our ride out to Miles College.

The first thing we saw on campus was a long trail of junior high school blacks marching across the lawn singing, "Miles College needs freedom!" Every glorious shade of black, they danced and clapped as they stepped, pushing each other playfully. Ironically, I was going to be singing to the most unpolitical blacks in all of Alabama. Everybody involved in the movement was in town getting arrested.

Perhaps it was better that way. The amazing thing that happened had already begun as we stood on the lawn, talking with some of our hosts. As we looked around we saw white folks arriving, here and there, in small groups, or two at a time. They just quietly walked across the green and up to the entrance of the main building, all of which shouldn't have seemed odd, but did. Our hosts were also staring at the silent arrivals. One of them said thoughtfully, "This is the first time whites have ever stepped foot onta this campus."

The auditorium slowly filled to capacity, the center section made up of whites and a few blacks, and the side sections mostly blacks. I was experiencing something more than stage fright. I was fearing for my life. There was a revolution going on all around us, and if a white businessman and his family wanted to hear me sing "Fair and Tender Maidens," they had to come and sit in this boiling hot room and integrate an audience. I walked out onstage, took a bow and fought the slamming of my heart. In the first song there was a loud bang in the balcony. Every muscle in my body jerked, my skin went all prickly, and I thought I would simply pass out from fright. A quiet exclamation of nodding and shrugging rippled through the audience ("Must have been a chair collapsing"), and then my heart began slowing back to normal. I sang and talked, and no one seemed bored. Perhaps it was partly because of the electricity we could feel emanating from the center of town, miles away, where the kids were at that very moment being arrested and filling paddy wagons, singing and praying, scared to their bones but bolstered by each other's presence and by the knowledge that they were doing right in the eyes of God. Images of the kids gave me courage, and the concert was beautiful. It ended with "We Shall Overcome," and the audience rose and held hands, swaying back and forth while they sang. The singing was soft and tentative and many people were crying.

Years later, I was told by an influential Washington liberal that she had been there that day, sitting next to a noted right-wing news columnist. He explained to her that he was only there out of curiosity, but at the end he rose with her and sang, holding her hand and weeping along with so many others. She said that that concert had an overwhelming impact on her life. And so it did on mine.

The fire hoses aimed and sprayed, the dogs charged and sank their fangs through raggedy sleeves and into flesh, the billy clubs swung and struck, and Dr. King went to jail. The world watched, and all the civilized people put their thoughts, prayers, energies, sympathies, and letters with the black community, which was, rapidly now, and with the great dignity of nonviolence, rising to its feet and standing tall for the first time in American history. "Y'see," said Dr. King, "a man cain't *rahhhd* your back if it's straight!" On the train going to the next city we learned that the Gadston Motel had been bombed, but that no one had been hurt.

The first time I had a serious talk with King was in 1965. Andy Young was taking me to see King in his room, during a Southern Christian Leadership Conference meeting in South Carolina. We stopped outside of King's door, and my stomach knotted up as I heard King's voice raised in anger and frustration. Andy waited for a moment before knocking and slipping us both in. James Bevel and Jesse Jackson were there, hollering on about something to do with loyalty. King had a drink in his hand, and his eyes were glistening with tears. He was going on about how he couldn't take the pressure anymore, that he just wanted to go back to Memphis and preach in his little church, and he was tired of being a leader. He let a tear roll down his cheek and slither to a halt on that powerful jawbone. A woman who worked with King was crying over the sink in the bathroom. I went in and hugged her, not caring whether or not she wanted to explain anything, only wanting to be of some use and comfort.

Perhaps I was shocked at first that ow-uh great leader would get drunk and curse and weep and talk crazy and, I suspected, attaching rumors I'd heard to the scene in the hotel room, have girlfriends. But I was more relieved than shocked to be a witness to his human frailties. I knew that he would be criticized for his "weaknesses," and I knew also that it was inhuman to expect more from him than he could do, or be, or than he was already giving. Maybe someday I would be in a similar position. I wanted understanding and forgiveness in advance.

King was smiling but sheepish when we met the next day.

"Well," he began, "now that you know Ah'm not a saint . . ."

"And I'm not the Virgin Mary," I said. "What a relief!"

The evening before the planning breakfast in Grenada (which King had slept through), I had been invited to go with James Bevel, a maniacal and wonderful and lesser-known preacher and aide to King, Jesse Jackson, Andy Young, and Hosea Williams to pick King up at the airport. I tried not to show my giddy delight at the fact that I would finally be with him, behind the scenes, hearing the planning and in talk of the leadership. I huddled by the window of the movement rent-a-car, looking out at the lush evergreens dripping with moss, and the undergrowth creeping up to meet the branches.

"Gosh, it's beautiful down here," I ventured. They all started to laugh and then thickened their accents for my benefit.

"Down heah we calls 'at beautiful scenery a swamp, an' folks that does'n pick enough bales o' cotton gits t'sleep down there . . ."

"Yeah, sleep fo' *long* tahm!"

I felt like an ass, but they all went into such gales of laughter that I had to laugh with them.

Bevel started telling survival stories about how he did the "Sambo." He said one time he was driving down this very road, and in the rearview mirror he saw a *po*-lice car pull out to follow him. He got nervous and sped up, and so, of course, did the *po*-lice. So he floored it and took off, in some wild fantasy that the junk heap he was driving could outdistance a sheriff's car. Naturally, the police caught up after a brief chase, lights flashing and siren screaming, and pulled Bevel over. Bevel jumped out of the car and ran up to the policemen, twisting his hat in his hands and doing what he called the "Sambo."

"Oh, Lawd," he started in. "Ah sho' am glad t' see you be de *po*-lice! Ah thought dey wuz some kids chasin' me and Ah done got so skeert Ah took off. Lawd Amighty, jus' whin Ah thot Ah wuz done fo' Ah seen yo' lights flashin', and oh, thank *yew*, off'suh, thank *yew! Sho'* feels lahk you jes save the life o' this po' nigguh . . ." My eyes must have been half out of my head listening to Bevel and watching everyone howl with laughter, even though they'd heard the story a hundred times.

We quieted down as we pulled into the airport. Traveling mixed was risky anywhere in the South, and picking up Dr. King was even riskier, even though the FBI was supposed to secure his safety. I never knew how I really felt about the FBI. In a way, I was glad they were there, because they were paid to keep us from being lynched by the Ku Klux Klan. On the other hand, many of them were just regular southern folks who couldn't stand us either, and would be happy for any accident that might befall us outside of their jurisdiction.

King's plane landed, and after he'd got past the folks in the airport, we bundled him into the car and headed off. To my utter surprise, no serious matter was discussed all the way back to town. The jokes started up again, and King had brought some fresh ones from the last stop. They were mostly about blacks, and though I tried not to approve, everyone was having such a wonderful time, laughing with each new joke till they had to get out their handkerchiefs, that I abandoned myself to the merry, highly imprudent entertainment until the next event, which was food. King loved to eat.

Walking into the tiny soul-food restaurant with him was like walking in with God. Every face in the room was transformed. He smiled at everyone, and they nodded and smiled back reverently. Some of them came up to shake his hand, and others couldn't stop thanking him, and still others just shook their heads in quiet amazement and brushed tears away. King ate with unrestrained gusto. I think I ordered just what he did, and apple pie and ice cream for dessert. The next day we would walk to school with a line of black elementary students who, up till now, had been refused admission to an all-white school. King would rally everyone in the church, and talk about how all folks were equal in God's eyes, and how we must love our white brothers and sisters, and understand that some of them were sick in their minds. It would be a scary little walk, but I would be right next to King and quite happy to die there.

Before King arrived, we had had rallies in the church and marches in town, led by the local organizers. In the center of Grenada, we had sung and clapped hands and prayed and greeted the local townspeople, including Klansmen who perched on little stools on the sidewalks, leaning against the parking meters, peeling apples and picking their fingernails with huge, ominous-looking switchblades. Once a blue-eyed freckled boy of eight hopped out of a pickup truck and came up to me.

"Hi," I said. I had seen children curl their lips before, but usually in imitation of movie gangsters.

"Nigguh-lovuh," he said, looking me square in the eye.

"Well, yes, I suppose so, if you have to put it that way . . . and what's your name?"

Startled at my friendliness he ran back to the truck. Most of the stores closed their curtains and the proprietors and salespeople pulled them aside cautiously and peeked out of chinks in the venetian blinds. At the umpteenth turn past the local beauty parlor, a tiny miracle took place, the kind that reminds one that life includes little victories among its big defeats. The door opened a crack and a girl's white hand thrust briefly and timidly out of the darkness making the V for victory sign. Should she read this, I thank her now for her bold action. Later on, all the women stood outside leaning against the storefront and there was no way to know which one of them had risked her job to offer us that fleeting moment of support.

Of the many photographs I have of myself and famous people, there is one which I had framed and have never forgotten. It is of King and me at the head of that line of schoolchildren in Grenada, Mississippi. Ira is in back of me, and Andy, and then a long string of kids, all black.

They were shining in smiles on that day, to be with their leader, and to be doing something important. King talked a lot about "historic moments," and they knew that this was one of them. A bright pigtailed girl was holding my hand. News cameras from every channel were there, and dozens of photographers. Across the street a clump of white kids headed to the same school. They looked particularly pasty, frightened, and unhappy on this day, not at all like a "superior race." I whispered to King, "Martin, what in the hell are we doing? You want these magnificent spirits to be like *them*?," indicating the miserable little band on the opposite curb. "We must be nuts!" King nodded majestically at an overanxious cameraman, and said out of the corner of his mouth, "Ahem . . . Not while the cameras are rollin' . . ."

When we were a block from the school, we were stopped by the biggest policeman in the world. King wasn't much taller than my five feet six inches, and I felt as though we were encountering an alien from another planet. I'm sure the policeman felt the same way.

"Good morning," I said steadfastly. "We're walking these children to class."

"Yew cain't go no futhuh than this point."

"Well, they'd like to go to school, and we're just helping them exercise their rights as citizens."

"Yew cain't go no futhuh than this point. Only the payents kin go futhuh than this point."

"Yes. Well, I have a letter here from one of the parents which puts me in charge. Like a guardian," I bluffed on.

"Sorry. No futhuh than this point." After several minutes of this dialogue, we turned back.

That evening several hundred million people watched the news and saw black school children in Mississippi denied the right to their formal education. And, due more to the presence of the news media, alas, than to the power of love, no rocks had been thrown or kids beaten, at least at one school.

The time came when King was confronted with a terrible decision. He had to decide whether or not to come out openly against the war in Vietnam. Blacks were fighting and dying on the front lines of that already controversial and unpopular war. The civil rights movement's slogan, "Freedom now!," was already taking on a new dimension.

King would choose to take a public stand against the war, calling it illegal and immoral. His direct line to Lyndon Johnson would vanish in a day, and his own people would be thrown into confusion and division. He had listened to the "still, small voice within," a Quaker expression for conscience or guiding light and, in my opinion, he paid for it with his life.

King and Andy came to visit Ira and me when we were in jail in 1967. I had sung in a big benefit for S.C.L.C. at the Oakland Coliseum. Harry Belafonte was there, and Sammy Davis, Jr. Sammy went up and put his arms around Harry and, looking up into his gorgeous face, said, "How come you're so tall and handsome and I'm so short and ugly?" And Harry had embraced him and said, "I guess that's just the way God planned it," and they had both laughed. After the show, Sammy went off to entertain the troops in Vietnam, and I went off to get three and a half hours of sleep before sitting in at the Oakland induction center in support of the antidraft movement. I was arrested along with about thirty-five other women and many men, and served the first of my two jail sentences over that specific issue, a short ten days.

Toward the end of our stay at the Santa Rita Rehabilitation Center, Ira and I got the news that King was coming to visit us. The "regulars," more than half of whom were black, were in a tizzy of excitement, and were told that under no circumstance would they be allowed to get near King. I tried to find a way to sneak one or two into the visiting room. Martin and Andy were sitting at a table in a little cubicle when I arrived. We embraced and talked. King looked tired. Tired and resigned. I felt guilty, as jail for me had entailed practically no sacrifice at all. I was gaining weight and making a lot of friends, and had plenty of time by myself. I made life miserable for the lieutenant and the guards by noncooperating with arbitrary orders, but then I'd sing them a song, or just chat, which confused them all the more. As my distinguished visitors and I talked, I spotted an animated black face peering around a partition and a hand gesticulating wildly to me. I winked at King and Andy and made a "shhhh" with my lips, and beckoned the girl over. She shook King's hand as he stood up to greet her, spread a tiny wrinkled paper out on the table and, in a frantic jumble, dropped her pencil, said

"Shit!," and asked him if she could have his autograph. He said, "Certainly," and she said, "Hurry!," just as the sergeant appeared, smiling woodenly.

"I invited her in to meet Dr. King," I said in my most kissy tone. "I hope I'm not breaking any rules . . ."

The girl ran off and, unable to contain her joy, let out a whoop when she reached her waiting friends.

"I got it! I got it! An' I shook his han'!" She wasn't allowed to go to the movies that night, but she lay on her bunk, glowing.

"I don' give a shit 'bout no fuckin' movie. I shook his han' and touched him and talked t' him . . . Nuthin' kin ever take that away from me!"

Forgive me, Martin, but when you died, I couldn't feel anything. David and Ira and I were on tour, speaking and singing about draft resistance. We were in a crummy little motel back east, and Ira knocked on David's and my room and announced that you had been shot. When the press came to interview me the next day, when you were dead, I talked mostly of our differences, how you wanted the black people to have their share of the American society . . . and how I thought having black sheriffs and city officials would not do much to transform corruption, and told them I didn't believe in funerals and would not be going. I did not watch the coverage of the funeral.

I wasn't ready to think about saying goodbye to you until eight years later. I was flipping the TV channels one afternoon after vacuuming the house. The cats and dogs were already settling down to stretch and scratch and spread their hairs all over the living room rug. I patted the rug next to me for the big shepherd to come and lie down. She complied, and I scratched her behind the ears and kissed her on the nose and thought about how cozy all the animals were, and how they kept me honest, cleaning up after them . . . and I poked the remote control again, hoping to find something mindless to relax to. Instead, I saw your face. You and Coretta were getting off a plane. She was beautiful and you were wearing your hat, and you both looked young and fresh as an Easter day. You talked to the press, explaining about your commitment to nonviolent change, and I could feel the impact of you on my life coming at me like a tornado. There was nowhere to hide, and anyway, I was already transfixed and beginning to relive those mighty times. Gabe walked into the room, and I realized that I was soaked in tears.

"Listen, honey," I said, "I'll be like this for a little while. If you want to see one of the greatest men in history, along with some of the toughest kids . . ."

Gabe sat with me for a while, and he saw the children being attacked by dogs. I pointed out Bull Connor, who had given the orders, and Gabe said he was a "fucker." I told him that King didn't even hate Mr. Connor, because he considered him to be just one of his brothers who was sick in his mind.

"Well, I think he's a fucker," said Gabe, and then he patted my knee and looked up at my face apprehensively, not because he'd said fucker, but because kids hate to see their parents cry, and I simply couldn't stop. I kissed him and told him that I was absolutely okay, and would stop crying when the movie was over, and he kissed me and told me he loved me, and went out to play.

The documentary ended with the funeral, and your voice-over, giving your own eulogy, ". . . Martin Luther King, Jr., *trahhhd* to live his life servin' others . . . Martin Luther King, Jr., *trahhhd* to love somebody, I want ya ta say that I *trahhhd* ta be right on the war question . . . I did *trahhh* to feed the hungry . . . I want ya ta be able to say that I did *trahhh* in my life to clothe those who were naked . . . that I did *trahhh* to visit those who were in prison . . ." I saw Andy dressed in robes, sitting in a huge thronelike chair, wiping away tears. I felt as though the two of you would tear my heart right out of my chest. I watched what I could see through veils of tears, to the bitter end . . . the procession, the mule and the wooden cart, the crowds. I saw the "dignitaries," who I thought had no business being there, and was glad I hadn't attended the funeral. And all the while, I kept trying to say goodbye.

And now, as I write these pages about you, another nine years have passed, and I see that I still can't say goodbye, and I see that it doesn't matter, and I don't have to. What I was concerned with was not your flesh, but your spirit, and it is as alive for me today as it was when I sang you awake in the little room in Grenada, Mississippi.

You, more than anyone else who has been a part of my life, are my hope and inspiration. When I hear the mountaintop speech, which is playing now, I long, more than anything, for the time and the place to come right again . . . that my path will be clear again . . . I long to regain the sureness of commitment and direction to go back out on the streets again, and know that the most important thing in my life is to do God's will. I long to end the preoccupation with age and death and all the pettiness from now till then, and to know that you must have known when you said, "I'm not concerned about that now. I just want to do God's will." Because He had allowed you to go up to the mountaintop, and you had looked over and seen the promised land.

Every time I hear your voice, it brings me back to the foot of the mountain. I don't lack the courage, Martin. It's just that in the eighties I can't seem to find where the path begins.

# 2

# "JOHNNY FINALLY GOT HIS GUN"

In 1963 my third album was out and doing well. My audiences had grown from small 1,800–3,000-seat town halls to Forest Hills (8,000–10,000) and the Hollywood Bowl (20,000). It was said that I made the ten- and twenty-thousand-seaters seem like living rooms and everyone there a personal guest.

I preferred singing to a lighted house or an outdoor venue because I could see the people. It was less scary when I was not singing to a black pit. I continued to appear in bare feet, usually wearing a simple dress and necklace. My hair was very long now, and straight, and the bangs had grown out completely. The effect was biblical but gloomy. I stood hunched over the guitar, a vocal coach's nightmare, still singing many of the soft ballads, but adding the songs and spirit of the civil rights movement: "Amazing Grace," "Swing Low," "Oh, Freedom," and the anthem "We Shall Overcome." I also added the sweet antinuclear song by Malvina Reynolds, "What Have They Done to the Rain?" "Joe Hill" became a favorite, along with the Dylan gems.

Despite this success, a sentiment harkening back to an essay on pacifism I wrote when I was fourteen began to haunt me. I was in a position now to do something more with my life than just sing. I had the capacity to make lots and lots of money. I could reach lots and lots of people. It would be a while before this sentiment would take root and grow into something tangible, but the intent was now evident and becoming stronger by the day.

I was shopping for groceries early one morning, just as the coastline mist was lifting from the quiet November streets of Carmel, and the checkout man said casually but importantly, "Kennedy's been shot."

I didn't understand what he was talking about, and nodded and smiled and lugged the groceries off to the car. But his voice kept running through my mind, and with a queer sensation creeping up my spine, I turned on the radio.

Kennedy had been shot, but he was still alive and the entire country was in a sickly panic. I felt the stirrings of hysteria within me, not really knowing why. I didn't believe the myths about him so much as I wanted him to be a heroic figure. Mimi and Dick and Kim and I gathered in the glass house and tried to absorb the shock together. I telephoned Ira.

"Darling, what a marvelous way to go! Rich, internationally famous, possibly the most powerful man in the world, sitting next to a beautiful woman, and 'poing!' it's over! Painless, quick . . . the lucky son of a bitch."

At first I was stunned by his callousness, and a little annoyed, because I too was caught up in the national hysterical heartbeat . . . but then, I'd like to go fast like that, I thought, in a blaze of glory.

The Johnson for President Committee didn't waste any time. The morning following the assassination, I received a telegram assuring me that the grand gala at which I had accepted to sing for Kennedy (a decision with which I was not very comfortable) would take place —the show would go on, only it would be for Lyndon Johnson, "just as the late beloved President Kennedy would have wanted it to be." The late beloved Kennedy was still warm. I thought about the invitation and decided, as occasionally I do, that to say "no" was too typically rigid and shut too many doors, so I answered that yes, I would appear.

There were the usual dignified liberal actors and comedians who had all modified their heartfelt speeches to John F. Kennedy and now said something appropriate but not at all heartfelt for Lyndon B. Johnson.

Dressed in a seven-foot-long mink stole, frilled one-piece camisole, net stockings, spiked heels, and arm-length gloves, Mitzi Gaynor sang some forgettable song. To end the number, she bent over and thrust the fur between her well-spread and firmly planted (and stunning) legs and then slowly rose, dragging the long fur back between her coyly squeezed-together thighs, and finally arrived up-right, arms in a V in the air, still singing, the poor overused mink loping about her shoulders and body, begging for a trip to the cleaners.

The production people were upset when they learned that I would refuse to join in a finale of the national anthem.

"But everyone'll be looking for you! You're gonna be a smash!" they pleaded.

I didn't sing the national anthem, and I was a smash anyway. Perhaps not with Lady Bird when I dedicated a song to Jacqueline Kennedy ("A bright ember of our recent past"), but I heard that I was credited by the President for "knowing how to take advantage of a situation." I started out with something diplomatic about his leadership, told him that he must listen to the youth, went straight for the jugular and voiced the people's desire to stay out of a war in Southeast Asia, and then sang all of "The Times They Are A-Changin.'" There was tangible electricity in the room when I sang the words. There was tumultuous applause. A nerve had been struck. Perhaps it was revulsion on the part of the younger people at the cavalcade of tinsel and bad taste which had preceded me, but I got the only encore of the evening and went back to sing "Blowin' in the Wind."

Back home in Carmel the Young Democrats for Johnson were trying to get hold of me through old Doner. Johnson was of course planning his campaign strategy against arch conservative Barry Goldwater. Doner's counsel was colorful and echoed my own instincts.

"Fucking morons," he said throwing his hands back over his head in a wave of disgust. "Dis lousy rotten bunch of sons of bitches, honey, der all idiots! Vel, vot the hell. You gonna do it?"

"Do what?"

"Dey vant you to *lead* dem."

"Don't be silly. Can I have a pencil and paper?" I replied, and sat down at his dining room table and drafted a letter to President Johnson. I told him that I would consider voting Democratic as soon as he quit meddling around in Southeast Asia and brought home the troops which were already there, and which the administration was calling "advisors." Doner looked on approvingly.

Like Doner's, my problem was not specifically with Johnson. It was with all of party politics and most politicians. Their allegiance was to the nation state. Whether they were Chinese, Russian, American, or Tanzanian, they took the chance location of their birthplace as the most serious event in the world, and made a living out of it. Other people took it just as seriously, but were not in a position to do as much damage. And how could anyone get serious about party politics after watching five minutes of any convention where people regressed to age six, wore stupid hats, got drunk, screamed and shouted, and played with balloons, at a time when they should have been doing some serious contemplating about their futures and the future of the world?

I have never been involved in the campaign of any major political candidate, preferring to work entirely outside of the party structure. Occasionally I have slipped a check and a note of encouragement to some brave congressperson who has defied everybody and risked his or her return to office because of principles. I did not vote in 1964 and would not go to the polls until it was time to vote against Nixon in 1972.

My fourth album, *Joan Baez in Concert Part Two*, was out and doing well when I decided to take part in a small antiwar rally in Carmel. I may have organized it with Ira; I really can't remember. There weren't more than thirty of us, and we looked pretty scruffy, but we marked the arrival of the peace movement in Carmel. My psychiatrist drove past and had a look, and told me later that we looked too grubby to have much credibility.

The organizers of the Free Speech movement at Berkeley got hold of me, and I went up to sing and speak. Ira and I raised the subject of nonviolence, and developed a small following. But when I was asked back again and again to take part in their marches and rallies it was not so much because of an overwhelming interest in nonviolence but rather because I drew huge crowds. I understood that fact and bashed on regardless, slipping Gandhi in between songs and winning a few hearts and minds and annoying the "radical" left with my "moderate" ideas.

One day I led an enormous march from the steps of Berkeley's famous Sproul Hall over to the grassy hillside opposite the building where the regents were having a meeting, the results of which would affect whether or not the students would get any of their demands. Ronald Reagan was one of those regents. Mario Savio was elected to go and speak with their spokesperson. While we waited, I led singing and others spoke. Mario came out of the meeting angry and disgusted, but worst of all, feeling beaten.

His discouragement may have been justified, but the protesters needed to feel fresh power at a time like that, as discouragement would spread quickly and turn into anger. I don't remember if I asked for or just took the microphone.

I told them that their power was theirs and no one could take it away; all they had to do was demonstrate it (or words to that effect). They could make this their university. They could do something as simple as claim Sprouse Hall, I ranted on, mispronouncing "Sproul." And that's precisely what they did.

I was there when they went into the hall. Up in front of thousands of kids and press from all over the country and the world, I told them to go into that building with "as much love as they could muster," and then I sang to them. Some of the more "radical" kids didn't like me talking about "love" at such a serious revolutionary moment. Inside, the halls and rooms were filled with students holding seminars on everything and a seminar on civil disobedience led by Ira and me. There were also plenty of informers, I assumed. I wandered around singing and enjoying the sight of people who were feeling their own power, some for the first time.

Ira and I planned to be arrested with them if the police came. We waited many hours, and by two-thirty in the morning decided that there would be no arrests made that night. We left the building, planning to return in the morning, and as we were pulling out of the parking lot, the police moved in.

I supposed they didn't want to arrest me because I was unfavorable publicity for them. We turned on the car radio, suffering with the kids, wondering if they would keep discipline and with it their dignity. Many did. Others tried. And others understandably panicked. But if there was ever to be a real nonviolent movement among white middle class kids in this country, they would have to learn that being nonviolent does not mean that you are protected from a policeman's billy club. That night some of them learned that panicking brings the club down harder and faster than might have been the case if they'd kept singing. But, to their credit, they were brave, and they were scared, and Berkeley marked the beginning of a new level of activism and risk taking in the universities of the United States of America.

In 1964, after the election of Johnson, what had started as the Free Speech movement turned into a radical movement against American involvement in Vietnam. Seeing that nothing could come of our presence in Vietnam except disaster, I had a quiet revelation and decided to refuse to pay my military taxes. This move was personal, political, and public. At the time our "defense" costs amounted to approximately sixty percent of the national budget. I wrote a letter to the Internal Revenue Service which I reprint here:

Dear Friends:
    What I have to say is this:
    I do not believe in war.
    I do not believe in the weapons of war.
    Weapons and wars have murdered, burned, distorted, crippled, and caused endless varieties of pain to men, women, and children for too long. Our modern weapons can reduce a man to a piece of dust in a split second, can make a woman's hair to fall out or cause her baby to be born a monster. They can kill the part of a turtle's brain that tells him where he is going, so, instead of trudging to the ocean, he trudges confusedly toward the desert, slowly blinking his poor eyes until he finally scorches to death and turns into a shell and some bones.
    I am not going to volunteer the 60% of my year's income tax that goes to armaments. There are two reasons for my action. One is enough. It is enough to say that no man has the right to take another man's life. Now we plan and build weapons that can take thousands of lives in a second, millions of lives in a day, billions in a week.
    No one has the right to do that.
    It is madness.
    It is wrong.
    My other reason is that modern war is impractical and stupid. We spend billions of dollars a year on weapons which scientists, politicians, military men, and even presidents all agree must never be used. That is impractical. The expression "National Security" has no meaning. It refers to our Defense System, which I call our Offense System, and which is a farce. It continues expanding, heaping up, one horrible kill machine upon another until, for some reason or another, a button will be pushed and our world, or a good portion of it will be blown to pieces. That is not security. That is stupidity.
    People are starving to death in some places of the world. They look to this country with all its wealth and all its power. They look at our national budget. They are supposed to respect us. They do not respect us. They despise us. That is impractical and stupid.
    Maybe the line should have been drawn when the bow and

arrow were invented, maybe the gun, the cannon, maybe. Because now it is all wrong, all impractical, and all stupid.

So all I can do is draw my own line now. I am no longer supporting my portion of the arms race . . .

Sincerely yours,
Joan C. Baez

I released this letter to the IRS and simultaneously to the press.

After the letter had been widely printed around the country and around the world, a representative of the IRS showed up at my front door, papers in hand, suggesting that I drop my whole silly idea and sign on the dotted line, pay up, and avoid a lot of trouble. I invited him in for a cup of coffee. He refused and asked me to please come to his office in Monterey. I went, like a fool, and the minute I was in his office realized that I shouldn't have bothered to come. I sat in a chair and sulked while he finished up a telephone call. When he turned his attention to me he astutely remarked that I didn't look too happy.

"I'm not," I said. "I don't like being here."

Not understanding what I meant, he began reassuring me that as soon as I changed my mind and paid up I'd feel much better.

"No," I said, "you don't understand. I don't intend to pay my taxes, and so coming here is pointless."

"But, surely, Miss Baez, you don't want to be a bad citizen, do you?"

"The way I see it you can either be a good citizen or a good person. If being a good citizen means paying to make napalm to dump on little children, then I guess I'd rather be a good person and refuse." He became agitated.

"Surely you don't want to go to jail," he warned me, ominously.

"Well, I imagine I'll go to jail sometime. It might as well be over something I really believe in," I answered.

"But jail's for bad people! Jail's for criminals!" he warned me, becoming still more agitated.

"You mean like Jesus? And Gandhi? and Thoreau?" I said, beaming.

"Huh?" he said.

The IRS put a lien on my house, car, and land. It made no real difference in my life, though the public didn't understand, and I got checks from all over the country from people who imagined me sitting out on a curbside with a tin cup in my hand. I continued refusing for ten years. Sometimes a representative from the IRS would appear at my concert venue and take cash from the register before it even reached the promoter. I was accused of being impractical, because, of course, the government got my money plus fines. But the point was that I was refusing to *give* it to them and that they were spending a lot of time and money to come and collect it. And meanwhile, the tax resistance movement was growing, as was criticism of not just the war in Vietnam, but all wars.

I did my first Johnny Carson show. The producer had a "little chat" with me.

"You know, Joan, we're so thrilled you could make it on the show, Johnny's just knocked out. Really. Fantastic."

"Thank you."

"We wanna make sure everything comes off smooth, you know, because the reason people love Johnny so much is that he makes 'em laugh, you know what I mean? It's the end of the day and they're gettin in bed, and well, you know, heh heh, that's a time when they don't want to have to *think* about anything. They just want to be entertained. So the point is to just keep it light, and everyone will be happy."

"What are you trying to say?"

"Oh, nothing in particular. Except for one thing, that is. Ummmm. Well, let me put it this way. As a favor to Johnny we'd like to tell you not to say anything about income taxes."

"Why did you have to say that?"

"Oh, just because, as a favor to Johnny . . ."

"Why don't you want me to talk about income taxes? I hadn't intended to, but now I'll have to know why."

"Oh, c'mon, Joan, be a good sport."

"I'm not a good sport. But if you'll tell me *why* you don't want me to talk about income taxes, I won't. Isn't that a fair deal?"

"Look," he tried, now a little desperate. "Say I'm your best friend. I have a dinner party and invite a bunch of people, and I invite you, but I ask you to do me a favor. I ask you not to wear the color blue. Would you wear blue?"

"If you were my best friend you'd know that unless you gave me a good explanation for your silly request I'd come dressed all in blue."

Just when I thought we were completely deadlocked, a Chicano producer, in a small office, whose name I remembered for years but have now forgotten, called me into his office.

"If you say, on Johnny's show, that you refused to pay sixty percent of your taxes, someone watching might want to do the same thing, and Johnny's show could be blamed, or even sued, for having influenced their decision."

"Thank you," I replied. I didn't talk about income taxes.

As our involvement in Vietnam deepened, I was asked to do more and more talk shows. The average scenario went like this: I'd be invited out after a Teflon display or a quilting bee or a talking dog contest, and the interviewer would ask me something about my position on the war (You've been a real activist. You must feel pretty strongly about this . . .), and before I could get a sentence out he'd say, "Oh, just hold it a minute, we've got Bonzo Gritt here fresh from filming on the set of 'Forever America' and he'd like to give *his* opinion," and Bonzo Gritt would sit down and say "Well, Miss Buyezz, I've always admired your singing very much, but personally, *I'm* not gonna sit back and let the red plague creep across Indochina and around the world to our shores and swallow *me* up," and the interviewer would say, "Thank you, Bonzo, and we'll be back in a minute, after this message, . . ." and there I'd sit. And then, after we came back on, I'd light into them like a cheetah, telling Bonzo that if he were committed he wouldn't be sitting in that chair, he'd be "over there" fighting on the front lines. Then I'd appeal directly to the roomful of middle-American mothers who had been on a six-month waiting list to see this show, asking them if they thought their boys wanted to go to Vietnam, and if those busses that went to the induction center every morning at five o'clock were filled with young men ready to give their lives for their country, or young boys who were terrified and were there only because they'd gotten a letter in the mail telling them they had no choice. And the moms wouldn't know whether to clap or boo, and then I'd sing, and no one would know *what* to think. I got over my shyness in a hurry, and began to actually enjoy the charade that inevitably took (and still takes) place on network television entertainment shows and to look at it as a challenge.

In my files is a 1965 picture of me in a bikini, walking along a lakeside beach. I look like a normal enough young woman, trudging along, a little preoccupied about something, and fresh out of the water. On the other side of the picture is a letter to my mother and father and, significantly, "everyone."

Dear Mum—and Popsy and everyone—
This was at Searsville Lake. I had an interview.
My life is strange right now. I'm sorry I haven't written. I always hope you forgive me for not writing.

I have a choice of things to do with my life. I think it is time to charge in head first. I want to start a peace movement. It began to hit me about two months ago. The time is ripe and I feel I could do anything I want. The sky is the limit. I think it will start in the fall. I don't know yet what exactly I'll do. Ira has some ideas he says he thinks could be tremendous but he wants me to see if I can come up with any first. He says he can get some of the best organizers in the country when we need them. I just feel that people are searching and groping for something real, something truthful—The movement will be nonviolent. It is terribly vague, but I see no harm in preparing yourself in spirit for something even when you are not sure exactly what it is. I have to be ready to sacrifice just about everything I have. Who can ever tell if he's ready to do that till the time comes? My car, my house, my sleep—I must take care of myself. I'm sorry there are so many I's and my's in this letter but I must get it down on paper for you guys. I must be ready not to die for something, but to live for it, which is really much harder. Like flying in airplanes and having the flu in jail sometime. That's pretty hard, but who knows. I have to keep my "head straight" as the beats say . . . To know what I am doing before I do it and while I am doing it—and to admit to myself and everyone else if it was wrong after it's done—a march—a vigil—a meditation—anything.

Wow. I got wound up——I am a leader
I love people
I will need help—yours and everyone's
OK? you guys?
I love you—
See you in jail—
I leave for a trip in two days—I will let you know—

Your egomaniacal<br>daughter—

Someone had to save the world. And, obviously, I felt I was the one for the job. I went through a period of self-purification to prepare myself for the "movement," by simply exaggerating my usual behavior.

Then one day I told Ira that I did not want to remain an ignoramus forever and asked if he would consider tutoring me more formally. Ira claims that *I* suggested the next idea, and I think that *he* did, but the discussion evolved into a proposition that we form a school called the Institute for the Study of Nonviolence.

We asked two friends to help us: Roy Kepler, owner of a superb local bookstore, and a WWII war resister who had spent time working in mental hospitals for alternative service and in prison during the Korean War, and still a sturdy pacifist and one of the world's most decent people; and Holly Chenery, who was possibly the brightest woman I'd ever met in my life. She was a rigid vegetarian, absolute nonviolence advocate, and had the only truly organized mind of the four of us.

The school was to be run in seminar style, unpressured and unhurried, and would cost a minimal amount to attend. We would use a reading list, and the various seminars would consist of discussions on the reading. We would subscribe to the journals and newspapers which could keep us best informed about world affairs, and also to various nonviolent action journals and bulletins. And we would have organized meditation.

The perfect little schoolhouse presented itself to us in the middle of Carmel Valley, only ten minutes from where I lived. It had a kitchen, a big room for the seminars, adequate toilet facilities, and a place out back for Ira to live. We bought it with my money and began holding seminars almost immediately. There was no problem getting students. There was, however, a problem with the couple across the street, who had up till that time lived relatively quiet and protected (and, I thought, boring) lives. Now they let it be known to the community, and, in fact, to the world, that they were in peril of losing their peace and security. Communist hippie weirdos were invading the valley and threatening their way of life.

We had to evacuate the school until we'd been up before the county board of supervisors. We were in court for weeks, and held classes everywhere from a local park, from which we were removed, to my own house, which was illegal for us to use as well. The area's staunch and starched conservatives showed up in court to defend the upright couple, while our supporters were people from all over the Monterey Bay area, some with influence and some just plain folks, and our students.

Holly spoke and was most impressive in her no-nonsense drab cotton skirt and Peter Pan–collared blouse, short-cropped hair and thick glasses. And Ira was irresistible as usual, appealing to the forbidden fantasies of the twittering, supposedly hostile, clubby wives. When it was my turn to speak, I was wearing a proper dress and shoes. We had been referred to as the "lunatic fringe"; I said that I supposed I was the lunatic and Ira's beard provided the fringe. Everyone laughed. Then I said that my opponents were worried about the property value on their forty-thousand-dollar houses going down but I was a homeowner, too, and had one hundred thousand dollars invested in Carmel Valley and I, too, was worried about my property value. Then I sat down.

In the end, the wife became so distraught that she destroyed her own case by listing the twenty ways, which she had written down on a napkin, that we had made her life unbearable. By around point sixteen—we "had forced her to seek psychiatric help"—it was clear that her problems extended far beyond the property line, and we were granted the permit to teach and study nonviolence in beautiful, peaceful Carmel Valley.

During the first four years of the Institute I studied regularly, and acted as "teacher's aide" to Ira. Speakers, scholars, and activists came from all over the world. Martin Luther King's people shared time with us, and Ira and I went to the South to take part in their conferences and planning meetings. We were visited, sometimes in the night, by frightened young men from nearby Fort Ord who wanted to know how to get out of the Army and into Canada.

Each seminar began with ten or twenty minutes of silence, and each day included one full hour during which everyone was asked to desist from distractions like reading, thumbing through magazines, chewing gum, smoking, wandering aimlessly, doing cross-word puzzles, or sleeping. One day a week we were silent for the whole afternoon. For some, the silence was difficult; for others, impossible. For me it was difficult, but very important.

And, of course, we studied the concept, theory, history and application of nonviolence in all its aspects, from use in personal relationships to internationally organized methods of fighting oppression. The more I read and talked and argued and discussed, the more devoted I became to the concept. What became strikingly evident to me was that in order to hold fast to the principles of nonviolence, one had to have unerring faith in them, and be ready to die in the course of holding to them. It was no good saying that "nonviolence works, up to a point." That only meant that when things got too difficult or the activist was threatened with punishment, or was not attaining victory fast enough, it was time to switch to something more expedient. The decision to abandon nonviolence is understandable but means that nonviolence is being used only as a tactical method of achieving change, and not as a principle according to

*Joan, Sr., 1942.*

*Almost-two-year-old Joan, Jr., 1942.*

© Albert Baez

© Albert Baez

*Popsy, 1942.*

© Joan Baez, Sr.

*Storytime for Joanie and Pauline, ages three and five.*

*Mom . . . sedate . . . and beautiful, 1940.*

*Chiquita Juanita, age seven.*

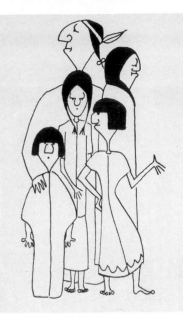

*Early family portrait, by me, 1953.*

*With the Royal Hunt Club, Baghdad, 1951.*

*Joanie (seven), Mimi, and Pauline. I am wearing my favorite dress ever: red velvet with plaid satin.*

Self-portrait from class photo,
age sixteen.

A revealing self-image . . . 8th grade.

My high school rendition of my second
screen crush.

*The Baez women: total noncooperation with the photographer, Popsy, 1953.*

*Faces from sketch pad, 10th grade.*

*Friends and family and the hearse that took me to Newport, 1960.*

*We were crossing Jordan River—Bob Gibson and me at Newport, 1959.*

*Tuesday night at Club 47, 1959.*

*Jordan Hall, Boston, 1961.*

**Time** *magazine cover, November 23, 1962. I felt like death and was depicted accurately. . . .*

*Postcard of a Romanian gypsy, sent from Popsy to Manny, 1965. "Dear Manny, Cover the mouth and it looks like a folk singer we all know (but the Roumanians don't)."*

*After the cross country ride with Michael, visiting the family in Claremont, 1961.*

*Eric Von Schmidt's famous poster.*

*Two shots of early "Renaldo and Clara,"
1963 (Bob's first Newport).*

*"How many fair and tender maids will love as she did then?" Michael and me, 1959.*

*Michael and me, 1960.*

*Lovely Kim.*

*And again . . .*

*Grenada, Mississippi, 1966. "You cain't go no futhuh than this point. . . ." the cop said to us. King went all the way.*

*Montgomery, Alabama, 1963. I started up the steps of the capitol building, and the police formed a solid line of resistance; it was very flattering.*

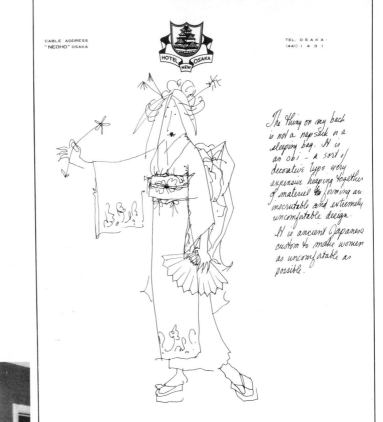

*The thing on my back is not a napsack or a sleeping bag. It is an obi - a sort of decorative type very expensive heaping together of material forming an inscrutable and extremely uncomfortable design.*

*It is ancient Japanese custom to make women as uncomfortable as possible.*

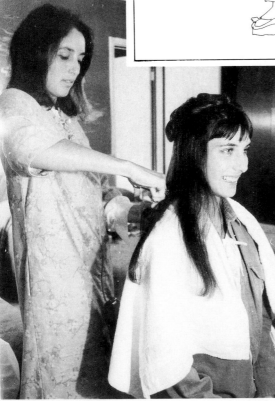

© Jim Coyne

*Japanese hair ceremony.*

Letter home from the ill-fated trip to Japan, 1967. Text reads: "The thing on my back is not a sleeping bag; it is an obi–a sort of decorative-type, very expensive heaping together of material, forming an inscrutable and extremely uncomfortable design. It is ancient Japanese custom to make women as uncomfortable as possible."

*My impressario, Manny Greenhill, 1974, in Santa Monica, California.*

*French television, 1966, with Mom and Manny.*

© Jim Marshall

*Ira, my devilish prophet and mentor, 1968.*

*In meditation with a Saigonese monk at the Institute for the Study of Nonviolence, 1966.*

© Jim Marshall

which the adversary, no matter how brutal or inhumane, is also in need of being freed.

I read the assigned books, but most of my learning came from listening and discussing. I became very spiritual. I spent days on end listening to Gregorian chants, and developed elephant skin on my feet from tucking them under me when kneeling in prayer. I continued touring, advertising the Institute while on tour, and recorded *Farewell, Angelina* and the Christmas record, *Noel.*

I was giving only about twenty concerts a year but was not, as some people assumed, trying to conserve myself for the future. I just found that life on the road was physically and spiritually unhealthy.

As the Institute flourished, I vascillated between being a star on the road and a servant of God at home. Most of the money I earned I simply gave away. Just about any request that came in, if remotely connected with nonviolence, would be honored with a check of between fifty dollars and five thousand dollars. Many of the concerts I gave were benefits, for cooperative nursery schools, Quaker Meetings, peace groups. The record royalties poured in steadily, so there was not much limit on funds, and there was no limit on how much I would give away.

There was a great deal of profound joy in my life, but there was practically no fun. I didn't know much about having fun. I felt too guilty, as though I wasn't supposed to start having fun until everyone in the world was fed and clothed.

I quit reading what the papers said about me because either they portrayed me as more self-sacrificing than I was, or they didn't like me and said, in a variety of ways, that I was a fake.

Al Capp, creator of the "L'il Abner" comic strip, launched the most imaginative of the negative attacks, introducing a character into his strip called Joanie Phoanie. She was a slovenly, two-faced, showbiz slut, a thinly disguised Commie, who traveled around in a limousine singing "songs of protest against poverty and hunger for $10,000.00 a concert." She put out albums like, *If It Sounds Phoanie It's Joanie*, which included "Lay Those Weapons Down, McNamara," "Throw Another Draft Card on the Fire!" and "Let's Conga with the Viet Cong." Looking back at both the strip and the situation, I have to laugh. At the time, I couldn't. Mr. Capp was slandering my name, my causes, my music, and, of course, my persona. I got huffy, and huff turned to rage. I never sued Al Capp. I asked for a retraction but did not get one. Al Capp publicly denied to all who asked that Joan Baez was Joanie Phoanie.

Many years later I would read: "The truth that's told with bad

intent beats all the lies you could invent," but at the time my righteous indignation came from feeling guilty about having money,
even if I was giving most of it away. In my heart of hearts, I thought
I should not have anything. And that's where he stung me.

Was Al Capp right? The puritan in me said that unless I learned
to live free of possessions, like Gandhi, I was less than perfect.
Gandhi's aim was to be detached from all desire. I tried to be detached, but did not succeed. I was attached to my house, my boyfriends, my ever-changing wardrobe, and my demons. Mr. Capp
confused me considerably. I'm sorry he's not alive to read this. It
would make him chuckle.

My confusion about being rich and famous was compounded
when I went to Europe in 1967. I had been there to perform only
once before, on a television tour in 1966. In Belgium I fell in love
with a Parisian photographer who was assigned to cover me for a
magazine. We walked all over Brussels and he took hundreds of
pictures of me. Then we went to Paris where he escorted me to an
Yves St. Laurent fashion show. He kept saying the show wasn't
verrry interrresting because it was the end of the season; I didn't
know which season he meant, and the show looked pretty inter-
rrresting to me. The last item of the day was a wedding dress which
was actually supposed to be a big white cake with satin ribbons and
veils tied around it and the model's arms and legs sticking out.

We went into the dressing rooms and he handed me a five-thou-
sand-dollar dress to try on. It was beautiful. "Everry wooman should
wearrr a drrress like thees at least once een zee lifetime."

Back at his studio I posed in it. It was white, and heavy with tiny
beads. I felt beautiful in it. I also felt mystical, spiritual, and queenly.
I loved it. But then I started to cry and couldn't stop until I'd taken
it off.

He took me shopping in the hidden fashion warehouses of Paris,
where I bought a classy blue gabardine pantsuit, and another in kelly
green. I bought silk blouses and scarves, and Pierre Cardin shoes.
Then he took me out in my new clothes and the insecure skinny
Mexican from my past was not even a shadow of reality, and the
hopsack and ashes, Joan of Arc, madonna was temporarily eclipsed
as well. We went to a private club where I danced with him, and his
friends, until they collapsed in exhaustion. The disc jockey played
one of my songs and everyone clapped. When I couldn't dance
another step we got into my friend's car and drove around Paris. I
was still dizzily happy when dawn broke over the Tuileries and we
breakfasted in a small cafe where I simmered down into a dreamlike

state and nearly fell asleep with my head in a big plate of eggs and croissants. I was having FUN.

He took the cover photos for the *Noel* and *Joan* albums, and for my little book, *Daybreak*. I was infatuated with Europe. I was infatuated with the photographer. I was infatuated with my new clothes, all of which I gave away and replaced with something resembling a nurse's uniform when I went to Japan the next year.

That same year I went to Austria and saw the Lippizaner horses. A hand-kissing, heel-clicking horseman insisted I sit in the reviewing stand with the head riding master and a couple of generals. I was delighted.

I went riding with a count. He was a handsome count, but not a very nice one, having as many ladies lined up in his parlor as he did horses in his grand stables. He wasn't too interested in me because after we were on our mounts, mine a gigantic Irish thoroughbred and his an even bigger something else, he discovered I couldn't take the jumps and his whole adventure was ruined. He left me in the charge of his more thoughtful sister and galloped back to find better pickings while there was still plenty of time for a royal romp in the woods.

Then I went to Italy.

Marco, whom you will hear about later, took me shopping on the Via Veneto where I bought two fine flowered silk dresses which clung to my body and fluttered around my knees like Arabian silk in a desert wind. In California one would have said, "I felt good about myself." But I would have said that I felt like the queen of the world.

That same summer I gave a short concert tour in the States. I had sold out two halls in Washington, D.C., and was closing the tour by returning to do a third. The D.A.R was refusing to let me use their very own Constitution Hall, which we had already supposedly rented. Manny and my road secretary and childhood friend Jeanne and I installed ourselves in the grand old Hay Adams Hotel and planned our strategy. One call from Manny and the press jumped on the story, giving me, for the first time in the States, extravagant amounts of sympathetic coverage.

Secretary Udall, of the Department of the Interior, instantly gave me permission for a free concert at the base of the Washington Monument.

Wearing one of my "queen of the world" dresses I danced in and out of our aging but plush sitting room, doing one television news show after another and every newspaper interview I had time for. Each television news team would leave the Hay Adams and go directly to speak to the grand duchess of the Daughters of the American Revolution, or whatever she was called, who was sitting in *her* parlor giving *her* side of the story—namely that Miss Buy-ezz was an anti-American demoralizing influence on our boys over in Veetnam, etc. To her credit, the grand dragon presented her case convincingly and well, but she was not queen of the world that day. I was.

And by 1967 much of the press was becoming very cynical about the war. The last thing I saw on TV before we left for the concert was a boy and girl walking to that very site with a picnic basket swinging between them, and the commentator was saying, "It looks like a beautiful evening at the Washington Monument, where the grounds are already crowded with spectators who have come to see the free concert by Joan Buy-ezz. . ."

When the queen of the world woke up the next morning, her manager had stuffed newspapers under her door. The most conservative said she had sung before eleven thousand people; the most liberal said fifty-five thousand. The police estimate was forty thousand. That was all wonderful, but it was the note from an Austrian count, who had arrived in Washington suddenly and by chance, which gave her the most lazy sense of glee she had ever had. Accompanied by a large bottle of Rémy Martin, the note requested that she join the count for dinner that evening. But the queen of the world leaned back on her plumped-up pillows and stretched and decided that even if she was doing nothing that evening she would be much, much too busy. She was learning how to mix fun, having nice things, and enjoying life a little, with doing what she thought was her calling. She went home to Carmel Valley and kept her silk flowered dresses.

Ira and I were on a pilgrimage to the Gethsemane Monastery in Kentucky to meet a holy man. Thomas Merton, a Trappist monk, he was a well-known pacifist and poet who had been writing more and more openly and strongly against the war in Vietnam. His order had already silenced him once. We had been reading his essays and poems at the Institute.

I don't remember being invited, but I do remember going. Ira and I teased each other about our closet desire to meet someone *really* holy who would magically touch our lives and change us into perfect people. Knowing we were fantasizing nonsense didn't stop us from dreaming.

I went into one of my religious states at the sight of the monastery. Then I wished the monks were hidden behind bars in great hoods, because the first one I saw was tripping over himself, acting suspiciously like a Joan Baez fan.

Thomas entered briskly and greeted us warmly. He was an absolutely lovely man. His face was good and cheerful and kind. He emanated warmth and honesty. Perhaps there was yet hope.

The first thing he wanted to do was get off the property and buy some junk food for lunch. Of course, I thought, he must be sick to death of gluten bread sandwiches and homegrown beet juice. At a local fast food joint he bought two cheeseburgers, a chocolate milkshake, and a large order of fries. Ira and I had hamburgers and Cokes. The three of us, sort of like Piglet, Owl, and Pooh, went out into the middle of a field and had a picnic. Ira was Owl, and I was Piglet. Merton looked considerably like Pooh.

The good monk enjoyed his cheeseburgers so much that our trip was surely worth it for his lunch alone. I believe we talked about Gandhi, nonviolence, the war in Vietnam, but what I remember clearly was discussing the subject of his discipline. He wanted more than anything to travel. He wanted to see Bangkok, but he was not allowed to. His superior, for whatever reason, had decided that it was in Thomas's best interest to stay at Gethsemane. I had the strong feeling that it was in the best interest of the Catholic Church. He was much too outspoken. Ira tried a string of arguments, most of them based on the foolishness of vows if they were interfering with the broadening of Thomas's life experiences, his art, his passion. Merton only laughed, his eternally cheerful face becoming flushed.

After our picnic we went back to the monastery, through it, and out the back. Through a little bit of woods, by a narrow footpath, we came to where Merton lived in a small cottage by himself.

He opened a little wooden cabinet and pulled out a bottle of Irish whiskey, which he and Ira began to down with amazing speed and alacrity. Ira began saying, "C'mon, Thomas, what's the *real* story, aren't you going nuts in this place with all these sophomoric boring junior monks looking up to you as God?" and Merton would answer quite solidly, though with a slur, that his calling was here, and here he would stay.

"What about women?" said Ira, waving his glass through the air in a big swoop, as if to indicate many thousands of women. Merton said something about a lady he had met and said he had, well, more or less, fallen in love.

"Aha!" Ira said, mean as a ferret. "What do you DO about this woman?"

"I can love her in the spirit!" shouted Thomas, waving *his* glass around the room, a little defiantly, I thought.

"Nonsense," I interjected. "What about her body?"

"Her body isn't here! And anyway, I don't need it to be here."

"What if it *was* here?" I plugged on. I wasn't drinking.

Merton indicated that he could still love her in the spirit, though he was sounding less and less convincing. Ira asked where she lived.

"In Lexington," Merton said, wistfully.

"But we're going to Lexington tomorrow evening!" Ira whooped, thoroughly caught up in the moment. "Why don't you skip vespers and come with us? We'll drive to Louisville and get the plane to Lexington! C'mon! You can do it!"

To my great surprise, Merton did not hesitate for a second. He was on his feet dancing around the room, saying, ". . . and then I could spend the night and then I could be back before matins the next morning and no one would ever have to know. . ."

I was mortified. I didn't want to be a party to devilment in the life of a good, intelligent, and kindly monk.

"Ira," I said reproachfully—but he was beyond reproach. And he was a little drunk. Needless to say, so was Thomas.

Well, Thomas Merton never came with us to Lexington. In the sober light of morning, in some little southern motel, Ira changed his mind. I made him place the call. Merton was disappointed, like a child. He was no doubt relieved, too. I think we told him the plane was full. We didn't have the nerve to say that we'd been crushing our own fantasies in urging him to break his discipline, and all three of us would regret it in the end.

# 3
# "HIROSHIMA OYSTERS"

In January of 1967, I went on a long-awaited tour of Japan. I'd put it off for many years, mainly because I didn't like traveling, was not keen on long flights, and I was particularly phobic about non-Western or Asiatic countries because the food was unfamiliar and would no doubt make me sick. But, Japanese requests to our office for concerts had been many and gracious, and I'd finally made the decision to go. I took along my manager, Manny; Ira and Susan the secretary, now married to Ira; my sister, Mimi; and my then-current boyfriend, Paul. We would be gone for two months, three weeks of which would be spent in Japan, doing nine concerts in four major cities.

I had just been home for a while and gone through one of my many attempts at purifying my spirit by throwing out all of the clothing and jewelry I owned and liked (except for my alexandrite ring and a bunch of crosses). I embarked on this tour without the typical entertainer's trunkloads of spangled clothing, T-shirts, boots, feathers, and offbeat coats. Instead I brought four plain dresses, made for me by Pauline, identical except in color: one white, one dark blue, one light blue, and one grey herringbone.

My hair was shoulder length, as was Mimi's. Mimi was not feeling austere. In a hat and green suit, she looked like a Saint Laurent fashion model, traveling with a nun who'd just been told the habit was no longer compulsory but who could not adjust to civilian clothes. Ira was in chipper form, as he always was when we traveled together, sporting a tweed suit, a tweed hat, a suitcase full of Brooks Brothers shirts, and one or two conservative black ties. (He would rip the labels out when we went on demonstrations.)

Susan, only twenty-one years old, had recently had her gorgeous honey-colored hair coiffed, and the back of her head looked like a huge chrysanthemum. Her china-doll complexion and Renoir body were encased in a trench coat and silk scarf. Susan was enormously bright and organized, and she irked the hell out of Ira, who had fallen in love with her on a previous tour, and now seemed constantly annoyed at having her in the same room. She and Mimi had been buddies for many years, and did a lot of giggling together throughout the Japanese tour.

Paul, whom I've referred to in a couple of my songs, was a lavishly handsome six-foot-four Irishman I'd met in Liverpool during the Dylan tour of 1964. He'd been standing on the front steps of the concert hall collecting money for a children's fund or some such thing. His words were gentle and ever so true. He was not yet "lost in the Irish fog." He was a decent and intelligent young man, who will perhaps always be in an austere period of his life, and he dressed in the remnants of a school outfit from Trinity College, Dublin.

Manny, looking like the proverbial kindly father, fresh off an immigrant ship, carried a great jumble of passports, visas, and vaccination pamphlets, and tried to decide who would act as road manager, as neither he nor Ira nor myself was capable of managing our own affairs. Whether Ira liked it or not, Susan was left to organize us.

I spent the overnight flight poring through my Berlitz Japanese book, trying to figure out how to really *say* what was written in phonetics for "hello," "how are you," "good evening," "good morning," "where's breakfast," and "I have to go to the bathroom," none of which was simple. How was one to know that the word "arigato," thank you, would be pronounced "eingato," and that when you add the "gozaimash-tá," very much, not to mention the giggle at the end, "arigato-gozaimash-tá" becomes very unlike French, Spanish, or Italian. But we were in jovial spirits, and nobody slept much.

As we touched down, we were punchy from jet lag and very pale from no sleep. As we left the plane, we were greeted by about twenty maniacal Japanese photographers, literally ready to kill each other to get pictures. They were all shouting my name, but stayed about seven feet in front of Mimi and me, as we walked arm in arm, smiling at the cameramen and looking desperately for the ladies' room. One man fell and was trampled by the others. We spotted a door with an insignia on it of a lady's kimono and excused ourselves, darted inside, and burst into giggles. I ducked my face into the cold water as Mimi disappeared into a cubicle. We tidied up, primped up, and headed out to greet more chaos. Not knowing who was a promoter, who was a friend, who was the local folksinger, or who was anything, I smiled and bowed at everyone, and everyone seemed warm and genuinely pleased to have our strange group visiting their country.

Carmen MacCrae was in the elevator at the Hilton. She had eyelashes three quarters of an inch long, and they weren't hers. Not knowing there was a Japanese side, we stayed on the European side of the hotel. Communication with the hotel personnel was difficult. Manny, who usually manages to speak Yiddish in any country when his knowledge of the local language runs out, found no way to communicate at all. There was a young woman named Deko-san who would be my part-time interpreter and helper; and there was the official interpreter, Takasaki, who would be with us at concerts, and do instantaneous translations at press conferences and other gatherings.

Our first major obligation after arriving in Japan was a press conference. Mimi was impressed with how careful I was in answering the questions, most of which were political and very intelligent, with only one or two like, "How long have you known Bob Dylan?" At the end of the conference, which covered everything from income taxes to the war in Vietnam, the Institute for the Study of Nonviolence, racism in the South, and more, someone asked me about rock music. I said it was too controversial a subject for me.

The first concert was in Tokyo. What repertoire would be right for the Japanese audiences was not clear yet, but some suggestions were made by Deko and the promoter, and the rest I did on intuition. The audiences were sweet, enthusiastic, and generous, bringing me gifts which they placed just beyond the footlights, making little bows. I learned to love the Japanese bow, and I use it to this day in concert to thank people for having come to hear me.

But something was going wrong, and it had to do with the language barrier. I couldn't seem to get points across to the people when I wanted to and was beginning to think there was a massive cultural gap between myself and the Japanese people. The problem was most acute during concerts.

The first incident occurred at the third concert. Deko-san had knocked on the door to signal it was time to begin the concert, and I'd given my little answering groan. Takasaki went out on stage and talked for five minutes to the audience. "Deko-san," I asked, "what is the man saying?" "What man?" she said. "The man who is interpreting—Takasaki-san." Deko replied, "Oh, him no say nothing." Flaring up, I replied, "How can him no say nothing for five whole minutes?" Deko said, "Pardon?" I felt rude, which I had been. I said, "How can he stand there and say nothing for five full minutes?" Deko said, "Oh, he tell them to please no smoking in hall, and other things like that." I was being manipulated. A no-smoking announcement can't last up to five minutes. My home team of Manny, Ira, Mimi, Susan, and Paul were becoming suspicious.

During the concert, I would say something mildly humorous, harmless, and probably pointless, it would be translated, and there would be a stone-faced response from the audience. Something serious (for instance, the fact that I didn't pay my war taxes in the United States) would receive a round of giggles after it had been translated. That night I exploded to Manny, and told him that I thought that Takasaki was all fucked up and didn't speak English *or* Japanese. As a group, we decided that I should talk to him, and actually tell him what I was going to say, so that he could practice his interpretation. I recall him sitting in the dressing room, nodding helpfully as I painstakingly, in pidgin English, drawn-out syllables, and sign language, explained to him the few political points that I wanted to make and the jokes that I thought were translatable. He nodded to everything, and I was hopeful we had made some progress.

The next concert, Takasaki seemed even more nervous than usual. It seemed to me that every time I said anything he was repeating the same sentence over and over to the audience. When I mentioned war taxes and Vietnam, the word "Vietnam" was not repeated in the translation. Was it possible that the word "Vietnam" could be so different in Japanese from what it was in English? Just as I was getting really flustered, a beautiful little Japanese girl brought a dainty, colorful gift up to the stage, and plopped it at my feet. I accepted the gift, and said "Thank you" into the microphone. Takasaki said nothing, so I turned to him and said, "Please tell her 'Thank you,' " and he said, "Aringato." I was about to start the next song when another young Japanese girl brought forward a paper origami bird, and also put it at my feet. Touched by her sweetness and shyness, and at a loss for words in the huge, silent hall, I said,

"Japan is full of surprises." Again Takasaki responded with total silence. I stared at him. "Tell them what I said: 'Japan is full of surprises.' " He smiled dumbly at me. I said to him, "Do you know what a surprise is?" and discovered that my right fist was clenched and that I had a strong urge to show him what a surprise would be like in front of a few thousand people. I unclenched my fist, and he mumbled something into the microphone—I'll never know what— and, again, there was no response from the audience. I went on to the next song, but not before I put my arm around his shoulder, saying, in effect, "Don't worry about it; we'll get past these little difficulties." I didn't know this was the most humiliating thing I could have done to a Japanese man. He turned rigid and blushed, I sublimated my rage, the audience maintained a hollow silence, and the plot thickened.

We flew to Hiroshima—first human-inhabited testing grounds for the American atomic bomb—still in a quandary about Takasaki. We had no assurance, or reassurance, from anybody bilingual—American, English, or Japanese—as to whether or not I was being translated at all in the concerts. When the plane landed at the Hiroshima airport, I was quite airsick, and sat recuperating for a minute with a wet washrag on my head, wondering what the local promoters had in store for me. (At some point in my career I had learned not to assume that the flowers at the bottom of the airplane steps were necessarily for me, having once lunged for a large bouquet of roses and had the bestower leap backwards, clutching them to her bosom, as they were not for me at all, but for some diplomat who was following three people behind.) I did, however, assume that the child with short-cropped, shining black hair and magnificent oval eyes, dressed in the Japanese kimono, could be holding the giant-sized bouquet of flowers for me. So I pulled myself together and, along with my entourage, alighted from the plane. The child was exquisitely beautiful, and I took her hand in one of mine and the flowers in the other arm, and walked with her into the airport lobby where the city fathers were waiting to greet me.

I wanted to stay with the little girl, or at least have her on my lap, but she disappeared, and I was left sitting in a circle around a table with some of my entourage and, at the head of the table, a man I did not recognize. On either side of him were other men I did not recognize. One of them was introduced to me as an interpreter. To this day I don't know whom I was speaking to, but the first question from the lips of a man who was obviously a local somebody was translated to me by a smiling stranger: "Didn't you feel, as you were flying over Hiroshima, that this is a city dedicated to peace?" I looked stupidly at him, felt the red tape encasing me in my chair, and replied, "Please tell the gentleman that, as I was flying over Hiroshima, I felt airsick." Something was translated, and the man smiled happily, which seemed strange. A series of similar questions followed, and I tried to give more respectful answers.

The meeting concluded, and we piled into cars and were driven toward the Hiroshima Memorial Museum. A vague and oppressive feeling overcame me, that I wanted to absorb Hiroshima at my own speed, and I might not be able to absorb Hiroshima at all. I knew there was a Quaker house in the city, and I wanted to visit the people there, knowing that one or two would speak English. Maybe someone could explain why I felt so alienated from the Japanese people. Perhaps I could learn what peace activities went on in the city, what grassroots projects might be taking place. Instead, I was being rushed to the most commercial spot in all Hiroshima, which was the war memorial museum.

When the car stopped, Mimi and I got out and walked slowly, with mixed emotions, and lay my flowers on the grave of the symbolic unknown Japanese human being. Fair enough, it seemed to me; now I wanted to be alone. "Come," our hosts said, "you must go in and see the museum." I knew well what was there, pictures of the devastation, fossils of people, shadows on the cement, photographs of broken bodies and of faces scarred and pulled into horror masks. I did not want to go in. My hosts were insulted, and I didn't care. I asked to be taken to the hotel.

In Hiroshima I was to do a benefit concert, the monies to be divided between two peace groups—one in Hiroshima and one in Nagasaki. We did have a chance to go and visit the peace center, where we talked with a white-haired American woman who had been living in Japan for a long time. Quakers always give me a feeling of relief and security. Wherever they are, whatever they've been through, they hold on to the one thing that is so dear to me: an unbending devotion to nonviolence.

The group was small and pleasant, and they served us tea. The room was cold, but it was a relief to have an interpreter who I felt was actually translating what I said, and a group of people who related to the things I wanted to talk about. I remember Paul bending through the tiny doorways of Japanese buildings and taking his shoes off, looking almost as tall when he sat down as he did when he stood up, and the Japanese girls blushing at the very sight of him. Ira was animated, asking questions about the background and current history of nonviolent activities in the area. Mimi, Susan, and I sat on pillows, sipping tea and wondering about Hiroshima. Some shy "Hiroshima maidens" apologized for their appearance, and gave us strings of delicate origami birds. I wondered where the money from the benefit would actually go, and realized it was futilely small regardless of where it went.

On the night of the Hiroshima concert, there was a battle with the local promoters, who did not want any of the money from the Hiroshima concert to go to Nagasaki. Apparently, there was an argument about which city was bombed first, or worst, and how many people died; in other words, a question of prestige. It struck me as so base to bicker over which city was best known throughout the world for having had people blown to shreds that I asked Manny if he could just please take care of it and split the money fifty-fifty between Hiroshima and Nagasaki. I did not want to sing until the dispute was settled.

In two hours of discussion Manny would hear long responses which unfortunately amounted to nothing. Expert at the time-honored custom of never saying no, the Hiroshima promoters and city fathers, with much politeness, smiling, bowing, and many cups of tea, never budged from their position. As it came time for the concert I could see that I would break my contract if I refused to sing; and with my bizarre interpreter, there was no way to explain my side of the dispute to anyone, let alone the press. Manny told me the city fathers would be happy to discuss the problem after the concert.

Onstage was an enormous sign in Japanese that included my name and the word "Hiroshima." I went onstage with mixed feelings, and struggled through another concert with my troublesome interpreter. By intermission I was developing a terrible stomachache and by the end of the concert my hands were clammy and I was sweating all over. I was, in fact, quite sick.

We were taken to the mayor's house. Raw fish was being passed around, and I got greener and greener. I wandered over to a window with Mimi and Susan. Below, schoolchildren were waving and calling up to us. I wanted to be with them, but because of all the stupid red tape I was stuck in a room full of elders who didn't interest me in the least, and even if they did, nothing would ever be translated properly so I could find out what they were really like. With the children, I could be assured that one or two of them would speak some English. If I hadn't felt so sick, I would have slipped away and joined the children. But by then my head was literally reeling, and we returned to the hotel. For an hour I lay on the couch with stomach cramps and a weakening spirit.

When the promoters arrived I fought for my right to distribute money to Nagasaki. The promoters responded to our arguments with nodding heads and the clipped "hai," which means yes, and never the "eyeh," which means no, and the usual smiles and nods. Each time they would nod and say "hai" and smile, I would feel encouraged, but there was no cause for encouragement. The final blow came when I was informed that the money would go toward building a small monument to honor the dead. I rose from the couch, screamed that I didn't want my hard-earned money going into some fucking pile of cement, and told Manny I couldn't stand it anymore and to do what he could.

I went into the bathroom and lay down on the floor in a cold sweat. Mimi and Susan put rags on my head. The bathroom floor felt too good to leave, but Mimi finally got me into bed, where the scene escalated into a "Queenie crisis," with Ira holding one hand, Paul lying on the bed holding the other hand, and me weeping and telling them all what to say: "Don't worry, dear, you won't throw up." Logical Susan was saying that of *course* I wouldn't throw up; if I hadn't thrown up for seventeen years, why should I start now? Mimi was sneaking across the room to grab a flowerpot (which I wasn't supposed to see) and emptying the flowers out "just in case." And Manny was wandering through the room with a stack of Don Ho records, trying to distract me. I didn't want to hear Don Ho; I didn't want to think about Japan, or the promoters, or the stupid money, Hiroshima, Nagasaki, bombs, or anything. I just wanted to have my stomach feel better or else to die.

Instead, miracle of miracles, just after I'd been reassured by Ira for the hundredth time that of course I would not throw up, I lurched forward and gave a massive retch. Mimi had the flower pot under my chin in a flash and everyone oohed and aahed, as if I'd just given birth to twins, or perhaps triplets. No food came up, as there probably wasn't any there. I leaned my head back on the pillow. "Good God," I said, "is that all there is to it?" "That's all," said Mimi, "just like having a baby." Everybody clapped, then quietly left the room, except Paul who, patient soul that he was, stayed to see me safely through the night.

After seventeen years of thinking it would kill me, even the semblance of vomiting was quite a triumph, and I secretly wished that it would happen again that night, in which case I would consider myself a professional. Somewhere around two in the morning, my wish came true, and with the pride of a father peacock, I retched all by myself into the same empty flowerpot. Perhaps this was the end of those rotten promoters! Who cared! I was free of my phobia for the time being and could now rest through the night with no reminder of the evening's agonies, except a painfully tender abdomen.

The next day involved a long train ride, most of which I spent sleeping, though I occasionally roused to munch on a banana. A doctor came to see me when we got to Osaka. He poked my stomach, and I yelped. He smiled benignly, and mumbled something to Deko in Japanese. She nodded and smiled. "What did he say, Deko?" "He say have no fever, only food poisoning. You can give concert." "Wonderful," I replied, and told Manny to cancel. Plans were made for me to return and give the concert on my day off. I slept for another night and day.

Meanwhile, Ira had been on the phone with a group of peace activists in the area. This was now the third or fourth day, and I was recuperating. The Osaka peace groups wanted me to attend a rally they were having that night. My adrenaline went up. I believe that adrenaline combats illness, and as the day went on, I had decided to commit myself to an evening out. I felt better and better, and Manny got more and more nervous about what the response would be to me leaping around with peaceniks two nights after a cancelled concert. I got gingerly out of bed, put on my dark blue dress, and went off to the rally.

In a medium-sized auditorium we squeezed our way through an overflow crowd of wildly excited people and, entering the main room, saw ahead of us onstage another gigantic sign, a welcome in English to Joan Baez. My throat tightened and my eyes filled. Why should I get a standing ovation? What did these people know of me? Less than I knew of them. Our whole group was seated at a table on the stage. An excellent interpreter, whose name was Tsurumi, accepted questions from the audience for us. The bulk of the questions were intelligent—about the United States, its involvement in the Vietnam war; about pacifism, leftism, rightism; about how my music related to my politics. All of that was followed by a heated discussion on the ticket prices that I was charging in Japan.

Tsurumi was a fantastic interpreter, from what we could tell, and it dawned on us to ask him if he could help us out with my concert interpreting with Takasaki-san still at the helm, which was growing worse with each performance. He accepted. It was not until days later, however, that Tsurumi came clean about what had actually transpired during my concerts; he didn't want to explain. He didn't want us to feel foolish or embarrassed, he said. I assured him that we already felt both foolish and embarrassed and he said, "Well, then, I'll tell you. Takasaki speaks perfect English. He interprets nothing of what you say." I was aghast. "During the five minutes before the concert, he says nothing about no smoking in the halls. He says, 'This girl has a lovely voice. You should listen to her sing, but as far as her politics goes, she doesn't know what she's talking about. She's innocent and young, and she came here to sing to the people, not to talk. So, simply ignore what she might have to say.' What his speech did was quiet everyone who was bilingual and lessen the number of protest letters which might come in." I sighed, and gave a groan, and swore. We were all in a state of shock.

My mind raced back to an evening with Mimi, Susan, Takasaki, and myself. We did not like him, and had decided that he did not speak much English, but we'd gone to sit at his table to make an effort to be pleasant with him, as he seemed lonely and under great pressure. "How do you say 'chopstick' in Japanese?" I asked him slowly.

"Chopstick?"

I said, "Yes, you know, what you eat with," and moved my fingers as though they had chopsticks in them. He looked around the table at the three of us, and back to me. "Chopstick?"

Takasaki was playing "I don't speak English," and I began playing, "Let's be rude to the dumb interpreter."

"Oh, well, chopstick," he said finally, and gave us a word which I wrote down phonetically on a napkin. Assuming that we had crossed the language barrier with Takasaki, we chatted some more and had a cup of tea and a bowl of strawberries. A few days later when ordering lunch on the train going from Osaka to Tokyo, I clutched the napkin in my palm and, using the word Takasaki had given me, asked the waiter for chopsticks. He was confused, but nodded politely with the usual "hai," and disappeared and came back with no chopsticks. Finally, I went to the kitchen section and repeated the word. A bilingual gentleman said, "We don't serve *lamb chops* on the train."

Returning from this flashback, I listened to more examples of how Takasaki had evaded or misconstrued or blatantly misinterpreted many of my remarks; Tsurumi admitted that he did not understand Takasaki's behavior.

Toward the very end of our stay, during the few days we had off in Tokyo, Manny approached me, saying that there was a request for one more press conference. I asked him what in the name of God there could be one more press conference about. He said he didn't know, except that the record company wanted to present me with a gold album.

I dressed up in my press conference outfit. In a room at the Hilton, I faced a small, conservative-looking group of people, including record company representatives, and went through the formalities of accepting the gold album, smiled, shook hands, bowed, then turned to the strange-looking group and asked them if they had any questions. Four hands went into the air simultaneously. They belonged to four men, all dressed the same in dark suits and ties and white shirts, all holding notepads and pencils. When I nodded in their direction, they looked at each other momentarily, before one of them acted as spokesman.

"The man would like to know if Miss Baez was ill in Hiroshima because of eating oysters." I was baffled by his question, and requested to know why he'd asked it. He hedged, and asked the question again. He said they were aware that I'd cancelled a concert just after my visit to Hiroshima, and was it true that I had eaten Hiroshima oysters? I asked the men what newspaper or journal they were from, and it turned out they were representatives of the Hiroshima Oyster Company. The rumor had been that Miss Baez had had to cancel the concert because she'd been at a seven-course dinner, which included Hiroshima oysters which had made her sick. The Hiroshima Oyster Company wanted to clear its name of the possibility that they may have poisoned me. The irony was that the only thing I had refused to eat in Hiroshima at the seven-course dinner the night before the concert was a bowl of Hiroshima oysters, because I don't like oysters. There was no way not to offend the Hiroshima Oyster Company, but picking the lesser of the two insults (which also happened to be the truth), I said I was allergic to oysters and so had been deprived of the well-known delicacy. The four men scribbled in their notepads, got up, and hastened from the room.

One afternoon, unable to bear the degree of public reaction that took place every time I walked into the hotel lobby, I wrapped my head up in a scarf, put on navy pants, a pea coat, and boots, and ran out a back entrance and up a hill to a little shrine. For an hour and a half, I sat quietly thinking and looking for the little patches of sunshine which crept across the gravel, wondering what strange phenomenon had infected this visit to Japan. The country was known for being beautiful, its people for being gracious. What had gone wrong? I didn't find out until after I'd returned home and was settling down to work at the Institute and to write a book.

• • •

*Excerpts from* The New York Times, *Tuesday, February 21, 1967:*

. . . Press reports allege that an American, identifying himself as Harold Cooper, a CIA man, had ordered the Japanese interpreter, Ichiro Takasaki, to substitute an innocuous translation in Japanese for Miss Baez' remarks in English on Vietnam and Nagasaki's atom bomb survivors. Mr. Takasaki was cited as the source for these allegations . . . This morning, *Asahi Shimbun,* a leading Tokyo daily, printed a long account of the affair. The newspaper quoted Mr. Takasaki as saying, "It is a fact that pressure was applied on me by a man who said he was from the CIA." Mr. Takasaki's interpreting surprised bilingual Japanese listeners when the national Japanese television network carried a tape recorded replay of Miss Baez' concert on January 27th. Miss Baez left Japan by air for Hawaii on February 2nd.

When Miss Baez had referred to Nagasaki and Hiroshima, Mr. Takasaki said simply that "the show would be televised." Explaining her song, "What Have They Done to the Rain?," about the atomic bomb, Mr. Takasaki again only stated that, "the show is being televised." And when she said that she had refused to pay taxes because she did not want her money to be used to finance the Vietnam war, Mr. Takasaki gave this translation: "Taxes are high in the United States. . . ." Mr. Takasaki explained that before the concerts began, a telephone call came to him on January 12th, apparently from the American Embassy. The caller said he was an interpreter for someone named Harold Cooper, of the American Embassy, and reportedly said, "You are free to act as master of ceremonies, but Mr. Cooper hopes that you will not make any political statements." . . . Next day, a man who called himself Harold Cooper, telephoned him directly . . . After saying that he was a United States intelligence agent, he asked that Mr. Takasaki change the meanings when Miss Baez made political statements . . . "If you don't cooperate, you will have trouble in your work in the future." Each year Mr. Takasaki works in the United States about two months . . .

Mr. Takasaki decided to cooperate, since he felt if he refused he might not be able to obtain visas for the United States in the future. Mr. Takasaki told the *Asahi Shimbun* that he had actually met Mr. Cooper four times, and that each time Mr. Cooper made strict demands concerning Miss Baez' concerts. He said that at one time Mr. Cooper said, "Japan is in the midst of general elections, so be especially careful about Miss Baez' statements. Since many of her fans have a right to vote, political statements made during concerts have a major influence . . ." On February 3rd, Mr. Cooper called Mr. Takasaki at his home, and reportedly said, "Thank you for your cooperation. I am now leaving for Hawaii . . ."

"It was a most strange case," said Takasaki. "I knew that Miss Baez was a marked person who was opposed to the Vietnam War and who had been tacitly boycotted by the broadcasting companies in the United States. American friends also repeatedly advised me not to take on the job. But I took it on as a business proposition, since the Japanese fans were coming not to hear her political statements, but her music. I met Mr. Cooper once in the presence of a *Japan Times* reporter, but even in that meeting he openly demanded that I mistranslate. I tried to reject the absurd demands, but he knew the name of my child and the contents of my work very well. I became afraid and agreed."

*Excerpts from the* New York Post, *Tuesday, February 22, 1967:*

The U.S. Embassy in Tokyo denied that any U.S. government employee had approached Takasaki, and said it had no employee named Harold Cooper.

# 4

# "FOR A WHILE ON DREAMS"

I began getting seriously interested in David Harris when he came to visit me at Santa Rita Rehabilitation Center in 1967. My mother and I, along with sixty-seven other women, had been arrested for supporting the young men who refused induction. The price for me, after all, was small: forty-five days in the equivalent of a girls' summer camp. During my first stay in October of that year, a short but informative ten days, David had been there as well, on the men's side. But this time, he had kept out of jail to prepare himself to refuse induction. When he came to see me in the cage (the little visiting stall where a half dozen of us were crammed at a time), he was wearing a cowboy hat and was looking six foot three, which he is. His smile was one of the sweetest in the world and his eyes were a shade that a friend of mine calls "unfair blue." Instead of a prison uniform, I was wearing my own dress which I had ironed inside the cage, and earrings made out of fresh red berries and broom straw. My eyes were painted up with mascara I'd made from charcoal and toothpaste. I was ready for something terrific.

When visiting time was over, a black inmate asked me who the cowboy was, and I told her he was a leader of the movement against the draft. My ears were ringing from the din of inmates shouting to their visitors. I went back to my bunk and thought about David. We were involved in the same political work. He had a good mind. He cared about little kids dying under our bombs in Vietnam, and sometimes all I could think about was those kids. I decided to see him after I got out.

Fifteen days before our time was up, my mother and I were kicked out of jail. The prison officials, torn between teaching us a lesson by keeping us the full forty-five days and disposing of us early, had chosen the latter. They wanted to avoid any more celebrity visitors and the press conference planned for our release date. When I tried to place a telephone call to arrange a ride home, the lieutenant said no and accused me of wanting to alert the press. "Don't worry," she said. "We have a ride for you." They had a ride for us, all right, all the way to nowhere. We were dumped at a nearly deserted bus station in Oakland. Mother and I ordered some breakfast, and I went to a phone and called the person who would arrange a press conference. Two hours later, we had our press conference in a small room filled to overflowing. Then I went to another phone and called David.

David. He was handsome and bright and appealing. He was clumsy, messy, and sweet. Most of all, he shared my passion for nonviolence. He was a brilliant speaker. He spoke of eliminating the draft in this country, and then tackling the military here and around the world. The military, as he put it, was a house of cards. America owned most of the deck. If you pulled out her cards, the house would automatically fall. He had a lovely mouth. When he stopped preaching long enough, it was a kissable mouth. Maybe he's what I need, I told myself. Someone as strong as me, or stronger. Someone I don't just crave because his hair falls a certain way and his lips have a cupid's curl.

I went to live with him for a while in the resistance commune in the hills above Stanford. I launched into my customary "Beware of Joanie" routine and warned him what a terrible tiger I was and how he had better not get any big ideas about owning me. He said if I attempted to castrate him, to please not wrap him around a tree first the way the last girl had done.

David and Ira and I went on the road. David had already received his indictment and we knew that jail would be inevitable in the near future. I would sing a song or two and give a brief talk about nonviolence, and Ira would speak, but David was the headliner. I loved watching him speak. I was infatuated.

We'd known each other three months and been on the road two weeks. One night in bed in a motel in Wisconsin, we started discussing children's names. I asked David if he realized what we were doing. He said, "Christ," and that's when we decided to get married. I called my mom out west. "Guess what? I'm gonna get married." She said, "To whom?" And I said, "David," and she said, "Oh no." The last she'd heard of David was about a fight we'd had when I was fed up with him and said he was a dumb ox. After I hung up, David developed a fever and complained of aching muscles, and by morning had to be taken to the local receiving ward where they said he had a bad case of the flu. I was, of course, convinced that it was psychosomatic. My time was to come.

A week later we were in New York. The hotel phone rang at seven-thirty in the morning. It was Associated Press, who wanted to know if David and I were getting married.

"David," I said. "A.P. wants to know if we're getting married."

He rolled over, scratched his head, and said, "What the hell?" So I told the reporter the rumor was probably true, but there were no plans as yet.

That afternoon the announcement of our marriage was on the front page of the *New York Post* with my picture, and was amply covered in the *New York Times* and most papers in the rest of the country. So we decided to wrap things up as soon as possible and began looking for a movement preacher, preferably a pacifist. We would have to have a real wedding, we figured, and that meant our four parents, my two sisters, my aunt, his brother, a few of my personal friends, and half of the West Coast draft resistance. We made plans to fly everybody east, and I went shopping for a wedding dress. I was deliriously excited and terrified at the same time. I began getting ghastly stomachaches. David held up pretty well. We found an actual pacifist minister and a funky little church with peace symbols all over it where we would be married on a stage set designed for a play. There was a beautiful tree in the center of the stage covered with paper flowers. Together with the preacher, we planned a combination of an Episcopalian and a Quaker ceremony. David bought a suit after much hunting and altering, and I flew around Saks Fifth Avenue gulping Kaopectate and outfitting my family and trying to memorize my half of the Quaker marriage speech. "I, Joan, take thee David, . . ." etc. We took out the word "promise" and said "will try," and changed "for as long as we both shall live" to something a little less terrifying, though I don't remember what.

The day before the actual ceremony, my stomach was a wreck, and I had regressed to about age six. Members of the family hung nervously around my bed and decided to call a doctor. The doctor came. I told him what was wrong with me. "I'm getting married tomorrow, and I'm scared stiff, and I have developed a spastic colon and diarrhea, but it's all psychosomatic and all you really need to do is tell me that I will be all right and I don't have the flu or something."

"Do you mind if I make my own modest diagnosis?" he asked, hoisting my nightgown and poking my abdomen. "I would like to rest assured that you don't need an appendectomy, for instance."

"I don't have a fever," I warned him. "That is, as long as I don't have a fever, I'll be all right. Anyway, I don't." He didn't say "Shut up." He just put a thermometer in my mouth and checked his watch. After a minute or two, he retrieved the thermometer, looked at it and grunted again.

"Well?" I said.

"Hundred and two point six," he announced, and washed off the thermometer.

"I want to die," I said. He looked very sympathetic.

"Would it help any," he asked, standing there with his head cocked, "if I told you that I had a fever of one hundred and three and a half the night before I got married?"

"Depends," I said. "Are you still married?"

"Yes, I am," he replied. I thought he was lying, but I didn't care. He had said the right thing.

He gave me some Thorazine, convinced me that it wouldn't make me throw up, got me to swallow it right there on the spot, and I entered the land of floating swans.

If I had ever wondered whether David would be kind or devoted, I found out that night. I floated blissfully in and out of sleep, waking occasionally to the nausea of an empty stomach. I would moan a little, and David would hulk out of his bed and slip a teaspoon of Jell-O or an ice cube into my mouth. Within seconds the nausea would subside, and I'd go back to sleep. I don't believe David slept much in between. He couldn't go down the hall and get drunk with his friends because I was demanding all of his attention, and probably also because it would be too embarrassing for him.

Dear David, did I ever thank you for that night? It wasn't a very fun way to spend the night before a wedding, especially our own, but even after our roller coaster years together and the tumultuous

times directly following, I've said that you were on the side of the
angels . . .

Wedding day. David was very nervous. He still had his walrus
sideburns and moustache. He wore cologne, his suit fit well, and his
shoes squeaked. I wore a Grecian-style, off-white, floor-length dress
and bare feet. I gazed at David a lot. I also swallowed a lot of Kaopectate. We realized that we hadn't bothered to get rings, so we
ripped off ones we were wearing and hurled them at my secretary,
and she went out and bought two gold bands. A little after the
appointed hour, we piled into a limousine and headed for the
church. I was wearing the black velvet cape that my mother had
worn to her own wedding.

A film crew was at the church. I think all they got of me were
shots of my hand raising the indispensable green medicine bottle to
my lips. David was talking politics in another part of the same room.
My sisters arrived. I remember thinking how beautiful everyone
looked. My mother and father resigned themselves to the marriage
of their second daughter and were truly dignified and stunning to
behold. David's mother looked lovely and benevolent in the best
sense of the word, and his father looked strained, but pleased. He'd
been seventeen years in the military and his son was marrying a
peacenik. David's older brother looked shy and sweet, which he is,
and my sisters looked like princesses, which they are. Tia looked
happy, because she is an optimist and because she was glad I wasn't
marrying a junkie or a tightrope walker from the local circus. The
minister's hands were shaking, and he was so nice that I wanted to
cry. I forgot the words when it came to "in sickness and in health,"
and I said, "Oh, shit," and the minister whispered them to me, and
the whole time David was smiling this immense smile, partly out of
nervousness and partly because it is truly the most natural position
for his face. We were gripping each other's hands for strength, and
we ended the whole ceremony with a prolonged French kiss which
was interrupted by a harrumph from my father and an outburst of
giggles from everyone else. Then everybody clapped and the champagne was brought out, and Judy Collins, a good friend of all three
Baez girls, sang, and my father took some rolls of photographs
which for some reason came out all black.

I drank champagne, glued myself to David's side between chatting
with relatives, and twisted the new gold band around the third
finger of my left hand thinking what fun it was to have a new name.

The concept of keeping one's name, not to mention identity, was not yet born in me. But the idea of becoming a wife, and, hopefully, a mother, was thrilling. I was going to be Joan Harris, and David and I were going to have bushels of babies and save the world at the same time. On the third finger of my right hand I was still wearing the gold and alexandrite ring.

How kind you were, David! I was a crazy person. You married a crazy person. I was out on the hillside one evening with your mother, the night she told me I could call her Elaine, and the moon started to come up and I thought it might suddenly go back down again if I concentrated hard enough. And that idea frightened me. When she went to bed, I lay down by the roadside between the garbage cans with my knees tucked up under my chin and might have stayed there for hours, but you came out and called for me, and I said, "Over here," and you carried me back into the house and lit a fire and read to me from *Alice in Wonderland*. One night, to please you, I smoked some dope, but it made me even crazier, and I got hot and cold flashes and was terrified by your mouth as you read out loud. I had to run around the house and stay away from the windows because I might suddenly jump out. You said, "C'mon, let's go outside and get some air"; I said, "No, I'm scared I'll be too cold." "Well, here, let's put this sweater on," you said, and I started to cry. "No, I'm scared I'll get too hot." Then I started to really boohoo, and you put your arm around me and talked me outside, where the air felt good on my face. I had to pee and you said, "Sure, why not?" and began to laugh but tried to stop yourself so my feelings wouldn't get hurt; but I was squatting down in the petunias and had begun to feel a little better, so I said, "What's so funny?" and you said, "We just spent ten thousand dollars rebuilding the bathroom, and you come out here to pee."

We lived in the Los Altos Hills on a quarter-acre of land we called Struggle Mountain. Ours was a shacklike house attached to another just like it. A couple hundred yards away was a very old two-story house in which eight or nine people lived communally. We were all vegetarian, and we all had gardens. David and I used to sit out front on the stoop by the petunia bed, and God-knows-who would come by and invite themselves to sit down. Most often we'd make them tea, and David would talk about The Resistance and I'd listen and then get up and wander around and go make bread. Next door lived

Robert and Christy. Robert was a draft resister, but his number never came up. He and Christy didn't wear any clothes in the summer. Later, when Robert and Christy were more like family, he'd come in to use the pencil sharpener, and sitting down at the kitchen table I'd be eye level and two feet away from his groin, and could watch or not when he sharpened his pencil. For a while after David's arrest, I stopped wearing anything either, and so did most of the Struggle Mountain commune people who shared the property. One day the fire truck pulled up outside the fence and about fifteen firemen pretended to be looking for brush fires, but while glancing into the telescope, they also glanced over the fence, and I didn't feel uninhibited at all. I felt the way you do in a dream when all of a sudden you are naked and walking down Broadway.

I tried so hard to be a good wife. My demons attacked me ferociously, and I spent hours at the psychiatrist's trying to change myself from being Queenie into being Wife.

David got a Samoyed named Moondog who was terribly appealing if not too bright. He was untrainable, but had a winning smile, and David let him wander in and out of our tiny house at will, smiling and tracking mud onto the kitchen floor and the triple pile rug that covered the living room. One day I blew up because I had just vacuumed the house when Moonie scratched once and yelped twice and David let him in. I cursed at the mud tracks, "Goddammit, David, I just finished cleaning, plus that dog is scratching holes in the door."

David asked which was more important, the dog or a plank of wood, and I said, "You are forgetting something. Me. I'm more important." But David said I was anal-retentive, and I said I needed to be taken out to dinner. He said being waited on in a restaurant was counterrevolutionary, and I said I still needed to be taken out. I said he bought books and buying books was a bourgeois luxury that poor people couldn't afford, and if he was spending thirty dollars a month on books, he could spend the same amount on me. It was mostly my money anyway. I just wanted him to make a fuss, over me!

One day three women's libbers came up to register some complaints. They didn't like the poster The Resistance had put out. It was a picture of Pauline and Mimi and me all wearing hats and looking like the three little maids from Gilbert and Sullivan's *Pirates of Penzance*, and the caption said, "GIRLS SAY YES TO BOYS WHO SAY NO." I thought it was clever. The feminists hated it because it said "girls" and because the women shouldn't have to answer to anyone, especially men, not yes or no. They wanted the poster taken off the market. I honest to God didn't know what they were talking about. But I kept running back and forth to the kitchen, fixing them sandwiches and lemonade, while they nudged each other and looked in exasperation at the ceiling. David raved on about The Resistance and called women "chicks."

In spite of our troubles, I was faithful, very faithful, even when nothing was working, and I cried a lot at night, and he was endlessly patient and hoped everything would work out. Sometimes it did work out, and I was so proud. Proud that I could actually be a wife and feel calm and happy for a while.

David's indictment had come quickly after he refused induction. By the time his trial came up, the judges had quit expecting everyone to stand when they walked into the courtroom. We did, though, out of respect for his lawyer, Francis Heisler, a well-known, much respected old man with Einstein hair and a wit like a saber, who could have gotten David off on a technicality. He was torn because he knew that David was making his stand in the trial on moral grounds, and Francis would have loved to show his prowess on technical ones. The courtroom smelled of patchouli, mothers nursed their babies, and we all wore flowers and sang in the halls.

David was beautiful. Once the prosecutor asked him if there had been anything obstructing his way into the induction center. Yes, David, I thought, closing my eyes. Yes, David, *you* were. *You* were obstructing your own way. David started to answer the question and stopped, and said, "Yeah, wait a minute. *I* was obstructing my way." When the jury came in with the verdict, I began to shake. There was a Quaker woman on the jury we'd all been hoping against hope would call upon her Quakerism and defy the judge's instructions. The verdict was Guilty, and David made them all say it one by one, and when she said "Guilty," we all felt betrayed.

We were on a speaking tour when I got pregnant. We went to colleges, and I'd sing and David would speak and the kids would get mesmerized. I thought David was going to turn the world around singlehandedly, and if he could have done it with charisma alone, it would have been done overnight. Sometimes I didn't understand what he was saying, and later I found out that other people didn't either, but it didn't stop us from sitting and watching him with our mouths open.

Anyway, we were in North Carolina, and I was taking my temperature every night and morning with the special get-pregnant thermometer, and the graph told me we were right at the crucial time. It wasn't the most romantic thing in the world, yanking the thermometer out of my mouth and saying, "Now!" The next morning, I was doing dishes with Betsy, an old friend. She had always loved my alexandrite ring, which I had worn since the days of Kimmie, and all of a sudden I took it off my soapy hand and asked her if she'd like to have it. She was astonished, knowing that I never took that ring off. In fact, she knew I had had four duplicates made of it: one in topaz, one padparaja, one a blue stone, and I forget the fourth. I never wore any of them much, because I preferred the purple one. She looked at the beautiful gypsy ring I held out in my palm, and took it. That's when I knew I was pregnant.

Eleven days after my period was due, I went to the doctor for a test. Afterwards we sat in her office and she said, "Well, I have some good news for you," and I started to cry. She said, "I thought this was what you wanted!" and I blubbered, "It is!" and called David, but he wasn't at home. I drove home lost in fantasies of cribs and sleepytime mobiles and David getting out of prison, though he wasn't in yet, and us leading a nonviolent movement through the highways and byways of the world, taking turns carrying our little diapered bundle on one hip till it was big enough to toddle on its own and then we'd have more and more and there would be children tumbling all over the floor riding big dogs and cuddling little cats.

The house was empty when I got home, and I dawdled around and made some tea and tried to calm down. I ran to the doorway when I heard the car pull up. David's mother came up the path with a load of groceries, and David was just behind. She was smiling like a summer morning, and David was too, until I blurted out "I'm gonna have a baby." Elaine nearly dropped the groceries, and David tried to be thrilled, but he was hurt that I hadn't told him privately first. I regretted it immediately, but it was too late. Two weeks later, in a concert at San Jose State, I did the same thing. I just couldn't contain myself for another minute, and toward the end of the concert I announced, "I'm pregnant!" and David read about it the next day back east where he was speaking. He would have liked the private things in our lives to have some real privacy. I'd like to think I've changed and would handle things differently now, but I wouldn't, I know. I'd just blurt it out again.

One day I decided to cut off my hair. My tresses had been a trademark from the time I'd begun singing. I took two Valiums and went to the hairdresser's and had my hair bobbed, and left feeling like an Italian movie actress.

David came home from tour and said, "You cut your hair off without asking me!" and then tried to make a joke about it, but was hurt again. Our lives rumbled along.

We were ready when they came to arrest David on July 15, 1969. The resistance community seemed to have moved into our front yard. I spent the days baking bread and making pancakes and fruit salads for endless numbers of friends and well-wishers. Their hero would soon be gone, out of reach for the daily coffee and cigarette he was so willing to share with any of them. The day we suspected the sheriff would come for him, we were awakened by the sound of a flute floating to our bedroom windows on the warm, hazy morning air. One of David's loonier devotees was sitting in a tree like Pan, playing for us. I was tired and edgy and told David I wished the guy would drop dead, but David said, "He's a good guy, a little whacky, but he means well," and I softened, only because of David's kindness. So I got up and began, with the help of Christy, to cook breakfast for the tree dwellers, sun worshippers, sprout eaters, children of the dawn of Aquarius, squatters, resisters, and other loyal friends. I stayed in the kitchen, turning hot and cold at the sound of each passing car and busying myself making coffee and herbal teas.

Mid-morning one of our spies came roaring into the driveway and announced that the patrol car was on its way up the hill. David had that big smile on his face. The waiting was about to end, and his life would become much easier after there was a reality to deal with and not just fantasies to wake him up at night. The sheriff and his assistant were baffled by us. We were friendly, welcoming them with offers of coffee and juice and homemade bread. They declined everything. David, seated on the couch talking with a small group and protected by flanks of welcoming committees, rose and greeted them with a warm handshake which made them feel more sheepish and silly than they already did. David went around the group and hugged everyone. I stood at a distance until the last minute. They put handcuffs on him and he held up his hands in the victory sign just before climbing into the back seat. I hugged him and said some things, but I don't remember what they were. When they drove off in the heat of that pretty day, the sheriff's car had a draft resistance bumper sticker plastered just above the license plate. We had our last laugh, and I felt quieter and quieter until I just decided to go for

a walk. I walked a long time over those hills, a long time in the heat
of that fine, pretty, lonely day up on Struggle Mountain.

My first job after David went to prison was to finish the film we
were making jointly, called *Carry It On*. The film crew followed me
on an entire tour of the United States, from Denver to Madison
Square Garden. I was charging two dollars a ticket and giving what
money I made to The Resistance. Two resisters were working with
me: Jeffrey Shurtleff, of the madras slipover shirts and rubber beach
sandals, who sang with a voice of honey and silver; and Fondle, a
tousle-headed slow-moving guitar player whose real name was
something else. Our road manager was the lunatic who had been in
the tree playing the flute on Struggle Mountain the day David was
taken away. He would leap up from the table at a truck stop and
start clearing the dishes, while a row of two-hundred-pound truck-
ers turned and stared. He would also remove all the furniture from
his hotel room as soon as he checked in, hang a picture of a mandala
on the wall, light up incense and candles, and sit in the lotus position for forty-five minutes. Jeffrey would join him and the two of
them would cook brown rice on some device they'd bought at a
health food store, and then they'd boil up some ginseng tea and
have themselves a little feast. Fondle and I would order hamburgers.
Jeffrey sat in the lotus position onstage and battled with himself in
outdoor venues when he was attacked by mosquitoes, not because
of his respect for life, I don't think, but because of his obsession with
self-discipline.

In southern California I decided, at the suggestion of some resisters, to include a demonstration in my concert. One young man
had deliberated a long time and decided to turn in his draft card. He
wanted to "go public," and was hoping that I would accept his card
in a little ceremony in front of the audience. I said fine, and worked
out a bit of theater. Midway through the program, I would announce
that the next song was dedicated to the draft resisters. If there was
anyone in the house who wanted to turn in his card right then and
there, I'd be happy to accept it. At that point, the young man would
come forward and hand me his card. It worked fine, except that
thirty other young men also came forward and handed in their
cards. I knew they were not ready to refuse, and I handed all their
cards back, told them where they could get draft counseling
(namely, backstage), and took an intermission.

I decided to make a record for David. It would be a nice gift. I
went to Nashville again and recorded twelve country and western
selections. I had drawn pages of David's profile in the evenings

when he sat reading, and I now chose the best of them and designed a record cover with his portrait in the center surrounded by a three-and-a-half-inch-thick border of multicolored images from tarot cards making up a flowering band. The background was silver. It was a big project, especially because I recorded a double album of all Dylan at the same time. I went home and got serious about the coming baby.

We have a picture of me sitting out in front of the house shortly before Gabe was born. It was taken just after a storm had blown things all over the yard and the sky was still dark. I am sitting on a toilet that Robert had been planning to fix for a long time. My hair is growing out and I am waving at the camera. Mom would say those were my "hippie days."

Gail Zermeno came to the Institute for Nonviolence from her college at Berkeley. She stayed on in California as a working member of our draft resistance and nonviolent community, eventually becoming my personal aide and close friend.

I took the Lamaze natural childbirth course with Gail as my helper. One night I woke up with cramps and my heart started to race out of control. I put my hand to my mouth in excitement and disbelief and said, "Calm yourself." I got up slowly to see if the cramps stopped. They did not. I decided to go into the kitchen and make some Jell-O. I filled a small pot of water, opened a box of strawberry Jell-O, spilled half of it on the floor, emptied the rest into a bowl, put the wrapping into the boiling water, and burnt my fingers fishing it out. I gave up and went back to bed, and the cramps must have stopped because I slept until about seven. They woke me up again. It was a Tuesday. David called on Tuesdays. Gail came over and we went down the hill to the clinic. The doctor said it would be a long wait, so we went back up the hill. It was a twenty-five-minute ride, but I was still hoping for David's call. I plunked myself on the couch and began breathing over the pains. Many hours went by, and friends from the commune came and went. When I was puffing too hard to talk, I'd signal by putting my hand in the air so they'd know I was busy. We waited until the pains were a minute and a half apart, and then headed down the hill again, my hand more often in the air than not. David called five minutes after we'd left.

I'd planned to have my baby while sitting up, but after the first big contraction, ended up on my back and stayed there for the rest of my labor. Some poor intern came in and covered me up with a sheet, and I kicked it off and said I didn't want any fucking sheet over me. He left and I never saw him again. I was breathing my Lamaze rhythms like a beached blowfish, and the doctor came in and told me to take it easy or I'd pass out long before delivery. I don't remember much after that except for a pain shot. I grabbed the doctor's hand and squeezed it and hollered "FUCK!" at the top of my lungs because nothing is more painful than a pain shot. They were wheeling me somewhere and the doctor kept saying, "Do you feel like pushing?" and I kept lying and saying no, because I was scared. I was hyperventilating, and I thought I heard a cat howling in the next room, but the nurses said it was me, and then finally I was pushing like mad. Oh God, I thought, I must be pushing a mountain out of me, and I heard the doctor say, "Looks like a healthy little boy," and I was wide awake and all ears and felt wonderful and had no pain and was crying and I wanted to see him. He was purple and gooey, but I reached up for him and started to sing, "Hello Little Friend," a Joe Cocker hit. They put him on my chest for a minute and I simply did not believe he was mine. Then I got hungry. I had my little boy, and now all I really wanted to do was eat. My mom was in the corridor when they wheeled me out. She'd driven up from Carmel when she got the word, and she kissed me and clutched her hands together, teary-eyed with excitement. I lay in my hospital robe thinking about food, and a nurse came in and said, "Have you tried a little water?"

"I've tried a lot of water, and now I want to eat."

"Have you been nauseated?"

"Yes, most of my life, but not right now."

She brought me food, and Robert and Christy brought me food, and I gobbled it all down and then called David. "We've got a Gabe," I told him. We had long since decided upon either Gabriel or Joaquin (we had no girl's name). A week later, I received the most beautiful letter David ever wrote me. He had been waiting for the call from the hospital, walking around the yard in the rain. After it came he just wanted to be alone, so he got into a broom closet and shut the door and sat there. He knew he was smoking because he could see a glow which would flare up now and then and after a while dim and go out, and then flare up again. "We have a Gabe," I had said to him. Born out of the sixties and out of our haphazard lives, born out of caring, born into our dreams, we had a Gabe.

I traveled a lot soon after Gabriel was born. I have pictures of him lounging in rubber boats in a St. Tropez swimming pool, after having eaten raspberries and champagne mixed together in the portable baby-food grinder. He was carried through the main square in Warsaw and sunned on the beaches of Italy. Gail was my constant companion and Gabe's surrogate mother. For Gabe's seventeenth birthday she gave him an emergency road kit for his car and a Chinese wok.

After David had been in prison for ten months and Gabe had been born, I had an affair. I sneaked around, got hot flashes when the phone rang, made mysterious trips to Los Angeles, and worried about being a terrible person. I was frightened of David's homecoming. One resistance wife called me to say that her husband had gotten out early. He'd just walked in the front door one day and wrapped her up in his arms and taken her off to bed. She sounded ecstatic. I broke out into a sweat. I coveted Gabe. Alone, with him in my arms, I sat at dawn and wrote him a lullaby. Way up there on Struggle Mountain, peering up into the oaks, waiting for the sun to hit the top branches of the eucalyptus trees, I escaped with Gabe on a silent, wingless, flying horse. *The grey quiet horse wears the reins of dawn . . . and nobody knows what mountain he's from . . . in his mouth he carries the golden key . . . and nobody knows him but Gabriel and me, Gabriel and me.*

It was chilly in Texas the morning we came to the prison to take you home ten months later. Gabe was dressed in blue wool knickers and a camel's hair coat. I had on a big fuzzy Afghan embroidered coat, and you were wearing the suit I'd brought you. The press was at the San Francisco airport en masse. There was a big party for you at the Institute. Gabe toddled around in the California sunshine and everyone was smiling and looking happy for us, and I was frozen in my own footsteps. Gail took Gabe so that you and I could have some time alone.

Our house was so small, David, and you were so big! I got angry when you told your macho prison stories about all of the seedier and most violent times you'd lived through or heard about. You told them over and over again to adoring groupies and never answered when I asked you what you wanted for dinner. (I was jealous of the adoring groupies, and you didn't know what you wanted for dinner, no one had asked you for so long.) I didn't mind sharing Gabe as much as I had thought I would. But that was because I considered him mine, and just on loan to you. When it dawned on me that you were actually his father and had rights to him and to his time and to his love, I was furious.

We didn't split up over Gabe, or over the affair I'd had, though it had been quite real and not at all a passing fancy. We didn't split up over politics. We split up, when we did, because I couldn't breathe, and I couldn't try anymore to be a wife, and because I belonged alone, which is how I have been since then, with occasional interruptions which are mostly picnics, honeymoons, overnight sprees on tour, and my dreams. What I knew in my bones at the crumbling finale to our erratic three years together I could express consciously to myself ten years later. I am made to live alone. I cannot possibly live in the same house with anyone. This is no longer a great problem for me. Sometimes I am very, very lonely. But I prefer this loneliness to the desperate feeling of failure that I had when I couldn't manage being your wife.

I am sorry, Gabe, that we couldn't be a family. I think I have been a good mother. I have loved you very much. Loving you was easy. People warned me about the terrible twos and the threatening threes and the frightful fours, but you never had them. You were fun. Wonderful fun. You were also a heartbreak. Seeing you sleeping peacefully on your back among your stuffed ducks, bears, and basset hounds, a glow of fevery red on your cheeks from playing so hard, would remind me that no matter how good the next day might be, certain moments were gone forever because we could not go backwards in time. So I began to lose you from the moment you were born. I could fill this book with stories about you as a baby, but you would hate that. So I'll tell just a few. Here's one you can hate me for: I refused to toilet train you. When we put you in the nursery school, you were too young and they said, "We don't usually take children who are still in diapers, but when he sees the other kids, you know, it will only be a matter of days or weeks." But it was weeks and months, and you were in your threes when you took the pins out and handed them to me, and wadded up the diapers and chucked them in the bathroom wastebasket. We never had an accident.

After David and I split up I lived in Woodside. David lived a half an hour away in the hills. Gabe grew up going back and forth between us. None of us liked the arrangement, but since David and I both wanted to spend time with him, this is how it ended up.

I never took Gabe on a peace march. I never took him to a farmworker's funeral.

One day he announced that the trouble with me was that I didn't play war enough. I said fine, let's go play war. We set up little metal soldiers and took up our positions.

"Mine are the good guys," said Gabe.

"I see. And who might they be?"

"The Americans. You have the bad guys."

"And who are the bad guys?"

"Ummm, Japanese."

"Really? You mean like Gene, our gardener?"

"Oh. Well, then they're Germans."

"Goodness. You must mean like Shorty. You know, that guy from Germany who made you those tarts on your birthday?"

"Well. Mom, c'mon, you're wrecking the game."

"Sorry, Gabe. Let's see, they are from Denmark, like Rachel in your class who sings to the whole school on birthdays and Christmas."

"OK."

"What do we do now?"

"Now we go to war!" he said gleefully.

Making battle sounds with his throat and tongue and gurgling spit, he proceeded to level my lopsided army with one man, slamming into my lines, *p'tewy*-ing down whole rows at a time. I tried feebly to attack his troops, but everything I did was wrong. Within sixty seconds, it was all over but the burial.

"That was fun, Mom! We should do that more often!"

"Anytime you like, sweetie."

I suppose I overcompensated in trying to free him of the oppressiveness of being the child of a fanatical pacifist mother and two famous social activists. When he was ten he relieved me by a statement which showed anything but a conventional acceptance of military consciousness. We were watching TV one afternoon, and the news of the day was the arrival and debut of a new missile. Many of the big brass were fondly looking on as it glided out of its shaft toward the camera. I said something appropriate like "Ugh." Gabe said condescendingly, "I *know* what you're thinking, Mom."

"What am I thinking, Gabe?"

"You're thinking, 'Look at the big new shiny penis and all the generals standing around getting hard-ons.'"

"You're absolutely right, son," I said, delighted.

And so how did we manage, at the breakup of what *Time* magazine called "The Marriage of the Century"? How did we manage with our son? Just the way everyone else does. By fighting and crying with frustration, and tugging and pulling at Gabe's loyalties, and then breaking down and seeing how miserably we were behaving, and then trying to learn how to trust each other. That trust came, little by little, and with an enormous amount of work. And we worked because we loved Gabe. Neither of us was right or wrong. Both of us were just hopelessly foolish, possessive, and loving parents. We did our absolute best. We are still doing it.

# 5
# "TO LOVE AND MUSIC"

Woodstock was drugs and sex and rock and roll. Woodstock was Janis coitus interruptus Joplin, and Jimi genius Hendrix, and the gorgeous sweating chest of Roger Daltrey of The Who. Woodstock was Country Joe McDonald, handsome as a wild Indian. "So it's one, two, three, what are we fightin' for, don't ask me, I don't give a damn, the next stop is Viet-Nam." Woodstock was Dirty Sly and the Family Stone gettin' HIGH-YUH! along with a half a million people. Woodstock was cockeyed Joe Cocker, bent up like a weird palsied street person but singing like Ray Charles. Woodstock was rain and mud, GI's in disguise, and cops putting their guns up and cooking hot dogs for hungry hippies. Woodstock was white ladies of the lake emboldened by the roadblocks set up between the golden city of freedom and their sororities, pulling back their river-rat hair with the lake dripping from their pretty elbows, not really unaware of the cameras grinding away on the shore, focused on their lovely breasts. Woodstock was Wavy Gravy and his Hog Farm, "How about breakfast for four hundred thousand people?" and his words to the wise, "DON'T TAKE THE BROWN ACID, YA DIG?" Woodstock was Abbie Hoffman shouting in my ear over Creedence Clearwater Revival to take this jackknife, which I wouldn't because he was poking fun at my nonviolence, or so I thought . . .

Woodstock? Hell, I was already pushing my luck. I'd been on the music scene for ten years and still didn't take dope or use a backup band.

But Woodstock was also me, Joan Baez, the square, six months pregnant, the wife of a draft resister, endlessly proselytizing about the war. I had my place there. I was of the sixties, and I was already a survivor.

We flew in over upstate New York. I pushed Mom in the helicopter after Janis Joplin, and we chopped our way above the patchwork farmlands and the hordes of roving backpackers. Janis clutched her ever present bottle of booze and everyone leaned out over the door, the wind blowing us into wild people, the blue and black clouds ahead of us and all around. Was it just the bizarre weather, or did we all sense history in the making?

They put me in the bridal suite of the Holiday Inn. People were crashed all over the floor in the lobby and *I* got the bridal suite. I must have given it away because I was in another room the next morning when I heard a great thundering racket and saw a helicopter landing in the parking lot just outside my window. I stuffed some toast in my mouth and flapped my arms at the pilot, who was grinning into my bedroom. He nodded that he'd wait. I bundled off with some press and I cannot remember who else. The whole event had me so wired up I didn't mind flying around cumulonimbus thunderbusters in a tiny helicopter. Ours was the last flight into the golden city that day. And my mom didn't make it till the next day because of the mud. Scoop, the lunatic roadie, was driving and kept getting stuck deeper and deeper, and telling Mom that everything would be OK. Finally he just stopped and smoked a joint, and everything *was* OK, at least for him.

Woodstock was Manny trying to get my mother to smoke a joint. She wouldn't. She was too scared, she said.

Sometimes famous people make fun of the glamour that surrounds us. And sometimes being famous is more trouble than it's worth. But there are times when it is marvelous! Woodstock was one of those times. I had the run of the entire fairgrounds, backstage included, special access to everything, no want for food and drink, and plentiful offers of a place to rest.

When one of the big thunderstorms hit (just after the crowd had chanted "NO RAIN, NO RAIN!"), I was instantly ushered into a van. It belonged to Joe Cocker. I (the square) hung out with his band (the junkies) and chatted and drank beer and felt very in-crowd, even if they didn't know me well enough to laugh at my jokes. At one point a stagehand stuck his head into the van.

"You all right, Joan?"

"Yeah, I'm fine!"

"You're sure?"

"Yeah, I'm sure . . ."

"We can't get you anything?"

"No, really. I got everything, thank you."

It turned out there was a rumor out that I'd gone into labor.

Yes, indeed, Woodstock was two babies getting born and three people dying. Woodstock was a city. Yes, it was three extraordinary days of rain and music. No, it was not a revolution. It was a technicolor, mud-splattered reflection of the 1960s.

I sang in the middle of the night. I just stood up there in front of the residents of the golden city who were sleeping in the mud and each other's arms, and I gave them what I could at the time. And they accepted my songs. It was a humbling moment, in spite of everything. I'd never sung to a city before.

You know what Live Aid did? It proved what I've been telling the press at every Woodstock anniversary for the last ten years. There can never be another Woodstock. Woodstock, in all its mud and glory, belonged to the sixties, that outrageous, longed for, romanticized, lusted after, tragic, insane, bearded and bejeweled epoch. It is over and will never return. I do not miss it. But sometimes I resent the eighties.

# 6

# "I WILL SING TO YOU SO SWEET"

Sometime in the mid-sixties Maynard Solomon at Vanguard had suggested an album of poetry both spoken and sung to music. In 1968, I recorded the album *Baptism*, which included selections from Rimbaud, Lorca, Treece, Prevert, Blake, Joyce, and others, set to classical accompaniment. It was on the charts for the last third of 1968: my audience could apparently withstand a broader range of musical experimentation than many people thought possible.

The next time in the studio was for *David's Album* and *Any Day Now*, a double album of all Dylan material. I loved recording in Nashville, and because of the richness and variety of Bob's music, it was one of the easiest albums I've ever recorded. I just spread his sheet music all over the floor of the studio, shut my eyes and pointed, and sang whichever song came up. *Any Day Now* plus *David's Album*, the collection of country and western songs took me and my now good ol' buddies, the Nashville pickers, exactly four days to make. *Any Day Now* went gold and *David's Album* roamed around the charts for months. The fact that *David's Album* sold was due more to my strong following in those years than to the fact that it was country and western as it never made the country and western charts.

In 1970 Vanguard released a retrospective two-album set called *The First Ten Years*. In 1970 I also made *One Day at a Time*, another record leaning toward country, which included three songs with

Jeffrey. Both *The First Ten Years* and *One Day at a Time* were on the hit lists for months.

During these years I did not know what it was to have pressure put on me to "be commercial," because my albums sold well, and because Maynard Solomon was more interested in art than he was in keeping me a hot item. The fact that I stayed hot was due to the times, which were still highly political, and the fact that I could sing.

In 1971, again in Nashville, I recorded *Blessed Are . . . ,* the first album to include a number of my own songs.

"A Song for David" was about waiting for him by the stony gate of the prison, with "the little one" in my arms, and about the stars being the same for him as they were for me, and about old man Earl, who was his prison mate, and who ended up being Gabe's god-father. I wrote the "Hitchhikers Song" about the backpackers in their beads and face paint, thumbing along the route through the Santa Cruz mountains. And "Blessed Are . . . ," a song to the parents of the kids like Janis Joplin who didn't want to bother being survivors. "The Last, Lonely, and Wretched" told of the crazy, filthy, godfor-saken guy who barged into our house one day and took a bath in our sunken tub. "Outside the Nashville City Limits" was about a magical day in the country with my secret but not so secret friend, when my love for him overflowed onto the beauty of the land— "and the leaves came out so tender at the turning of the winter,/I thought my eyes they would brim over as we talked." "When Time Is Stolen" was about when the love affair ended, and as though trying desperately to settle back down, I dreamed up the lullaby "Gabriel and Me." While traveling through Europe with Gabe on my hip I wrote "Milanese Waltz," and "Marie Flore," about my little ten-year-old friend from Arles. Some songs came fast and suddenly, some in the middle of the night. Some were laborious efforts. They were very personal, and in my opinion none rated much over a five. But writing gave me a kind of satisfaction I'd not felt from singing other people's work.

David painted the cover to *Blessed Are . . .* while he was in jail. It was in the top twenty for a while and eventually went gold. I re-leased "Let It Be" from it, which rode alongside in the top fifty.

Through the late sixties and early seventies I continued to tour either alone or with Jeffrey and Fondle. I continued giving away most of my money. Some of the royalties from my records went to the draft resistance. My public image was clear: a girl, a guitar, her songs, and a message. My hair was short by then, but I don't think most people saw it that way. To the diehard fans, I was still Joanie with the waist-length tresses and achingly pure soprano. I was not only anticommercial, I was impossible. In my concert brochure I wrote things like:

[I] . . . wanted to be, when I grew up,
   a nurse,
   a veterinarian,
   a cellist,
   a hero,
   beautiful.
Never a singer.
I'm not a singer.
I sing,
I fight,
I weep,
I pray,
I laugh,
I work and wonder.
   . . . The entertainment industry would have me tell you about "Joan Baez, the Folksinger." How I "got started" and where I've sung and what laurels I have gathering dust under my bed.
   But I'll tell you simply, that there is no "Joan Baez, the Folksinger."
   There is me, 28 years old, pregnant, my husband just beginning three years in prison for draft refusal and resistance organizing. . . . Me, sitting here listening to Merle Haggard's "Sing Me Back Home" and thinking . . . about children dying in Vietnam, Biafra, India, Peru, U.S.A. . . .
   . . . In the midst of all these things, how could I pretend to entertain you?
   Sing to you, yes.
   To prod you, to remind you, to bring you joy, or sadness, or anger . . . And I will say . . .
   Consider life.
   Give life priority over all things.
   Over land.
   Over law.
   Over profit.
   Over promises.
   Over all things.

As I read this, seventeen years later, it appears excessively grim. It was a long, long way from the petunia beds of Struggle Mountain to the Raphael Hotel in Paris and the Via Veneto in Rome.

All the while David was in prison, work continued on the film *Carry It On*, our beautiful little documentary about two people with a mission. It shows David speaking, us traveling or just sitting in the mottled sunlight in the yard on Struggle Mountain planning "the Revolution." It shows my concerts while he was in jail, carnations on the stage at the Madison Square Garden two-dollar-a-ticket concert. The title comes from a song by Gil Turner which says:

> There's a man by my side walking
> There's a voice within me talking
> There's a voice within me saying
> Carry it on, carry it on . . .

Just before David and I split up, *Carry It On* was released, a sound track album from the documentary. At about the same time Maynard Solomon of Vanguard and I decided that it was time to part company. Perhaps he felt the beginning of the end of the time when I could sing whatever the hell I pleased, put it out with a homegrown picture on the cover, and have it make the charts.

It was a genial split, as those things go. He has since packaged and repackaged my thirteen years of music with him, *Hits, Greatest and Others* (which I wanted to be called *Hits and Misses*, but he didn't think that was funny), *Joan Baez Ballad Book, The Joan Baez Lovesong Album, Greatest Folk Singers of the Sixties*, and others. Each time Maynard wrote and announced another release I'd feel like an old cow being milked when I'd already gone dry, but I must confess the records were always well packaged, and to this day they continue to sell all over the world when many of the newer models do not. As I was leaving Vanguard, we released "The Night They Drove Old Dixie Down," which became my only big "hit" to date, going up to number five on the pop charts and staying in the top forty for fifteen weeks.

I signed with A&M records. It was a refreshing change. I felt as if I'd crossed over into the big-time—offices and studios in L.A., limousines, and star treatment. On the other hand, I felt I would be given more artistic license at A&M because of its size and personnel than I might have at a larger, even glitzier company.

I was right. My first album with them was *Come from the Shadows*, a title taken from a line in the French Resistance song called "The

Partisan." It was not a commercial album. The cover is a photograph of an elderly white, middle class couple being arrested at an antiwar demonstration. The concept of a less than very political album had not yet occurred to me, but in two of my own songs on this album I was climbing from the "five" category to the "six or seven": "Prison Trilogy" and "Love Song to a Stranger."

At the end of that year, 1972, I had my Christmas visit to Hanoi, and put together a record company's nightmare when I came home. I promised A&M that on the next album there would be no bombs, sirens, antiaircraft, or weeping mothers. Miraculously, *Where Are You Now, My Son?* made it onto the charts in 1973 for a few months. I happen to think the album is brilliant, but it was pushing a good thing pretty far. The American public had not yet begun the massive trend toward "feeling good about itself," or that album would have been buried alive.

In 1974, in reaction to the coup in Chile, I recorded an album in Spanish as a message of hope to the people who were suffering under Pinochet. The album was called *¡Gracias a la Vida!* (*Thanks to Life!*). Highly musical, using backup that included a mariachi band from the restaurant next door to the studio, a group of farmworkers on the chorus to "No Nos Moveran," and a Chilean harpist, it is one of my favorite albums. It sold moderately well in the States, and very well in Spanish-speaking countries.

All in all, A&M was inordinately good to me. Yes, I still sold well for who I was, but the times were beginning to change. Though I had not officially sung "folk songs" for years, I was still called a "folksinger."

_PART_
_FOUR_

# "How Stark Is the Here and Now"

# 1

# "LYING IN A BED OF ROSES"

Although I later fell in love with France, and now consider it my second home, the first country to win my young heart and seduce me with its language and beauty and fashion and flowers and intellect and men was Italy. Entering Italy for the very first time in May of 1967 was like entering a Fellini film as one of the stars. My reality, by any normal standards, was a fantasy: I was sought after by intellectuals, wined and dined by writers and filmmakers and politicos, pampered as the darling of the leftist intellectual circles in Rome and Milan. I met Furio Colombo, whom I called Marco, and who may be the smartest human being I've ever known. A journalist for *La Stampa*, one of Italy's two largest newspapers, author of a book about Kennedy's America and one on the American theater, he was then also working for Italian television. He took me to tiny restaurants where everyone knew him, and everyone knew me, and he talked about politics, philosophy, art, and religion, while I sat starry-eyed and in awe of his stupendous mind. I was taken to the most prestigious shops and given outrageous discounts on the latest fashions. I was given beautiful suites overlooking parks and gardens, and actors, writers, poets, songwriters, painters, senators, and professors sent me bouquets of roses.

I sat up in bed in my magnificent suite in the Excelsior Hotel, in an ocean of white linen sheets and a mountain of pillows and quilts, and ordered croissants and jam and caffè con latté for breakfast. I'd

practice Italian songs on the guitar until it was time to order a big
bowl of spaghetti al dente for lunch. Basking in the attention, confused at first, I soon became spoiled and addicted to the splendifor-
ous scene.

The concerts were not so much concerts as they were spectacles,
gala events, political forums. I sang in the Teatro Lirico, a beautiful
opera house in Milan. It was filled to capacity, standing room only,
with a crowd that could be described as exuberant. In the middle of
the first half there was a great commotion in the balcony but I just
continued singing, hoping the noise would subside. A political
group had unfurled a Viet Cong flag in the top row of the balcony,
and when I hadn't responded to it, had become angry. They began
noisily demanding recognition, part of the audience supporting
them, others just as noisily telling them to shut up, and still others
expressing their impatience and disgust at the whole scene. Eventually, the commotion turned into a near riot, and I took an early
intermission.

I hadn't seen the flag, of course, as I looked into a spotlight, but
the flag-wavers were now demanding a statement from me on 1)
why I had ignored their statement, and, 2) my position on the war
in Vietnam. When I went back out I gave a short speech related to
the American invasion of Vietnam, which Marco translated. Unfortunately, in an attempt to spare me the reaction of the conservatives
in the crowd, Marco interpreted "American invasion" as "American
involvement," and a second shouting match ensued, with people
standing up on their seats and hurling wadded up programs at each
other, shaking their fists, and, I gather, cursing each other's family
lineage, putting a heavy emphasis on the maternal side. Finally I
asked Marco to leave, then stretched out my arms imploringly and
sang "Pilgrim of Sorrow"—a heartrending spiritual I'd sung to King
in Grenada—which, if done in the right key, allows me just enough
sustained high F's to win over the most difficult of crowds. The
Milanese forfeited their deep love of confrontation for their equally
deep love of the human voice, and, perhaps remembering that theirs
was the birthplace of Puccini and Verdi, succumbed to my untrained
but impressive vocal gymnastics, decided to sit down, and listened
to the rest of the concert.

I finished up with four encores, left the stage carrying armfuls of
bouquets, and fell exhausted onto a tiny velvet couch in a dressing
room already so overflowing with flowers that the new ones had to
be put into the sink and toilet bowl. Everyone left the room in a
hush, and I fell asleep; ten minutes later they came back, polite but

animated: the public was still on its feet cheering, demanding another encore. I went onto the stage barefoot and sang a capella and my love affair with the Italians was sealed by my unabashed acceptance of their wild flattery.

In 1970 I sang in L'Arena, a soccer stadium in Milan. I had been on television and spoken in Italian about Martin Luther King, about the war in Vietnam, about demonstrations, about nonviolence, and had sung a song in Italian called "C'era un Ragazzo," about two youths—one Italian and one American—who both play guitar and listen to the Beatles and the Rolling Stones. One day the American gets a letter from his government and goes off to Vietnam, and now the guitar is forgotten and instead he plays a new instrument, which has only one note. It goes *Ta ta rrra ta ta, ta ta rrra ta ta.* It was a current hit sung by Gianni Morandi, a teenage idol who had one of those scratchy, sexy voices which sells millions of records. My singing "C'era un Ragazzo" on TV, a suggestion of Marco's, was a coup. The first night, sixteen thousand people came to the stadium to hear the outspoken, radical, anti–Vietnam War, pacifist American singer. I read introductions in Italian off little pages scribbled with phonetics, and sang a one-and-a-half-hour show, including "Where Have All the Flowers Gone?," "The Ghetto," "Swing Low," "Sweet Sir Galahad," "C'era un Ragazzo," and other popular Italian songs. The crowd was excited but well behaved, and the evening was a success.

The next night, the audience had doubled in size. Kids jumped the fence to get in free, the police were everywhere, and I was determined to maintain control over thirty thousand mad Italians. Marco had a microphone offstage for when I needed help, because the politicos had also turned out en masse. The Maoists, Stalinists, Trotskyites, and anarchists were the most vocal, and regularly interrupted the concert by shouting or chanting anti-American, anti-Nixon slogans. While the students and the more manipulative politicos jammed the lawn the entire 360 degrees around the raised platform where I stood, the conservatives, local politicians, mayors, stars, and normal people sat in the bleachers quite a distance away. Right-wing fanatics sat in small groups and occasionally countered the Maoists, etc., with brave shouts of "Viva Il Duce" (Long live Mussolini). Up close, red flags dotted the crowd, and between songs I humored, cajoled, and tried every trick I knew to keep the evening calm.

In a sudden spontaneous and collective move, the young people sitting on the ground rose up in unison and shouted, pointing at something in back of me on the playing field. I turned and saw a young man running full tilt from a carabiniere, who was, I assumed, going to "capture" him for having jumped the fence. *"No carabinieri!"* I shouted into the mike, my voice booming out across the field. *"Per piacere, no carabinieri!"* The poor policeman walked away in disgust and embarrassment to join his fellow policemen. The crowd gave a victory roar, and the young gate-crasher was hailed and seated in the audience, hugged and kissed, and generally received as a hero.

The elders in the bleachers watched the phenomenon of the political princess and her unruly hordes with amusement, and, I am told, with admiration. Every time I mentioned nonviolence, the antipacifist leftists would shout and scream their own slogans to contradict me, but I was as fearless and tenacious as an old schoolteacher, and, with or without the aid of Marco, would simply lecture them back.

A wind blew up, and I suddenly felt the incredible vulnerability of being alone on the stage. Indeed, the weather was rapidly turning bad. I sang "The Ghetto," and got to the last verse:

> And if there's such a thing as revolution
> And there will be, if we rise to the call,
> When we build, we build, we build the new Jerusalem,
> There won't be no more ghetto at all.

At the word "revolution" two things happened. The students went berserk because the word inflamed them, and raindrops began to slap down onto the crowd and the uncovered stage. Thirty thousand heads tilted skyward. The bourgeoisie headed for the bleachers, and the young and the reckless headed for the stage. My platform was about four feet high, and the kids were either moving or being shoved toward the stage in waves, as the sky opened up with lightning, thunder, and a flash flood. My mind raced for a song which everyone could sing, as it might be the only way to calm the mounting hysteria. Rain arrived in sheets, and by the time I started "Kumbaya" the first battalion of kids was crawling up to mount the stage. A great gust of wind blew the stool, notes, and water glass off into the night. My last words over the speakers were: "Manny! Manny! Manny, the stool!"—and the electricity went dead. I knew I was in the hands of God, and of maniacs. The Italians were suddenly upon me. I kept smiling and holding the guitar in the air, thinking it would be safer in the rain above my head than crushed between the chests, arms, and legs below. I saw Marco shoving his way through the soaking, screaming crowd. I saw Gail, who was usually quietly playing with Gabe offstage, elbow her way toward me with the ferocity of a mother cheetah.

A few faces from a student nonviolent group appeared, kids I'd met with earlier during my stay. They calmly tried to link arms, in the hopes of encircling me and getting me off the stage. There was, of course, no backstage, only a soccer field which was rapidly becoming a lake. Someone managed to wrap me up in a large cloth. I looked down and saw that it was an anarchist flag, and shouted "No, grazie, no!" and began trying to disentangle myself while still keeping the guitar in the air. I caught another glimpse of Marco, who was bobbing around like a cork in a bathtub, as were all of us, and he was shouting something to me about the guitar.

Francesco, a great bearded giant of a boy from the nonviolent student group, picked me up in his arms and, bumping people out of the way, hulked down the makeshift stairs. Reaching a surprisingly clear, if soggy, area of grass, he began to run, splashing across the field, past screaming fans, and hurled me into a sound truck. Gail followed just after, shouting, "Lock the doors!" As we did I felt a tiny shock. I tucked my hands under my cold, miniskirted bottom, and sat like a nervous river rat, caught in an unfamiliar bunch of reeds. There was a great pounding on the window. Francesco shouted to open the door, which I did, and he yanked me out, the way a mother yanks her child from a mountain precipice.

"Eelectreecity!" he bellowed, and off he ran with me in his arms again, this time to a waiting car.

Back at the hotel we sat, dripping, on the floor of the lobby: Manny, Marco, Francesco, Gail, and myself. Colleen (my friend from the Carmel days—we last saw her in turquoise silk at the hospital curb looking at her new car . . .) arrived with Gabe sleeping in her arms, her story just as incredible as ours. When the rain started, she had gone into a room off the hallway which ran between the bleachers. There she and a few other women decided to stay dry and away from the crowd. As the storm whipped up, more people left their seats seeking shelter. One of the women with Colleen panicked and shut the door, fearing the crush of the oncoming crowds. When the crowd started banging on the door in a fury, Colleen took it upon herself to open it and invite them in. It was the decent thing to do, and besides, they might have broken in and vented their understandable rage. Ten-month-old Gabe was the hero of the moment, for as furious as the soggy Italians were, characteristically they were just as protective of a baby as they were of their own pride, and Colleen was eventually guided through the crush of bodies and helped to a taxi.

So there we sat on the tile floor, recounting every incident and laughing until we wept.

"You know why we're still alive?" I ventured.

"Why?" everyone chorused.

"Because I insulted the police and they went on strike! If they'd tried to control the crowd, we'd have been killed!"

I remembered Marco's glasses crunching noiselessly under a shoe.

"By the way, Marco, what were you shouting at me the whole time?"

"I was saying, 'Don't hold the guitar een the air!' "

"But why, for Christ sake. It was going to get squashed!"

"Yes, I know. But you must understand, that when the Eetalians see something held over their heads, out of reach, een the air, like that, they theenk eet ees sometheeng to capture, like a flag een the meedle of a battle. Every time the geetar went another eench higher, they more and more wanted to have eet, to capture eet, to claim eet. That's why, Giovanna."

The next morning at breakfast the headwaiter came over to our table.

"*Et, il concerto. Come vai? Successo o fiasco?*"

"*Fiasco,*" I teased.

"*Ha!*" he retorted, proudly whisking a newspaper out from behind his back. Rave reports of the concert dominated the front page.

"*Successo, non fiasco!*" he grinned back at me.

"Yes, I know. *Un gran successo.* It was wonderful," I said, and kissed his hand.

# 2

# "SILENCE IS SHAME"

In 1972 Ginetta Sagan appeared on my doorstep. She was tiny, pleasantly chubby, with short black hair, huge luminous brown eyes, and the countenance of a sunburst. Under her arm—or rather, in her lap, because as I remember, she was sitting on a huge stone near the garden—she held a big messy bundle of documents. I remember very little of that meeting, except her heavy Italian accent, and grisly pictures of tortured prisoners from places like Turkey, Greece, South Africa, and Cuba.

Ginetta told me about something called Amnesty International and its work on behalf of all political prisoners, regardless of ideology, race, or religion.

Over the years that followed I learned about Ginetta's incredible past. I will print only a few details here, because she is finally writing the book we have all urged her to write for many years. In it will be the details of the horrors this tiny woman went through at the tender age of nineteen. A member of the anti-Nazi, anti-Fascist resistance in the north of Italy, she was arrested, and spent forty hideous days in prison undergoing every form of torture used in those days to elicit information. She survived, barely.

Ginetta was born with the gifts of an active mind, a love of life and of beauty, an unquashable spirit, and a faith in people very much like that of Anne Frank. Her favorite expression, "There are so many beautiful people in the world!," reminds me so much of "I still believe that people are good at heart." I think she is speaking of herself.

Amnesty International, I finally understood after two or three visits by this persistent little Italian, was an organization which worked for the release of prisoners of conscience, namely, anyone imprisoned for reasons of ethnic origin, or religious or political beliefs, and who had never used or advocated violence. Amnesty also worked to free anyone from torture, no matter what the nature of their crime, and to abolish the death penalty. Amnesty had its headquarters in London, England, and a large office in New York. Ginetta wanted to create a thriving Amnesty International on the West Coast. And she wanted me to help her.

I do not need retrospective wisdom to know why I was so attracted to Amnesty: I needed to do some kind of work that produced tangible results. The things I had worked for all my life, and would go on working for, were things I would never see, like fewer nation-states and an end to the arms race. The Institute no longer stimulated me; it was filled with good souls who, since I traveled so much, had come to feel that it was in fact theirs, and that I was rather a nuisance of an absentee landlady. Ira and I had not been close since my marriage. Ginetta was a fireball of energy and compassion and a European intellectual, eager to share her knowledge and experiences with me. She had three sons; perhaps she would have liked a daughter.

I took a year out of my life to organize Amnesty International West Coast.

Oh, how we would laugh! I sat in Ginetta's guest room which we had made into an office, surrounded with documents and leaflets and pamphlets and indexes and files and literature on political prisoners. One day I answered the phone "Amnesty International," and when Ginetta came on the line the caller said, "Who's your secretary? She has such a pleasant speaking voice!"

We tore up and down the coast fund-raising, meeting with editorial boards, going to private homes and giving talks on how to form an Amnesty group.

Amnesty works as a network of groups. To be a group you had to get together, meet at least once a month, and register with Amnesty in London, which would send you the names of three prisoners: one from a left-wing country, one from a right-wing country, and one from a Third World country. Then you began a letter-writing campaign, doing anything you could think of to rattle the authorities in charge of your prisoner enough to let him or her out of detention.

One group invented the idea of telephoning the jail collect and asking for their prisoner, person to person. A call was placed every hour on the hour around the clock. This trick would almost certainly put a halt to torture, at least temporarily, and often resulted in a release.

Groups began popping up like daffodils in springtime. I became a member of the National Advisory Board.

A CIA-backed coup took the life of Salvador Allende in Chile on September 11, 1973, and the repression which followed was monstrous. We concentrated on Chile as I devoted myself full-time to Amnesty, giving benefit concerts, accelerating the fund-raising. Exiled Chileans helped me plan my Spanish album.

We needed two thousand dollars to send a doctor and a lawyer to Santiago. We'd heard rumors of torture and murder and hoped to get information from inside the stadium where victims of the repression were being kept. Ginetta plowed through her Rolodex and out popped a card, like Cinderella's fairy godmother making a glass slipper appear with her magic wand.

The man was a distinguished, liberal, millionaire Italian, and he lived ten minutes away. I grabbed the address, jumped in the car and tore off without my shoes. Oh well, I thought halfway there, maybe he won't be stuffy. He was not. He was kind, elegant, served me tea, and pretended not to notice my bare feet. I left forty-five minutes after I'd arrived, with a personal check for one thousand dollars in my hand.

I learned what my limits as a fund-raiser were. I didn't have any.

Ginetta's husband and I went to see another local millionaire who turned out to be more interested in flirting with me than learning about Amnesty. Leonard and I, feeling we weren't getting anywhere with him, just kept insisting that he *must* meet Ginetta. Fine, he said, at last, and addressing me directly said, "Invite me to dinner."

"My pleasure," I replied. Then he proceeded to dictate to me his preferred menu. He obviously thought that I would be cooking.

"I want raw cucumbers sliced on a microtome."

"Fine," I said, with a wave of my hand, wondering what a microtome was.

"Then, I'd like braised brains."

"No problem."

"Puréed spinach with a dash of nutmeg."

"Yes, of course."

"And for *dessert*," he said, leaning forward, "for *dessert* I'd like a chocolate soufflé. But I want you to cook two of them, placing the second one in the oven one minute after the first, so that if the first one collapses we have a back-up."

"Let me write all this down," I said dutifully, and did so. I couldn't glance at Leonard or we'd have collapsed into giggles.

"That all?" I asked cheerfully, and he responded by naming the wines of his choice.

Leonard and I nearly died when we finally got out into the fresh air.

"Do you *believe* that guy? Oh, my God! I can't wait to tell Ginetta! Good thing I've got Christine to do the cooking! He thinks *I'm* gonna cook! That'd be the bloody end of Amnesty West Coast! Ha Ha Ha! Boy, I hope he makes this worth our while!"

Christine, my guardian angel, British factotum, child-rearing expert, and cook, obliged. With certificates from any number of European cooking schools she was not the least bit fazed, but felt no love for our guest of honor. I told her it didn't matter, just to cut those cucumbers mighty thin, because whether or not we got a generous donation might depend on our being able to hold up a slice of cucumber and read a newspaper through it.

Dinner went flawlessly, except that, knowing he wanted to witness me gag over the braised brains, I had a hamburger. And Christine drew the line at one chocolate soufflé, which dropped, I assumed, because she had hexed it. But she served it with perfect aplomb, as though it were meant to be sticking to the sides of the bowl and sunken like mud around the roots of a rose bush.

After dinner I whisked out my guitar and sang to him over aperitifs in the sitting room, while Ginetta and Leonard looked on dotingly.

He was not a generous millionaire. Perhaps he had expected more than I could, in good taste, offer. If he's reading this, he might like to know that the same amount he gave us for our trouble, I can make twenty times over at a brief appearance in a rock concert, even now. Oh, well, it was all in the game.

Night after night the four or five of us who constituted the office, plus volunteers, drove the hour to San Francisco to leaflet at the film *State of Siege*, by Costa-Gavras. The film exposed, among other things, the corrupt element in the AID program, which funded the teaching of torture techniques in Latin and Central America. We solicited signatures against the use of torture, and educated people to the fact that torture was more prevalent than it had been since the middle ages, that the danger was its common use as government policy, and that, though at one remove, the hands of the U.S. government were far from clean.

I gave a concert for Melina Mercouri on behalf of Greek political prisoners, and went to New York and Paris for the first Campaign to Abolish Torture. It was attended by people from all over the world, and no one knew which direction it might go. At one point I took the microphone from a group which was trying to disrupt the meeting and discredit Amnesty, and sang a song. Order was restored, and I have been credited with having helped to squelch a potential disaster for A.I. At my concerts I arranged to have leaflets handed out containing the names of three prisoners, or the name of one special, urgent-action prisoner, with instructions as to whom and where to write demanding his or her release.

I decided to work directly with Amnesty until the day when any newspaper or radio talk show I approached would know what Amnesty International was, and when the facts, coming from London, were no longer disputed. It took only a year.

I have continued to go to vigils, concerts, and demonstrations for Mothers of the Disappeared, Andrei Sakharov, Anatoly Scharansky, and others, and against the death penalty. I remain on the National Advisory Board. Having brought up and nurtured Amnesty from when she was a baby, I feel very close to her. What a thrill to have been on the "Conspiracy of Hope" concert tour in 1986, A.I.'s twenty-fifth anniversary tour, with U2, Sting, Peter Gabriel and others. A.I.'s membership grew by 25,000 as a result of that tour.

Nearly fifteen years later, Ginetta and I remain very close. She has taught me diplomacy and restraint in my dealings with government officials, heads of state, and others I have often wanted to thumb my nose at. "Never close the door, you may need this person some day," is one of her favorite expressions. In 1983, at *Newsweek's* fiftieth anniversary celebration, I was seated across from Mary McCarthy at the head table. The big feature of the evening was a videotaped speech by Henry Kissinger. When he appeared on the big screen I stuffed my stockinged feet into their high heels and left the table, and stood in the lobby until it was finished. My moderation and diplomacy end where Henry's nose begins.

# 3
# "DANCING ON OUR BROKEN CHAINS"

Spring of 1972.

It was Ira's idea.

The women and children of America would go to Washington and join hands around the Congress of the United States. In a symbolic act of solidarity with the women and children of Vietnam, we would demand that no more funds go to continue the war. No more funds to bomb, napalm, strafe, gas, torture and massacre the crossfire victims in that country. We wanted the violence, at least from our side, to stop.

It might have been one of the largest demonstrations Washington had ever seen. As it turned out, it was the most difficult, demoralizing, battering, discouraging task I have ever taken on in my life. But I learned how strong my faith was when I knew I was right; and I learned something about what it's like to be sabotaged.

I asked Coretta King to join with me in sponsoring the demonstration we later named Ring Around Congress. We were one black woman and one brown, both dedicated to nonviolent action. We met in New York. She was quite swept off her feet by the idea, and in her words, it was the historic moment for it.

We asked Cora Weiss of Women's Strike for Peace if she would help us organize. Years later she and I would split over my open criticisms of Hanoi's human rights record. She is strongly left-wing, and by no means a pacifist. But she was and is one of the finest organizers I've ever met. She said yes and recruited four other women: Amy Swerdlow, Edith Villastrigo, Barbara Raskin, and Barbara Bick. They were tough. We were a formidable group.

We divided our territories and tasks around the country. My first task was to contact Another Mother for Peace and see if they would sponsor us and promote our march through their newsletter. They were not known for radical action, and had never promoted civil disobedience. We were not planning on civil disobedience, but it was something that had to be considered should anything go wrong in Washington.

They adopted the idea with no hesitation. How could they lose? It would be American moms and kiddies saying no to war. The peace movement no longer consisted solely of "dirty hippies and KGB agents." The dirty hippies were there, naturally, many with wigs paid for by the FBI, and the KGB agents were there, too, trying to figure out who the CIA and FBI agents were. But the honest movement now included priests, housewives, lawyers, educators, businesspeople, politicians, students, and even a few entertainers.

Coretta gave the project whatever respectability I couldn't. Another Mother for Peace held up the mailing of their newsletter long enough to tuck our announcement into every one of its hundred thousand copies. And the responses started coming in to our offices almost immediately. Yes, the mothers said, yes, and a thousand times, yes.

Responses to the East Coast offices were equally enthusiastic. Very soon Ira and I began to wonder if we would have a logistics problem. It looked as though there might be a hundred thousand people ringing the Congress.

The first blow came two weeks into the planning when Coretta King changed her mind. Coretta's secretary had called Cora. I was stunned and requested a four-way conference call with Cora, Amy, Coretta, and me, in New York, Washington, Atlanta, and Carmel Valley. Whatever had gone wrong we could surely make right. During the call I pushed for a reasonable explanation of Coretta's change of heart, but she would only say that she had changed her mind and thought the timing for the demonstration was not right. She would be a participant like the hundreds of other women and groups already on our list, but wanted to be off the leadership position of cosponsor with me. I reminded her that two weeks before she'd said the timing was not only perfect, but historic! She was unmoved. I wracked my brain to figure out who had gotten to her. And why. Surely the march could do her, or her image, no harm. She asked me for a list of names of sponsors so that she could write and inform them of her new position.

With the wind knocked out of my sails, I called Ira and discussed whether or not to continue. We decided to go ahead. And I made the very un-Gandhian decision to take my time sending the list of sponsors back to Coretta.

Ira and I flew east. We set up headquarters in the Georgetown Inn, a little one-star hotel down near the C. and O. Canal. It had no room service and only one phone we could use, but that little hotel would provide for us, both figuratively and literally, a shelter from the storm to come. One of Washington's worst floods was slowly gathering momentum in the muggy overhead clouds, and a campaign against our march was gathering momentum somewhere in the Capitol

Unaware of impending trouble, we had our first big meeting. It was thrilling at first. The room was filled with strong women, both white and black, spilling over with ideas and ready to go to work. Then, all of a sudden, out of nowhere, someone accused me of paying one of the black women for the work she'd done. The disruption had begun. I smelled power plays and tried to sort them out so that tempers might be assuaged and egos properly pampered. I couldn't find the source of the trouble. Some women demanded a special meeting. We must, they said, get permission from the "black community of Washington" to have our march. Fine, we said, let's have a meeting.

In the meantime, groups, clubs, church members, school kids and families were signing up by the scores. I was sure we could patch up the local infighting in no time at all.

Coretta's secretary called and asked me if I'd sent on the list . . .

The next day the skies opened up over Washington with a vengeance. Many parts of the city were flooded, including the basement and parking lot of the Georgetown Inn. We opened our hotel room to a group of soaking wet, angry, rude, and vindictive blacks who claimed to be "the representatives of the black community of Washington, D.C." Ira and his band of organizing women were all present. When everyone was seated, there was a momentary and very stiff pause during which we could hear the pounding and splashing of the rain, a sound which in other circumstances might have united a group of strangers by its ferocity. I started to say something by way of a greeting, but was quickly and in no uncertain terms interrupted by Mary Treadwell, a formidable tank of a woman, at the time married to Marion Barry, the other apparent leader of the group.

"AHHH . . . am speakin' first," she announced.

And speak she did.

She told us that we had no business in Washington. That the blacks in Washington were sick and tired of cleaning up the streets after white demonstrators and peaceniks had left town. She said that the issue of the day was not the war in Vietnam, but rather the black/white issue, which we should be addressing. We must, she announced, call off our irrelevant march and demonstration. The others all nodded in agreement.

I was confused, but not intimidated. In fact I was furious. Forgotten was the claim that I was paying off blacks. The accusations seemed to change with the winds of the storm outside, as though our adversaries were searching for the most vulnerable spot within us. We listened as one after another they issued their ultimatums. We must pack up and leave Washington, they said. It was not our city. I wondered who in the hell they were. One thing I did know. If this baloney kept up it would sap our energies completely. I didn't know the half of it.

I was sitting crosslegged on the floor and my purse fell out of my lap. One of the things that tumbled out was the picture of Kim, the ten-year-old girl covered with napalm, running naked down the streets of Saigon. A skinny black man sitting near me in a three-piece suit picked up the picture and grunted scornfully.

"Huh. I s'pose you impressed with this picture."

"Well, yes I am," I responded.

Well, let me tell you, girl, that this ain't nothin'. She got napalm all over her back an' so what? Dey drop that stuff ever'day in mah neighborhood. You folks prob'ly not aware of that li'l fact. This picture means *nuthin* to me, *nuthin!*"

At last it was my turn to speak. I tried, and so, one by one, did the other organizers of Ring Around Congress. We were ridiculed, shouted at, and denied. It became clear that our visitors intended to stay with us in our modest flooded-out hotel until we submitted to them and told them we'd get out of Washington.

When none of us budged, the "representatives of the black community of Washington" said they were planning a "summit" meeting on the same day as our march, to deal with the *real* issues, and if we were foolish enough to go ahead with our march they'd come out and throw bricks at us. Barbara Raskin got so frustrated that she stood up on a chair and screamed at the top of her lungs, "SUMMIT! WHAT THE FUCK IS A SUMMIT?!" We laughed, but our laughs were met with icy, arrogant, and disdainful looks.

By three o'clock in the morning they settled for a compromise: we could think about everything they'd said, and we'd call them in the morning. They got up to leave.

One man who'd said nothing all night whispered to me as he passed, "I'll be back in an hour." We wondered who the hell he was, and if we dared trust him. Ira and I turned out the lights. Two men who'd been standing across the street since we'd arrived went home. An hour later there was a knock at the door.

Perhaps if this man had not come back to see us in the wee hours of the morning, we would have been so discouraged and confused that we would have fallen for the whole Mau Mau act and gone home. But he said, very softly, "There's somethin' fishy goin' on. Ain't no Washington nigger gonna git up at nine o'clock in the mornin' on the twenty-second of June and go down to the Capitol buildin' an' throw bricks at you. Sumpin's behind all this. Never you mind that part. Your march is right. You are right. Keep on with it. Don't let 'em stop you," and he left.

We kept on with it. We didn't let them stop us. But they sure as hell slowed us down.

First, we lost every black we'd had on board. One lovely woman who had volunteered found all of her tires slashed. She showed up in the crowd on the day of the march, at what I must assume was serious risk to her personal safety.

Julius Hobson, a black Washington organizer, was in the hospital dying of cancer. We found him in his bed smoking a cigar. He said the smell of the smoke was so revolting that it made his nausea a little less awful in comparison. He was furious with the goings-on and claimed folks were being paid off by somebody up higher to stop our march. He said that if he was the only black in Washington to be there, he'd come and march with us on June 22. On the morning of the twenty-second the nurses found him trying to sneak down the hall on his crutches, and they put him back in bed.

Coretta's secretary called and asked me to *please* send that list . . .

Our "opposition" now contacted every major name in the antiwar movement to invite them to the "summit" on the black/white issue on June 22. For anyone already signed on with us it created enormous confusion. Most good white liberals, and *certainly* most good white radicals, deserted us. Or, out of deference to the blacks, felt the diplomatic thing to do was stay home on that day. One of our original organizers, who lived in Washington, was unable to take the pressure put upon her, and quit. We couldn't get any new recruits because we had just enough time to contact the old ones and reassure them that the march was still on. I began doing television news every chance I got and when I was offered a spot on one of the morning shows almost cried with relief. National television would be above and beyond the Washington scuffle, and would provide a platform for me simply to talk about the march and invite all the mothers and kids in the country to join us. My spirits picked up.

I called Angela Davis and invited her to be a sponsor. Her name would panic some American housewives, but she was, in fact, a woman, a black, and against the war in Vietnam. Her secretary said yes without my even having to speak to Angela. I explained what was going on in Washington, and that Angela might be pressured to back out. The secretary said Angela knew all about it and didn't care. I called Marion Barry.

"Marion?" I said, from a pay phone. "There's something you ought to know about. Angela Davis has signed on with us."

There was a long silence at Marion's end. Finally he said, "You just don't quit, do you?" and I said, "You wouldn't respect me if I did, would you?" I don't remember if he answered.

That evening Ira and Mom and I had dinner at the Raskins'. Seymour Hersh was there. He was funny, sarcastic, cynical, and fast. I was letting off steam by imitating Barbara when she'd stood up on a chair during the all-night meeting and screamed, when a phone call came for me. I straightened up and climbed off the couch to take my call.

"Yes?"

"'Dis Joan?"

"Yes."

"Listen here, Joan, I wanna TALK to YOU! Who the FUCK you think you are? I mean you don' have no right callin' ANGELA! ANGELA ain't your property! If she belong to anybody it's US, you dig, and you ain't got no business layin' han's on ANGELA!"

"Angela's not anybody's property," I said boldly. "She happens to support our march, that's all."

"YOUR MARCH, FUCK YOUR MARCH, GIRL, ANGELA DON' KNOW NUTHIN' 'BOUT YOUR MARCH, YOU LISTEN TO ME, GIRL." I held the phone away from my ear. Then I covered the receiver and, in a stage whisper, told the roomful of friends what was going on at the other end of the line.

"Why don't you hang up?" was Seymour's timely and sensible

suggestion. I put the phone to my ear and listened for one more moment and then hung up. I felt refreshed, but I also felt as though I'd been physically assaulted. And I felt afraid.

Coretta's secretary called about the list.

With only a few days left Cora began receiving telephone calls from a man named George Wiley, the head of Welfare Mothers' Rights and a friend of hers. He tried to reason with her to stop the march, and when she didn't acquiesce he implored her. She came to me, wavering for the first time, wondering if we were doing the wrong thing to continue, and I told her if she quit on me I'd lie down and die. She was torn every time he called. We turned the calls into a joke. I'd come into the office in the morning, having almost regained my spirit during the night, and Cora would greet me with "George Wiley just called," and I'd scream "NOOOOO!" and we'd all laugh, except it wasn't funny. The only woman who never flinched or hesitated was Edith Villastrigo. She was about five feet tall and tough as nails. It was she who suspected that we were being attacked from higher up than a group of hostile local blacks.

The sabotage continued until and through the twenty-second of June. The two black men remained on the corner across the street from our hotel. The "representatives of the black community" quit calling us and concentrated on calling everyone else in the country and inviting them to their "summit" meeting. I traveled around doing television and radio. The rain continued to pour down on Washington. I was packed and getting ready to fly to New York when the morning show phoned to cancel.

"We're real sorry, but we've had to put someone in your place. It was the timing . . ."

"But you can't! You told me—"

"Well, yes, I know, but these things happen. Anyway you should be glad, because it's Ralph Nader, and he's basically for the same things you are . . ." I don't remember the rest.

I went up to the roof of the hotel where Mom and I had put chairs so we could sit in the sun between cloudbursts and listen to the sound of the city's air conditioners. I was too stunned and dejected to do anything but stare at the gathering clouds. I didn't even cry. When I look back hard at my life, I can think of no time when my spirits sank so low, and when I felt so battered and powerless.

Ira, in his resilience, was my best medicine, reminding me cheerfully that at times like this one must continue to work against all adversity, if one feels that one is morally correct. He pooh-poohed the morning show, and told me of all the latest developments: A train of mothers and children would be coming from New York, and another from Baltimore. Candice Bergen was going to march with us. Mimi flew in to join us. LaDonna Harris, much respected wife of Senator Fred Harris, would chair the rally on the steps of the Capitol. Women were coming from as far away as Idaho, Iowa, Kentucky, Mississippi, and California. There would be simultaneous demonstrations in San Francisco, Palo Alto, Minneapolis, and Boise. I couldn't help but wonder what might have happened if Coretta had thrown her weight behind us, and if "the representatives of the black community of Washington" had had something better to do with their time for the month of June 1972.

On the twenty-first, Coretta's secretary called. Coretta was threatening to have a press conference if I didn't send her the list of sponsors. I apologized and said it would be in the mail within the hour. It didn't matter anymore. (Coretta and I have since mended the breach between us, but have never discussed what actually happened. I have developed a huge respect for her over the years.)

On the morning of the twenty-second, Hurricane Agnes had left nothing dry in her wake. We considered renaming the march "Surf Around Congress." We went to our posts, putting Edith and Ira on the phones to reassure callers that the march was still on. The rain stopped long enough for us to gather our grand total of twenty-five hundred women and children in a church, and march from there to the Capitol. The train bringing hundreds of marchers from New York's Penn Station got as far as Baltimore, then turned back because of the flood. The women organized the trainful of people, and upon their return to New York, they raised their banners high and had a "Ring Around Penn Station."

Barbara Raskin's ten-year-old son, who had given us the name Ring Around Congress, spoke at the rally, with LaDonna Harris and me holding him up to the microphones. Mimi and I sang, played with the kids, and taped messages for Vietnamese children. Others lobbied their congresspeople. Cora Weiss took the microphone when we actually encircled the Capitol building and shouted, "WE HAVE RUNG THE CONGRESS! THE WOMEN AND CHILDREN OF AMERICA HAVE RUNG THE CONGRESS!" as we nearly yanked our arms out of their sockets trying to form a chain. We were covered by all three networks, Time, Newsweek, and the Associated Press.

Later we laughed about that single string of folks making a ring around Congress, but under the circumstances, it wasn't a bad showing.

The following year a friend of mine called me and said he had just read in the proceedings of the Watergate hearings that Ring Around Congress was one of the demonstrations the Nixon administration had tried to stop. It must have been a pretty small honorable mention, because I have not been able to locate the quote. But Mimi still thinks they seeded the clouds.

# 4
# "WHERE ARE YOU NOW, MY SON?"

It rained when I was in Hanoi. It rained into the bomb craters and made brown swimming pools. The people were carrying their bicycles over the ruins, packing up with nowhere to go.

After the first few nights of bombing, most of the city was evacuated. During the seventh and eighth days of bombing, the city began to fill up again. The B-52's were hitting the countryside at the edges of the city, and I suppose people felt they'd rather die at home. I didn't want to die anywhere.

This is the story of my thirteen-day stay in Hanoi, eleven of them the days of the Christmas bombing, the result of the "most difficult decision" President Nixon had to make during his term in office. That Christmas bombing was, as it turned out, the heaviest bombing in the history of the world.

In December of 1972 I was on the road in the eastern United States when I received a telephone call from Cora Weiss. The group The Liaison Committee, which Cora headed, had been sending a steady flow of American visitors to North Vietnam to try to keep up some kind of friendly relations with the Vietnamese people even as our country continued to bomb the hell out of them, burn their villages, and napalm their children. Before Watergate, anyone who talked or wrote about the atrocities the U.S. military was performing in Vietnam was looked upon skeptically, or with great annoyance and anger, by a high percentage of the American population.

I would be the guest of a North Vietnamese group called the Committee for Solidarity with the American People. No serious fighting had taken place in the north for many months, and four Americans were being invited, among other things to deliver Christmas mail to the POW's in Hanoi. Gabriel would be with his dad at the time. I could return home by Christmas day.

I sat alone in a motel room in Erie, Pennsylvania, chewing on my cuticles and wondering if I could haul myself and my truckload of neuroses halfway around the world to see things I was afraid of seeing, eat food I was afraid of eating, take night flights which are anathema to me, and travel with three other people I'd never met. I was practically paralyzed with fear, and disgusted with myself. At the same time, the prospect of the trip became more and more irresistible. Little did I know while sitting in that crummy motel room with the snow falling outside, my three-year-old child off at a coffee shop in the arms of his loving grandma, that I would come within eight blocks of never returning home.

I made a couple of hundred calls from a New York hotel room, telling everyone I knew that I was going to visit Hanoi.

I would be traveling with a conservative lawyer, ex-Brigadier General Telford Taylor; a liberal Episcopalian minister, Michael Allen; and Maoist Vietnam Veteran Against the War Barry Romo. We met for the first time a couple of hours before departure, in the SAS lounge at Kennedy airport. Displaying the big sack of mail that we would be delivering to the POW's, we bluffed our way through a press conference. We were carrying cameras, tape machines, batteries, film, and a minimal amount of clothing. Tucked in our bags were personal messages to members of the Solidarity Committee from people who'd gone before us, and lists of what people wanted brought back, chess sets being the big priority.

We flew at night, Mike Allen and Telford downing a few and chatting noisily in the row behind me, and Barry dozing off across the aisle. As I think back, the preacher and the general, as we came to call them, were a little anxious, and Barry, who had been in Vietnam in battle and under fire, was (in my opinion) terrified of what he would feel coming back as a friend where he had once been, frankly, a paid killer. I was feeling pretty good, due to a smooth flight and plenty of Valium.

I vaguely remember a hotel in Denmark where we floated in and out of the restaurant, nodding at each other and looking jet-lagged. On another flight I remember leaning over toward Telford as we watched the sun making its hazy way up through the clouds. Telford said, "On the road to Mandalay, where the flying fishes play, . . ." and I finished, "And the dawn comes up like thunder over China, 'cross the bay," and felt like a terrible hypocrite because I was afraid Telford would think I knew something about poetry, or that I read books. I simply have a good memory, and my mother and father used to say that poem whenever we were driving to the beach.

In Bangkok Barry started to get sick with what I figured to be his internal conflict about returning to Vietnam, and I began pumping him full of tetracycline and trying to talk to him. I got cramps in the Bangkok airport and a uniformed woman from Thai Airlines managed to find me a Tampax, the last of that luxury I was to see during nature's long and eerily early visit to me that month.

Somehow we were in Vientiane, Laos. We had dinner with the terribly sweet *New York Times* correspondent, who was bitterly disgusted that nothing he sent in ever got printed without being massacred first. Jet lag hit with all its force at dinner, and I excused myself and went to bed. The next day we obtained visas from the Provisional Revolutionary Government to enter North Vietnam the week before Christmas.

We boarded our final aircraft along with a gathering of dour-looking Russians and some Japanese. The flight was short and hot and the Russians remained dour throughout.

I remember the landing on the short runway, piling out of the plane, and being met by a group of the loveliest people one could imagine. Our hosts were all men, and they gave us flowers and invited us to sit down while our things went through customs. Quat was the leader of the group, lively and intelligent and full of jokes. During the time we were there, Quat's wife would give birth to a baby during a bomb raid; one member of the committee would lose his wife and eight children; another would lose track of his wife's whereabouts and spend all of the time he wasn't with us trying to track her down, not knowing whether she was alive or dead; but they looked after us as though they were our personally assigned guardian angels and had nothing else in the world to do.

I rode with Telford to the Hoa Binh Hotel, past thousands of people along the route and miles-long traffic jams. I was looking at the children, of course, and what I had heard about them was true so far: they were delicate and reserved, yet full of laughter, and they thought we were hilarious. While our car sat pinned in traffic, the children began to gather. One of them gave me a flower, and all the rest laughed with amusement. Later I tried to give the same flower to a shy little girl who looked on from the edge of the group, but the

others would not allow it. They said (and it was translated to me)
that the flower had been given to me and I must keep it.

Telford was much more interested in the automobiles that were
passing us going in the other direction. "That one's Czechoslova-
kian, I believe, isn't it?" he'd say to the driver. I was amused by the
way we were seeing things. "Look at those beautiful kids," I said to
him, and he replied with a very genuine, "Where?"

I saw Barry get out of his car and walk off. Of course, I thought,
how stupid to sit here. I got out and was immediately surrounded
by ten or fifteen children who were grabbing at my hand and apparently trying to lead me somewhere. I laughed and let them tug me
along, and it wasn't until they took me off the regular dirt bicycle
path to an even smaller footpath that I began to understand what
was happening. We were approaching a combination lean-to,
chicken house, and outhouse. It had two "walls" of rusty corrugated
steel backed up against a frail fence. The facilities themselves were
even more sporty, a couple of broken bowls, properly being put to
use instead of thrown out. I had no choice. I made a little bow to the
children and left them standing about fifteen feet from the structure,
went steadfastly forth and squatted with as much dignity as I could
muster, hoisting my tweed skirt and causing much mirth among my
small audience. Unfortunately, due not only to the peanut gallery,
but also to the Russian convoy inching past about seventy-five yards
away, I wasn't able to produce anything, but I pretended to be very
relieved and pleased as I stood up and smoothed my skirt and
bowed a thanks to the children.

Traffic thinned out as we came into the city. The streets were lined
with trees, and the sidewalks were lined with people. The beauty of
the women was stunning. Dressed in white blouses and black pajama pants, they held a baby or a bundle resting on one hip, their
heads cocked in placid curiosity under a pointed straw hat. Wisps of
hair blew loosely around their faces, the bulk of it gathered into a
magnificent braid. The women aged quickly and mercilessly. The
faces of the old showed hundreds of lines and their teeth flashed
empty gaps and silver. The young men had skin which would be
coveted by Western women.

We had all seen the Vietnamese men in the marketplaces, saunter-
ing about the streets, and staring into the intrusive cameras. We'd
seen their eyes in a thousand daily papers. And we'd seen them—
these soft men of steel—with bullet holes in their flesh, lying dead
in their own rice paddies. On the streets of Saigon, they seemed
Westernized in the worst possible sense of the word. Here on the

streets of North Vietnam, their eyes were not suspicious, but amused. We were intruders, but must be friends or we would not have been allowed to visit, so most people smiled immediately upon making eye contact.

We arrived in Hoa Binh at mid-afternoon. Our hosts suggested that we wash up and rest, and then gather for dinner. My room, like all the others, was spacious old French architecture, with ten-foot-high ceilings, wooden floors, and a modest balcony looking out over a tiny street. Across the street were tiny houses of the poor with mud courtyards and tropical-looking trees hung with laundry.

My room was furnished with a single bed, with a mosquito net drawn back for daytime. Next to it was a small table with an ashtray, matches, a white candle, and a bottle of drinking water. Near the balcony two chairs were placed on either side of another table holding a Thermos of hot water, a small container of tea, and two cups.

The bathroom was a huge tiled affair, with a big lion-footed tub, stained at the bottom from the yellow and brown water that usually preceded the flow of clear water. Hanoi had been bombed before, and it was difficult to keep running water operating at all. The toilet was a pull-chain, and worked in its own good time. There was another bottle of water above the sink, a piece of soap, and a couple of worn but clean towels.

I lay down on the creaky bed and listened to the sounds of a busy city almost devoid of cars. Some Vietnamese music was coming from a loudspeaker across the alley, and I fell into a heavy sleep.

I was awakened an hour or so later for my official chat with a member of the committee. Each of us had separate talks at that point; mine was at my coffee table with Quat, who told me of the plan they hoped to follow for us: trips to local places of interest, visits to war memorials, and talks with North Vietnamese who would, I assumed, try to impress upon us the horrors of America's invasion of their country. On the third day they hoped to pile us into jeeps and head out into the country for Haiphong. The ride was supposed to be beautiful . . . Haiphong had once been beautiful.

I watched Quat's face as he spoke. It was a gentle and considerate face. It was patient. We talked a little about pacifism. He seemed to respect me for my beliefs, and like people I meet everywhere in the world, reasoned that it had no place in his own country. I asked him if he knew that the National Liberation Front had once used nonviolent tactics against the French with some success. He laughed politely and said that things were different now. I told him that I had not come there to proselytize, but to meet people and make friends. Later on in the bomb shelter it would be for Quat and a man named Chuyen that I would weep, because I couldn't bear the thought of them coming to any harm. Chuyen was one of the very few people I would see cry during my entire visit. And Quat and Chuyen were the ones who consistently halted the traditional toasting of a fallen B-52 if I happened to be in the room when the news came. I think Chuyen was a pacifist at heart.

At dinner there were fifteen to twenty people. I remember the yellow vodka which I refused to drink, and dish after dish of delicious food. The only dish I couldn't cope with was a whole bird with its head flopped over the side of the bowl, beak open. Aside from that, I had my neuroses under control and began to enjoy watching everyone loosen up. Quat drank like a fish, and Telford and Mike joined him. Barry hadn't been challenged yet, but his turn was to come.

The level of gaiety rose to new heights with the telling of jokes: first a Vietnamese joke which would need a dozen explanations to cover the culture gaps, and then an American one that got the same treatment. When the joke was finally understood, there was triumphant and uproarious laughter, not so much at the joke as at the feat of having figured it out. Quat dashed over to my place with two little glasses of vodka. I couldn't refuse his offer, nor could I guzzle it down with a "bottoms up." Eventually, Quat thought of a way to let me off the hook by saying that vodka was injurious to my throat, and no one must make me drink anymore. Barry was challenged and rose to the occasion like a trouper, drinking two, three, four, I'm not sure how many little glasses of that awful yellow stuff, his shyness diminishing and his cheeks reddening with each glass.

At the height of the noise and laughter Quat raised his arms in the air and said, "Now, music!" Two Vietnamese singers rose to their feet. Their voices were trained, crystal clear and powerful. The men sang like Irish tenors and the women like nightingales. I got my guitar and asked them what they would like to hear. They liked Pete Seeger songs and anything recognizable as an antiwar song. Quat liked traditional music, and in the end the song which was his favorite was "Hush Little Baby, Don't Say a Word, Daddy's Gonna Buy You a Mockingbird."

In the midst of our rumpus I suddenly noticed that Barry seemed extremely tense, as if the guilt he had been burying had slowly unearthed itself, and now, with the help of the vodka was suddenly unbearable. I dedicated a song to all the Vietnamese and Americans who had died in the war, and then to all the men who had refused to fight it from the beginning, and finally to those who had quit fighting when they had become disillusioned (or, illuminated). I said it was necessary that we forgive them what they could not forgive themselves. I sang "Sam Stone," the story of a Vietnam veteran. Barry put his head down and wept through the song. I supposed he was seeing private reruns of the horrors he'd lived through, that the rest of us had sat home and paid for. I sang my heart out to him. When the song was over, Quat offered him another vodka, and Barry blew his nose and laughed and cried at the same time. Then the Vietnamese did a strange thing. They took him to the head of the table and sat him down, as though to protect him from any harm, hovering about him chatting and joking casually for a few minutes until he dried up. And in this way, Barry Romo, ex-marine, was forgiven, no questions asked, for his part in what had taken place in these people's jungles.

We joked and sang for a little while longer, until it was time for bed. We would be up at seven for breakfast and then taken to see a war memorial. They asked us if we would like to eat American, French, or Vietnamese food during our stay; we all said Vietnamese. I went to bed exhausted under my mosquito net and floated off to the sound of the loudspeaker still playing the haunting melodies that had played all afternoon.

The next morning we saw the war memorial. It was boring. I hated the pictures of babies with bullet holes in their heads and women with their intestines falling out into the mud. I hated the horror stories. I'd heard and seen them for years. It was my business to know them. I also hated the maps and long descriptions of what was bombed and when. Chuyen could feel my restlessness, and he gave me a sympathetic glance. I shrugged and smiled.

Most of the details were directed at Telford, who was there as a lawyer to determine whether or not war crimes had been committed. Legally, I was of no use, especially because of my deep-seated opinion that war itself is a crime; that the killing of one child, the burning of one village, the dropping of one bomb sinks us into such depths of depravity that there's no use bickering over the particulars. But Telford was a terribly conscientious man and was carrying out his duties to the last detail with endless questions about logistics, dates and so forth. I tried to be patient, reasoning that Telford was probably the most important member of our group as far as credibility at home was concerned. I also liked him very much and was, in spite of my boredom with maps and details, fascinated at the way his mind worked.

We were given tea and tangerines and eventually let out of the little building. Later, in between propaganda sessions, there were lovely walks, and a visit to a restaurant on the lake where the waitresses sang to me in exchange for my song to them. Chuyen took me to a music school where the students and I exchanged songs for over an hour, and where we ended up having a political discussion about American involvement in Vietnam. By then I was taping everything.

Always there was Quat, smiling and laughing and animatedly telling stories and jokes, but listening attentively to any questions we might have and trying to explain things to us. It was during one of these talks that Quat innocently said the things which would haunt me in the shelter later on. We were sitting in the lobby of the hotel, where we gathered before and after meals to drink and talk, when I asked Quat what he would do if the insanity ever stopped and he had some free time.

"Oh!" he said. His face lit up and he looked past his glasses and past me to what he was imagining. "There are islands north of Haiphong which I have never been to. I would take a little boat, and go around to all of them, taking my time and stopping at each one. They are supposed to be so beautiful. All of Vietnam was beautiful once. But these islands are supposed to be special." It was as if he knew the islands, and they were his Shangri-la. It was also clear that there had been no time for Shangri-las in his lifetime. He finished talking, and with a smile, said, "Yes, that's what I would do." His smile was not sad; it wasn't a forced stiff-upper-lip smile. It was a truly optimistic and cheerful smile. So that's what this lovely man would do. Take a small boat to some islands. Not very much to ask, it seemed to me. Not very extravagant. I said I hoped he would someday have his dream. "I don't know," he said and laughed.

The second night in the hotel dining room we were shown patriotic films about the people of Vietnam. There was one about the Viet Cong in training, sliding down poles and swinging from ropes and shooting at targets, looking an average age of fourteen, though I know they were older. A pleasant-looking officer gave a demonstration in Vietnamese to his juniors about antiaircraft, and he used two little plywood planes to show how one shoots down the other most efficiently. Heroic music played between narrations. I excused myself and went to my room. When I came down later, one of the committee said, "Were you tired? You must have needed a nap."

"I wasn't tired," I said to him. "I just didn't like the film." He smiled.

And so the first two days went, more visits to places with reminders and explanations of the war. We ate three good meals a day, and drank jasmine tea. (I can no longer smell jasmine tea and not think of Hanoi.) I was looking forward to the trip to Haiphong, as our days were too organized. I was longing to walk the streets of Hanoi alone, without a group, and without a schedule. Until now what I had liked best was sitting alone on my balcony and listening to that strange music, or talking with Quat or Chuyen alone without the propaganda.

On the third night I cleaned up and went down to dinner. From that point on, my mind contains only strong flashbacks of what took place. I remember that we were again shown films, but these interested me because they were about children and what the different kinds of poison chemicals used by the United States military had done to unborn infants. I remember a sequence of a cat in a cage dying from a kind of gas, and a monkey dying from the same thing. I remember an American soldier shooting fire from a hose at a small hut and planes spraying miles of jungle with poisonous white clouds. There was a picture of a baby born abnormal because of chemicals. She was lying on her stomach and appeared to have no muscles. A nurse and doctor were standing next to her; they lifted her arm and when they let it go it dropped to her side like a piece of butterfish.

Nervous and afraid that I would feel faint if I watched any more, I was about to retreat, make myself small and apart from the things and people around me, set up the armor that would keep me from seeing, when right in the middle of that whole familiar series of regressive emotions the pattern was jolted.

The electricity in the building failed, leaving us sitting in the dark. Everyone stiffened, the Americans uneasy, the Vietnamese speaking rapidly to each other in quiet tones. Then, as though I'd been whirled back in time, like Dorothy in *The Wizard of Oz*, I heard a siren coming from a distance, starting at zero bass and rising evenly to a solid, steady high note where it stayed for a second or two and then slid back down through all the notes like a glider. All I could think of was the civil defense drills we'd had in grammar school. I sat still, aware that my heart had doubled in pace, and waited for instructions from the Vietnamese. By the time the siren began its second wail, one of our hosts had lit a candle and broken out of Vietnamese to say to us, calmly and with a smile, "Please excuse me. Alert."

How ironic. Please excuse *whom?* But I didn't think of the irony yet. I thought of standing up carefully and not banging into anything in the dark. I also thought that we were having a drill, a routine drill, being led at a careful but rapid pace out the door and down the hall. At the end of the hall there was a turn, a small room filled with bicycles. We were bumping into each other and making wisecracks about I don't remember what.

The flickering from the candle half helped and half hindered, blinding the eyes when it came too close, but giving us our only light. The tiles were uneven, and we walked by feel. The rest of the hotel guests were appearing from other halls and floors, forming a bottleneck at the rear door of the hotel. The candles were put out, and we poured and stumbled into a courtyard bright with moonlight.

There were Mike and Telford. Now I saw Indians, Latins, and others whom I later learned were Poles and French.

"What's going on?" I asked a Latin man. He was Cuban.

"They don't know anything. Maybe planes. I don't hear them. We'll just wait. Hasn't been any bombing for a long time."

*Bombing?* I heard the word, and I had surely suspected that's what the sirens were all about, but hearing this man say it as he looked so matter-of-factly at the sky was something different. I realized that we were standing just outside of a bomb shelter. The Indians began making jokes and everyone laughed. I thought I was the only one who was nervous. Telford had been in war zones before. Barry was not around. Mike may have been as nervous as I was, but he was chatting away and seemed fine. I relaxed a little.

A tall Indian held up his forefinger and said, "Shhh." In the distance I heard them . . . the planes. Everyone went on standing there in the moonlight, but now we were not talking. The sound faded into the distance and the voices came back, only much softer. People let out sighs. My heart was slamming again. I felt alone with my panic. There were a few more jokes, the voices almost back to normal.

And then it hit.

The planes were coming fast, and they were loud. The group jumped as a unit, heading for the door of the shelter down the narrow stairs. A big boom happened somewhere, and it shook the shelter walls and sent a wave of adrenaline through all of us. People hurried down the steps. The Cuban sat me down at the end of a long narrow bench which faced another long narrow bench. I had to go to the bathroom. There was another blast.

"That was close," was all the Cuban said. He and the other veterans were trying to assess the seriousness of the situation.

I didn't know what was happening. My ears were fluttering and popping as if I was on a plane gaining altitude quickly. The Cuban was telling me to lean away from the wall, to keep swallowing and pop my ears. I grabbed his arm with both hands. For a while all I could think of was my straining sphincter muscles. The bombs were coming down continuously. The Cuban was shouting in my ear. "It will be all right. They are not as close as they sound. Don't worry."

But I could see that I was not the only one who was worried. The big Indian sat forward with his head down. He was very dignified. People would look up at each other and shake their heads. When there was a lull they would look at the ceiling. When it started up each time it did so with such force that we were almost knocked out of our seats with the plain shock. Every muscle in my body was tight and ready to move. I must have cut off the blood to the Cuban's hand. With every fresh concussion I bent over his lap, feeling that I would be protected next to his chest. I was desperately afraid. I said to him, "I am scared."

"I know," he said. "That's okay. After a while you get used to it. You'll be a veteran after a few more raids."

A few more raids! I'd be dead by a few more raids! More concussion, more fluttering, more deafening roar. Down went my head. I didn't like losing control like that; I decided to try to keep my head up.

There was a lull. We heard the planes getting softer. I loosened my grip. Murmuring started up among the group.

"Maybe they are leaving."

"Yes, perhaps. But they could be circling."

"Had you heard any rumors of this?"

"Nothing."

"An early Christmas package from Nixon, perhaps." And we all laughed.

I looked around the shelter. We'd come down a concrete stairwell, wide enough for one person to pass at a time. There was a narrow eight-foot hall which turned left at the end. A few steps later there was a small door on the right leading to the cement room where most of us sat. The room was about twelve feet long and so narrow that when you sat on one of the two long benches that were placed lengthwise against the walls, your knees almost touched the knees of the person sitting opposite you. There was a bare bulb dimly lit in the middle of the ceiling. At the far end of the room was a door leading to an annex, the shelter for the Vietnamese who worked at the hotel. They had a separate entrance. It was only many raids later that Barry and I rebelled and took blankets in to sit with the Vietnamese.

There were about five Indians who were with the International Control Commission and had been in Hanoi for sixteen months. The Cubans were off of a ship that had been hit by our bombs in Haiphong harbor. There were three Pathet Lao (the Laotian Communist Liberation Movement), and the wife of one held a three-day-old baby in her arms. Most of the French didn't come down to the shelter. They were with Agence France Press, and they remained on the third floor of the hotel watching out the balcony window or wandering the streets trying to guess what was going on so that they could report it.

I introduced myself to the Cuban. His name was Monti. I told him that I was trying to stop shaking and thanked him for the loan of his arm. We Americans exchanged glances, shaking our heads in amazement. The Vietnamese in their annex sat patiently, the children now beginning to play. I was coming out of shock. I'd forgotten how badly I'd needed a bathroom.

CRACK-BOOM! This time the bomb exploded before any of us heard the planes. I took a deep breath and felt like vomiting. I took Monti's hand again, breathed deeply and waited. This time I made a conscious effort to keep my head up. I was only partially successful. Monti explained that we were hearing carpet bombing. It was like thunder, the kind of thunder that rolls and rolls when you see purple lightning like strobe-lit twigs hurled into the air at the edge of a desert horizon. The intermittent cracking of antiaircraft seemed to be coming from the hotel patio. I didn't understand that it was ground-to-air, and its volume added to my panic.

We rode out the minutes. Carpet bombing is relentless. I realized with shame and horror that to pray for the planes to go away was to pray that they would drop their bombs somewhere else. I was kneading Monti's hand and sweating all over, my body shaking again as badly as before. But I was beginning to get a grip on myself. As soon as the noise became less than deafening, I felt like making a joke.

"I wonder if Macy's is open till nine this evening."

"What is Macy's?" asked the big Indian.

"It's a department store in the States. There's some last-minute Christmas shopping I have to do." They began to laugh. The bombing was in the distance now.

"Oh yes, Christmas. Your country has an amusing way of celebrating." It was not said bitterly.

"I think it's stopped," Monti said, and again I let go of his hand. My body began to unclench, a long process of relaxing muscle knots like untying an old-fashioned buttonhole shoe. Then I was limp. The fear was gone and all that remained was a light anxiety.

The Vietnamese stirred from their squatting positions in the annex. The siren started its low rumble and soared to the all-clear note, staying there for about fifteen seconds. Everyone stood up, talking, joking, speculating, and we walked back up the stairs into the moonlight.

I followed Mike back through the hotel, past the room where we'd been watching the film before the lights went out. I peeked in. The Vietnamese were setting up to roll the movie again. They acted as though nothing had happened.

"Christ," I muttered to Mike. "No thanks, I'm going to bed."

I passed the lobby where all the people from the shelter were gathering to drink yellow vodka and beer, and trudged on up to my room. Barry's door was closed. He'd slept through the entire raid.

The music from the scratchy little speaker sounded like Russian marching music. I laughed. It wasn't completely Russian, but the influence was obvious. I leaned over the balcony feeling strangely calm. People were moving about as usual. The only difference was the sound of sirens in the distance and the fact that the sky was eerily bright.

I remember taking a bath and getting into a long woolen nightgown. What innocence! I didn't even lay my clothes out so they would be easy to find, but dumped them over a chair on the other side of the room. I lit the candle and climbed under the mosquito netting. I must have been asleep in three minutes.

A strident voice was squawking at me in a language I didn't understand. From somewhere inside the hotel, through the window, enveloping everything, encasing my head, came the siren. It was so matter-of-fact. There were footsteps in the hall. I was out from under the mosquito net reaching for the candle. There was a knock at the door, and Mike Allen came in.

"Want some help? Want me to take you down?"

"Yeah, okay. Thanks. Just let me get some clothes on."

Mike stood near the door holding his candle. "Okay," he said, "but hurry."

I was feeling around for my clothes, finding only a pea coat, leaning over the chair groping for my long johns, when the sky lit up and there was a RATTA-TAT-TAT which seemed to come from the balcony. I jumped back from the window, grabbed the pea coat, and Mike came hulking over to grab my arm.

"Screw the clothes! Let's get moving!" My heart was bouncing around the back of my throat and head. My candle was out. We bumped down the hall in the dark. The sky was bright: when we passed a window we could see. Something happened, and I was alone on the stairs. I think Mike went to find Barry and Telford. I saw the black and white tile floor of the lobby like a checkerboard with men dashing across it. Very suddenly I became disgusted and angry and sat down on the bottom step. I'm not going this time, I thought, it's stupid. A group of Cuban sailors passed. One of them said: "Come. You mustn't stay there. It's dangerous."

"It's all dangerous. It disgusts me."

"Please come. The bombs could start any minute. Come, I'll take you." I got up and walked with him.

My bravery dwindled to nothing at the sound of the planes. We began to run. The Cuban had me by the elbow. The planes were overhead, and we were scrambling like rabbits across the courtyard. The sky lit up just as we made it to the stairs. This time the shelter was full, the entrance and hallway jammed. Mike and Telford hurried in. The concussions started. The sound was deafening. I remember distinctly that my nightgown was fluttering. Again I was shaking uncontrollably. I wanted to bend over and curl up on the ground. Fortunately, there was no room, so I went on standing. My nightgown continued its mysterious fluttering. (I learned later that the fluttering was caused by drafts made by the concussions.) There was a lull. Mike Allen was right next to me; I was pretty sure he was praying.

The planes were back. Down went my head, this time onto Mike's chest. He put his arms around me, but there was not a thing to say. If anything, this was the worst the bombing had been so far. It seemed to last forever. Even some of the French had joined us. Finally, the racket stopped and there was only the sound of the planes droning away from the city. There weren't any jokes this time. The Vietnamese appeared at the shelter door just as the all-clear sounded. We left solemnly. The Vietnamese asked where Barry Romo was, and Mike said he had wanted to stay in bed. They smiled.

I said goodnight to Mike and the people in the hallways, went to my room and got dressed in long johns, a turtleneck, blue jeans, boots, and my pea coat. I made myself some tea, lit the candle, turned out the lights, and sat in a chair trying to think. But the music was like hypnosis. Just before I climbed into bed, I put my little cassette machine on the night table.

I couldn't have been asleep more than half an hour when I heard the voice on the loudspeaker again. I sat up and waited. The voice came again, that singsong, clipped, woman's voice delivering its elaborate message. I climbed out from under the mosquito net and put my cassette under my arm. The hall lights went out at the same time the siren started. I blew out the candle and felt my way toward the door. The sky lit up, and I heard a plane approaching tremendously fast. It didn't sound like the other planes. I began to run, trying to turn the tape recorder on as I ran. I was alone in the hall. Either the others weren't up yet or they'd all gone downstairs. I passed a window and there came a white flash accompanied by a RATTA-TAT-TAT and I hit the floor on one knee, the tape recorder dropping onto the tiles. What am I doing down here? I thought. I didn't know what was happening. I huddled low to get past the window and wondered if anyone had seen me. Then I stood up and realized with great lucidity that I did not want to die running. I could die scared, but not running. I tested the recorder and found it was working; it had picked up the siren, the running footsteps, the RATTA-TAT-TAT, and the clunk as it dropped to the floor. My unheroic flight had all been recorded. Good. I'd keep it to remind myself that it's embarrassing to run like a puppy. In the eleven days of bombing which followed, I ran only once, and it was at the instructions of and alongside members of the Swedish Embassy who had to cross two streets to get to their shelter.

There were ten raids that first night. Monti was right: by dawn I was a veteran. I had even started singing to everyone during the less intense raids. When we stumbled out into the air after the last raid of the night, the sun was up and there was a rooster strutting around the yard, crowing. Women were hanging out wash and children were puttering in the yard.

To my amazement, I was told that the trip to Haiphong was still on. We brought all our things downstairs and stood around the lobby. Quat's men handed us each a helmet. I immediately left mine behind a door because I knew I could never wear it.

And then, looking tired and distressed and apologetic, as though they were parents who had just ruined a weekend for the kids, the Vietnamese informed us that the roads to Haiphong were dangerous, both in their condition and in their location, and we would have to stay in Hanoi. I was relieved and disappointed at the same time. I was already addicted to the bomb shelter. Being under fire on the open road did not appeal to me, but a sense of adventure lingered on, pushing me to get out into the country, out of Hanoi.

We went to the outskirts of the city, Telford and I in the same car, passing through what had been a village the evening before. Now small huts were left standing between huge craters filled with muddy water and people were busy hunting for the remains of their things in the ruins. The Vietnamese always gave us the impression that few people were hurt. I know now that they did not want us to know the death toll.

Telford asked a series of questions of the guide while I stood silently at the edge of a bomb crater, looking down into it and then up at the people. They paid us no mind. We got back into the car. As we were bumping slowly back over the bricks and mud which had once been a country road, a girl passed by the car, carrying her bicycle. She looked in the window and said something to the driver. I had to pump a translation out of him. I heard her say, "Nixon."

"What did she say about Nixon?" I asked.

"She say, do they come to take a look at Nixon's peace?"

We returned to the hotel, having been spared seeing anything but a sampling of what fresh bomb craters look like. There was a raid during lunch. We all said "shit," and grabbed some food and headed for the shelter. The Air Force was setting a pattern for the days to come: raids all night, one at noon, one in mid-afternoon. We rested as much as possible in between. Those funny Viet-Russian marches played over the speaker all day long now. After the noon raid I slept.

The second night of bombing was similar to the first, only not quite as severe. I asked Barry if he would help me out. I have never found a way to thank him. He was a fanatic Maoist who disliked the pacifist rhetoric that armed-struggle advocates referred to as "sunshine talk" as much as I hated his endless jabber about the fascist racist imperialist pigs. Each time the siren rumbled to a start and all the lights in the city went out, Barry would come to the door and say, "Are you ready?" would take my hand and walk me to the shelter. I told him to make me keep my head up during the heavy bombing. When there was a loud concussion it would often be followed by a "tsk, tsk, tsk," which was Barry reminding me to get my chin up. One night we stayed in the shelter to continue a discussion we'd begun on violence versus nonviolence. We were frustrated that we could get nowhere with each other's dogmas. We'd both heard it all before, and each believed vehemently that the other was wrong. It ended in a state of near tears and at that point we made a pact never to talk about it again. I don't know if I was of much help to Barry, but he was the person in the group who was most able to help me with my terror. I spoke no more about Gandhi and he never again referred to bullets of love. And we laughed a lot. I was especially grateful to him for spending so many long hours in the shelter because I found out later that if he had any fears at all, they were of being caught and sealed into a shelter to die of suffocation.

For me, the mercury that measured fear and anxiety soared up and down totally out of my control. Eventually, even with the bombs crumping nearby I would find myself joking and singing, adding ridiculous verses to lighten things up. One night as we waited in the shelter, someone asked me to sing "Kumbaya." As the verse progressed, we heard the planes in the distance, heading toward the city. I'd been squatting and singing near the tape recorder. The planes droned onward, getting louder. The next verse was "Save the children, Lord." In the middle of the second line the bombs began raining so close to our bunker that the tape recorder fell over with the concussion. I rose to my feet, grabbed on to Barry who was standing, and went on singing. When the bombing finally stopped, someone said that was the last time they'd ask *me* to sing when the night was quiet.

On the third day the Bach Mai Hospital was bombed. I saw a dead woman laid out by the roadside. There were corpses around her carefully covered with mats. She had not yet been covered up. She was old. I wanted to go and lie next to her and put my arms around her and kiss her. I would have done it if there had been no people around but I was afraid that I would offend someone or that the press would take a picture and I would be accused of being theatrical. We walked around what had been the largest hospital in North Vietnam. The head of the hospital was speaking rapidly, pointing to the wreckage of three-sided rooms on second stories where beds hung partially over the floor's edge, bits of sheet dangling in the breeze.

"This was X-ray," he said, waving toward the remnants of a wall, as we labored over slippery debris. Telford had his notepad out and was asking those awful questions again.

A woman hurried by carrying a bandaged boy on her back, her face set but the tears undried on her cheeks. Telford was asking the dates of when certain craters had been made. Was this one fresh or was it from the June bombing? The Vietnamese spoke quickly, explaining everything. Quat was there. He asked me to sit down and not go any further while the others went ahead. Barry stayed with me. From around the corner came the smell of burnt flesh. Near the

entrance of the grounds we could see a crane and some small equipment struggling to lift concrete and bricks from the mouth of the
shelter in which a number of people were still alive. The last I heard,
the attempt was not successful, and eighteen people died there.

It was at the hospital that I saw Chuyen cry. He simply walked
away from our group where he had been translating. Someone
called him, and when he kept his back turned another member of
the committee took up where Chuyen had left off. When he joined
us again, his eyes were red and full. I put my arm around him for a
moment. He just shook his head. It wasn't until the night after we'd
seen the Bach Mai disaster that I finally began to feel what I had
absorbed.

I had gone down to the shelter. Barry spread my blanket in the
Vietnamese quarters. I was catching a cold and my body was uncomfortable and restless. Sleep seemed impossible. One of the Indians
had brought his blanket down and was lying in the guest section of
the shelter. Barry fell asleep. The little bunker was so damp and
cold, so unhealthy. Our guardians were upstairs now, taking turns
resting three on a bed near the rear entrance to the hotel. They were
the most patient people I'd ever known . . . and the bravest. Chuyen's tearful face passed before my eyes. And then Quat's face,
animated and cheerful . . . : "There are islands north of Haiphong
. . . I would take a little boat and go around to all of them . . ." Very
suddenly I was sobbing. Barry was awake, sitting up and encouraging me to cry.

"Get it out. You've been holding it in there too long. Go ahead
and cry."

My racket woke the Indian and he began telling me *not* to cry, that
I was upsetting myself. "No! You must not. Here. Here's a tangerine. Eat something. You will feel better."

"I don't want any fucking tangerine," I mumbled, and Barry
began to laugh. He was encouraging me to cry, and the Indian
wouldn't hear of it: a cultural difference, I assumed, and took the
tangerine.

"Here, I'll peel it for you," the Indian said, grabbing it back. It
occurs to me that he just wanted desperately to help out.

"Thank you." I sighed.

Well, I had scratched the surface. I wondered what was really
going on inside of me. I wondered about the children who spent
their lives ducking bombs. The ones I'd met seemed very stable.
Perhaps it was better to have something real to deal with than to
conjure up, as I had, symptoms and phobias all of your childhood.

Here was the difference I'd thought so often about, between victims of ourselves and victims of circumstance. Me and my years of therapy. Me and my friends who went in and out of psychiatric hospitals, trying to decide whether to live or die. And here, where the children had always known war, perhaps here life was a little more precious, just the opposite of the nasty cliché I'd heard all my life about Asians—"life is cheap over there." Perhaps there was no time for phobias here on the battlefield.

And so it went. Eleven days and nights of bombing, and then going out to see it in the mornings. I came to know the French press people, Jean Thoroval and his wife, who lived on the top floor of the Hoa Binh Hotel. They seemed fearless. Mike Allen suggested I spend some time out of the shelter so I began going up to the Thorovals'. The French were fun and distracting. They gave me great courage. I took my guitar up and we sat around, Mike, Jean and Marie Thoroval, Telford, two other members of the French press, and Barry, and I sang. Thoroval's favorite song was "Até Amanhã," a Brazilian carnival song. His face would light up and he would do a little dance. When the voice came over the microphone, Jean would go to his desk and mark down the number of the raid. When the bombing started, I would put down the guitar and pick up a cigarette. I don't smoke.

One night we were up in the Thorovals' room chatting, drinking beer and waiting. I was nervous. There had already been several raids that night which I had sweated out in the shelter. When the next raid began, Mike called me over to the window.

I went unhappily to the balcony and looked out over a city already burning from the preceding raids. The planes were on their way. Mike stood there, boldly cheering me on. We could hear the droning of the B-52's getting steadily louder, bringing the war closer. I wilted and took his arm. "I don't want to see," I said, and went over to Marie, who was perched on an armchair, smoking casually. I could see her by the light from outside that was bouncing around the room. I took her hand.

"*J'ai peur*," I said.

"*Moi aussi*," she said. She patted my hand. "There is nothing to do but wait."

A fresh wave of carpet bombing rolled persistently. Marie uttered a "*mon Dieu*." Then came a crash which set the windows flapping and objects dropping from desks. I was on my feet.

"*Ah. Bon. Descendons à l'abri.*" It was Jean, the stoic, saying, "Let's go to the shelter," as he walked at an even pace to his bedroom and came out with a carton of Gauloises. We went slowly down the three flights of stairs. Marie was telling him to hurry, but he would not. He had never been to the shelter. It was again filled to capacity, and we crowded in under a display of fireworks.

The Indians were in the hallway looking somber. They did not make light jokes or ask me to sing. Jean kept rushing out into the courtyard to see if any planes were being shot down, and Marie kept calling desperately for him to get back inside. I was breathing deeply again. I remembered an expression I'd heard from old Doner, ten years before. I turned to Mike.

"You speak French, don't you?" I yelled in his ear.

*"Oui, un peu."*

"You'll like this one. *Je n'ai pas peur—Je tremble avec courage!"* ("I am not afraid—I tremble with courage!") He loved it. It began doing the rounds of the shelter, translated into various languages. Meanwhile, Barry was out running around the streets counting B-52's as they exploded in the sky.

There was much publicity over the first six pilots shot down. What a tiny victory, I thought, as we began to see their faces on posters all over town. We were invited and taken to the press conference to see them. Heavy security surrounded the building where the pilots were to be shown to the international press. There were city officials, military personnel, and tons of cameras and tape machines. I did not want to sit in the front row where places had been saved for us; all four of us sat a couple of rows back. Barry was on one side of me, and was not in good shape. Perhaps he was afraid he would see himself when the pilots came out. Barry called people in the U.S. military "pigs." Perhaps he was wondering if he had made a total transition himself. Telford was taking notes, and Mike and I were getting our tape recorders ready for whatever was about to happen.

What did happen was unspectacular. The prisoners were driven into a courtyard adjoining the press room. One at a time, they were led around in a circle in the patio while people took pictures of them. They were bandaged and in shock. I was astounded that they hadn't been torn to shreds by the Vietnamese. They looked young, and I felt sorry for them. One by one, they stepped up to the microphone and gave their name, rank, and serial number. If they had a message to give the press, they could. One of them said he hoped "this terrible war would come to an end real soon." Another sent his love to his wife, Sally, and wished his family a Merry Christmas. My God, they were oblivious. These guys were guilty of genocide, and I don't think it had ever occurred to them. In spite of the fact that I hated the press conference, I thought it was carried out with great restraint by the North Vietnamese. And I, too, hoped the war would end soon and Sally and the family would be joined by their daddy, and he would get a nice civilian job—like a fireman or forester, and burn his uniform and send all his medals back to the White House.

Our visit to the POW camp was even more bizarre than the press conference. It began with the same red tape I'd been through at prisons everywhere, except that I was never before given tea in the warden's office. The sun was going down, which meant that the evening raids could start at any minute. I had my guitar, Mike had his Bible, Telford had his notepad, and Barry had a stomachache. It didn't really matter what we had with us or what we planned to say or do. In this prison, as in all others I've ever seen, the main issue was boredom and loneliness for home and one's friends and family. We were closely supervised as the pilots showed us around their barracks. Flying shrapnel had severely damaged their bunkhouse the night before, and they were irate about not having any shelters provided for them. So was Telford. They were scared. They didn't understand what was happening. One of them held up a large piece of shrapnel.

"This thing came right through the ceiling. We was hiding under the beds. We've kinda made our own shelters, but they don't amount to much. I don't understand."

"What don't you understand?" I asked.

"This," he said, holding up the deadly looking piece of steel again. "I mean, I don't understand what's happening." He was absolutely serious.

"Well," I ventured. "There are these planes flying over here every night carrying bombs."

"I know that. But I don't understand what's happening," he repeated for the third time.

"Well, it's really very simple," I explained. "These people drop the bombs out of the planes and the bombs fall to the earth where they explode and cause tremendous damage to people and things. Apparently one or several of these bombs landed close enough to your compound to send that piece of metal flying through your roof."

"But what I mean is," he persisted, "Kissinger said peace was at hand, isn't that what he said?" The sarcasm drained out of me like milk pouring from the tipped cup of a child. I wanted to cry.

"That's what he said," I told the expectant pilot. "Maybe he didn't mean it. They lie a lot."

Mike kneeled and said a prayer. They kneeled with him. I sang the Lord's Prayer, thinking I should keep things Christmas-like. Then I asked them what they'd like to hear. The consensus was unanimous: "The Night They Drove Old Dixie Down."

I laughed out loud and sang it. Then we all sang "Kumbaya." Fighter pilots, lost in a strange land, standing with an American brigadier general, a preacher, a Maoist, and a pacifist, all under supervision of the "enemy," joining hands and singing with tears in their eyes, "No more bombing, Lord, Kumbaya . . ." I embraced them one by one and we left. The last thing I heard one of them say was "Get us out of here . . . if you can."

On the ride home, Telford announced to me that the POWs' having no shelters was the most disgusting thing he'd seen since he'd been in Vietnam. The prison officials had assured us a number of times that shelters were being built; in fact, the prisoners were digging them themselves.

At dinner Barry and Telford exploded at each other and Barry finally moved to another table. I felt he needed support and took my plate over to where he was sitting. It was not the first rent within our group, nor the last. Mike refereed, and Barry and Telford seemed to make a silent agreement similar to the one shared by Barry and myself. Mike held things together through his good nature and a bit of preaching and storytelling. Barry hated the church, but he, too, seemed relieved at Mike's boisterous good spirits.

Toward the end of the week, we learned that the airport had been bombed, causing considerable damage to the runway as well as the airport building. There would be a slight delay in our departure.

As Christmas drew nearer there was no letup in the bombing. Occasionally, a Chinese plane would land and take off. We did not have visas to go through China, and it became clear we were going to celebrate my favorite holiday in the Hoa Binh Hotel.

The Vietnamese put a two-foot-high replica of a tree in the middle of the hotel lobby on a table, and hung bits of decoration on it. It sat fifteen feet from the bar as our only visual reminder that the Prince of Peace had come into the world to redeem all of our sins, in the hopes that the people of the world would be a little kinder to each other. Mike and I planned a small service to take place in the lobby for the hotel guests and for our hosts, who I thought would at least be amused. There had been a lull in the raids, and I was hoping that a twenty-four-hour cease-fire had begun.

All the stories about Christmas have been written. They are of abounding love, sacrifice, rebirth, and forgiveness. They are about children in their time, their joy, their magic. Every year they are told again and again, and they are fresh and warming to the souls of the weary and the old. They become true even if they are only wondrous fantasies. Because it is the one time in the year that those of us who celebrate it have an unwritten alibi to be nicer to each other. An extra inch or two of love. Christmas to me is exquisite.

I don't know what Christmas was to the United States President and Secretary of State in 1972, but some of the true spirit escaped them. Surely there is a time zone chart somewhere in Washington, D.C. They must have known that it was Christmas Eve in Hanoi even if it wasn't yet Christmas Eve in the "real world."

Mike led a prayer in English and gave a short improvisational sermon to suit our situation. There were no more than twenty-five people in the lobby. I was ready with my guitar to share in whatever the Christmas spirit dictated on that, the strangest of all Christmas Eves of my life. I sang "The Cherry Tree Carol," and after Mike did a reading in French, I sang a calypso version of the Lord's Prayer.

My head was stuffed up with a cold, but the voice was coming out fine. *Our Father who art in heaven, hallowed be Thy name.* What a strange and pitiful Christmas. *Give us this day our daily bread. Hallowed be Thy name.* Perhaps Quat would eventually get to his islands. That will be my prayer for him. *Forgive us all our trespasses. Hallowed be Thy name.* God, bless and keep Gabriel. Give him a good Christmas. And keep his daddy well. *As we forgive those who trespass against us. Hallowed be Thy name.* I wonder if my family got the last telegram we sent out. It told them we were all right, and wished them a Merry Christmas. Best not to think of home. *And lead us not to the devil to be tempted. Hallowed be*—a bomb exploded somewhere in the city. I went on singing—*Thy name. But deliver us from all that is evil.* The lights went out. I stopped my song. The French were telling me to keep going, and the Vietnamese were asking us to go to the shelter. The siren commenced. Mike was swearing. People lit candles and I tried to go on singing. My voice came out so weak that I thought it was someone else's. I realized later that I was trying to keep quiet so that the bombs wouldn't know where we were. I strummed on the guitar, waiting for the hotel to be blown to bits or my voice to return. Either would have been a relief. I cut a verse, and amidst the shuffling of feet, encouragement from the French, and the closing notes of the siren, finished the Lord's Prayer. *Amen, Amen, Amen, Amen, Hallowed be Thy name.*

"Those bastards," I said to Mike as we hurried to the shelter. "If there's one thing I can't stand it's being interrupted in the middle of a performance." Mike had been swearing steadily under his breath ever since the bombing started.

Later that evening we went to a midnight mass. I was in a near panic. The church was full, the streets outside lined with soldiers and police, obviously an emergency unit to lead people to shelters in the event of a raid. The service was awful. The priest gave the sermon in Vietnamese, French, and German. Each time he ran through his lines he appeared more pompous and cold than the time before. This was one time I was some help to Barry: I think if I hadn't kept him joking with rude remarks under my breath he might have run up to the rostrum and throttled the priest. When the collection plate came around he was delighted to see Quat ignore it. Mike was so excited to be inside a house of God that he managed to work himself into a state of religious fervor; I think he even took communion. Telford looked serious and reminded me of my father in Quaker meeting. There were roving news cameras with bright lights which also kept me from being a public outrage. The choir sang familiar Christmas carols in French, and I taped them on my cassette recorder. When the service was over, I didn't feel one bit holier than I had when it began but only wanted to go home and go to bed and not hear any sirens, planes, or explosions for a full day.

I got my wish and slept for sixteen hours straight. I think we all did. Even our hosts took a break. A twenty-four-hour truce is an amazing feeling.

There is something I feel I must say here. During this "truce" a great psychological, and probably physical, change took place in me. The exhaustion, the sleep, the calm were, by the end of the twenty-four hours almost boring. It was like the letdown that follows a long-prepared-for performance in a play or an exciting tour of concerts. Odd as it seemed, and frightened as I had been for so many days, something in me actually missed living on the edge of the knife. I would be ashamed of saying this, but I have heard others express the same feelings about their experiences in the Second World War. At least I knew I was alive during those raids, because I was treasuring my life as I had never done before. Why be ashamed to admit that I missed the excitement? Because to wish it back was insanity, was wishing back death for hundreds more people and possibly myself. And, sure enough, as soon as the raids began again, I wanted to be out of Hanoi, and my thoughts returned more and more to my home and to Gabe. And once again, I became afraid.

One morning after a particularly bad night we were taken to a business district called Kan Thiem that had been devastated by carpet bombing. It shook us all more severely than anything else had so far. Even our hosts seemed shocked. Maybe it was because the raid had occurred near dawn and there hadn't been time to clean things up. People were dashing about or just standing and facing the ruined area, talking rapidly and shaking their heads. Within a few yards of the road we were walking on mud, brick, and debris, staring into the small rooms which lined what had so recently been a street. There was a woman quietly picking up a few scraps of her life. There was a man weeping to himself, and a surviving family moving about their small area like zombies. Everywhere were headbands of white cloth, the symbol of mourning for a relative.

After the long row of what had been buildings the night before, we struggled over an area of even more jagged and slippery terrain leading out into the open. Hundreds of people struggled past us carrying their bicycles. Some looked at the ruins, others simply kept walking. I glanced up and saw, amidst the flow of people stumbling toward me, an old, old man. He had a long white beard and a kind face and was bent forward with his hands low to the ground so that when he slipped he could catch himself before he fell. Just as his footing became unstable again, I reached out automatically to take his hand. He allowed me to help him and then looked up. He peered deep into my eyes, straining for a second, and then smiled cheerfully and nodded his head. He said, *"Dankeschön! Dankeschön!"* and clasped my hand in both of his. I bowed to him as he bowed to me, and off he went.

I saw a woman sitting on a small heap of rubble, pounding her fists on her thighs and crying with a despair that was ferocious. She would go from a wail to a moan to almost a growl, then sob wretchedly from her island of misery. Her husband was tugging her gently by the hand, looking somewhat embarrassed, scolding her softly to get up and come with him. She would attempt to rise to her feet and then she would give in to the anguish which had taken away all her strength and pride and sensibilities. Cry, I wanted to say. Cry, for God's sake. Keep crying until there is nothing left in the well, until the next turn of the hourglass. All my common sense told me to stay away from her, but I could not. I squatted next to her, putting my arm around her. Some people looked on, as they looked on at the many other scenes taking place all around. For one desperate moment she wailed and put all her weight against me. Then she looked up and saw that I was not only a stranger but a

foreigner as well, and she became visibly uneasy, though her sobbing didn't change. I got up immediately, found my way back to
Barry and took his hand.

We came to what looked like a large expensive movie set of a piece
of the moon. Men were standing atop craters banked with mud and
trash, shouting out the number of the dead. Today they wanted us
to know. The number was mounting into the hundreds. The white
headbands were a part of the moon people's costume. Some of the
younger children were laughing excitedly and scrambling from crater to crater like extras. Many people walked in slow motion. Barry
guided me around the edges of a crater. We were walking on top of
what had been people's homes. Here was a shoe, here a half-buried
little sweater, a piece of broken dish jammed into the earth, a book
lying open, its damp pages stuck together. The press were there
with their cameras. Barry and I were walking just behind Jean Thoroval and his interpreter. On the other side of a thirty-foot abyss I
saw a woman bending low to the ground singing a strange little
song as she hobbled back and forth over an area of ten or twelve feet
of ground. At first I thought she was singing a song of joy that she
was all right and her family had been spared. But as we got closer
her song grew strange to my ears. She was alone. Thoroval asked
his interpreter what she was singing. The interpreter listened closely
for a few seconds and said to him, "Elle dit, *'Mon fils, mon fils, ou êtes
vous maintenant, mon fils?'*—My son, my son. Where are you now,
my son?"

Oh, heaven and earth. Such depths of sadness cannot exist. I
crumpled to the ground and covered my face and sobbed. That
woman's boy lay somewhere under her feet packed into an instantaneous grave of mud, and she, like a wounded old cat, could only
tread back and forth over the place she'd last seen him, moaning her
futile song. *Where are you now, my son?*

Barry raised me to my feet and said, "Let's go now." I couldn't
walk very well, and he supported me. I was sick of mud, sick of
craters, sick of death. Not for me, but for these people who had been
living here for so many years. We passed a younger member of the
French group. He was furious. "*Ah, bon.* Now what do you say, eh?
You still think like a pacifist? After all this you would still say to put
down your arms?" I waved my hand to indicate the moon set. "This
is supposed to change my mind?" I said in a quiet fury. "You are a
fool." But he was beckoning to Barry. I was not supposed to notice,
but what he pointed out was a child's hand lying a few feet from us
in a pile of debris. It was like a doll's hand which pops out at the

wrist, and the rest of the doll was nowhere to be found. Barry took me back to the car.

After our visit to Kan Thiem an air of desperation spread over all of us. Thoroval became ill. His wife said he could not eat. He called it indigestion, but it was more like a case of revulsion. He'd been in Hanoi for two years. The Vietnamese children looked drained and colorless. I had begun to dress like the Vietnamese, wearing black pajama bottoms and sandals with my shirts and pea coat. I was afraid to think of home. Telford read books patiently during the raids by the light of a candle. The Frenchmen looked tired. The Pathet Lao couple with their tiny child couldn't make it up and down the stairs anymore. The mother was too sore. I bought five chess sets and jewelry from a woman who had lost her brother the night before. She let me hold her a minute. Our Vietnamese hosts went out and bought a jumper for Gabriel, as though to reassure me that I would see my child soon. We'd already made two unsuccessful trips to the airport, being turned back at a checkpoint. No planes. And the ghastly unspoken fantasy slowly formulating in the minds of all of us finally began to be voiced.

I think it was first spoken, in broken English, up in the Thorovals' quarters over beer and cigarettes. It made perfect sense. By now it was clear that the American administration's strategy was to bomb the North Vietnamese back to the bargaining table. The strategy was not working. There was the insult of the new Russian missiles which were shooting B-52's out of the sky like fat crows. By now Nixon was so insulated from the American people that there was no way for him to sense that he was losing their confidence, and that he had completely overstepped the boundaries of everyone's sensibility, except the extreme right wing and idiots. On Christmas day a tree had been delivered to the White House, its branches broken and all the ornaments smashed. The message was clear.

Why was the administration sticking to a strategy of losing B-52's and Phantoms by the score when Hanoi could be wiped off the map forever with one nuclear bomb? Certainly China or Russia would not retaliate over such a small item as Vietnam. No, dear Barry, China would not have done a thing. We were, as the expression goes, sitting ducks.

At this point, Quat began a campaign to restore our good spirits and hope. He planned a series of farewell dinners as though we were actually going to leave Hanoi alive. I distinctly remember two of these parties at which we again drank, laughed, made music, and said goodbye to many people we'd met during our stay. At one of the parties a woman sang to us in Vietnamese, and then told us in a tearful voice that her son was at the front, and that she would sing her favorite song in English for us and for her son. She clasped her hands together and stood rocking back and forth next to me, choking back the tears and singing an old Stephen Foster song, verse by verse. She knew the words phonetically and it was only because we all knew the song from high school music class that it was at all comprehensible, but it was unbearably beautiful and moving. Mike began a seizure of throat clearing, and even Telford's eyes could not stay dry. I tried to sing with her, but could not hold the notes. She soared to the high notes and broke on the lower ones, and with each break tears rushed from her eyes. She ended on a wavering note, and then reached her arms out to me saying, "Sank you, sank you," to which I could respond nothing. I sang too, all of their favorites, and Quat passed around the vodka.

At the other farewell dinner there were raids, and we went singing into the shelter. Beneath the bombs, two women sang steadfastly and clear-eyed, in two voices which sounded like one, in perfect harmony, accompanied by an accordion drowning out the sound of the planes. I think during the few minutes that they sang I would have been able to face death with some dignity. That night after the party was over, I stood out on the Thorovals' balcony, at Barry's prompting, and breathed in the night air while waiting for the planes to return. He had persuaded me that I would feel better if I faced up to the fear and watched the sky.

"If you really want to have courage," Barry said softly, "you will sing."

I began to sing "Oh, Freedom," quietly at first and then more and more boldly. "And before I'll be a slave, I'll be buried in my grave . . ." The notes were coming out loud and sure. I sang a few verses, and when it was over there was the sound of clapping from the little street shelters below us. I smiled at Barry.

"You see?" he said. "You made them feel good."

I sang some more. I sang through the entire blackout, feeling many things as I went along. How I would miss my son if I died; but then no, I would be dead: he would miss me. I still didn't want to die. I was not brave like the people walking below. I was hanging on desperately to my life. But I was singing.

"Ain't gonna let nobody turn me around, turn me around, turn me around, walkin' up to freedomland . . ."

No bombs came down during that raid. Perhaps it would have

been very different if they had, but as it was I came in from the balcony feeling triumphant.

It was decided that we would try to leave Hanoi through China since the Chinese planes were still the only ones attempting the Hanoi airstrip. This would mean a trip to the Chinese Embassy to obtain transit visas.

Telford, Mike, Barry, and I arrived fifteen minutes early in the afternoon. We were ushered into a dark and gloomy old French building, down a hallway hung with pictures of Ho Chi Minh and Mao, and were seated in the receiving room which was also hung with pictures of Ho Chi Minh and Mao. There were two interpreters; one to get us from Chinese to Vietnamese, and the other to get us from Vietnamese to English. Barry was sitting across from me trying to hide his delight at being in the embassy of his beloved Mao. We were served Chinese beer, offered cigarettes, and at long last the ambassador arrived. We stood up to greet him, and all he said was, "Hmmmmm." He was wearing little round glasses and a Mao jacket. He seated himself and said, "Hmmmmm," again. He spoke to the interpreter, who in turn spoke to the other interpreter, who then spoke to us.

"The ambassador says he hasn't been sleeping too well lately."

We shifted around in our chairs trying to think of appropriate responses to his statement, but he spoke again.

"He says perhaps it is because of the bombing that goes on all night."

"No doubt, no doubt," said Telford.

"Tell him we haven't been sleeping so well either, and apologize about the bombing," I ventured. It was interpreted and the ambassador said, "Hmmmmm."

"The ambassador wants to know why you have come here to see him today." He knows damn well why we're here, I thought.

"Well." It was Telford's turn now as spokesman of the group. "The ambassador is surely aware of the fact that it is very difficult to find a way out of Hanoi, and we understand that the Chinese planes are the only ones which seem to be functioning with any regularity at all." More interpreting.

"The ambassador wants to know, is this the *only* reason you came to visit the Chinese Embassy?"

"Oh!" said Telford hurriedly. "No, of course not. But we did think it would be a wonderful experience for us to see even a *small* portion of your great country on our journey home."

Telford, you hypocrite, I was thinking. And who do you think you're fooling? At this point Mike Allen commented on the beer. Marvelous beer, the Chinese beer. Made in Peking? Marvelous! Barry was squirming in his chair and probably plotting how he could get a Peking beer bottle for a souvenir. The ambassador was looking almost comically inscrutable and was no doubt enjoying nailing us all into a corner.

"I don't wish to be rude," I blurted, "but please tell the ambassador that speaking for myself, I'm scared stiff and would like to get the hell out of this city as soon as possible, and that's why I came to see him today." The ambassador smiled faintly with his next "Hmmmmm." Mike and Barry laughed, and I don't remember if Telford responded.

After more small talk, the ambassador had our passports collected for what he had probably intended to do all along, which was to give us visas for the next day. We tried to muffle our excitement and relief. I wanted to rush up and hug him, but that seemed definitely out of order. We all stood up and made gratuitous gestures and speeches and shook hands and bowed. Barry had been silent the whole while. His moment had now arrived. Just as we were filing toward the exit, he plunged his hand into his pocket and gathered a fistful of Vietnam Veterans Against the War buttons. Walking stiffly up to the ambassador he placed the buttons on the tea table, saying, "I am with you in your fight to stamp out the fascist imperialist aggressor." The ambassador looked baffled, peering at the pile of tiny buttons with their incomprehensible logo, which had been delivered with the equally incomprehensible short speech. "Oh, for Christ's sake, Barry," I mumbled to him. "He doesn't know what the hell you're doing."

"He'll understand," said Barry.

Back in my room at the hotel I packed for the third time. It was beginning to look as though we would actually leave Hanoi, and I wanted to listen to the music from my balcony window and think about the people and enjoy feeling hopeful about returning home. There would be raids all night, but there was a general air of optimism about the arrival of the Chinese plane.

In the morning we ate breakfast and met for the final time in the lobby, dragging our bags, tape recorders, cameras, gifts. Once again, I tried to leave my helmet behind, but when I got in the car I found it had been placed by my feet. For the third time we headed off in three cars for the airport. Again we passed the skeleton of a train depot, the wrecked huts, the craters. We came to a pontoon bridge.

I popped two Valium. The pontoon bridge was the only way left to cross the river. The traffic went one direction for a half hour and then the other direction for the next half hour. I shrank down in my seat and waited for the sound of sirens. Getting caught on that bridge during a raid was my idea of hell. It would mean getting out and climbing under the car. There would be a fight about the helmet. But worst of all was the great expanse of open sky above the bridge. I felt sure we were a perfect target. The ride across the bridge took about an hour.

At the airport, the chairs were lined up the way they had been when we'd arrived two weeks before, but the room had only half a roof and part of its walls. Debris had been pushed into corners and the room swept and wet-mopped, but there was a dull finish everywhere, an endless amount of dust. The bar was standing. I asked for the ladies' room and was directed to a cubicle just intact enough to ensure partial privacy. The plumbing was out. From the broken window I could see some Russians, some Vietnamese, and a group of wounded Polish soldiers arriving outside for the same flight.

We wandered outside looking at the damage. While I was strolling around peering at the rubble, I saw partially buried in the thick mud, halfway down the inside of a crater, a piece of metal which had a startling shape to it. I climbed in and pulled it out of the dirt. A piece of an airplane, no doubt, had melted into the shape of a bird sitting on a branch. I slipped it into my purse. The lobby was filling up and I knew there would be a raid. A phone rang, and everyone sauntered across the pockmarked area in front of the terminal, toward the airport shelter.

There were eleven Polish soldiers, counting two who were in coffins. Like Monti's, their ship had been hit in Haiphong harbor. When we reached the area just outside the shelter, people struck up conversations. Some of the Poles asked me for autographs and I obliged and shook hands with them; others were very much in pain, and just looked on.

We were ushered down into the shelter. It was pitch-black until someone lit a candle. There was a fat lady who was embarrassed about trying to make it down the stairs. The shelter was like a catacomb, each new room black until a candle-bearer caught up with us. Ten or twelve of us reached a small cubbyhole and sat down to wait. A Pole stood in the doorway. I was next to Barry and Mike. Near me sat a wounded Pole with his head sunk into his knees. All the Poles looked exhausted and shell-shocked. We heard the planes in the distance. Every soldier in the bunker stiffened. One began to cry. I reached out my hand and stroked the head of the one nearest me. He looked up wearily and put his head back down. I began to sing, "Hush, little baby, don't say a word, Papa's gonna buy you a mockingbird." I kept stroking his head. "If that mockingbird don't sing, Papa's gonna buy you a diamond ring." Get those goddamned planes out of the sky and let these guys get out of here. "If that diamond ring is glass . . ." I finished the song and the planes were gone. No one spoke as we got up and headed slowly for the open air.

The Chinese plane was landing. The soldiers were too tired to smile. We walked back to the runway and lined up. The coffins were loaded first, then the Poles, and next the Americans. We turned around at every other step to wave goodbye again and again to Quat, Chuyen, and the others. The plane was small and hot. Directions were given in Chinese, and Chinese music played over the speakers. The engines started up. As we taxied down the wreck of a runway I looked out the window and saw our little band, still waving. Suddenly, en masse, they all turned their heads around and skyward, and I knew that the B-52's must be coming back. And then, as though nothing had happened, they turned back and continued to wave to us until we were airborne and they were specks on the pockmarked land below.

We arrived home safely on New Year's day. My son stepped out of the crowd at the San Francisco International Airport and handed me a bouquet of acacia which was as big as he was, and he said, "Hi, Mom." I picked him up in my arms and said, "Hi, sweetheart," and gave him a fire truck I'd bought at the Tokyo airport.

The first two weeks I was back I stayed at David's house, where I slept most of the time and spent the remainder giving interviews to newspapers and magazines. Every time I fell asleep on the couch I could hear Gabriel hollering around the house, and the only thing that woke me up was when he'd drop a Tonka truck on my head or the cat on my stomach or himself on my chest. Then I would grab him and hug him and tell him I'd play in a few days when I was back on my feet. At night I left a candle lit so that when a plane went over and I found myself sitting up in bed reaching for my pea coat, I could orient in a hurry to the fact that I was home. But part of my psyche was still in Hanoi.

When I had fully recovered my physical strength I went to my own house and listened to the fifteen hours of cassettes I had taped in Vietnam, including the sirens, the bombs, Phantoms, B-52's, anti-aircraft, the children laughing, Monti talking, the Vietnamese singing, myself singing in the shelter. I did a rough edit and took the results to the record company to record as best I could the story of my Christmas in Hanoi. It is one long poem partially sung, and begins with a run to the Swedish bomb shelter during a raid, some bombing, and then the old woman at Kan Thiem chanting, "Oh, my son, where are you?" The last verse of the title song goes:

> Oh, people of the shelters
>     what a gift you've given me
> To smile at me and quietly let me share your agony
> And I can only bow in utter humbleness and ask
> Forgiveness and forgiveness for the things
>     we've brought to pass.
>
> The black pajama'd culture that we tried to kill
>     with pellet holes
> And the rows of tiny coffins we have paid for
>     with our souls
> Have built a spirit seldom seen in women and in men
> And the White Flower of Bach Mai will surely
>     blossom once again.
> I've heard that the war is done
> Then where are you now, my son?

The album is called *Where Are You Now, My Son?* and it is my gift to the Vietnamese people, and my prayer of thanks for being alive.

# 5
# "WARRIORS OF THE SUN"

I met Ambassador Harold Edelstam at an Amnesty International lawn party and fund-raiser in 1973. He had been the Swedish ambassador to Chile at the time of the coup in 1973. And I had heard this story about him.

One night, in the bloody weeks following the assassination of Allende, when the streets were filled with fear, lost hopes, and bodies, someone got word to Mr. Edelstam that the tanks of the junta were rolling toward the Mexican Embassy, threatening to fire on it if the people inside didn't surrender and come out. Guns poked from the windows of the embassy, and a determined but futile resistance was about to be put up. Ultimatums were being issued from bullhorns on the tanks, and since this was a totally lawless coup, there was no doubt that the people in the embassy were in danger of their lives.

Holding the Swedish flag above his head, the ambassador walked with his staff past the tanks and into the Mexican Embassy, brought everyone outside and escorted them, under the protection of the flag, to the Swedish Embassy. And there they stayed until their passage back to Mexico was arranged.

"Do I have the story right?" I asked him.

"Yes, more or less," he said in his singsong Scandinavian accent. The ambassador is tall and skinny and aristocratic. His hands are paper-clean.

"Why did you do it?" I asked.

He laughed, as if enjoying a good joke.

"It's simple," he said. "I've never been able to tolerate injustice."

And I've never been able to forget that simple statement.

My 1974 concert in Venezuela got off to a ragged but adrenalated start when the governor opened the gates to the stadium early, perhaps to win popularity with the students, or perhaps because he didn't want to pay for new doors—these were about to be demolished by the enthusiastic crowd. The promoter, a left wing, multiracial, extremely bright and tough young woman named Maria, was enraged because, naturally, she was losing money as a result of the governor's whim.

The concert rules at the school stadium were: no one on the playing field, everyone in the bleachers. From previous similar experiences I knew that the rules were entirely unrealistic, and they appealed to me as little as they did to the largely student audience of six thousand.

The bleachers filled as a young Venezuelan folksinger opened the show to whoops and yells and foot stamping. Her songs were very political, like most of the audience. Her set was followed by a brief intermission. When I was introduced, I walked across the great expanse of field with a small huddle of people and climbed up onto the platform. With the very first note the audience began flowing out of the bleachers and onto the field, gathering momentum and running toward the tiny stage. The kids' faces were animated and beautiful. We had a shouted conversation from stage to ground and back. At this rate we would be a family before two songs were up.

I had just launched into the second song when the electricity went dead. A chorus of boos went up and was followed by much confusion and bustling around the sound equipment. I squatted at the edge of the stage chatting with different individuals in the crowd in their grammar-book English and my ersatz Berlitz, rudimentary Spanish. No headway was being made with the electrical problem, nor did anyone seem very upset. The evening was progressing happily on Latin tempo.

Rumors began circulating that the president of the university had ordered the sound off until the kids returned to the bleachers. Manny elbowed his way through the crowd to the side of the platform. After a minute of saying "Huh?" and "S'cuse me?" he finally understood what I wanted and went to negotiate with the president for one minute of electricity. I went on conversing with the kids up front, rising occasionally to tap the mike. Word came back in a flurry of excitement that the president had agreed to the minute of electricity, but only for me to announce that everyone must return to their seats. I felt as though I were trapped in a junior high school pep rally with the dean saying we'd have to return to class unless all the seventh-graders went back to their assigned section in the auditorium. The electricity came on.

"I would like to thank the president of this university," I blurted out in my broken Spanish, "for giving us back the electricity. As you see, the audience is well behaved and does not present a problem here on the field." ("Thank you señor president for to give me electricity. The students do not a problem here next to me.") "I would like to express my gratitude by dedicating a song to you, and if you like the song, you will let me know by leaving the sound on. Thank you very much, we are all grateful to you." ("I want to say thank you by to dedicate you a song and if you this song like you will for us make electricity. Thank you of us to you.")

Perhaps he felt I was so illiterate that I could do no harm. The sound stayed on, and a wonderful evening was had by all, the audience and myself enjoying a bizarre victory in the name of the people, and the president of the university ending up something of a hero for the night.

I dedicated much of the concert to the *refugiados* and *prisioneros* of the bloody regime in Chile, as it had been only a year since the coup, and many Chileans had fled to Venezuela for their lives. I didn't yet know what a golden representative was seated in the bleachers next to the governor.

I had been invited to a private dinner after the concert at the home of a Venezuelan woman writer named Frezia Barria. There were only about ten people attending, including her children, and a man named Orlando Letelier.

I had heard about Orlando the way you inevitably hear about exceptional people, in stories told with love and a touch of awe. The former ambassador from Chile to the United States had been imprisoned during the coup and was a source of strength to everyone who knew him.

When he arrived and we were introduced, I was surprised to see that he had red hair. If Goya had been commissioned to paint a cheerful redhead with freckles, it would have been Orlando Letelier, for he had the slender height and demeanor of Latin aristocracy which Goya had depicted so frequently and so well. Orlando's hand was still healing from being ripped on the fence as he and his fellow prisoners were herded at a run from one yard to another. He wanted to play the guitar and sing, though playing made his hand hurt, and he wanted to dance the *cueca*, a Chilean folk dance. He was with friends from years past, and he was happy, filled with stories and laughter and songs and jokes. I was cajoled onto my feet amidst laughing and clapping, and danced the *cueca* with him, not caring that I could only wave a handkerchief around in the air and imitate Orlando's footsteps and grin like a happy fool at the joy and fun of it all.

The dancing slowed as energies were spent, and Orlando began to talk more seriously, and much more softly. The children went to bed, and the crickets chorused outside in the humid night. My Spanish being what it was, I contented myself with listening to the syllables, the rolling *r*'s, and the sibilant *s*'s, and thinking about the ferocious stupidity and evil of imprisoning a man like Orlando on the freezing islands of his own country. Miraculously, he had not died. He had fought the cold and hunger, the beatings, humiliations, the deprivations, and the terror with his plenitude of spirit, and with his disciplined mind. Just as miraculously, he was not murdered, and was here now, mending, smiling, and whispering stories. Every now and then he would almost weep, and his friends would wipe their eyes, and I would feel my heart bursting with tenderness for this man. Then, in a wave of silence, something in the room shifted, as though we'd all taken in the same breath of air at the same time, and all of us were suddenly and intensely aware of the ghastliness Orlando had so recently left behind. At that moment, as we held our breath in the stillness of early dawn, other murderous crimes were occurring in a long white scream, beyond our power to stop them.

Back home, I decided to try to write a book. I had not written in many years, and, uncertain of what I wanted to say, found myself returning over and over again to the theme of the long white scream.

One morning in 1976 as I alternately wrestled with words on my typewriter and gazed out the window, my secretary came unannounced down the path through the oleanders, her head thrust forward and her brow in a troubled frown. She was an extremely efficient, highly emotional woman with a kind heart, and everything in her posture told me she was bearing bad news. Sitting down in front of me, she spoke in shaky but controlled tones, and her eyes filled up in anticipation of my reaction to her words. The next thing

I remember is sitting in the kitchen, staring at the coffee jittering in my mug, and listening to my own teeth chatter uncontrollably. I had just been east to sing at a benefit for Chilean prisoners, and had again spent time with Orlando, finding him as unique and refreshing and special as I had on the first meeting, when, as complete strangers, we'd made and sealed a friendship by dancing the *cueca*.

I flew to Washington, D.C., for Orlando's funeral and sang in a park before the march, circulating through the gathering of stunned and profoundly hurt diplomats, academics, poets, bureaucrats, exiles, workers, students, and politicians. The march was stately and heartbreakingly sad. A deep voice called out over the bullhorn through the misty morning sunlight, *"Compañero Orlando Letelier!"* and the thousands of trudging mourners replied, *"Presente!"* The voice again: *"Ahora!"* (Now!); and the crowd, *"Y siempre!"* (and forever!). Those of us with flowers stepped out of line to lay them on the spot where Orlando had died. His car had been booby-trapped and exploded on Embassy Row, killing him and his young coworker, Ronni Moffitt. The assassin was a professional hit man from Chile's secret police, D.I.N.A., who plea-bargained his way to star witness for the prosecution. Two officials from D.I.N.A. were indicted but never stood trial, and two Cuban exiles were convicted. The United States government's position was dubious at best, since the CIA had helped finance the military coup and supported Allende's overthrow, as well as the installation of Latin America's most efficient dictator to date, General Augusto Pinochet.

The march ended at St. Matthew's Cathedral. Before the service I helped seat people, battling obnoxious members of the Communist Party who tried to occupy the first and second rows of pews. I ushered them away firmly, as though it were my designated job, saying that the area was reserved for family. They hated me a little more than usual, and I returned their fury knowing they were trying to claim the spirit of this brilliant, dancing diplomat for themselves. But he was bigger than a political party; his spirit belonged with the poets.

I sang in the high mass. Looking out over the packed congregation I saw Orlando's wife, Isabel, and his four handsome sons. Isabel's doe eyes were swollen from weeping. I sang "Gracias a la Vida" and kept my eyes high above the crowd, because many people had begun to weep. I remember Ronni Moffitt's young husband struggling to speak from the pulpit, eaten up with fury and sorrow, his tears and his words becoming one.

• • •

When I came home I thought about Isabel and her four sons and dreamed I couldn't get out of the archbishop's way as he moved from place to place during the funeral mass. I saw Orlando laid out in his coffin again, only this time his face was a skull and some shreds of flesh, drenched and glistening crimson with fresh blood. When I tried to kiss him my lips came away soaked and the skull turned slightly toward me, as though to ask for something, but could only moan in despair.

For a few weeks I tried to keep writing my book. Then I put it away and didn't try to write again for ten years.

The first time I met Betty Williams and Mairead Corrigan, winners of the 1977 Nobel Peace Prize, they said "Hellay, Jane!" and I thought, Oh Christ, they have me mixed up with Jane Fonda. But it was only the Belfast accent.

Two remembrances of my visit to Northern Ireland in 1976:

The frost was crystalized on the hedges along the roadside above the city. A mother of twins was telling Ira, his new wife, Molly, and me about the first spontaneous peace march they'd had in August 1976. The mothers came toward each other, she said, Catholics from one direction and Protestants from the other. They had no idea what would happen when they met. She'd been shoved up front, she said, because she had a big pram, with the twins in it. No one would want to harm the twins, they thought. Well, she said, they just kept on coming, mothers, kids, and prams, all in silence and fear and wonderment, past the big oilcan barriers that separated the two territories. It had never been done before. No one had ever crossed the barriers, and here were two thousand people tumbling toward each other on the Falls Road.

And then they met. They cheered, embraced, and wept, unable to believe the extraordinary thing they had just done. Then they went into the park to talk and talk, and invite each other to tea, and to try and make plans beyond that day. But none of them wanted to look beyond the day. Afraid the spell would break, they did not even want to leave the park.

There was a woman, they said, who'd gone mad and sat at her son's grave and cried day and night, refusing to leave. Her son had gone to visit friends. They had heard the knock at the door, and called out that they were on their way. But the knocking became suddenly frantic. Then they heard a machine gun. When they got to the door and opened it, the boy fell forward into the hallway, dead, with the uneven design of a cross blown into his jacket, pouring blood from every little hole.

With the Irish peace people we marched with our frostbitten toes in the name of unity, peace, freedom, and an end to the ancient divisions that had so devastated Ireland. When we got into a car to go home to Belfast and turned the key in the ignition, there was a little bumping sound, and then nothing. The only other time I can remember being so frightened was on the pontoon bridge which led out of Hanoi. I was positive that the car was booby-trapped and we'd all be blown to hell, but my Irish companions hesitated for only a millisecond, and then picked up the conversation where it had left off. They had already told me they didn't even bother to check under their cars anymore. If you're going to go, you're going to go, they said.

And I remember Mairead. The breath of God ran through her like a fair summer breeze. She was a smile. She was a prayer. She was endlessly brave, going into the streets and homes of "the enemy" unarmed and with cheerful countenance. No evil could envelop her or even touch her. I'm sure she is all those things still. She will hate to read this, because she is also self-effacing, like some other saints. God bless you, Mairead Corrigan. And God bless the brave women of Ireland who, for a brief but exceptional moment in time, waged mass nonviolent warfare in one of the most violent countries in the world.

One day before Andrei Sakharov and Elena Bonner had been exiled to Gorki, I telephoned them just to say hello and wish them well. I thought reaching them would be terribly complicated. It took three minutes.

"Your party is on the line in Moscow," the operator said, as though I were talking to Los Angeles.

My God, I thought. How efficient. And then, I thought for the first time, what the hell am I going to say, and in what language?

"Hello?" I started out boldly.

"*Da?*" came the response from ten thousand miles away.

"Um . . . Do you speak English?"

"*Nyet.*"

"*Parlez-vous Français?*"

"*Nyet.*"

"*Sprechen Sie Deutsch?*"

"*Nyet.*"

"Oh." I am an idiot, was all I could think. "Joan Baez, here. Umm. Amnesty International?"

"*Da.*"

"I think I'd better call you back," I shouted, feeling utterly stupid, and hung up. I imagined a roomful of guests in the Moscow apartment scratching their heads and figuring it must have been the KGB up to some tricks. I called Ginetta.

"Boy, am I an ass," I said. "I had him right there on the line!"

"Call eem back and sing eem a song!"

Of course. I called back, waited three minutes or less, got Mr. Sakharov on the line and yelled, "JOAN BAEZ. AMNESTY INTERNATIONAL. HELLO, ANDREI SAKHAROV. HELLO, ELENA BONNER!" and proceeded to sing five verses of "We Shall Overcome." At the end of each verse I would hear from their end, "*Da!* Please, yes! Good, good, please, yes, my vife!" and I'd sing on as they passed the phone from person to person. At the end I shouted "GOODBYE! *DA SVIDANYA!*" They were all shouting at once. I hung up, and sat down on the bed and cried.

In the summer of 1978 I went to Russia and met the Sakharovs.

There was supposed to have been a big concert in Leningrad Square featuring Santana, the Beach Boys, and me. I had taken Russian lessons, learned a beautiful Russian song by a much loved poet named Bulat Okudjas, arranged for Gabe to be in camp, packed mountains of chewing gum, candy, cassettes, records, and everything I owned made of denim, and contacted Sakharov's stepdaughter (Elena's daughter, Tanya) in case I could arrange to visit him. The trip was announced in a big press conference, at which the Beach Boys displayed a surfboard and Carlos Santana talked about peace and love. I said that I was going with no preconceived notions of what the USSR was like, and made no comments on human rights.

The Russian government called off the concert two weeks before it was to have taken place. No explanation was given. I assumed that they figured out, belatedly, that there would have been a crowd as large as the one at Woodstock, everyone wearing blue jeans and dancing to rock and roll, and behaving like Western degenerates.

I was furious, and decided to apply for a tourist visa and pay Sakharov a visit.

That's how I met him and Elena. I went with John Wasserman of the *San Francisco Chronicle,* and Grace Warnecke, a photographer and translator. We had prearranged a time, and simply walked into their apartment building, took the little elevator as planned, turned to the right when we got off, and knocked on a door that looked as if it had been kicked in and broken down a hundred times.

I know the Nobel Peace Prize winner and his wife as a grandmother and grandfather. In silence, and very movingly, they took the letters and tapes we had brought them from their kids, and devoured them slowly, page after page, side by side. I wanted to disappear and come back the next day, to let them indulge privately in the fresh contact with the people they must miss in a way unknown to most of us.

We were given dinner. Andrei said two things which I will never forget. One was just after I'd finished singing a song. "The KGB is listening, you know," he said.

"Yes, I suppose so," I answered.

"Oh well," he said, "Why not? They are human too."

The other was what he thought I ought to do when I got back to the States. I must encourage the buildup of our arsenal of weapons, nuclear and otherwise. It was the only way to deal with the Russians.

"Aren't you the guy who won the Nobel Prize for PEACE?" I asked.

He laughed, but not very hard. I've always thought there should be one prize for peace, and another one for human rights.

And there should be a third for courage. Mr. and Mrs. Sakharov should have had the last two.

*PART
FIVE*

# "FREE AT LAST"

# 1
# RENALDO AND WHO?

Bob wore scarves, a grey felt wide-brimmed hat wreathed with flowers, pin-striped shirts with tiny mandarin collars, vests, blue jeans, and cowboy boots. He played a two-hour set with band and friends. Other people were featured at different times in the show. There was an anorexic palm reader named Scarlett Rivera who had black hair cascading to her waist and maroon lipstick and who played the gypsy violin, swaying back and forth in feathers and sequins and peering up occasionally at Bob. A small angel named David Mansfield played the steel guitar, the violin, and the piano. He had a pretty white face framed with curls, and one day the Rolling Thunder ladies dressed him in wings and a halo and nothing else but his shorts, and made him play the violin for us. A tall albino southerner with clear skin and black circles around his eyes sang a seven-minute song about a Japanese maiden who, I think, committed hara-kiri. Roger McGuinn came on and sang "Chestnut Mare" and got lassoed on the last note by Ramblin' Jack Elliot, who one night ran through all the trailers stark naked. Cowboy Kinky Friedman whooped out onto the stage dressed in a ten-gallon hat and chaps, and sang "Asshole from El Paso." Ronee Blakely, looking like a cross between Greta Garbo and a Midwest prostitute, sat at the piano every night singing a long sad song with a heartbreak chorus which repeated over and over like a wolf's howl. Her lips were pooched out like Marilyn Monroe's, as though waiting for someone to poke a straw into the little round hole and offer her a milkshake. I told her I'd give her a hundred dollars if I ever caught her with her mouth shut. Providing laughter and insanity was Neuwirth. (My savior on the London tour so many years before. I had in fact been friends with Neuwirth long before I met Bob. He used to come visit Mimi and me when we lived in Belmont, near Boston, to cheer us up and make us laugh.) He put on a clown face, the kind with the big red nose and bald head and hair tufts of green nylon, and went onstage and sang "Where Did Vincent Van Gogh?" with Bob, who wore a clear plastic mask which made him look like a wax facsimile of himself. When Ronee saw everyone getting dressed up, she put on rhinestone flame-shaped pixie glasses and a beret, and painted red hearts on her cheeks and a big black moustache over her pretty upper lip.

The band leader, Rob Stoner, was a handsome ambitious lad with sexy eyes and pockmarks, and he did a lot of acting in the film Bob was making of the tour. I heard about the film; unlike "Don't Look Back," the documentary made of the English tour of 1964, this one would supposedly have acting and plots and scenes and characters. I heard a rumor that I had refused to be in it. Everyone else was in it, the guitar pickers and drummers and light and sound people. So one day I put on a curly red wig, a long, belted T-shirt and high boots, slapped on some makeup (including a couple of oversized black beauty marks), popped some green gum into my mouth, and slinked, chewing and clacking, onto the hotel balcony where a scene was being filmed. Dashing Stoner was dolled up in a black sequined cowboy shirt, pompadour, and shades. I went up and perched myself on the balcony railing, wrapped my legs around him, took the wad of green gum out of my mouth and stuck it to his cheek. Then I grabbed his pretty pockmarked face and French-kissed him. That's how I let it be known that I wanted to be in the movies.

One day I was trudging around in the snow on a farm in Canada with Dylan, doing a "scene." I had spent half an hour gluing on synthetic eyelashes and had been given a new wig, long and dark and curly. Naturally, I was playing a Mexican whore—the Rolling Thunder women all played whores. The scene opened with Bob shoving me through the snow toward a shack. In fact there was neither a plot nor a script so the characters "developed" as we went along. I went into the shack and sidled up to the hero, Harry Dean Stanton, the only real actor we had with us. He'd been called in from Hollywood to play the good guy, and he and I were supposed to sing "Cucurrucucu Paloma" and talk in Spanish and fall in love and then start kissing. Then, to our horror, in would barge Dylan (or maybe it was Jack Elliot, I don't remember), and emboldened by the newfound hero at my side I would chastise him in my heavy Mexican accent. It was a cold day, and I wondered what I was doing in this monumentally silly project, and if Dylan was taking it seriously. Sam Shepard was there, supposedly directing it, or writing it, but it was never written, and barely directed. Bob would stand in back of the camera and chuckle to himself and get everyone to run around and act out his mind movies. The filming happened in gleeful little happenings, enacting whatever dream Dylan had had in the night.

One day in the hotel in Portland, Maine, Allen Ginsberg read a poem to a ballroom full of mah-jongg players. The cameras filmed his performance, and the reaction of the startled Jewish community. They didn't know how to respond to this world-famous literary figure with the long beard, who started out mildly enough but ended up shouting about bearded vaginas, his eyes growing round and wild behind his glasses.

Another day we all got in busses and went to see Arlo Guthrie at a gypsy's place in upstate New York. It was a restaurant with a bar, and while everyone sat around drinking hot toddies Bob was wildly trying to get a scene to happen, and the old gypsy lady spotted me and said I must go up to her room. There she showed me the small embroidered smudgy pillow she slept with containing the ashes of her late husband. She told me she was never lonely. On the bed lay a faded, beaded white satin evening dress. It was ankle length and had lace straps over the satin bodice. Next to it were a little antique embroidered opera purse and a choke necklace of fake pearls and rhinestones.

"Put the dress on," she said cheerfully, and I did. It fit perfectly. She brushed a tear from her grubby cheek and shook her head sagely, saying that she had known I would be coming that day, though she had no idea who I was, and that the dress and purse and necklace were mine. Then she kissed me and said to go down and join the crowd. I felt positively magical gliding down the stairwell, and everybody spotted me at once and said "Ooh" and "Ahh," and Bob decided to do a "scene" with me. Before the scene started we walked down to a little lake. It was a cold fall day with a low sun in a grey sky. I was barefoot, and we stood under a tree and spoke softly (I don't remember about what), like two normal people. For a very few minutes we went back to another time, when we were nineteen years old, standing with brown leaves falling all around and snow in our hair . . . I knew the magic would stop when we

turned around, but I didn't mind. We walked back up the hill to do
the "scene." In front of the cameras I said everything that came into
my head. I asked Bob why he'd never told me about Sara, and what
he thought would have happened to us if we'd gotten married way
back then. He couldn't improvise very well, so I answered my own
questions. I said it wouldn't have worked out because I was too
political and he lied too much, and he just stood there with his hand
on the bar smiling and embarrassed because he didn't know what
else to do, though what I said was no news to him.

On the train Sara sat on Bob's lap. The kids were scattered up and
down the seats, four Dylans, Gabe, and Gabe's friend, Iggy. I was
not jealous of Sara, as I thought I'd be. In fact, I felt protective of
her. She was too frail to be a mom. Her skin was white and translu-
cent, and her eyes were huge and black. Everything about her face
looked frail: the rings under her eyes, the tiny dents in her forehead
that would come and go when her mood changed, her hair thin and
fluffy like black angel hair, her pouting lips and perfect nose, her
high arched eyebrows. Sara was cold in winter; she didn't seem to
have enough energy. We smiled at each other, and one day began
to talk about everything—meaning, of course, Bob. She was careful.
She was loyal. But I felt somehow that we had formed an alliance of
survival against her husband.

Bob and Sara were ill-equipped to handle the practical matters of
everyday life. I was forever handing them towels, bringing them
glasses of water and cups of coffee, lighting their cigarettes, looking
after their kids, and trying to get them seated together at dinner
tables. I don't know what I meant to them. Sometimes I thought I
was the male figure, or perhaps a caretaker for two floundering
things from another space and time, slow-moving and strange
beings, pale as wolves in winter, whom the gods had thrown together to fend for themselves.

Sara was afraid of standing on a bridge over water that didn't
move. I thought hers was a much more poetic phobia than my own
fear of throwing up and I wrote her a song called "Still Waters at
Night."

One day I dressed up as Bob, complete with matching hat, flowers
and scarves, shirt and vest, a cigarette and painted-on beard stubble,
and cowboy boots. I ambled into the room where Bob was filming,
sidled up to one of the security guards and said, in Bob's voice,
"Gimme a cuppa coffee." The coffee appeared in a millisecond.

"Gimme a cigarette," I said. Presto! A lit cigarette materialized in front of me at a respectful distance.

"You like it?" I asked in my own voice, grinning up at the guard.

"Christ! Is that you, Joan?"

"Uh-huh. Isn't this a blast?"

Even Bob was impressed. We did a goofy scene which concluded with me singing, as Bob Dylan, the song I'd written about Sara. Bob was playing an unknown musician who'd come to pitch his songs to Bob Dylan, and I was playing Bob Dylan and being rude to the unknown musician. Sara wandered into the room, cocked her head and then shook it and laughed, and sat down to watch with her foggy quizzical look. I ended my song and made a few abrupt Dylan-esque remarks and the scene was over.

"Ok," said Bob. "That's it."

"I gotta do it again," I said in his voice. He looked furious.

"Hey, c'mon. Bullshit, it was fine, it was great."

"Hey, c'mon. Bullshit, whose fuckin' scene is it anyway? It wasn't no good, I gotta do it again." I dumped some cigarette ashes on the floor, yanked at my wig hairs and looked nasty. We did the scene over again. Pleased with myself, I went to my room, put on a white turban, and practiced being Sara.

"You gonna sing that song about robin's eggs and diamonds?" Bob had asked me on the first day of rehearsals.

"Which one?"

"You know, that one about blue eyes and diamonds . . ."

"Oh," I said, "you must mean 'Diamonds and Rust,' the song I wrote for my husband, David. I wrote it while he was in prison."

"For your husband?" Bob said.

"Yeah. Who did you think it was about?" I stonewalled.

"Oh, hey, what the fuck do I know?"

"Never mind. Yeah, I'll sing it, if you like."

In Montreal I was supposed to be the whore again. Wearing a new wig, some fresh eyelashes, and a fire engine–red camisole with black garter straps and laces, I was lounging in my room, smoking and drinking red wine, getting ready for another step toward stardom on the silver screen when Bob called and said he'd changed his mind: I would be Sara and she would be the whore. I suggested that I be him and he be Sara, but he didn't think I was funny. He was in a creative frenzy, visualizing the scene with the three of us. The wardrobe lady brought me Sara's clothes, a white turban and winter coat and gloves. I was practicing Sara to myself by a couch in the lobby when a small voice asked me a question. It was not Gabe, but one of Bob and Sara's kids, who continued telling me his little concerns. Keeping my back turned, I mumbled a response and then told him to run off, that I was trying to concentrate. He did, never knowing I wasn't his mom. Pleased with myself, I stayed in character and headed off to do whatever the scene demanded. Sara was dressed in a slip and the long wavy wig, and was smooching in bed with Bob. I was supposed to walk in on them and cause a scene. To my disappointment, they kept stopping the cameras and telling me to change one thing and another. Apparently I was giving them the creeps being Sara, and since I couldn't switch characters that quickly, the scene ended up even more ragged than usual.

That first Rolling Thunder tour ended at Madison Square Garden on December 9, 1975. With Bob's agreement, the wardrobe lady fixed me up with everything, including new hat and flowers, Bob's clothes, whiteface, and painted-on stubble. The second half of the show opened with two Dylans, with identical guitars, outfits, voices, and gestures, the only visible difference between us, seen from ten rows back, being the side view of our blue jeans. Mine were filled out in back.

During the show I did a twenty-minute set which included dancing to the old Martha and the Vandellas' "Dancing in the Streets," and, of course, "Diamonds and Rust."

The second Rolling Thunder tour did not start out well. I was feeling impetuous, thinking my status in the show, and the pay scale, should be altered to my benefit. Bob had a thing about wanting me to grow my hair long, the way it was in the beginning. He once told me I'd start selling albums again if I let my hair grow. But I had cut it all off between Rolling Thunders, and when I walked into the rehearsal room in Jacksonville, Florida, Bob said, "What the fuck have you done to your hair?"

"What the fuck have you done to your face?" I answered, and plunged into a pout. He wouldn't rehearse with me or even set a time for later. I caught a cold and went to bed wallowing in self-pity, and wrote a dumb song about Bob. Somewhere it said, "We haven't got too much in common, except that we're so much alike." That was the strangest part of it all. We have, and had, almost nothing in common, except that he was my mystic brother; we had been street twins, bound together by times and circumstances.

There I lay in bed, sniffing and glowering, just as I had done in

England ten years before. Louis, one of Bob's good and faithful servants, a Jewish fisheries tycoon who collected antique cars for a hobby, came over to see what he could do with Queenie. Louis was slightly perverted, but always kind and thoughtful to me when push came to shove. Push was now at shove, because the first concert was coming up in two days, Bob and I had not rehearsed, and I was threatening to go home.

I was easily cajoled back to reason and to the tour. Bob came to visit and was even sort of nice. After he left, Neuwirth came leaping into my room yelling in an Italian accent, "She ees going to LEEVE (live)! THE QUEEN EES GOING TO LEEVE!" and he threw open the window and shouted it across the whole grounds of the large and rambling hotel complex. I suddenly felt fine, but embarrassed at all the color that had flooded my face, and at the fact that I couldn't stop laughing.

I poked my head outside like a mole in spring. In Bob's compound a girl with henna hair and Salvation Army clothes was walking on a tightrope she'd stretched between two big moss-covered trees. She practiced her cult meditation discreetly and was a practical sort, and stayed with us for most of the tour. Musicians were everywhere. Bob was now wearing a sh'mata in place of the pretty cowboy hat, and everybody was wandering around with bandanas and torn sheets tied around their heads. I didn't succumb until the end of the tour, and then only with an eight-foot-long red silk scarf from Spain, wrapped into a turban and adorned with a gaudy brooch over the center of my forehead, the spot where rajahs stuck their royal jewels. This Rolling Thunder wasn't as pretty or as fun, I thought, and I began to realize that musically, spiritually, politically, and in every other way, I was limiting myself severely.

Sara showed up late in the tour, wafting in from a plane looking like a madwoman, carrying baskets of wrinkled clothes, her hair wild and dark rings around her eyes. In two days, she had regained what I called her "powers." Bob was ignoring her, and had picked up a local curly-headed Mopsy who perched on the piano during his rehearsals in a ballroom off the main hotel lobby. Sara appeared airily at the front door dressed in deerskin, wearing her emerald necklace and some oppressively strong and sweet oils. She greeted me with a reserved hello and talked distantly about nothing in particular, all the while eyeing the closed door to the ballroom. I had the impression that she had her magic powers set upon that room, and that whatever plans Bob had would soon be foiled. The door to the room opened and Mopsy tumbled out.

"Who's that?" said Sara, looking at the girl sideways with her big, lazy, suspicious eyes.

"Some groupie. No one likes her," I answered. It was true. We liked the tightrope walker, who vanished quietly when Sara was around, but Mopsy was a lawless intruder and I realized how much I supported Sara.

The next thing I remember is backstage at that night's show. Through a curiously wide-open dressing room door, tucked back from the neon lighting, I saw Sara in her deerskins and oils, perched on a straight-backed chair. Her husband was on one knee in front of her, bare-headed and apparently distraught. It was like a silent movie, Bob in whiteface and Charlie Chaplin eyeliner, Sara all ice and coal and bits of rouge. That night I sang "Sad-Eyed Lady of the Lowlands" and dedicated it to Sara.

Bob's birthday came and ten thousand people sang to him in a stadium in the rain. He stuck his face into his amplifier until the song was over, and then plowed into "A Hard Rain's A-Gonna Fall." That night we had a disjointed party for him complete with a cake, but he got drunk and looked dead tired. I decided to walk him to his room. He started flirting ever so slightly, and I told him to wait right where he was and dashed off to find Sara and delivered her to Bob. They both laughed sheepishly and looked mildly pleased, and I said "Happy Birthday," and went back to my room quite proud of myself.

The tour wound down rather ingloriously somewhere in the Northwest. The weather was turning cold. I didn't like my room and was getting homesick and feeling that my life was being wasted in a madhouse. At the very last I hadn't seen much of Bob and was surprised when he came to the table where I was dining with some of the other inmates. He tried to convince me to extend the tour, saying we should just keep booking concerts down the West Coast, and then, after that, go on booking wherever we wanted to go. He said we were the greatest road show ever. I said I wanted to go home.

"Why? What's home got that Rolling Thunder ain't?"

"My kid and my garden. And things I gotta do."

"Yeah? Like what?"

"Start getting uncrazy, for one."

"You ain't tellin' me that you're gonna be any less crazy at home in your house, c'mon!" He was gulping something out of a hotel bathroom glass and had begun teetering.

"We kin git a bunch of maids and teachers and tutors and stuff and just stay on the road forever. It's great for the kids. They'll just turn into a little pack. Be great for Gabe. Can't do it without you, Joanie." It did sound exciting . . . And he went on a stunning tirade about how wonderful and special I was. In fact, I was the *only* one, and all them others didn't never count anyway. They didn't mean shit.

"You're it," he said, nodding definitively.

"Thanks, Bob. And you're drunk." He went on like that for a while longer, and wound up on one knee fumbling around for a pocket knife, saying we should be blood brother and sister. He had the blade out and was sawing away aimlessly at his wrist. I asked him to wait a minute and got a clean steak knife from the waiter, dunked it into the Scotch and made some little scratches on our skin, just deep enough to draw blood, and we stuck our wrists together. He nodded happily and drunkenly and said that now it was for life.

"What's for life, Bob?" I asked.

"Me and you," he said quite seriously.

In spite of everything, the Rolling Thunder tours had been a success, at least musically. I suppose it was because of them that years later I thought Europe 1984 would work out. Bob and I had talked occasionally over the years about touring Europe, and I figured he would like to tour if it were totally convenient and he could make piles of money. At our European promoter's urging, I proposed a short tour with him, but he'd said no, no way. He was goin' t' Latin America with Santana cuz it was easy and cuz people down there didn't know nuthin' 'bout nuthin' anyways, meaning, I guess, that he was less pressured to do music they demanded and freer to do as he pleased.

My promoter, Fritz Rau, and his associate, José Klein, both of whom I loved and with whom I'd worked for years, had a fifteen-year-old dream of organizing the great Dylan/Baez reunion in Europe. So when, a month after Bob's and my conversation about Latin America, they called me and said, "HE'LL DO IT! HE WANTS TO DO IT!," I assumed they had come up with a good enough offer to make the reunion attractive to Bob. I was suspicious because the tour was already being planned as a Dylan/Santana tour.

I insisted on approval of everything from size and order of the names on posters and ads to order of the show and length of sets. Mainly, I insisted that Bob and I have equal billing and perform together somewhere in the show, and that Santana open the show.

Much was promised.

Nothing was in writing.

Everything was insinuated, assumed, or simply wished for.

For weeks before the tour, I tried to reach Bob, but he was never available. I pinned José down.

"I need some reassurance that Bob intends to sing with me."

"Bill Graham's speaking to him about that today."

"What's the story on the order of the show?"

"Everything's set for Frankfurt, and I think the others are coming together." A personal manager would have pulled me out of the show at that point. I had not had a personal manager since parting with Manny in 1978.

At the request of Fritz and José, I did a press conference, a TV rock show, and special interviews to promote the great Dylan/Baez event. Like Fritz and José, I was heading into the reunion blind, and with growing excitement. I didn't reach Bob until two days before the first show. Trying to reach my blood brother by phone went like this:

"Hello, this is Joan. I'd like to speak to Bob."

"Oh, hi, Joan. Gee, I don't know, he was around here earlier. I'll have him call you back."

"No, I'd like to talk to him now. I can wait."

"Gosh, ummm. I just saw him somewheres, ummm . . ."

New voice.

"Hi, Joan. This is Stanley. What can I do for you?"

"Probably nothing, Stanley, because I don't know you. Unless you can produce Bob . . ." Much clicking and covering of the receiver. Bob, realizing he can't get me off his back, finally deigns to speak.

He sounds awful, but I jolly him along and tell him I heard he'd had a great opening concert in Venice. He is only grunting today. I suggest that we rehearse a couple of songs for the show. He has a terrible reaction and I realize that he is allergic to the word "rehearse." He finally says we can "go over some stuff."

I flew into Hamburg to meet him and "go over some stuff," only to discover that he was not at the same hotel, and would not be in town until the next day. In fact, he would arrive in his private plane just in time to go onstage for his own set.

So started Fritz and José's balancing act between Bill Graham's organization and their own "schmetterling" (Fritz's affectionate nickname for me, meaning "butterfly"). And so started one of the most demoralizing series of events I've ever lived through. It compared only to Ring Around Congress under Hurricane Agnes.

Somehow the first concert stuck to a crumbling semblance of all the things I had been promised. Carlos Santana, bless his heart, threw his ego out the window and opened the show. My set was very successful, even in a half-sold stadium in the rain. I went up to Bob during a break in his set. He had been unapproachable before, surrounded by bodyguards. Now he was standing by himself, picking his nose.

"Hello, Robert," I began.

"We supposed to do sumpin together?" he said.

"Yeah, I think it would be appropriate to do sumpin together. I think they kind of expect it."

"Shit. My fuckin' back is killin' me." He stopped digging in his nose and began to rub the base of his spine. He hobbled off grimacing. I assumed that I was giving Bob a terrible pain in the back, but, still thinking that we were having a reunion, I told him I'd walk onstage and join him and Santana on "Blowin' in the Wind," as Bill Graham had desperately suggested.

"Sure, if you feel like it," said poor Bob.

The results were ragged at best. My tour manager, Big Red, began a campaign to separate me from him. Soon I lost the battle to appear after Santana, who is also Bill Graham's property, and I became the opening act. I was not in a financial position to walk out on eight well-paid concerts, but each new demotion overwhelmed me.

One evening in Berlin Fritz and José tried to get me to start my set fifteen minutes before showtime. There was a problem with a curfew, they said. The local act was on and off, and by half an hour to showtime, seventeen thousand soggy Germans were standing in the rain, blaming me for their discomfort. I went on ten minutes after showtime, and the audience was soaked, miserable, drunk, and nasty. Later, when the night had fallen and the rain had stopped, I went to watch Bob's show. The stars were out and twinkling, and bright colored lights danced on the stage. I'd long since stopped bugging him about singing together. The curfew didn't affect him, of course: he did his usual straight two hours. That night I lay in bed hurting from head to toe, mainly in the throat, behind the eyes, and in the stomach. At three in the morning I got up, went out and walked the streets of Berlin until six.

My suite had a picture window looking out on a huge maple tree. I lined up the couch pillows on the floor so that I could lie down and look directly into the leaves which were flipping gently like the pages of an abandoned book, their two sides of slightly different hues, and I entered those lovely branches and rested there in the kindly arms of that tree for four hours, dozing lightly, healing slowly.

At noon I got up and decided to concentrate on salvaging the

French concerts. I called José and made him promise to personally investigate the posters and advertising for our three French shows. I demanded fair billing or I wouldn't appear. He promised. He probably tried. He failed. In a sauna in Vienna, over the bony white knees of some distinguished Austrian, I saw an ad in an issue of *Liberation*, a Paris daily newspaper: In print barely large enough to read, Joan Baez was once again billed as a guest star.

I called Bill and told him I wouldn't be going to Paris. He thought I wanted more money. I didn't. Did I want to sing with Bob again? No, I said, it's too late; I would probably never want to sing with Bob again. I hung up as Bill began to raise his voice. I felt as if I'd had a steam bath, an ice dunk, a facial, a manicure, and then been to Quaker Meeting. I was at peace for the first time in nearly four weeks. A storm of phone calls, telegrams and threats followed. I sent off a telex to the French press giving some diplomatic excuse for the unfortunate cancellation of my appearance in Paris. The Paris promoter called his own press conference and said that Madame Baez would *indeed* be appearing, and any rumors to the contrary were false.

Happily, for once, our own sloppiness worked to my advantage. We had no binding contract with Bill Graham. When it was clear that I was not making idle threats, the Paris promoter announced that if Ms. Baez didn't appear it was because she was impetuous and felt like snubbing the Parisians and that she'd never play Paris again.

He was winning the public relations battle; I was losing sleep but staying clean. I went to Italy. Bill flew in from Spain to try to talk me into changing my mind. I was flattered. The way I had been treated I didn't think anyone would notice if I left the tour. Bill tried everything, between pleas and lures setting me up for possible legal proceedings saying things like "I wish you thought you were *capable* of walking out on that stage," and "Of course, there was never a *guarantee* that you were going to sing with Bob, it was just a *hope*." When he finally gave up, I ordered him a big bowl of ice cream, four flavors, because he was not used to losing battles and needed some sort of compensation. In the end, I paid him a monetary forfeit, which I had expected to do. But paying money was nothing compared to the battering my ego and spirit had taken for over a month.

The last time I saw Dylan was backstage, in Copenhagen. That night I'd had a wonderful set and I was listening to a little of Santana, before catching the plane to Italy, where I had my own extremely successful tour in process. Bill came up and said he'd heard I was leaving.

Bob's heavies began materializing.

"If you're *really* leaving, Bob wants to talk to you."

I laughed. "Not if I'm just pretend leaving?"

When "Bob wants to talk to you," it means that you go to where he is. He never comes to you.

"Here I am," I said cheerfully.

"He's in his room, over past the stairway—"

"If I happen to pass his room on my way out, grab me. I'll be leaving in about ten minutes, but I'll be in a hurry."

Guards were stationed between me and the sacred room, and as I passed, they converged upon me.

"He's in here," they pointed and I was ushered through his door in a reverent hush, as though I were entering a cathedral.

Bob was lying on a sofa with his head toward the door, dressed in what looked like a formal suit. His eyes were shut and his feet were up on the arm of the sofa. He had jumped when I walked in, so I knew he was awake.

"Don't get up," I joked. He didn't move, except to look up as I approached.

"Oh, yeah, hey wow, I'm tired, real tired."

"Yeah, well, you don't look so hot. Have you been taking care of yourself?"

I leaned over and kissed his sweaty forehead. It was covered in whiteface. He looked, as the British say, as if he'd been dragged through a hedge backwards.

He peered sleepily around the room.

"I think I dreamed I seen you on TV. At least I think it was a dream. Hard to tell the difference anymore. You was wearin' this blue scarf. That was some scarf!"

"It wasn't a dream, Bob. That was a broadcast from Vienna."

"Shit, you're kidding. I must be more tired'n I thought." Bob started running his hand up under my skirt, around the back of my knee and partway up my thigh.

"Wow, you got great legs. Where'd you get them muscles?"

"From rehearsing," I said. "I stand up and rehearse a lot." I took his hand out from under my skirt and placed it on his chest.

"So," he said, stretching his arms out straight with a cat shiver. "You leavin' already?"

"Yeah, I gotta go."

"How come?"

"I have to catch a plane. It's the kind of plane you have to go and get. It doesn't come and pick you up."

"You don't wanna hang around and maybe do sumpin together later?"

"You mean sing?"

"Yeah, do sumpin together."

"Naw, I don't think so, Bob. Not that way. I wanted to do it right, you know, but it didn't work out. Maybe some other time. I gotta go."

"That's too bad. You bin enjoyin' yourself?"

"Yeah, Bob. It's been my favorite tour in the world." And I kissed him again and left.

Goodbye, Bob. You looked happy on Farm Aid. I thought maybe I shouldn't write all this stuff about you, but as it turns out, it's really about me anyway, isn't it? It won't affect you. The death of Elvis affected you. I didn't relate to that, either.

# 2

# "LOVE SONG TO A STRANGER"

I was on my way to Berlin with Jeanne, my friend and former business manager Nancy, Nancy's friend, Fritz, and José. Jeanne had a crush on José. Nancy had her friend. Fritz drank schnapps and found beautiful women to sleep with. And I was lonely.

At the Frankfurt airport I commented that everybody had someone to sleep with except me. Nancy, who would have swum the English Channel to get me fresh cream if she thought it would make me happy, puckered her face up and started pacing around the waiting lounge, plunged into thought. Suddenly she stopped short, cupped her hand over her mouth, and focused on something across the lounge.

"Do you see *that?*" she said, poking me in the ribs and staring.

"What? Do I see what?"

"That!" she said excitedly, pointing. "That!"

Sitting quietly with a piece of cheap luggage at his feet was a young man, a boy, I suppose, with a beautiful suntanned face and shoulder-length brown hair streaked with summer blond. He was small and dressed in a light leather jacket, not nearly warm enough for winter in Germany. He was indeed lovely.

"Want me to get him for you?" Nancy said in a much too loud voice.

"Nancy, shush!"

"Well, DO you?? He's gorgeous!" and she marched off. I was in the heat of a blush, and mortified. I didn't watch. Nancy returned dragging the sweet suntanned beauty by the arm. He had huge brown eyes, a pouting cherubic mouth, a lovely body, and the passivity of someone who floats with the wind, like a leaf. He was clean and, I thought, not in any way harmful. I was embarrassed, but found him irresistible.

"This is Andy!" announced Nancy proudly. "He likes folk music."

Andy smiled shyly. He had terrible teeth. I didn't care. Nancy sat him down next to me.

"Chone? Chone Betz?"

"Yah. Joan Betz," I said.

José and Fritz came over and talked to him in German. Their faces softened as they spoke, and I asked Nancy what the hell she had said to the young man, since he didn't speak English. Nancy was noisily excited over her coup, and began to laugh as she repeated her story. Nancy's laugh is unparalleled for sheer hysteria, volume, and contagiousness. The waiting room passengers shifted around to watch.

"I just walked up to him and said, 'Mind if I sit down?'" She cackled. "He said he didn't *sprechen* English and I said, 'That's perfect! Do you know JOAN BAEZ?' He didn't understand right away so I went like this, with my hands, as if I was playing a guitar, until he finally caught on and smiled and said, 'Yah, yah, Chone Betz!' and then I grabbed his arm and hauled him over. Isn't he adorable? I think he's wonderful!"

Andy was going to Berlin on our flight, so Jeanne switched seats with him and he sat next to me in first class. We were like two kids running away from home.

"Der sonne?" I ventured, indicating the tan on his hands and arms.

"Oh, yah. I am difing. Sri Lanka. I luff ze zun. I hate Chermany. So kalt."

"Do you want to come to my concert in Berlin?"

"Yah. José tells me. I come."

I slipped my arm through his, took his lovely bronze hand in mine, and fell asleep with my head on his shoulder and his head resting on mine. When we were landing, I took off a big gold and turquoise ring I'd worn for a long time, and put it on his finger.

"What is your last name, Andy?"

"What?"

So we always called him Andy What.

Andy What stayed with us for the entire tour and joined us on the following tour to Spain. He kept to himself, took walks, smoked, listened to his tapes, enjoyed the concerts, loved his "femily," as he called us, dreamed about Sri Lanka and the sun, and made love to me. It was ideal.

# 3
# "NO NOS MOVERAN"

I had refused to sing in Spain under Franco. In 1977, one year after his death, I made my debut there. Now that they had won power, after forty years of struggle and many losses suffered during the civil war and the Franco regime, there was much exultation and confusion among the Spanish liberals, socialists and communists.

I had been in Greece within weeks after the colonels fell, in 1974, and after a two-day spree of wild celebration the population had gone nervously back into its shell. People could not adjust to freedom; they feared that as suddenly as it had come it would vanish and, like butterflies emerging on a spring day, they would be whisked into a political net where their terrors would resume. The same appeared to be true in Spain; many people were disoriented and afraid. As they had needed each other's courage and bravado to survive Franco, they now needed it to reaffirm that he was finally dead.

Conservative Spaniards had always bought my records, especially *Gracias a la Vida*, although two songs associated with liberation struggles had been censored from the original.

In Madrid we stayed at the Ritz, where Andy and I had a suite. There was a sunken tub in the bathroom, and we sank into it on arrival, drinking the champagne we found in the room, alongside roses from the promoter, from the hotel, and from the Communist Party.

*If only I could have laughed at this when it came out . . . Phoanie Joanie, her mom, and sister leaving Santa Rita Rehabilitation Center after first stay, 1967, greeted by Popsy and Pauline.*

*A call to disarm—written by me and designed and printed and distributed by the American Friends' Service Committee, 1968.*

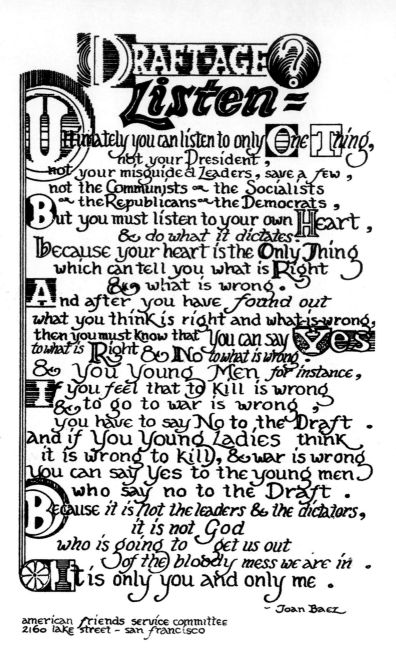

**DRAFTAGE?**
**Listen:**

Ultimately you can listen to only One Thing, not your President, not your misguided Leaders, save a few, not the Communists or the Socialists or the Republicans or the Democrats, But you must listen to your own Heart, & do what it dictates. Because your heart is the Only Thing which can tell you what is Right & what is wrong. And after you have found out what you think is right and what is wrong, then you must know that You can say Yes to what is Right & No to what is wrong. & You Young Men for instance, If you feel that to Kill is wrong & to go to war is wrong, you have to say No to the Draft. And if You Young Ladies think it is wrong to kill, & war is wrong You can say Yes to the young men who say no to the Draft. Because it is not the leaders & the dictators, it is not God who is going to get us out of the bloody mess we are in. It is only you and only me.

~ Joan Baez

american friends service committee
2160 lake street ~ san francisco

*Joanie, Pauline, and Mimi, unwittingly alienating the women's movement while raising bucks for a cause we held dear.*

*David and me recruiting for draft resistance, 1967.*

*1968*

*"The Marriage of the Century"* . . .
*according to* Time *magazine.*

*Short time before David's arrest.*

*Us horsing around in front of our house on Struggle Mountain.*

© Jim Marshall

© Jim Marshall

*First family photo, Safford prison, Arizona, January 1970.*

*Barry Romo, Telford Taylor, Joan Baez, Mike Allen, coming out of Hanoi, 1973.*

*Mike, Barry, and me walking through the rubble of Gialam International Airport, after it had been bombed by American B52s during our visit to Hanoi.*

*"Honey, you've got a mother who sings to you . . . dances on the strings for you."*
*Love, Mom.*

*Two Bobs.*

*Joan and the other Bob.*

*One Bob.*

*Mimi and me at Concord Pavilion, California, 1981.*

*Me, Judy Collins, and Mimi, Newport Reunion, 1985. Still friends after all these years!*

© David Gahr

*Jeanne Triolo Murphy.*

*Gabe, the littlest Dead Head, age eight.*

*After the concert, President Carter and his aides congratulated Jeanne and me on our work in behalf of Cambodian refugees. Afterward, Rosalynn Carter visited refugee camps at the Cambodian border.*

© Ginetta Sagan

*And we hear you, Lech Walesa! In the Brigitta parish house, Gdansk, Poland, November 1985.*

© Ken Regan/Camera 5

*At press conference for the Amnesty International Concerts, 1986 with (left to right) Aaron Neville, Bono, Sting, Bryan Adams, Peter Gabriel, Fela, Lou Reed.*

*Jack Nicholson welcomes me to Live Aid.*

*Clockwise, left: Belmont, Massachusetts, age seventeen; Claremont, California, age twenty; Japan 1967; Nashville.*

© Tommy Wright

*Clockwise, right: Nashville; photo for an album cover, not used, 1977; home in Woodside, California, 1981; Muscle Schoals, Alabama, age thirty-nine.*

© George Wedding

Courtesy of Henson Associates

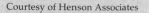

*Mom in England, around 1980 (when I did "the Muppet Show").*

*Popsy, home in California, around 1980.*

*© David Montgomery; courtesy of Diamonds & Rust Productions, Inc.*

*Publicity photo, 1981. Recognize the ring?*

*Gabe as a jock—a short-lived phase at St. Mark's School, Southborough, Massachusetts.*

At Christmastime, I gave Fritz a huge book of drawings of our tour, cartoons I'd done lightning fast in fine-line ink. One of the pictures is of the Madrid press conference.

"Señora Baez, why do you come now to Spain?"

"Señora Baez, why you didn't come before to Spain?"

"Do you like Madrid?"

"Is Mr. Bob Dylan with you? If yes, why? And if no, why not?"

"I understand you don't care anymore the politics, only to make money."

"Why do you charge money for your concerts here? Don't you think they should be free?"

"Are you married?"

"Why your contract says that you must be driven in a Rolls Royce?"

"Señora Baez, why you are doing this commercial television show tomorrow? Do you know that it is the most commercial show in all of Spain?"

I had never heard so many rumors in my life. The most colorful fabrication was the Rolls Royce. Trying to be funny, I told them that I had asked for one Rolls Royce because the Spanish promoter couldn't get me two of them. When I saw everybody scribbling that on their pads, I quickly announced that I had made a joke, and neither rode in, nor ever requested, a Rolls Royce. But to this day, the myth of my white Rolls Royce lives on in Spain.

The next day was the TV show, and it was going to be strenuous. I had imagined it to be a combination of the Johnny Carson Show and a Vegas nightclub. It was. Fritz had gambled on this show because everyone said that "all of Spain" stopped in its tracks at five in the afternoon to watch it. The first act would go on to flashing disco lights and lip sync to canned music. Then would come Boney M., a well-known European rock group, and then a black curtain would be lowered in front of all the glitter to change the mood to one of somber dignity, and I would appear, and sing three songs, ending the show. There would be no interview, and no one following me to break the mood.

I had worked hard to put together the most appropriate and powerful set possible in three songs, two of which would be sung in Spanish. I memorized introductions in Spanish.

The studio was nerve-wracking. Andy stayed with me in the underground labyrinth which housed tiny, claustrophobic dressing rooms. I paced around, working on my Spanish and trying to anticipate the evening. The show would be broadcast live. Suddenly, I heard Fritz screaming. It was not rare to hear Fritz scream, but tonight his voice bordered on the manic.

"SHE ISS ZE SHTARR! WHO ZE FUCK ISS BONEY M.? NOBODY GOES ON AFTER MEIN SHTARR!" There were rapid translations, frantic footsteps, pleading voices, and then more screaming.

"SHE SINGS ONLY MITT ZE BLACK CURTAIN, AND SHE VILL FINISH ZE SHOW, EXACTLY HOW ISS PRINTED IN ZE CONTRACT, OR ZER VILL BE NO SHOW, MUY BIEN?"

He appeared in the doorway. "Zer iss nossing to vorry about, only zat zeez ash-holes must undershtand I vill kill zem mit mein own two hands . . . Oh, yah, nonwiolently, of course."

We had our black curtain, and I closed the show. It was a small studio, and the more visible public up front was carefully chosen from the Spanish upper middle class. There were a few kids, also, I thought, of the rich.

I remember vividly the pearl necklace on the woman sitting nearest the stage. She ran her fine long fingers along and around it and, though dubious of my politics and image, prized her choice seat and would have much to tell her friends about over cocktails that evening. The faces around her were well tanned, the hair well groomed, and the healthy bodies elegantly dressed. It was not an easy audience to sing to. I had to remind myself that I was being broadcast live to millions of people outside of the studio, to a very different Spain from this select group. I understood the grumblings of the left-wing journalists at the press conference and went ahead with my planned program.

What happened next turned out to be one of those rare events which no one can ever really plan, and which are never forgotten.

I spoke of the best-known heroine of the antifascist resistance: "I wish to dedicate a song to a very brave woman who is known for her courage in the resistance. I, too, am a soldier for justice, but I fight without guns, with nonviolence. But with much respect, I sing this song for La Pasionaria."

The words had the effect of a stun gun. The lady in the pearls stopped fingering them, and some of the well-bred couples glanced at each other with expressions I could not decipher. I began the song I had chosen to honor La Pasionaria, which was "No Nos Moveran," one of the anthems of the resistance, known and sung in English as "We Shall Not Be Moved." It was one of the songs censored from my Spanish album and had not been sung openly in Spain for forty years. I sang, *"Unidos en la lucha, Unidos en la vida,"* and *"Unidos en la muerta,"*—Together in the struggle, together in life, together in death. It began slowly, rhythmically, a plaintive and emotional and simple statement. We shall not be moved. Just like a tree, standing by the water, we shall not be moved.

At the time I had no idea of the impact this simple song would have on so many people. I knew that the bejewelled women and their suntanned men had mixed reactions to it; I could see it in their downcast black lashes and tiny smiles, but at the end of the song even they, like the cameramen, brushed away tears and and rose to join in the chorus. There was strong applause and my contribution to Spanish commercial television was over.

There was a sudden crush of people on the backstage stairway. They swarmed in from nowhere, weeping, trying to embrace me. Fritz was puffing and shouting, and he, José, Jeanne, and Nancy were trying valiantly to block the hallway. I shut the dressing room door and shrugged at Andy. I don't remember most of what followed, but Jeanne told me recently she was afraid the crowd would go out of control in the tiny hallway. There was only a single exit in back of them and they had filled the corridor. Nor do I remember the trek to the car, with people pushing and shoving, yanking hairs from my head and trying to touch my face, shoulders, and hands. Somehow Fritz was next to me, calmly guiding me toward our car, punctuating the scene with his few words of Spanish delivered in an unmistakable German accent.

As we settled into the car a man in a Mercedes pulled up next to us and called out to me. I rolled down the window. I didn't like his face, but smiled and waved to him.

"You shouldn't get involved in the politics of Spain," he said.

I indicated my confusion by cupping my hand around my ear. He repeated his ominous warning, smiled stiffly, and glided off at the next green light.

"Was that a threat?" I asked, stunned.

"Fucking fascist," said Fritz. "Remember Franco iss not even one year dett."

The overwhelming response to the TV show overshadowed the incident and reduced the Mercedes driver to his proper status. I was told that hearing "No Nos Moveran" and La Pasionaria's name had broken a spell, or perhaps broken through a layer of protective silence that still surrounded the great, though entombed, Generalissimo Franco. There was wild celebration, hugging, kissing, weeping, and toasting in the living rooms and bars of Spain. Fresh strength was lent to, and derived from, the ghostly memories of the armies of the poor. The children in their rows of tiny coffins were remembered again and through the tears were rocked again by their mothers and kissed on their foreheads by their fathers. I had brought healing and jubilation as my gift to Spain, and the left wing forgave me for appearing on the most commercial television show in Spain.

The producer of the show was fired. He had known my choice of songs and his decision not to interfere cost him his job.

We left the relentless noise of the city, breathed mountain air, and visited cathedrals. I lost myself to a chapel filled with lighted candles, kneeling devotees, bloody hearts, stained glass windows, crèches, crowns of thorns, a stilled pipe organ, brilliant ironwork, the musty smell of centuries-old stone, and whispered supplications. *Ay, que terrible en las cinco de la tarde.* I kneeled and prayed for the souls of the children of Guernica and for their mothers and fathers. *Gracias a la vida.* Thanks to life, which has given me so much; smiles and tears, my feet which are tired from so much marching . . . I prayed for the fascist with the slicked-back shiny hair who had told me to stay out of Spanish politics, and gave thanks for my weapons in battle—my voice and the desire to use it.

We didn't know that our driver had either taped our conversations or taken voluminous notes when we were out of the car, that a photographer, posing as a fanatic fan, was being paid by a newspaper to get some juicy photos, and that the room service waiters at the Ritz must have been offered something worthwhile to spy on us. We found out a few days later, reading all about ourselves in a gossip column. It explained who was sleeping with whom (they had José with me, and Andy with Jeanne, but never mind), about what we ate and drank, what we wore, and what we talked about. Any reality that wasn't interesting was spiced up and embellished.

When the article came out, we were already in Barcelona. And I already had new things to worry about.

I, poor idiot, hadn't understood that Barcelona was in Catalonia, and that naturally most of the people spoke (or preferred to speak) not Spanish, but Catalan, a language supposedly similar to southern provincial French, but utterly unclassifiable to my ears. I had prepared the concert with Spanish songs and introductions. When I strode out onstage I was greeted with wild cheering, but when I launched into my well-rehearsed phrases and expressions, they were met with less than enthusiastic applause. I sang in Spanish, to only lukewarm response. It is a terrible feeling to try every trick in the book, all the honest ones first, and still feel yourself slipping backward into mush.

That evening my life was saved by Joan Manuel Serrat, a Catalonian singer-songwriter whose music I knew, and who had a beautiful face, a beautiful voice, and an understanding heart. Before the second concert Manuel came tumbling into my dressing room with his entourage and an enormous bouquet of flowers, hunkered down by my chair and explained that I had to say just one or two things in Catalan, and the evening would magically come together. I told him that I had memorized his own song, "Rossinyol," and he said that it would be perfect. Then he gave me the words to "No Nos Moveran," which I wrote out phonetically. I did the same with "good evening," "thank you," "you're welcome," etc. Then Manuel had a real stroke of genius. He told me that when Franco came to power the president of the government of Catalonia, Josep Farradellas, was exiled to France. He did not see his beloved homeland again until after Franco's death, at which time he had a triumphant homecoming and was reappointed president. Apparently, when he appeared in front of his people, he said, *"Bon anite, amigas y amiks! Ja estoc aqui!* (Good evening, ladies and gentlemen! I am here!)" And they went wild with happiness.

All I had to do, said Manuel, was walk out on stage and say, *"Bon anite, amigas y amiks! Ja estoc aqui!"* and everything would be fine.

I was excited and moved by the story, and frantically scribbled phonetic Catalan phrases for everything I wanted to say. Manuel embraced me and wished me well, and I went out for another concert. When I reached the microphone and opened as he had suggested, the house came down. These people's pride in being recognized verged on hysteria. I said my few phrases, and after that it didn't really matter what I chose to sing. At one point during "Poor Wayfaring Stranger," I heard the plaintive notes of a harmonica straining up from the crowd. Eight thousand people catcalled and shushed to silence the intruder, but I said, "Oh, no. It's okay! Let him play!" and for one long and exquisite verse, a Catalonian musician poured out his soul, and there was not a sound except for a guitar, a voice, and a weeping harmonica.

Toward the end of the evening, I sang "Rossinyol," and the hall turned into day with the lighting of thousands of candles. The Catalonians were hearing not just a song in their own language, but one which, to my delight, they all knew by heart, and they sang every verse, standing up under the bouncing light of their own candles. Childlike glee and jubilation followed, and I began "No Sarem Mugoots" ("No Nos Moveran") over the happy din. This was now almost too much. There were tears as the candles were relit, and flowers were thrown onto the stage. A senator who had openly denied Franco during all his years in office came up onstage at my invitation. Joan Manuel came out, too, and we all sang "We Shall Overcome," and Catalonians who were long since dust rose up clean and held hands and swayed and sang out as well, and, their earthly struggle over, became the smiles between our tears. And Franco's car, driven by the fascist with the slicked-back hair, and loaded with white bones, leaving only a small spot for the General to sit, was lost somewhere in the valley of death.

Madrid.
The concert.
Too much press. Too many photographers. Andy was there to comfort me, and I had a better list of songs. I wore a heavy brown leather skirt and brown boots, and a nappy little sweater and a Saint Laurent scarf of rose, beige, and dark green draped around my neck, and out I strode to sing to ten thousand more Spaniards in a stadium.

The photographers fired flashguns at me like a trained militia. I ignored them for two songs, and then asked, please, if they could, *por favor*, just work for one more song and then stop. Their anger and readiness to fight shocked me, but at the end of the next song I tried again, this time in broken Spanish. Please, siente te, usted, por favor, es mucho ruido para mi, los fotógrafos. My endearing little smile got me nowhere and was beginning to tremble at the corners. The cameras clicked on over a sea of maniacs pushing, shoving and shouting, "*¡Aquí! Mira, Joan, aquí!*" Over here, Joan, look over here! The crowd shouted at them to sit down and they shouted back, and I felt my composure dissolving. In the chaos I sang another song and hated it and hated them and felt desperate and small and frustrated. The security guards began to move in on both sides. Christ, I thought, now what, as they began doing the only thing they knew how to do—forcibly shove the swarm of photographers away from the orchestra pit. The public understood my plight, and were themselves fed up with the chaos which was wrecking the concert, but each of them also carried, in his or her own memory, images of repression and brutality and a sense of powerlessness in the face of the police. The scene was becoming complicated beyond my experience and capabilities to put it right. The cameramen were now shouting in fury, and the guards were pushing more and more violently. Just as they were almost cleared out, one little obnoxious bastard ducked under the arm of a tall guard and prepared to snap one last flash. In a spontaneous gesture of fury, I axed my left arm with my right hand at the elbow, bending it into a fist, a gesture the Spanish refer to as the *butifarra*, expressing what I thought was a forceful "Screw you." The flash went off, the crowd roared with laughter, the photographer looked as if he'd been shot, I felt momentarily relieved, and the show went on and was a fine success, ending with the lit candles and great choruses. I had nearly forgotten the ugliness of the early incidents. But the real show had not yet begun.

A press conference had been scheduled at a hotel. I was excited, ready to expound on any subject, and anxious to get started. I trotted off leading my entourage.

"Don't go in there," said a woman, suddenly appearing alongside us.

I stopped short.

"Why not? It's my press conference," I said, annoyed at her intervention. My Spanish promoter looked sheepish.

"They are angry," she continued.

"Who is angry?" I demanded, myself furious. "Whatever it is, I'll handle it."

What no one could bring himself to tell me was that my charming gesture to the photographer had meant something more serious than "Screw you," something rather more to do with all of their mothers, and an only recently liberated Spanish press corps found itself reacting from its roots of Catholic puritanism. Insulted by my unladylike gesture, and further aggravated by the guards, the press had formed a *sindicato* against me, and were on strike. Well, not completely on strike, because they were *there*, a hundred or more strong.

Not understanding all this, I strode impetuously up to the microphone, like a spoiled child at her own birthday party, and, thinking I could charm them out of their silly snit, smiled and asked if they would like me to pose for pictures before or after the questions.

My million-dollar smile was met with expressions ranging from amusement to rage, and I tried to remember what the lady in the hall had been trying to tell me.

"Would someone like to tell me what the problem is?" I asked finally, and a man burst from his seat and began to read from a typed page, punctuating the text with his own feelings, urged on by nodding heads and grunts from his cohorts. I invited him to the microphone. He stomped up and read the long list of complaints, which in brief, were that they had been insulted, by a woman and a foreigner.

Did they think I had called the guards? They knew I had not. Was it really the gesture alone, here in newly liberated Spain? He ranted on. I peeked around at Fritz. He looked terrified. So did my Spanish promoter. I was not afraid; I was confused and impatient. A translation was made. The final point of the two scribbled pages of gripes was to demand an apology.

"Of course, I will apologize to you," I said instantly. "I had no idea that my gesture, made in a moment of anger, anger which I feel was justified, carried such a serious meaning here in Spain. I apologize that I have been rude, and that I have insulted you."

Silence.

Nothing was more unexpected or deflating than an apology. They obviously wanted a fight. A man stood up and waved his fist at me and shouted in Spanish. "What do you mean you didn't know the meaning of that gesture? Of course you did. You travel and have been around. I cannot accept that you are ignorant of such an obvious fact."

Grunts of approval issued from the crowd.

"I am sorry, but you are wrong. Why would I have wanted to alienate the press, whom I need, and expose myself to such an attack as this if I had understood the implications of an offhand gesture? And yes, I have traveled extensively, and, in fact, this is not the first time I have lost my temper and done similar things, and they were always forgotten in five minutes. Again, I apologize for my ignorance."

Silence.

"It is not enough that you apologize to us! You must apologize to the public. Why didn't you apologize to the public?"

"Sir. As we have discussed, number one, I didn't know the true nature of my insult. Two, the audience laughed. I thought they were amused. It was only you who were upset, not the crowd."

They grumbled some more to themselves and each other.

"However," I ventured, "I will certainly say to any and every Spaniard who was hurt or insulted by me that I humbly apologize for both my insult and my ignorance."

Still more grumbling.

"And now, if you'd like to have a press conference, I'm more than willing."

Many more questions were asked, but no photos taken. I was shaken, and I'm sure there was hurt written on my face, but I'd be damned if I would show more than what sneaked through. Had I really done something wrong? How tough I was in front of a crowd!

And tonight I would cry when everyone had gone to bed. Andy would understand, and he would hold me.

The next morning was worse than ever. We walked out onto the Paseo to buy some newspapers, and saw, hanging from every newsstand wall holder and clip, a most uncomplimentary photograph of La Señora Baez, in a pretty outfit and ugly humor, her nasty expression barely legible in the fuzzy newsprint, and the famous fist. *"Butifarra con la guitarra,"* one of the funnier titles read. I was devastated. I had worked so hard and sung so well and thought that everybody in the whole world, or at least in all of Spain, loved me, and here they printed this horrible picture, making my whole trip to Spain seem like one giant faux pas.

My poor face grew longer and longer as I walked the rows of newsstands with my "femily."

Fritz was trying to tell me that the articles themselves were wonderful, that I was a huge success in Spain and had Madrid in the palm of my hand. The picture, he said, would only ensure the sales of thousands of copies . . . But I heard nothing, cried my eyes out, and left Spain in a miserable little black cloud. Boarding the plane, I bought a copy of the *International Herald Tribune,* and found staring up at me the same nightmare photo with a short caption under it saying that La Baez had lost control of a crowd in Spain and called for the police.

# 4
## "FOR SASHA"

Ulm, Germany, August 1978.

It was a bright, sunny day, and fifty-five thousand people, mostly kids, were sitting, standing, and lying down as far as the eye could see. I arrived at the festival grounds in a Mercedes and was taken to my little trailer, where I met Frank Zappa, whom I'd known only from the poster of him sitting on the toilet with his drawers down. We chatted amiably. I went and sat on the trailer step, in the roped-off area, and tried to tune my guitar over the sound of Zappa.

Today was an experiment. I would appear in a rock show, between Zappa and Genesis; I would do forty-five minutes as the sun was setting. Unbeknownst to me, Fritz was placing bets with the other promoters backstage, they betting that I'd be booed off stage, he telling them to go fugg zemselves, that I was ze shtarr.

But this was a rock and roll show, where people came to get high, neck, dance, "get into the music," get drunk, and pass out. What could I sing to them? I could do some Beatles, some Dylan, Simon and Garfunkel. "Where Have All the Flowers Gone" in German . . . My hands were icy and my bones were cold. This appearance could be a major disaster.

Fritz tried to buoy my confidence.

"Zey vil LOFF you, mein schmetterling," he said. He put his big arms around me, and then held me away and furrowed his brow

and peered like a madman into my face. His glasses were lopsided
and he had a chunk of German noodle nestling in his beard.

"Yah," he said tenderly, "zees ash-holes hasn't seen nossing yet."

Heart slamming, knees shaking, breath coming much too short, I
trekked with Fritz, Jeanne, and Andy across the lawn. Zappa was
bounding offstage, exhilarated, following a third encore. The
crowd was standing, giddy from an orgy of sound. Deeper into
panic I went. I would be alone with my six strings and two vocal
chords.

The sun was slipping down toward the horizon as we mounted
the stage and stood back in the rafters, hidden by stacks of sound
equipment. A black curtain was lowered in front of the drum sets,
keyboards, and amplifiers which cluttered the stage. Respectful but
curious stage personnel cast glances in my direction as they dashed
to and fro reorganizing the stage for Genesis, who would follow me.
Out in the audience I could see drunken GI's and a lot of glassy-
eyed kids who thought they were at Woodstock. It was time to go
on. I put myself in the hands of God.

It was a skinny stage, between the black curtain and the microphone, skinny and unfamiliar. The crowd was busy; still mesmerized by Zappa, they welcomed me with polite applause. I said good
afternoon and wasn't it a lovely day for rock and roll. At the words
"rock and roll," a cheer came up. At least I could communicate with
key words and phrases.

The first song flopped because it was unknown. I don't even remember what it was. I cut it short and talked about the sixties
(cheers), Woodstock (cheers), and young people (small cheers; not
key words). Then I sang "Joe Hill." Something began to happen. A
chord was struck deep in the hearts of the older people, and the
younger ones, the ones who had been ten years old the summer of
Woodstock, sensed this. A drunken GI fell backward into somebody's arms. Someone else shushed him. Groups of people on the
sides began to chant "Sitzen, sitzen!"—Sit down, sit down—to the
rolling crowd in front.

"Yes," I said in language teacher diction. "If you can sitzen, everybody can see." They sat in disorder and disarray and on top of each
other, shouting and shushing and grumbling, but they sat.

"Sing, Joan!" someone cried out, and I said, "This is a song by
Bob Dylan." Another great cheer went up, and I sang "Love Is Just
a Four-Letter Word." They didn't really know the song but they
clapped along in rhythm, and their eyes and attention began to focus

in. It was the right time for "Sagt Mir Wo Die Blumen Sind" ("Where Have All the Flowers Gone"), and they roared approval and sang along. I noticed tears welling up in the eyes of many. Why? For the years they missed? For the "flower children" in America about whom they had romanticized and whom they imitated? For the memories that belonged to their parents and aunts and uncles, but not to them? Perhaps.

I sang "Swing Low, Sweet Chariot." The sound system was the finest in the world. My voice carried across the sea of bodies and seemed to bounce off the sun and echo back. Across the river, maybe a quarter of a kilometer away, I noticed hundreds of people standing at the riverbank, listening. I faced them, raised my hand high in the air, and shouted, "One verse for the people way over there!" They waved and gave a big cheer, tiny by the time it reached us, but all the kids craned their necks to see them, and waved and cheered back. I faced the riverbank and sang a verse. There were more tears now, and people were clasping hands and holding their arms in the air.

"Chone! Chone Betz! Sing 'We Shall Overcome!' " Now I felt my own tears starting and I glanced offstage and saw Jeanne and Fritz smiling and swallowing and nodding me on.

I sang a few more songs and then closed with "We Shall Overcome." The kids rose to their feet, clasped hands with each other, arms high in the air, and we sang and wept in our own special German sunset service. I bowed and said *dankeschön* and left the stage to a deafening roar of applause. Fritz was red-eyed and shaking his head. Jeanne's beautiful doe eyes were red-rimmed too, as she took the guitar from me.

Then a new noise was added to the roaring and stamping of the crowd: the sound of beer cans landing on the stage.

"Gott im Himmel!" shouted Fritz. "Ziss iss vot zey do ven zey vant you to come BECK!" and he stood proudly extending his arm to indicate the beer cans which were clattering off the curtains and flying in every direction.

"Schmetterling, vot about an encore, yah?"

Fritz walked through the hailstorm of flying beer cans to tell them that I was coming back as soon as it was safe. The cans stopped. I sang "Blowin' in the Wind," and the dream went on. I watched the tears, cheers, and beautiful red cheeks and smiles. Most of the drinking had stopped during my set, and the rowdy behavior had stopped completely. I bowed again at the end of the song, but as I left, I felt that the party was only beginning. The beer cans flew, and the chants started, and the stamping and yelling and whistling continued.

I gave seven encores before Fritz finally announced that there would be no more, and everyone must get ready for "Chenesis." We walked back across the field in a daze. Frank congratulated me, and I smiled numbly. It was time for some German sausage and chips.

The next day the papers said that I had stolen the show. I was recognized more than usual at the airport, and the man at security brought out news clips he'd cut out, of the day, the bands, the kids, and the lady with the guitar who had stayed onstage for an hour. I hugged Fritz, brushed some breadcrumbs from his grey V-neck, and boarded the plane.

# 5

# "THE WEARY MOTHERS OF THE EARTH"

Beautiful Laura Bonaparte was a psychoanalyst from Argentina. On June 11, 1976 her husband, a biochemist, was dragged out of the house in front of her eyes and she never saw him again. When she went looking for her daughter, who had also "disappeared," she was given her daughter's hand in a jar for identification.

When I visited Argentina, in spring of 1981, I was teargassed, thrown out of my hotel, prevented from singing publicly, and interrupted twice at a press conference by bomb threats. The bomb squad came and carried off two bombs.

The Mothers of the Disappeared say that the lucky ones among them are the ones who know their children are dead. Then they can mourn and get it over with, and try to start a new life. They say the hardest part is the night, when the images of their missing children pass before their eyes in the dark.

I was banned in Chile, too, but students organized an evening of music, and the police came in big vans and just surrounded the hall and listened to the concert over the outside speakers. Seven thousand people showed up after just two days of leafleting and word of mouth. Sprinkled throughout the hall were piano players, violinists, comedians, singing groups, dancers, poets, professors, writers, and actors. There were people who had been censored, imprisoned, detained, tortured—people who had not performed in public since the coup of 1973. I was told there had not been such a cultural event in seven years.

The strangest place was Brazil. It had an open press, and I could talk all I wanted, but I could not sing in public.

I almost went to perform at a student concert, but the police showed up at the hotel and said my papers weren't in order. We put them in order, and the police chief was on the spot, what with all these foreigners standing in his station waving documents in his face. I made him say that he was refusing to let me sing, and then I went out in front of the building under the precinct sign and sang "Gracias a la Vida" at the top of my lungs.

Then the lovely congressman with the drooping blue eyes, who once had been beaten up in that very same police station, took me over to the hall and sat me in the audience. All of a sudden, there was complete silence, and I began to sing. Everyone in the packed house sang with me, and when we got up to leave they stood up too, and sang "Caminando," their "Blowin' in the Wind." Sometimes it's impossible to stop goodness from happening.

On the way home we went to Nicaragua.

"The ambassador can wait," General Tomas Borges, Minister of the Interior, said to me in Spanish during the intermission of my concert while his teenage bodyguards finished poking around the corners and closets of my dressing room with their gun muzzles. Borges was shorter than I. He sized me up while puffing defiantly on his cigar. I had told him I was obliged to visit with the American ambassador after the concert.

"I'll have dinner with you on one condition," I told him. "You put out that disgusting cigar."

He not only put it out, he never smoked it again in my presence. He returned after the concert.

He took me to dinner, and after dinner to the prisons packed with national guards from the Somoza regime. He walked up to a grimy black cell crammed with unhappy, bored, dirty inmates, told the guard to open it, and his bodyguards to stay outside. Then he walked right in, a small stump of a man next to the taller prisoners. He peered into the face of a boy.

"How old are you?" he demanded.

"*Dies y seis.*" Sixteen.

"How long have you been in here?"

"*Tres años,*" the boy said wonderingly.

"What is your crime?"

"My father was a *guardista*. I was with him when he was arrested so they took me too. I have no crime other than that."

"Pack your things. You're going home."

The boy stood staring for some seconds, and then began snatching up his few belongings.

Señor Borges looked very pleased with himself and repeated the performance in two more cells. Then he took us upstairs to a special block, and became very emotional. He stopped at an empty cell and was silent. I knew what was coming.

"*Aquí está donde* . . . Here is where they kept me for three years. For six months my wrists were chained together and attached to these bars, so I could not lie down. My head was covered with a sack, and for six months I saw nothing."

"Why do you come back here to torture yourself all over again?" I asked.

"So that I won't forget what it's like. I promised myself that I would not forget."

We stayed just long enough to see history repeating itself. Marxism began to take root in every field of workers, every rally of young people, every drill practice in the town square. And the United States administration was, as usual, and as though communism were something it secretly wanted to nourish, doing everything possible to make the Nicaraguans build an army against us. Speaking of forgetting . . . has the administration forgotten Somoza? Or will he go down in our history books as a good guy?

PART
SIX

# "THE MUSIC
STOPPED
IN MY HAND"

# 1

# "BLESSED ARE THE PERSECUTED"

In the living room of a small home on the outskirts of Los Angeles I sang "Oh, Freedom" to a roomful of Communist Vietnamese. From the moment I walked into that room everything reminded me of my time in Hanoi seven years before—the touch of their soft, clean, yellow skin; the precision with which they set their eyeglasses; the modest and tidy grey suits looking as if they'd been tailored by a special designer who worked in miniature; their voices, soft and clipped, humming in Vietnamese, French, and broken English. When we left almost all of us had tears in our eyes or rolling down our cheeks. The spoken farewells were cordial; the looks, heartbreaking.

I do not remember Hanoi often or easily. Sometimes at night I lurch upright in bed, waking myself, heart pounding, chest and forehead damp with a sudden crazy sweat. As my mind races to discover who and where I am, I hear the rumbling of a jet sweeping lower than usual over the quiet town of Woodside.

Five years after the end of that war and seven years after my time under the bombs, I was once again rallying for the people of Vietnam, this time against the Communist government to which we had lost the war.

In 1979, I had no more desire to think about Vietnam than anyone else in the world did. The West, anxious to forget about Southeast Asia, let the horrendous massacres in Cambodia pass almost unnoticed. Though the massacres in Cambodia were reported by conscientious press, little protest was raised against them. The left wing was reluctant to make an issue of yet another disgrace being conducted by a "revolutionary government." The right wing didn't have much to say except for its usual "I told you so," which is never very helpful. I had not become involved, and knew only vaguely about the devastation wreaked by Pol Pot's scorched earth policy. I didn't want to know. I was even less aware of what was taking place within Vietnam. The exodus of boat people into the South China Sea had begun but was by no means at its peak.

One quiet morning I was visited by two boat people. One of the men was named Doan Van Toai, an ex-student from Saigon who, in the sixties, had been imprisoned under Thieu for antigovernment activities. The other was Hue Hu, a Buddhist monk who'd been defrocked by the Communist government. They were soft-spoken and terribly gracious. Where, they asked, were all the Americans who cared so much about the Vietnamese people in the sixties? The Vietnamese people needed their help again, but could not find it. They began a long description on the human rights violations in Vietnam. I groaned inwardly. Overflowing jails, starvation diets, suffocation in "connex" boxes. Intellectuals, doctors, dentists, architects, artists, old people, anyone who had had ties with the Americans, anyone suspected of being less than enthusiastic about the new regime, was being taken away to re-education centers. Some returned home, but many did not. They wanted to know if I would help them.

I remembered the pressure put on me in 1976 when I'd signed a mildly stated letter to the government in Hanoi requesting that Vietnam improve its human rights conditions. The request was accompanied by an apology for our long and destructive presence there, but a campaign was started to stop the letter. Cora Weiss and I had had a huge row. When the letter received little notice the pressure eased, and the issue faded into the background. Perhaps it was time to bring it back to light.

I formed a research group of five people, including Ginetta. We worked extensively, mostly in Paris, seeking out well-known French journalists of the left who as early as 1976 had begun to realize and denounce Hanoi's policies. We turned to members of the Buddhist and Catholic communities, to diplomats, both French and Vietnamese, to former fighters from the National Liberation Front, to exiles, and to refugees. Some of them had supported the Provisional Revolutionary Government, and had assumed that after the liberation they would be welcomed home as heroes. They discovered that they were now persona non grata, and that it was impossible to get a visa home, period. Over and over and over again, the stories repeated what I'd been told by Toai and Hu.

Everything the United States had done in Vietnam, following in the bloody footsteps of the French and Japanese, had created a political climate in which it was impossible for a peacetime society to evolve and flourish. We had mercilessly bombed, strafed, and burned the mountains, cities, and countryside and now refused to recognize Hanoi. We would not give Hanoi the reparation money once promised, and Vietnam had accordingly broken her promises of no reprisals, reconciliation for collaborators, and, of course, self-determination and democratic freedom for everyone.

According to our findings, Hanoi was destroying her own resources. The people who could be rebuilding Vietnam from within were being locked up. The numbers of political prisoners ranged from Hanoi's own figure of 50,000 to the figure given by many refugees, 800,000. Our calculations and best educated guesses put it at around 200,000, a large number when compared with any country in Amnesty's files. We would attempt to reveal our findings as soon as possible. I still have friends who think that the proper time has not yet arrived to criticize Stalin's gulags.

I wrote an open letter to the Socialist Republic of Vietnam and began collecting signatures in support of it. Getting signatures was not easy. In the end, eighty-one people signed. I was not shocked when I was turned down by most of the left. I was not even surprised when Jane Fonda chose not to sign.

I wrote her a long and careful letter explaining how important it was that she join us. Jane and I knew each other only from brief meetings. We had never worked together. I wrote to her as an actress whom I admired, and someone who had shared my strong protests against the war in Vietnam. Her response was a letter written to me and sent to twenty-five of our co-signers. It was written in a sympathetic tone, but declined our offer.

"I do not doubt that there is some degree of repression in Vietnam and I recognize it is even possible that I am blind to the practices you allege. However, I have tried to do my homework and to see with both eyes and I am not convinced that your charges are true." She went on to say that my sources were questionable, and that the repression was not as bad as the predicted bloodbath might have been, had it happened. Then she, or whoever wrote the letter for her, was extremely careless, and wrote, "I don't know if we can expect the Vietnamese to turn free those millions of people overnight . . ." Our estimates were much more modest. She hoped I would "reconsider your allegations," as it aligned me with the most narrow and negative elements in our country who continue to believe that death is better than communism. "While I do not agree with your analysis and I worry about the effect of what you are doing, I still look forward to sharing in a dialogue with you. Your iconoclasm intrigues me and I wish we could understand each other more fully." I had to look up "iconoclasm," and now I've forgotten it again. At least she wasn't pious.

A campaign was launched to stop me. I felt as if I were living in a vise. People appeared from my past, "just wanting to talk." They tried everything to get me to stop the letter. I woke up in the middle of the night in cold sweats. The phone rang off the hook with ultimatums and suggestions that I was naive, that Doan Van Toai was a CIA agent, that I was being used by the right wing, that I had lost all judgment.

Ginetta tried to speak with Vietnam's U.N. ambassador in New York. He brushed her off. After weeks of preparation, we were ready to release the letter:

Open Letter to the Socialist Republic of Vietnam

Four years ago, the United States ended its 20-year presence in Vietnam. An anniversary that should be cause for celebration is, instead, a time for grieving.

With tragic irony, the cruelty, violence and oppression practiced by foreign powers in your country for more than a century continue today under the present regime.

Thousands of innocent Vietnamese, many whose only "crimes" are those of conscience, are being arrested, detained and tortured in prisons and re-education camps. Instead of bringing hope and reconciliation to war-torn Vietnam, your government has created a painful nightmare that overshadows significant progress achieved in many areas of Vietnamese society.

Your government stated in February 1977 that some 50,000 people were then incarcerated. Journalists, independent observers and refugees estimate the current number of political prisoners between 150,000 and 200,000.

Whatever the exact figure, the facts form a grim mosaic. Verified reports have appeared in the press around the globe, from *Le Monde* and *The Observer* to the *Washington Post* and *Newsweek*. We have heard the horror stories from the people of Vietnam—from workers and peasants, Catholic nuns and Buddhist priests, from the boat people, the artists and professionals and those who fought alongside the NLF.

• The jails are overflowing with thousands upon thousands of "detainees."

• People disappear and never return.

• People are shipped to re-education centers, fed a starvation diet of stale rice, forced to squat bound wrist to ankle, suffocated in "connex" boxes.

• People are used as human mine detectors, clearing live mine fields with their hands and feet.

For many, life is hell and death is prayed for. Many victims are men, women and children who supported and fought for the causes of reunification and self-determination; those who as pacifists, members of religious groups, or on moral and philosophic grounds opposed the authoritarian policies of Thieu and Ky; artists and intellectuals whose commitment to creative expression is anathema to the totalitarian policies of your government.

Requests by Amnesty International and others for impartial investigations of prison conditions remain unanswered. Families who inquire about husbands, wives, daughters or sons are ignored.

It was an abiding commitment to fundamental principles of human dignity, freedom and self-determination that motivated so many Americans to oppose the government of South Vietnam and our country's participation in the war. It is that same commitment that compels us to speak out against your brutal disregard of human rights. As in the 60s, we raise our voices now so that your people may live.

We appeal to you to end the imprisonment and torture—to allow an international team of neutral observers to inspect your prisons and re-education centers.

We urge you to follow the tenets of the Universal Declaration of Human Rights and the International Covenant for Civil and Political Rights which, as a member of the United Nations, your country is pledged to uphold.

We urge you to reaffirm your stated commitment to the basic

principles of freedom and human dignity . . . to establish real peace in Vietnam.

Joan Baez
President, Humanitas/International Human Rights Committee

CO-SIGNERS:
Ansel Adams
Edward Asner
Albert V. Baez
Joan C. Baez
Peter S. Beagle
Hugo Adam Bedau
Barton J. Bernstein
Daniel Berrigan
Robert Bly
Ken Botto
Kay Boyle
John Brodie
Edmund G. "Pat" Brown
Yvonne Braithwaite Burke
Henry B. Burnette, Jr.
Herb Caen
David Carliner
Cesar Chavez
Richard Pierre Claude
Bert Coffey
Norman Cousins
E. L. Doctorow
Benjamin Dreyfus
Ecumenical Peace Institute Staff
Mimi Farina
Lawrence Ferlinghetti
Douglas A. Fraser
Dr. Lawrence Zelic Freedman
Joe Fury
Allen Ginsberg
Herbert Gold
David B. Goodstein
Sanford Gottlieb
Richard J. Guggenhime
Denis Goulet, Sr.

Bill Graham
Lee Grant
Peter Grosslight
Thomas J. Gumbleton
Terence Hallinan
Francis Heisler
Nat Hentoff
Rev. T. M. Hesburgh, C.J.C.
John T. Hitchcock
Art Hoppe
Dr. Irving L. Horowitz
Henry S. Kaplan, M.D.
R. Scott Kennedy
Roy C. Kepler
Seymour S. Kety
Peter Klotz-Chamberlin
Jeri Laber
Norman Lear
Philip R. Lee, M.D.
Alice Lynd
Staughton Lynd
Bradford Lyttle
Frank Mankiewicz
Bob T. Martin
James A. Michener
Marc Miller
Edward A. Morris
Mike Nichols
Peter Orlovsky
Michael R. Peevey
Geoffrey Cobb Ryan
Ginetta Sagan
Leonard Sagan, M.D.
Charles M. Schultz
Ernest L. Scott
Jack Sheinkman

| | |
|---|---|
| Jerome J. Shestack | Grace Kennan Warnecke |
| Gary Snyder | Lina Wertmuller |
| I. F. Stone | Morris L. West |
| Rose Styron | Dr. Jerome P. Wiesner |
| William Styron | Jamie Wyeth |
| Lily Tomlin | Peter Yarrow |
| Peter H. Voulkos | Charles W. Yost |

We raised $53,000 to have the letter printed in four major newspapers: the *New York Times*, the *Washington Post*, the *Los Angeles Times*, and the *San Francisco Chronicle*. But, before it was printed, I felt that I, too, should meet with the U.N. ambassador. And that's what I was doing singing to the roomful of communists in Los Angeles.

Ginetta and I met with the ambassador and his many aides over tea and cakes and bouquets dotted with hidden microphones. We chatted pleasantly for a while. Then I presented the ambassador with a polite ultimatum: Either Hanoi make a written promise that Amnesty International representatives would be allowed into Vietnam within six months, with free access to go where they chose, or we would print our full-page letter.

The ambassador assured me that I was completely misinformed and misguided. He insisted that human rights in Vietnam were the best in the world. I listened patiently, and then smiled sadly and said that he had done his job, and now I would have to do mine.

The meeting had its light moments. The ambassador conceded that after a revolution there are always, regrettably, a few isolated cases of mistreatment of prisoners; he would be glad to personally look into any we might know about. Ginetta, who is only four-feet-nine, dragged out a small carryall suitcase full of documented cases of prisoners currently detained in Vietnam. She placed it on her lap, unlocked it, and sat practically hidden behind the mountain of grisly evidence, chatting gaily, her huge brown eyes sparkling mischievously. Those eyes, at age sixteen, had seen the violation of her friends and co-workers, and had closed against the dark atrocities performed upon her young self in the cells and dungeons of the fascists. They had known her nakedness and their shining boots, her filth and their morning freshness, her youth and their defiling of it, but in the end, her mind and will and their defeat in the face of it . . . She flopped the suitcase open and revealed a stack of documents which alone would have put the Hanoi government in disgrace. The ambassador composed himself, raised his hand as though to calm a schoolchild, and said that perhaps this was not the right moment. And Ginetta, knowing she had made her point, said, "Oh, of course! You must be so beezy! I weel send dem to you later."

We left the little white house nestled in the orange blossoms and smog and waved our last goodbyes. My head was tight with conflicting thoughts and feelings, my nose clogged with tears wanting to be shed. We flew home, and I went directly to bed with a cold and fever, unable to face the onslaught I knew was coming until I had regained my strength and spirit.

All hell broke loose when the letter was printed.

I was called a CIA rat.

"It's an honor to be called both a CIA rat and a KGB agent," I responded. "I must be doing something right. And if they'd both pay me, I'd be rich."

I was accused of "betraying" the Vietnamese.

"Which Vietnamese?" I asked.

Would I not at least consider the possibility that my facts were wrong?

"I would rather err in intentionally offending government officials anywhere in the world (to whom I would happily apologize later if I have been mistaken) than offend one political prisoner whom I might now conceivably help and whom later I may never be able to reach."

William Kunstler, the noted left-wing lawyer, called my singling out Vietnam a "cruel and wanton act." But he followed that up by saying, "I do not believe in public attacks on socialist countries, even where violations of human rights may occur." At least he was consistent and honest, if, in my opinion, ridiculous.

I much preferred Kunstler's response to that of Dave Dellinger, a well-known pacifist. I agreed with the first part of his statement. "You have to be naive to believe that a Leninist revolution will allow any independent thought. Many Americans were wholly naive about what was coming in Vietnam if 'our' side won. I had no such illusions, although I did not oppose that criminal war any the less. So don't expect me to be shocked now." Why, then, wouldn't he support the condemnation of human rights in Vietnam? "Because, any such statement will be used to try to harm a government not only trying to cope with the enormous problems for which we're responsible, but also a government that is surely going to greatly improve the lives of the Vietnamese."

A full-page ad came out in *The New York Times* modestly entitled "The Truth About Vietnam." It was signed by fifty-six liberal leftists, and accused me of calling thousands of people "prisoners of conscience" without having a "scintilla of documentation. [They are in fact] 400,000 servants of the former barbaric regimes. . . ." The signers assured me and the American public that "Vietnam now enjoys human rights as it has never known in history," and that the people of Vietnam now "receive—without cost—education, medicine, and health care, human rights we in the United States have yet to achieve."

Another public letter was circulated by David McReynolds, Don Luce, Philip Berrigan, and others, taking no particular stand on current human rights violations, but urging reconciliation with Vietnam. I, in fact, supported recognizing the government of Hanoi. Tyranny has certainly not stood in the way of reconciliation before, if reconciliation was to our advantage. In this instance, however, it was not.

The only official response was from Vietnam's observer to the United Nations, Dinh Ba Thi: my charges were "groundless" and constituted "calumnies against the people of Vietnam."

The response from the right wing was, of course, even more obnoxious. William F. Buckley called me and my co-signers "new found humanitarians," but showed enormous generosity in forgiving us our transgressions. "The prodigal son, scripture and reflection teach us, is always welcome, never mind his tardiness or his procrastinations." Governor Reagan mentioned me in glowing terms on his weekly radio broadcast. My position as darling of the right was short-lived, however. It ended when I went to Argentina and Chile to visit the Mothers of the Disappeared in 1981.

There was also a very healthy, moving and reassuring response on the part of many people around the world who regarded the issue without ideological blinders.

And what, if anything, were the effects of the letter within Vietnam?

I have heard that some immediate changes took place. The government of Hanoi responded the way most governments do: it disliked international criticism intensely. Many prisoners were released, and the mystique that had cradled Vietnam was no longer impenetrable. The situation, in 1987, sadly, is still grim.

# 2

# "THE BRAVE WILL GO"

I was on tour on the East Coast in 1979 when Jeanne and I hatched the idea of sending the Seventh Fleet into the South China Sea to pick up boat people.

We went to Washington, D.C. At my request, I was introduced at a cocktail party to the then Undersecretary of the Navy, a soft-spoken man who seemed to have no problem dealing with the fact that I was Joan Baez, antiwar activist.

"What would it take to put the Seventh Fleet into the South China Sea to rescue boat people?"

"Orders from my boss."

"Which one?"

"The President."

"How would one go about getting those orders?"

"Why don't you ask him?"

That evening I spoke with Ginetta in California.

"Why don't you geev a beeg concert for dee boat people on dee White House lawn?"

Well, not the White House lawn, I thought, but perhaps a concert close by, and a candlelight march to the White House.

It took only a few days to plan the concert at the Lincoln Memorial, July 19, 1979, and arrange for permits for a march. I wrote a letter to President Carter, which was delivered to him by hand, explaining that the march was not in any way a protest, but rather a show of support from the American people who would back him in any humanitarian effort he made on behalf of the boat people. I suggested sending the Seventh Fleet out on a rescue mission, and then invited him the concert.

He didn't come, but the concert was attended by ten thousand people. When it ended, we marched to the White House carrying lit candles. We prayed at the gates, then I went back to the hotel. I got to my room just in time to turn on the television and see Jimmy Carter come out on the White House lawn, hoist himself up on the inside of the great iron fence, and announce that he would send the Seventh Fleet into the South China Sea. I called the navy undersecretary to see if it was true, and he said it was, and that the President would call me the next morning at around nine o'clock. He did and we exchanged mutual congratulations.

Later, in October 1979, we returned to Washington, D.C., and with the aid of Eunice Kennedy Shriver organized a fund-raiser. The evening ended up taking place in the twenty-four-hour period that Ted Kennedy was expected to announce his candidacy for president.

We panicked at the thought of our evening for the boat people turning into a Teddy for President rally so I called Chip Carter and asked him to come stand next to me all evening, which he, bless his heart, was kind enough to do. The pictures in the paper the next day were all of Ted, Chip (wearing a Carter for President button), and me. We lost money at the fund-raiser, but created a lot of talk about boat people.

Laos had been invaded by Vietnam, and thousands of people were walking or swimming their way "to freedom." Cambodia was still suffering under the Khmer Rouge, who were thriving in the ruins and chaos the U.S. bombs had left. The Laotian and Cambodian "land people" were not yet considered "news." Jeanne and I decided to go to Southeast Asia and visit Vietnamese, Laotian, and Cambodian refugee camps. Perhaps we could bring attention to their plight.

We flew to Thailand and from Bangkok we took an overnight train, filled with refugee workers, journalists, an television crews to northern Thailand. The press was coming north to the Hmong refugee camp where I would visit and sing a concert the next day. The Hmong were Laotian hilltribe refugees who had escaped into Thailand.

The doors and panels of the sleeper were dark mahogany, and the lighting shone from old fixtures and ancient glass. We squeezed past each other in the hallways, imagining Ingrid Bergman sitting in one of the private Pullmans, smoking and dreaming of Humphrey Bogart. After I'd had enough drinks and still not found a Humphrey Bogart, I retired to the lower bunk of Jeanne's and my cabin, and slept to the rattling and thumping of the oriental mystery train. Waking at dawn, I dressed, left the cabin, and stood in the hallway gazing out at a red sun rising over rice fields already being worked by farmers and oxen. The fields were indescribably calm in the faint morning mist, and I watched the sun turn yellow and then white, and become too bright to look at.

We bounced over the hills in a crowded van, sweaty and hungry, listening to the Thai driver's tape of Joan Baez singing "Kumbaya." He showed me the cover of the cassette. It was a photograph of an oriental girl with long black hair. I supposed she was Thai.

"What's the writing say?" I asked.

"Says, 'Joan Baez Greatest Hits.' "

"You're kidding me!" I said incredulously, wondering who was collecting the royalties.

As we neared the camp we came to a group of people at a crossroads, our own film crew among them. They hailed us over excitedly.

"There's a group of Laotians trying to get to shore. They've just swum across from Laos and the Thai border patrol is threatening to send them back or shoot them."

I asked who was giving orders, and they named some Thai colonel out at the camp. They would go to the river and try to inhibit the border patrol with their cameras.

When we arrived at the camp I asked to see the colonel. He was a short, fat, shiny man who was content in his position and well aware of the scene at the riverbank. He spoke English.

"It must be a wonderful thing to have the power over life and death, as you have at this moment," I ventured after we'd been introduced. I studied his smile and his eyes to see where his vulnerability lay. In his pride, no doubt, I thought.

"What kind of man would you say you are?" I asked him, and he laughed. I answered myself.

"Well, no matter. Whatever kind of man you are on other days, why not be a man of God today and give the lives back to those miserable souls at the river. As you know, they are at your mercy." He laughed again, and asked me if I was really so concerned.

"I am concerned enough to get down on my knees before you and beg for their lives," I said, and promptly knelt in front of him, embarrassing him enormously. His smile disappeared and he leaned over to grab my arm and help me up. A crowd had gathered around us. I wondered why I had been so impulsive, and realized it was because time was short. By now everybody in the group at the river could have drowned.

"Will you be coming to my concert?" I asked. "You must come. When I hear that all those people are safely ashore, I will sing a very special concert, and dedicate a song to you." I reached out for his hand and pumped it heartily. As I walked off, my knees were shaking. I did not know if I had succeeded in my mission, but it was time to leave the colonel alone with what I hoped was his conscience.

I had tea in a hut, and did a lot of press interviews. One of the network TV men said, from behind his humming camera, "You have been accused of getting involved here in order to create publicity for your record sales."

"Is that so?" I responded. You silly ass, I thought. You are out here at the end of nowhere, balancing fifty pounds of machinery on your shoulder, surrounded by enough human interest stories to fill an issue of the *Enquirer*, and you are asking me this stupid question.

"Ah, yes," I said. "I always come to the Laotian border to hawk my albums. Big market up here, especially in the camps."

The camp officials gave me a bright blue linen dress, handwoven, with a beautiful Hmong embroidered design on the bodice. I would wear it in the concert.

Thousands of refugees came to hear and see the big event. They sat in the dust, coiled with excitement, wondering who I was and why I was singing to them. I never knew how I was perceived, and therefore, how I was introduced in places like this. Laotians performed wild dances of great seriousness, their expressions demanding respect from both their own people and the many strangers watching. We were accomplishing what we'd set out to do! We were getting the "land people" of Laos (they were called "land people" as opposed to "boat people") on the evening news, and giving them a good time in the process.

At dusk, we left the camp and stopped at a big house on a hillside to see the two hundred or so wretched souls who had swum the river from Laos. They were in shock, ill, cheerless, and damp. They wandered around in slow motion, or sat staring. Who knows how many had drowned on the way over? But here were some soggy survivors, alive for the moment, their lungs taking in air and pushing it out again. Someone was giving them food, which their stomachs would accept and digest, and then their eyes would close, and the tiny spark of hope, hidden in the ashes of their lives, would begin to glow, fanned mostly by the children, who, the next day, if it didn't rain, would begin to chatter and snoop around and finally laugh at something in their new surroundings. Perhaps the colonel slept well that night.

We met another colonel, this one thin and dark and smooth from the inside out, good-looking, but dangerously slick. We'd gone to a cocktail party in Bangkok to meet him, because he had a helicopter which we needed.

He liked ladies. He pulled down maps in front of a blackboard and pointed. "You want to go there," he said, and we smiled and batted our eyes and said yes, that's where we wanted to go.

"The only way you can reasonably get there is in a helicopter," he told us.

"What would it take to convince you to give us a helicopter for a day?"

He laughed. "You are a very famous singer, no?"

"Yes." A helicopter for a song, just as I thought. I sang him "Swing Low," and he sat there, pleased as punch. I should sing antiwar songs to the bloody Vietnamese, he said. He would get us a helicopter and a pilot to take us to two camps.

First and foremost, I remember the beetle. It was bigger than any beetle I'd ever seen, even in Baghdad, where I was only ten and the beetles looked bigger than Tonka trucks. The one crossing the dirt path in front of us was black and shiny and had horns advancing before him like a Viking helmet. I bent over him and saw the spiky details of his brittle legs, and shivers went up and down my back like snakes. The camp officials gave me a dead one to take with me, and I was delighted, but had to throw it away after a week because it began to stink.

I was tired to the point of fainting, but stayed on my feet and went through the formalities of meeting people, listening to their private horror stories, always wondering what to say when they were finished talking. It was announced, as usual, that I was a famous singer, and that I would perform for them. The children gathered around expectantly while I wracked my brain for a ditty that would amuse and cheer them. "I Love My Rooster" was my most successful rendering. It is filled with animal noises: I love my sheep, *Baaaaa*. I love my cow, *Mooooo*, etc. I felt like an idiot, but managed to get the children smiling, and in the end, tumbling over themselves, grabbing onto each other's elbows for security against the mad foreign lady, giggling in their parakeet voices, their black eyes on me and their attention on my stupid but marvelously entertaining song.

We repeated the routine in the next camp, taping grim and ghastly stories of flights from tyranny, imprisonment, torture, and death. The children were always there defying pain, defying death, defying hopelessness. The children, always ready for a tomorrow, even when all was lost.

In the second camp we got word of Cambodia's hemorrhaging borders. Thousands of people were pouring into Thailand that very evening. They were sick and starving, some of them half-dead. We left the second camp and bartered with the pilot to take us to the Cambodian border. He called his superiors, who said no, but the no did not sound final. We persisted. The pilot continued to protest, but flew toward the border and dropped us off. We managed to get a car to the checkpoint where we were told we could go no further. It was dangerous, they said; Vietnamese soldiers occupying Cambodia were firing rockets toward the border. We nagged, strings were pulled, calls were placed. A lovely man from the State Department who spoke Thai and whom we'd met at a cocktail party went to bat for us. The border police shrugged as we walked past the checkpoint and toward the hills.

The dirt road was suddenly filled with scrambling photographers. Just as suddenly, we could see people all along the side of the road and far into the bushes, lying down and hunkering on stumps. Some were making lean-tos out of bits of cloth, others were cooking something in tin cans over makeshift fireplaces. A boy lying by the roadside caught my eye and I went over to him. He didn't move, though his eyes were open. He was very dark and very thin; his clothes were rags and he was coated with layers of dirt. I squatted down beside him. When I looked up it seemed as if all these people were moving in slow motion. In contrast, the photographers were racing to and fro, hunting for a story. As I watched in dumb shock, two Japanese photographers tripped over each other, chattering like magpies, barely missing stepping on the boy's head. "Son of a bitch!" I shouted and jumped up, ready to physically hurl them away. "Stop! Just stop! Get out of here!" They backed off a few paces, filming me, of course, and I got control of myself. We needed a story of the little boy on the wires, not a story of an impetuous star chasing a Japanese photographer into the bush.

I got up and grabbed Jeanne by the arm. "Who can get this kid to a hospital?" I mumbled frantically.

She singled out a young man who worked for Reuters. He came over, squatted down, smoothed the boy's forehead, went "Tsk, tsk," and picked the boy up in his arms. He walked only a few feet before he was surrounded by Thai soldiers pointing their guns at him and telling him, in Thai, not to go anywhere with the boy.

"This little boy is very sick. I'm taking him to the hospital," was all he said, and without hesitating, he turned around and trudged down the road with his dark and listless cargo. They surrounded him, all shouting at once, but he said he was very sorry, he didn't speak Thai, and kept walking. The little boy watched and listened to the two strange languages being spoken and shouted over his head, and never moved. The soldiers angrily pointed their guns at the renegade and his prize, but gave up in exasperation as he strode away from them. We all kept watching, and the photographers kept taking pictures.

I stood in a ditch chatting into a CBS camera, with my back to the hills and the border and the slow-moving exodus from the "killing fields," the phrase made famous as the title of the film about the fall of Pnom Penh and the ensuing devastation. A rocket exploded nearby. I nearly jumped out of my skin but immediately recovered my composure: sounds of war generally ensure a story on the evening news.

Jeanne was walking toward me, her eyes wide and filled with tears. "There's a baby back there, Joanie. I swear to God it's dying, right there in the mother's arms. Can't we *do* something?"

In fact, the baby was dead, and there was nothing to do.

I put my arm around her as we bumped along in a van in silence to a nearby village, where we went to sit with our film crew, friends, and reporters. In the middle of drinks that were slowly bringing us out of shock, the lovely young man from Reuters popped his head into the bar and announced cheerfully that the little boy was doing fine: he had eaten four meals since his arrival at the hospital.

Back in Bangkok, we ran into a friend on the street.

"You gotta come over to Peter Collins' apartment tonight! There's this guy from *The New York Times* who's been looking for his Cambodian friend for four years, and he's just found him! It's sort of a miracle because we all figured the guy was dead . . . He's been in the jungles for months, living on tree bark and stuff . . ."

I will never forget Sidney Schanberg and Dith Pran, sitting together on a couch in a room filled with press and embassy people. Neither of them talked much. Sidney is shy and Pran kept covering his mouth with his hand because his teeth had rotted badly from malnutrition. We could not know the journey of Pran, nor the agony and guilt of the American who'd left Pnom Penh when his friend could not, nor their joy at this bizarre reunion. We could only sense the profound tenderness of their friendship which had survived the four unspeakable years of the killing fields.

Jeanne and I sat in the beautiful bar of the hotel called Lenox Hotel on the left bank of Paris; sunk way down in overstuffed chairs, drinking vodka tonics and talking about our lives and what we had just witnessed in Southeast Asia. Jeanne had her legs up on the coffee table. She was wearing my old brown leather Ferragamo boots, which I gave her. She'd shined them up so they looked brand-new.

There we sat, still numbed by our experiences in the camps and at the border, discussing what we could do when we got home to continue the work we'd begun with the refugees. I still had a spirited group of people actively trying to keep up with the responses to the open letter: we called ourselves Humanitas. I could tell by the way Jeanne's foot was wagging back and forth that she had something on her mind. We were getting a little drunk.

"How would you like a director for Humanitas?" she asked.

"Huh?"

"How would you like a director for Humanitas?"

"Love one."

Under Jeanne's directorship, and working together with KRON-TV and the *San Francisco Examiner*, Humanitas launched a fund-raiser for Cambodian refugees that raised a million and a quarter dollars in ten weeks over Christmas of 1979. After the first major organizing meeting she hung up her real estate license, and then made two more trips to the camps to oversee the expenditures of the money we'd raised. Every penny went directly into nutrition, food, and medical programs. I know, because she took the money herself, and if she didn't see programs she liked, she created them, like the one for lactating mothers and children under five which we co-sponsored with CARE.

When the campaign was ending, Jeanne's sponsored Vietnamese family arrived in San Francisco.

Janny Thai, her husband, Cuong Huynh, and her brother, Minh Thai, had sold everything they owned and crammed themselves with forty-six other people into a fifty-foot boat which would take them away from Vietnam and into the unknown waters of the South China Sea. With Janny was her eight-year-old son, Tai, who was frail and sick. The night they left he had a fever of 103. They, and the other people in their party, were among the lucky ones who eventually made it to a camp alive. We had met them during our visit and Jeanne had decided to adopt them.

When they arrived in California they stayed with her. For the first few days they huddled under blankets, shivering. No matter how many clothes or blankets we piled on them they could not stop shivering. Jeanne turned the heat up and put extra heaters in their room, but they still shivered. Despite the shivering, Janny's brother had a job within forty-eight hours, and her husband was working within one week at a Chinese restaurant. Soon Janny was working at the local junior college (ESL program) and Tai was a tiny new member of a Sunnyvale elementary school.

Six years later in January of 1986 the family took Jeanne and me out to celebrate their new status as naturalized citizens. Tai is of average height, cute, a good student, combs his hair in a sort of waterfall, speaks Cantonese and English but no Vietnamese, and has changed his name to Andy. He calls me Auntie Joan, and he still remembers the rooster song.

# 3
# "MOTHERHOOD, MUSIC, AND MOOG SYNTHESIZERS"
## 1975–1979

In 1975, with the encouragement of Bernie, at that time my road manager/laughing buddy/ex-lover (also the young man for whom "Love Song to a Stranger" was actually written), I decided to record an album that was decidedly "nonpolitical." In the making of *Where Are You Now, My Son?* I had personally edited fifteen tapes, written one entire side, played the piano, and helped sequence bomb raids and music.

With *Diamonds and Rust* for the first time I became deeply involved with the music for the sake of the music alone, composing and playing the synthesizer. I wrote a little jazz ditty on the guitar, and when the band obviously liked it went home and wrote three verses of words and turned it into a real song, "Children and All That Jazz." I did not fight producer David Kirschenbaum and his suggestions about what would sell and what would not. I made my compromises and relaxed with them. Inevitably a discussion took place about finding "up" songs. You gotta have some "up" songs. "Up" songs are not a part of my musical history and they don't come naturally unless I'm hanging out with someone else's band, having a drink or two, or singing in Spanish. We looked through twenty or thirty "up" songs and the one I disliked the least was "Blue Sky," a pleasant little number, written by Richard Betts of the Allman Brothers Band, that didn't interest me but was not offensive. I had to admit that it rounded out the album very well and that in many ways *Diamonds and Rust* is the best album I've ever made. It eventually went gold.

If I did not want to have a wide, international audience, I would not have had to bother ever making compromises. The fact was then and is now, that I am not willing to accept being on an obscure label with limited distribution. Until recently, that decision kept me out of a record company in the States. Back then I did not know how difficult it would be to survive, as an artist, through changing musical trends. Folk music, on a commercial scale, was now a thing of the past.

I began a decade of taking the only unprescribed drug I've ever used. I *loved* Quaalude, and found that a tiny dose would decrease stagefright and enhance lovemaking. I stopped taking it only when it became impossible to get. I miss it, but am relieved that it is no longer accessible.

Bernie was becoming more and more of an influence on my life, encouraging me to lighten up and have fun and sing for the sake of singing. When I went out on the road in the States with a band he even introduced me to a gorgeous roadie named Carlos. Carlos was a curly-haired Mexican ten years my junior who had skin like silk, big black eyes that would melt a glacier, a way of joking that kept me laughing for days at a time, and stormy mood changes that kept me properly on edge. The tours were successful, all things considered—such as weeping folk purist fans who felt betrayed, politicos who felt dismayed, and new, updated fans who felt I still wasn't loose enough. We recorded *From Every Stage* on tour, and released it in 1976. It was a double album, two sides of acoustic and two sides with band and vocals. It's not a bad album, but it's dotted with embarrassing little statements like "The best way to look at this is . . . that I'm having a vacation. I haven't had a vacation in ten years." In other words, I feel guilty for eating three meals a day, not living in a jail cell, making money in concerts and making love to Carlos.

About this time I began having trouble with my voice. It had never occurred to me that anything could go wrong with my "achingly pure soprano." Now two things were becoming apparent. One, I was no longer a soprano, and, in fact, was having difficulty hitting any high notes at all; and two, I was clearing a constant tickle out of my throat between notes. Assuming I was indestructible, I ignored these problems for the next three years.

On the Rolling Thunder tour in 1976, I wrote a number of songs, the best one being "Gulf Winds," which was what we titled my next, and last, record for A&M. An album of all my songs was, in fact, not terribly exciting, but the cover was beautiful. It was taken in a studio and superimposed on a Santa Monica beach with a Hawaiian sky.

Bernie succeeded in wooing me away from Manny. Manny was, and is, essentially a folk music impresario. I wanted to be updated. Without knowing it, I had begun the race against time and age, and suddenly wanted to be hip and groovy and cool and all the things I had not been in the past. Encouraged by Bernie, who had been right about a lot of things but was wrong about this one, I made the stupidest "career move" of my life, leaving A&M and going to a hotshot little label called Portrait, which was supposed to become a subsidiary of CBS.

I recorded *Blowin' Away*, a good album with a terrible cover. Bernie and I parted ways, to become friends again years later. Nancy, the old friend who eventually traveled with me throughout Europe and the States as business manager, took over. The fact that I had no manager was becoming evident to everyone but me. *Blowin' Away* came out with a picture of me wearing a silver racing-car jacket, World War II flight goggles, and an American flag on my jacket sleeve. It was supposed to be funny but only reflected my state of total confusion about my music and the direction of my life.

In the thirty-ninth year of my life, I decided I needed a vocal coach. Three people recommended the same person, so I trotted down to Ramona Street in Palo Alto, and when I heard a stringy voice struggling up and down the scales, I walked in without knocking. When the pupil with the stringy voice had gone Robert Bernard gave me his total attention.

"What seems to be the problem?"

"My voice is not working right. I'm having trouble with the high notes."

"Do you sing professionally, or just for your own pleasure?"

"I sing professionally."

"Ahh. I see. Well, why don't you fill out this form here . . . what's your name?"

"Joan—"

"Oh, ha ha, Joan what, Sutherland? Ha ha!"

"No, Joan Baez."

"Oh Christ! Oh my God! Oh, how funny! I had no idea!" He turned as red as a tomato and put his hand over his mouth, trying not to laugh out loud. Laughing is terrible for the singing voice.

Maybe that's what makes voice lessons with Mr. Bernard so much fun: all the laughing we're not supposed to do.

As my voice began to come together my relationship with "the industry" began to fall apart. *Blowin' Away* hadn't done very well. I had a horrible evening with an executive from Portrait who was supposed to be a "great, great guy, you'll love him," who insulted me beyond my flimsy levels of tolerance by suggesting that the next album should be written by current writers who could sell. I was not included among them until I suggested myself, and he said, "Oh, sure, one song of yours wouldn't hurt." I went into a long, unyielding rage, hating the big slob from Portrait, who had fat fingers and bad manners.

I simply did not grasp the fact that I was no longer considered a "hot item." I went to Muscle Shoals to record *Honest Lullaby*. I killed myself over that album. Nancy and I went up to Ottawa in fifteen-degrees-below-zero weather so I could pose for a cover photo by Josef Karsh. It was a beauty. The choice of songs was mild, and the album might not have survived the changing times and the coming of heavy metal, but I went on every talk show available to present it. I hated pushing an album, but finally understood that I had to do it, and so I did.

There are varying opinions as to what actually happened to *Honest Lullaby* aside from my belief that Portrait dropped it the day it came out. One theory is that I paid dearly for a fight I'd had with the then-president of CBS records in New York.

I was going to sing in Israel. CBS had booked me into a famous festival, which sounded like a superb idea, until I found out that it was being held in what was at that time occupied territory. As a matter of principle, I cancelled my engagement there and instead sang two sold-out concerts in Tel Aviv and Caesarea, which were picketed by a few people and appreciated by more open-minded Israelis than I thought existed.

In New York, on the way back from Israel, I had called the president of CBS to talk about the record, and mentioned, almost as an aside, that his people (CBS) had tried to book me into occupied territory. He went berserk. What did I mean, "occupied territory"? That land had always belonged to the Jews and he would fight to the death to keep that land from the fucking Arabs who were going to push him into the sea.

"Don't you mean the Hudson?" I said stiffly.

One of us hung up, probably him. I didn't stop to think that I no longer had enough leverage to talk like that to a company president and also keep my job, though it wouldn't have made any difference.

It was around that time that I began the painful and humiliating process of discovering, ever so slowly, that though I might be timeless in the world of music, at least in the United States I was no longer *timely*.

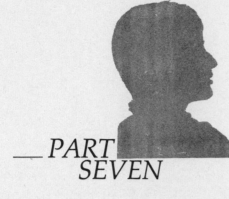

_PART_
_SEVEN_

# "Ripping Along Toward Toward Middle Age"

# 1

# "A TEST OF TIME"

There is a line in the 1966 movie *Morgan* when the psychotic and endearing hero says, in a mournful apology to the colorfully nutty woman he loves, "You are the only thing that lives up to my fantasies."

I first saw Marlon Brando in person during the civil rights march on Washington, in 1963. He was standing about twenty feet away, surrounded by newsmen and stargazers; I was barefoot, leaning against a pillar on the Capitol steps, wearing a purple dress. I tried to see his face clearly, hoping he would glance over just once and look straight into my eyes. As he evaporated into the crowd my heart pounded so hard my body shook.

When I was thirteen my seventh grade art teacher took me to see the movie *Julius Caesar*. On the screen a young punk with a bent nose strode back and forth saying, "Friends, Romans, countrymen, lend me youreahs . . ." while Elvira Teresa Pulombo, my art teacher, clutched the armrests and moaned. I didn't understand her reaction to him. He did have fierce eyes. And he did have a beautiful chest. We got to see his chest at the beginning of the film before he entered the Roman cabinet and began wearing robes. I teased Miss Pulombo all the way home.

It must have been two years later that someone took me to see a double bill of *Streetcar Named Desire* and *On the Waterfront*. Shortly after, I saw *The Wild One*. Goodbye world. I was struck by blue lightning. There he was, the magnificent dark horse who was a winner, the punk, the hurt child, the rebel. The most appealing man I'd ever seen. A veritable sex extravaganza, tough and tender, granite and satin; on top of that he seemed to be able to act, or else he was so loaded with charisma that one was left with the impression that he was an incredible actor. To this day, I don't know which is nearer to the truth. It doesn't matter.

I was hurled into my first totally consuming movie crush. I had hot flashes. I moped and daydreamed. I fantasized and prayed that he would come riding by on a motorcycle and be swept off his feet by the sight of my long black hair, brown skin, and limpid, knowing eyes. He'd want to take me somewhere. Anywhere. And when we got there, at the end of a long and thrilling ride, my hair all tangled and my face flushed, Marlon Brando would kiss me. In my fantasies, over and over, tenderly and passionately, he'd kiss me. On the beach he'd kiss me. Under the elms and oaks he'd kiss me. In the desert at sunset he'd kiss me. We kissed my way through seven periods of school a day, through three hours of homework a night, through the dishes and whatever chores I could do alone. I called a reluctant halt to it all at mealtime so that my family would not suspect my secret. This love was for real, and it was mine.

In those fantasies I wore beaded Indian garb of soft deerhide adorned with tassels, thongs, and feathers. The tassels, thongs, and feathers were ingeniously placed so as to hide my hopelessly flat chest, and the whole outfit cleverly ended somewhere in the middle of my thighs, giving full exposure to my thin but basically good-looking bronze legs. We never went any further than just kissing. (In the middle fifties there were still many others like myself who, at the age of fifteen, were still virgins, or very nearly virgins. "Very nearly virgins" meant that, in an uncontrollable state of passion and confusion, in the back seat of a raked Mercury or the like, preferably on tuck and roll upholstery, we had abandoned our precious maidenheads to the steady hand of some senior who had "plenty of experience," but understood that sexual intercourse, referred to as "going all the way," was out of the question, at least for the time being. Maybe next summer.)

My phantom Marlon understood all this, and was content simply to run through scenario after scenario of drawn-out plots and wild motorcycle rides, always culminating in the same old kiss. In spite of the drop in my school grades and body weight, this affair was much simpler than having to suffer through a real relationship with some tedious adolescent whose pimples and inadequacies I had once found easy enough to accept but which were now at best annoying, and at worst positively revolting. All local heroes paled in the blinding shimmer of Marlon.

This passion lasted a couple of months, and was rekindled to a fiery glow with each fresh viewing of a Brando movie, whether a new one, a repeat of a new one, or an old rerun. He was the king. When I was eighteen, I sneaked off with my mother to see *The Young Lions*, where, over our melting bonbons, we confessed to each other that we had shared the same crush for years. My father made wisecracks about the slight retreat of Marlon's hairline, but his attempts to slander my idol affected me not at all. I saw *The Young Lions* four times, mainly to gaze at the silvery blond peak which nestled at the back of Marlon's neck.

Sometime late in the sixties I finally met Marlon Brando under the legitimate guise of raising money for some cause. When I stepped up to his front door to greet him, he handed me a gardenia. I see the white gardenia now through a wistful, fragrant haze. I can say that he was a gentleman, and that he was funny. He seemed a little weary of everything, a little sad, though he told me that he was happy. We shared stories about crazy people we'd met as a result of being the object of other people's fantasies. Though he was aging somewhat it was not difficult to match up his eyes with the eyes of the young lion, the wild one, and all of my phantoms. Time was a veil. My memories of that meeting are as heavily laden with pathos as the gardenia was with its heavenly perfume.

Someone once said that meeting other celebrities was for the most part like ships dipping their prows to each other as they pass. I have found it so. But some phantoms seem to linger for a lifetime, and through many veils.

Recently I went with a friend to see *On the Waterfront* for the fifth or sixth time. It was billed with *The Wild One*. *The Wild One* was already on. Back through the veils I tore like the wind, back to adolescence and my phantom. During the close-ups I moaned audibly, and was joined by a chorus of other women. I hooted obscenities at Johnnie's persecutors and waited for his smile in the closing scene as he speeds off into nowhere on his bike, the camera pulls back and the ancient reel flickers to a halt. The audience clapped and cheered and felt they knew each other. Then I sank into a reverent trance as the crackling old grey, black and white print rolled for the millionth time. *On The Waterfront*. And there I sat for an hour and a half, victimized by the magic happening before my eyes, tears pouring bountifully and shamelessly down to my chin and onto my coat.

Bring infinity down to me one more time. Make it tangible. Put it in my hand, or hold it up before my eyes. Make it an emerald necklace, or make it an old classic starring Marlon Brando.

A month after seeing *On the Waterfront* that last time, I saw Marlon Brando again in person. The occasion was a benefit concert held in a stadium filled with over sixty thousand people. The day was grey, windy, cold, and verging on rain. Marlon was there to make a pitch for money for the American Indians. I heard his voice from the muddy campsite that served as a backstage, a vaguely familiar nasal tone issuing with a gusto and force that could well have been a matured version of Mark Antony's "Lend me youreahs." Curiosity overcame me and I headed for the stage. He was talking emotionally about giving to the cause. He would give five thousand dollars; if you couldn't give money, then give your spirit. I saw the back of his head. His hair was long, white and combed back. He was saying things about nonviolence and brotherhood, and smoothing his hair back with cupped fingers. When he finished his speech he raised his arms in the air, fists clenched in the "Power to the People" sign. There was a great roar and thunder from the audience, as sixty thousand people screamed and yelled. Marlon walked off into a crowd of waiting press and groupies. There was a tiny break in the crowd clinging to him, and I saw his face. It was pale, tired and dignified. It was old. The veils were gone. The astonishing thing was that he seemed so pale, almost transparent; I had remembered him as dark. He was wearing a light blue Mexican shirt and an open jacket, nondescript pants and black cowboys boots, and he was over-weight. I was still drawn to him as though he were a lifelong friend whom I hadn't seen in years. It was more than that: he seemed to be my blood brother. Or perhaps I was his mother right then. Those thoughts were in my mind as he caught my eye, and I was smiling because I knew I would get to hug him. He smiled back and pro-ceeded toward me, Moses parting the seas, as the people moved away and let him be. I embraced him, and felt as if we'd been through a dozen wars together. He told me I was looking great, and asked me what was keeping me young, was it my brain, or what? I told him it was my brain and embraced him again. He was damn fat, but it didn't seem to matter. I wanted to tell him how much he'd meant to me over the last twenty years. I wanted to see his sweet smile. I wanted to say something ridiculous to make him laugh. I heard the emcee introduce me, and went out into the wind to face the microphones and sixty thousand screaming and yelling people.

After my set I broke through the lines and was with Marlon again.

I looked at him carefully as we shouted to each other over the noise of the rock group which was now on stage. Veils fluttered past. I saw the lines at the corners of his mouth, the tiny straight teeth, the eyes I'd gazed into a thousand times in big theaters and small theaters and even once in person. We were standing in wreaths of time. We were encased in years. We were talking all the while about the crowd, about the causes, about this and that. It was impossible to complete a thought because we couldn't hear each other. I wanted to ask him why he'd decided to get old so early. I wanted to ask him how he felt, how his life was and had been, who he thought he was now, and if he was happy. Marlon may have been a ghost of the former screen hero, but he was dignified and even a little wise. Marlon was like an old lion. He was still king of the jungle.

I don't give up a lifelong love very easily. I leaned toward him and talked in his ear. I told him that he'd been a big part of my life, and that I often dreamed about him, though sometimes he didn't show up, even in the dreams. I thanked him for everything he'd been to me. He looked confused, a little distant, as though he didn't really understand me. The day was so loud, and so cold and confusing, and now I saw that we were surrounded by photographers, so I just smiled at him. I was full of love. Perhaps people don't thank old lions enough for having given away their entire youth to a million eyes they will never see.

# 2

# "RECENTLY I WAS IN FRANCE"

On Bastille Day, July 14, 1983, the president of France stands at the foot of the Obélisque in the Place de la Concorde and reviews his troups. He will salute from a huge wooden platform erected by the city. Permission has been granted to leave the platform up so that I can sing a free concert on July 15. It will be a concert dedicated to nonviolent struggle.

I am in a flurry of excitement. We must have radio ads, posters, television spots, and gossip to create "an event."

I leave France for a tour of Germany and take my stomachache with me. What if I give a concert at the foot of the Obélisque and nobody comes? Me, alone on a big wooden platform with as many police as spectators. Ugh. Marie Antoinette was executed there also.

In Würzburg, I hear from Paris. There is trouble from a ministry. Sorry, Madame Baez. There is no police permit. Without a police permit there can be no concert.

Voilà la France.

I have offended someone. Perhaps the minister of culture by refusing his invitation to sing at the official Bastille Day celebration; perhaps his wife by deciding not to sing a song she taped for me.

I call the Ministry of Culture.

*"Je suis désolée, Madame Baez, mais nous n'avons pas la permission de la Préfecture de Police."* I'm sorry, Madame Baez, but we have no permission from the police.

Perhaps it is the fault of my French promoter, who curses at officials over the phone. Nothing I can say will stop her.

The days go by. I am on tour. Each morning I hope the call will come from France saying the concert is set. Until then there can be no publicity. We are pulling every string I ever had in Paris to get the police permit.

I need a rest after Germany.

I go to Canisy, to my beloved castle in Normandy. Well, it's not actually *my* castle. It's been in the young count's family for 800 years. He just lets me *feel* it's mine. He is away. There is only one week left and no permit. All the police will be tired from working on Bastille Day. Two thousand police would have to be brought in from the provinces.

Six days left.

I wander around in another century, picking wildflowers, riding horses, and dreaming.

Five days.

I call Madame Mitterrand, the wife of the president of France. She is a friend.

She has just left for the country, her secretary says. In broken French I explain my dilemma to the secretary: Madame is the only chance I have left, I say (and it is true).

I hang up and look dismally at the royal red curtains of the seventeenth-century room. They mock my impotence. Madame will never get my message. I give up the whole bloody effort and go lie on the lawn of the little house where the guardians of the castle live, and pick daisies and blow a kiss to my beloved stable boy, Cher Ami.

Cher Ami climbed onto a horse when he was eight years old and, holding on around the huge warm neck, flew like the wind at the edge of time, hearing only the barrel echoing gulps and pounding hoofbeats, and feeling only mane and tears on his face. He slept in the snow with his dog when he was ten, and left his heart in the forest when he went home, to work and eat in silence. Before he was Mon Cher Ami, he was Mon Sauvage. He still traps poisonous snakes and talks to them as he frees them in the tall grass by the lake. To hell with the ministries. I will lie here and listen to the humming of the bees. And tonight, when the castle sleeps, I will put a fur coat over my nightgown and walk in the moonlight with Cher Ami. He will wait for me in the long grass between the lakes. We will go to his loft over the horses, and I'll lie with my head in the turn of his neck and my nose against his fine jawbone and downy cheek, and I'll smell the hay and the wheat dust. Who needs Paris and stomach cramps?

A smile spreads across my face as I watch a hundred suns dancing in the slate panels of the castle roof.

Here comes Cher Ami with his sleeves rolled up over Heathcliff arms.

"*Téléphone, Madame Baez.*"

"*Pour moi, Cher Ami? Qui ça?*"

"*Le président de la République de la France,*" he mocks, but through his long hair I see his father waving excitedly from a window in the stone house.

"*Ha!*" he shouts. "*C'est pour toi! C'est François! Oui! Il a dit François! Ooo, la la!*" and the leathery imp grins at me with one tooth missing. He has the beautiful eyes of his son, only they are blue, and set in creases. He winks and hands me the phone from the wooden box.

"*Halloo?*"

"*Bonjour, Joan Baez?*"

"*Oui, c'est moi-même.*"

"*C'est François ici.*"

"*François qui?*"

This must be a joke.

"*François Mitterrand, le président.*" And he begins to talk, but my mind has flown out the window. What on earth is he telling me?

"*C'est à dire, calmez-vous, tranquillisez-vous.*" He is telling me to relax and not worry. When an intellectual talks to me in French, I can understand one half, on a good day. I think he is telling me that the concert is on.

Now he is inviting me to lunch at the Palace. For Wednesday. That much I understand.

I can't ask him to explain about the concert again, so I thank him enormously and hang up, wondering if the concert is on for this year or next.

My promoter screams. "I don beleeve eet! *EE* call you direct? You are keeding! Zat eez rrreally somesing!"

"But I don't really understand what he said."

"I weel find out eef ze police has our permit." Click, she hangs up.

Jangle.

"Zee police, zay don know nossing. I'm going cghrazy. Zay says no show."

I go to my room and take a bubble bath. There are clumps of weightless flies trapped in the light on the ceiling, high above the tub. I'll put on something pretty and go visit the old countess in her house across from the stables. While we drink champagne I'll tell her my miseries and make silhouette designs with my riding boots on the tile floor.

She is in her sixties. A doctor, a conservative, and, of course, an aristocrat. She has no use for this sloppy bunch of Socialists who run the government now. When she was young the Germans occupied the castle and used it to house the inmates of the local insane asylum, which had been bombed into rubble.

"In the full moon you would see them jumping from the windows." She points toward my room. "They were completely mad, of course."

We eat dinner together in the castle kitchen, enveloped in the dank smell of centuries and of cobwebbed wine bottles.

I walk the ancient hallways past lingering shadows and gloomy paintings. They usually make me laugh. The ugly lady in the white wig with a bird perched on her useless white hand smells cheese and watches me over her bird. I stick my tongue out at her. It has been a disappointing day, as I am now sure that the concert will be next year. I gaze out my window at the lake below. The swans glide miraculously, like two white feathers.

My room is a mess. I must pack for Paris and lunch at the Elysée. A dejected face stares at me from the bathroom mirror. There are footsteps in the hall.

It's the countess, hurrying along in her jodhpurs. *Swish, swish.*

"Joanie! It's for you! Someone is saying that the concert is on!"

"Who?"

"I don't know." She puffs, out of breath in my doorway, her hair sticking out in red wisps. "Some frrrrightful little man from one of the ministries."

Back we go through the endless, echoing corridors, back in disbelief. I sigh and take the phone one more time in my clammy hands. Yes, the man says, the police got their orders and we will have a permit.

I can't help myself. I say, "Oh, I wonder who gave the orders . . ."

"Oh!" he says, "they came from very high up."

"Yes, I imagine so." I gloat. I am happy. I am more than happy. I am giddy.

• • •

Cher Ami drives me into Paris for lunch at the Palace. He hates Paris, but has memorized the route from the castle to the Hôtel Raphael.

I take a shower, but the sweat comes back in little dots on my nose and forehead from the heat and the approaching lunch with the president. There is a smudge on my linen slacks and the only belt I brought doesn't match my high heels.

That morning Cher Ami and I raced horses on the beach at dawn. Then we pranced them into the waves to cool their steaming flanks. I wore my purple Indian full skirt which blackened and doubled in weight when the white water rushed up to claim it. But that was the other me.

Across the gravel and up the grand steps I go. I've been here before, and I know the man with the plasterboard shirtfront and the gold keychain around his neck. Leading with a white-gloved hand he smiles me to the waiting parlor. I am left alone with day ghosts and tapestries until the penguins come to lead me through hallways to the fireplace room.

The first time I saw this room was when I had tea with the conservative president. There were just the two of us, and he sat so far across the room I could barely hear him.

The first time I visited the Mitterrands, the same room was filled with family, and dogs lolling and scratching cozily on the rug.

This time there is only the Official Family Friend, and he chats with me until Monsieur and Madame arrive. When they are announced we stand up and I go right to Madame and hug her. Thank you so much for coming to my aid, I say, from memory. How do you do, M. le Président? Forgive me on the phone, but I was afraid I would forget the formal tense, you see, and use the familiar and cause a big scandal. M. le Président smiles just a little.

We all sit down. The room fills with television cameras and more white gloves bring drinks on a silver tray. I have a gin and tonic, forget about the smudge on my slacks and talk about Gandhi.

The president is polite. He is a soldier, he tells me.

Yes, I know, I tell him. So am I.

Danielle is smiling, but she always smiles. She is a pixie.

What about the black curtain? I ask.

Yes, you will have your black curtain.

I understand the police will not allow the design of a broken gun on the curtain . . .

Madame intercedes. No, really, my husband cannot allow that.

"The day after Bastille Day!" he reprimands me. I smile. There's no harm in trying.

The cameras go away but the formality remains.

I love the whiteness of the dining room and the exquisite bouquet of pastel flowers in the center of the huge table. Danielle is a mile away, the president on my left, and the Family Friend on my right. There's nobody else today except the translator.

The president tells stories and Madame leans on her elbows and gazes across the table at him. Her fingers push dents into her cheeks and sometimes cup together around her nose. She catches herself and shakes her head back abruptly. She asks him a question. I think she is in love with him.

The president asks me if I dream in French. Yes, I say, when I am in France. He likes me but doesn't know what to say to me. He is a cultured intellectual. I am a cultured gypsy.

Coffee in the fireplace room.

I sing one song for the president because he will not be at the concert. He looks pleased, and his wife smiles like a little girl, pleased that he is pleased.

On the way out I kiss both of them on both cheeks. The penguin with the keys ushers me to a desk and asks, please, would I autograph an album for him. I do. Then I kiss him, too.

That night I go on national TV. They show the fireplace room and ask me what I talked about to the president.

"Gandhi," I say.

The president goes on the other channel. Among the many questions a head of state is asked before a national holiday, they ask him what we talked about at our lunch.

"Gandhi," he says. "Joan Baez is a serious artist and a serious fighter."

The next day Cher Ami and I walk the Champs Elysées. I am relieved when the ice-cream vendor says, *"Vous êtes Joan Bezz, n'est-ce pas?"* and tells her friend that I am singing at the Place de la Concorde the following night.

The fourteenth of July. Early in the morning, the city rumbles with tanks. Cher Ami and I peer out of the hotel window in disbelief.

The fifteenth of July. I have terrible stomach cramps. Only five thousand people will come to the concert, I am sure. There was nothing in any of the papers.

Cher Ami laughs at me and bets there will be more than fifty thousand. He helps me to the bathroom, where I lie on the tile floor and soak in the coolness, but the cramps stay. I take a pain pill.

Fritz and José have flown in from Germany. They come to see me, but I am pale and half-dressed and have a blue hot water bottle on my stomach. They are German men and don't know what to say, so they leave and go to check the stage. I call the countess at the hospital where she works. She comes immediately with her squeaky bag.

"Oh, my poor Joanie. But of course, you must be ex-*trrreme*-ly nervous," she says, putting her hand on my forehead.

"I'm not nervous. I'm petrified. I have only five hours left."

She checks my appendix and then gives me a pill. She has been looking at my wrinkled slip, and suddenly sees it in a different way. Her eyes flick around the room. I can see the image of Cher Ami in the mirror of her thoughts. She never knew before today; she suspected, but she never knew.

"He has another room, Brigitte," I tell her.

"Yes, of course," she says, and calls him in and scolds him what to do.

"*Oui, madame, oui, madame,*" he says, stubbing out his cigarette. She will check me in two hours, and tells me to take another pill if the pain persists.

Cher Ami walks me in and out of the bathroom. I lie back down on the tiles, and take another pill.

The nausea begins to fade. Cher Ami hints that the floor is too cold, and helps me to the bed like a hospital orderly. We speak only French.

"How can you love me when I look like an apple witch, pale as a potato?"

"I will love you when your teeth are all gone and you have only three hairs left on your head."

I begin to laugh.

"Like my grandmother, who sleeps with her mouth open and lets the flies buzz in." I laugh some more.

"Her head is empty now. When the wind blows in one ear leaves come out the other."

He slides down next to me and holds me. Feeling a tiny bit better, I listen to his heart beating back my hysteria, not to reason, but to sleep.

We drive to the monument at seven o'clock. There are already five thousand people there, sitting as close to the stage as possible.

The concert will be at nine. I shut my eyes and let out a whole chest of air through a whistle mouth.

Moving slowly from the pills I go up to test the microphone.
*Tap, Tap.*

A curious policeman, called to work from vacation in another province, ambles up to watch. I am ashamed when some kids jeer.

*"Ne sois pas bête!"* I say. "Don't be stupid! The police are here on their day off, three sweaty hours in a bus in the middle of summer, not by choice like you. And the concert is for them also." Later I sign their hats. Lots and lots of police hats.

People are coming in a steady flow from every street and sidewalk. They sit noisily or quietly and make a bobbing ocean around the monument. The moon is two thirds of a silver coin suspended at the blue edge of an orange sunset. The Arc de Triomphe, where I bicycled with my father when I was ten, in the mad circle of honks and angry elbows, is still in full sunlight, three kilometers away, quiet as a mouse, posted at the orange end.

I sit in a trailer trying to tune my guitar, but keep jumping up to look out the plastic door at the rivers of people: Japanese, German, American, English, Scandinavian, East Indian, Italian, and many others, who will soon be a family singing a joyous grace, and I will be America's answer to Edith Piaf. I am already halfway transplanted onto French soil, not a sparrow, but a mockingbird, which can, if you please, imitate all the languages of the birds. The evening will be a glorious song of the birds.

The moon rises into a darkening sky. Lights sparkle on the route to the Arc de Triomphe and my songs bounce from rooftop balconies and dissipate in the air.

There are no "incidents" with the police. Instead, the police listen and even clap. I sing songs to Gandhi, Martin Luther King, the Women on Greenham Common, the Mothers of the Disappeared, and even to the president of France for abolishing the death penalty.

I put on my white wings and fly up over the crowd, and when I look down, everything is shimmering on earth. I watch tens of thousands of people standing up to sing the encores. They are full of hope. Hope is contagious, like laughter. I see hope and song and laughter from my wings in the night sky.

Back at the hotel in the glow of success, I hold Cher Ami in my arms. He worked hard today. And he won his bet. The crowd estimate was one hundred and twenty thousand. I'll settle for an even hundred.

All the tiny muscle knots in Cher Ami's body are twitching as sleep undoes them, but there is no chance of sleep for me.

I go over to the ornate window and open the huge velvet curtains and tie them back with the fat gold braid and faded tassels. On the couch I prop up three pillows for my head and a fourth for my knees, and lie down deliciously in my good old crumpled slip to watch the streetlit leaves outside my window shudder in the night breeze, whispering for my attention against the grey building across the street. I sink into images of effortless thought, or unthought, while a thousand dawns yank me back with a jump, over and over again. Each time I come back I'm smiling, ecstatic to be awake for the first peep of the birds rising from the grey streets of Paris.

Marie Flore comes over in the late morning with her white skin and huge brown eyes, wearing scarves and gauze over her tiny frame, an undersized Titania in last summer's gown. Marie Flore was a small girl of ten whom I met in the south of France fifteen years ago. I am in a dream, staring at the wall and smiling. Marie Flore and Cher Ami and I sit in the morning sunlight, holding cups of steaming café au lait, framed by the massive red drapes.

We pack slowly and order croissants and strawberries and crème fraîche.

Today is free.

Absolutely free.

Cher Ami is driving us to the castle, but there is no rush. It is afternoon when we tumble giggling out into the hall.

"I could have danced all night," I sing suddenly in a high soprano, twirling down the hallway of the fourth floor, dropping my bags along the way. "And still have begged for more." My voice flutters in an arch on the word "for." Now we are at the top of the stairs. Two maids poke their heads out of the linen room and watch and cluck, and then just smile and lean. After all, I can do just about anything I want today.

I spin in a circle at the top of the banister.

"I could have spread my wings and done a thousand things." I am halfway down the first flight, with Marie Flore and Cher Ami just behind. And on I go, nodding and bowing to the guests at their doors, all the way to the main floor. In a run and a leap I am at the reception desk for the finale. "I could have dahnced, dahnced, dahnced . . . All night!" One hand is in the air and the other wrapped around the brass banister post, as I lean out into an imagined crowd of passers-by.

The two people at reception clap. We pay our bill. And I start the song all over again because there is a huge bouquet of flowers at the end of the elegant hallway, and it needs singing to. And after that there is the street, and I don't stop until I have danced through the hairdressers next door and patted all the wet rats on their heads, and kissed all the homosexuals standing with their scissors in the air.

Outside it is a gorgeous day and we collapse in laughter on the curbside, my head flopping into Cher Ami's lap.

"I'm sorry about the nasty experience you had, Ms. Antoinette," I say to Marie Flore. "Personally, I had the time of my life at the Obélisque!"

# 3
# "HOW BRIGHTLY GLOWS THE PAST"

At New Year's of 1985 I went to my first reunion, the twenty-fifth anniversary of people who had performed at Club 47, a three-night celebration of concerts held at Boston's Symphony Hall. I had not intended to go, but Mimi encouraged me, reminding me that after all, I was the first folksinger to have sung at Club 47, and somewhat the mother of it all. As flattery will get you anywhere, at the last minute I packed up and flew with her.

It was a well organized, cleverly promoted production put on by Tom Rush, folksinger gone to market, that included some new groups which had never seen the inside of Club 47, and a great number of oldies like myself, Mimi, Eric Von Schmidt, members of the Jim Kweskin Jug Band (including Maria Muldaur), the Charles River Valley Boys, Keith and Rooney, Jackie Washington, and others of bluegrass and pure-folk fame. I watched the show from the stage, which was smartly set up with tables and chairs and looked quite homey. Manny was there at a table nearest the performers, like a grandpa at a birthday party. This was his city, his venue, and his music, and these were his people.

I hung out in the dressing room and met people I hadn't seen for ten and even twenty years. For the most part we were well preserved.

Betsy Siggins, who was going prematurely grey a few years back, was now as white as a snowbank. She had found herself at last by running a soup kitchen in New York City which feeds two hundred and fifty people a day.

Eric Von Schmidt, artist, painter, musician. His hair and beard, which had been bushy and red, were now like silver and black silk, and the upper left missing tooth had been replaced with shining gold. Since the smile seldom left his face, the impression I had was all of sparkling: eyes, hair, teeth, and soul.

Dear Goodie had gained some weight which made his face quite round, and the dimples in his cheeks into great canyons. He lives with Dorothy, makes films for public television, and spends time in the fast lane—he traveled with Jesse Jackson when he was on the campaign trail.

Billy B. is a set designer now, and had made the big sign which said "Club 47" and hung as a backdrop for the stage. As I had suspected, he had barely changed, his hair thick in tight curls and his cut-glass eyes just as blue. I didn't feel any of the old wild attraction, however . . . maybe because his answering machine says, "Hello, you have reached the home of Billy and Sue Burke."

And there was Cooke, skinny as ever, looking like a Wells Fargo bank teller from the early 1900s, complete with moustache, vest, black hat and all. "Well," he toasted at New Year's Eve dinner, "I'd better say it now before I drink too much and get all sloppy, how much I love all of you . . ." Cooke had just finished a novel, and he said that it's hundreds of pages long and he can't really explain it.

Jim Rooney drank a lot and was the funniest person there. I hadn't known him very well in the old days, and now he's gained a lot of weight, too, and lives in Nashville and still plays the guitar left-handed, that is to say, upside down and backwards.

Fritz plays jug, washboard, and washtub, among other things, has a humor dry as an old oak log, and at dinner ordered the twenty-one-dollar lobster dinner and sucked clean every leg, claw, and elbow.

"Surfer Bob" Siggins, a research biochemist transplanted from M.I.T. to San Diego, banjo picker, and pedal steel whiz, had the tiniest, friendliest wrinkles around his eyes, and an aura of lightness to his thinning hair and eyelashes, as though he had tinted everything except his California bronze face.

Urban hillbillies, all. I hadn't realized before that this group of folkies had been the family I had not been able to develop in high school. They were my first second family, gathered during the years of my love affair with Michael and Harvard Square. And they were all still singing. Perhaps that's what impressed me most of all: loud, soft, onstage and off, solo, duet, trio, chorus, fifties rock, sixties country and western and ballads and folk, hymns; all of us sang—right-wingers, liberals, pacifists, reformed druggies, yuppies, and upwardly mobile guitar pickers; we all still sang.

The last night ended with Tom Rush leading us in a ragtime number. Then we all shifted around to different microphones, for a totally unrehearsed version of "Amazing Grace." I sought out Mimi and Maria, and Cooke got just back of us so he and I could lead in the verses. Everyone came forward from the tables onstage, and the smiles were dazzling. I hugged one of the "new guys," not remembering exactly who he was. Geoff Muldaur ushered his kids on with us. I put one arm around Mimi and the other around Maria. Maria, born-again Christian, more or less, looking like Mary Magdalene, San Francisco Mabel Joy, a white Tina Turner: flashy in hand-me-down clothes—flaming yellow chamois overblouse, punk belt, black skirt, and Ferragamo heels; cheeks ablaze with the love of Jesus and fire-engine-red blush-on; her huge black eyes rimmed with natural lashes so long and manicured they looked like dime store acquisitions; and underneath it all, always the look, the tiniest look of a hungry match girl who's just been slapped for gazing too long at a window display of dresses and fine shoes.

> Amazing Grace, how sweet the sound
> That saved a wretch like me.
> I once was lost, but now I'm found,
> Was blind, but now I see.

How we all sang. I thought Maria would leave the ground, Cooke sounded like the bass in the Sons of the Pioneers, and Mimi and I dared not look at each other for fear of stopping to think about this bizarre angel band, and how gorgeous it was, how like a Baptist church choir. After "Amazing Grace" came "Wasn't It a Mighty Storm?," which inspired dancing, swaying, rocking, and more harmony. The audience loved it and was hollering for more, but the time was 11:28 p.m. and overtime started at 11:30 p.m., so we rallied in the dressing room, where the atmosphere rapidly became like that of the winning team's locker room at the Cotton Bowl.

A party was being thrown at the Copley where I had the great fortune to find the best dance partner I've had since some pint-sized

Venezuelan swept me off my feet in a discotheque in Paris over fifteen years ago. I was ecstatic and could easily have danced all night. Unfortunately, we were in Boston and the music had to stop at two o'clock, and I was so disappointed I could have cried, right there in my inside-out black Joan Baez T-shirt, pushed-up sweatpants and sneakers, gasping for breath and steaming like a country fresh cow pie.

Something else stands out in my mind about that reunion, involving an entire separate story that resolved itself on that special New Year's.

Mimi and I don't see each other too much now, at least not the way we did when her husband, Dick, was alive. She was still my "little sister" then. After he died, Mimi's life had to begin all over again at age twenty-one, only this time built on her own foundation. She hadn't even known how to drive a car.

She'd left the nest at eighteen to marry Richard Farina, and in his exuberant way he'd been happy to make all of his own decisions and most of hers—about everything. He was killed on her twenty-first birthday, and for years she seemed on the brink of suicide and lived enshrouded in loneliness and sorrow. She told me that on her first night completely alone in her own apartment, she woke up from a dream screaming for help, and continued screaming and banging on the floor with her shoe until the tenant below came rushing up.

I remember her second marriage, held during the Big Sur Folk Festival. She was exotically beautiful, and fragile as Tiffany glass. Mylan was sweet, and the sight of his Abe Lincoln frame and long shocks of shining black hair, all dressed in velvet, and Mimi with a ring of daisies around her head, in a lawn-length white wedding dress, inspired the words to the first song I ever wrote, called "Sweet Sir Galahad."

Mimi and Mylan lived up on Telegraph Hill in a wonderful lopsided apartment which has since been torn down. Mimi began to see a therapist and dig deep down into the fabric of her undiscovered self. She learned to drive. She worked with the Committee, the famous San Francisco satire group, and since she didn't have much of an identity outside of Dick and me, and then Mylan, she began to create one. She and Mylan divorced after three years on reasonably good terms, and she called herself Mimi Farina.

Mimi had been a dancer when she was young. A natural, it's called, when someone is born with her kind of grace and precision. We all thought that she would want to "be a dancer." Perhaps it was after she saw the ease with which I became "famous," and after she had tasted stardom on stage with Dick, and after she understood that to be a prima ballerina meant a kind of dedication she did not have, in a milieu she really didn't like that much . . . and perhaps also because she is a good musician, Mimi chose what I thought was the most difficult of all paths possible: she chose to sing and accompany herself on the guitar. She chose the path which would doom her forever to a lifelong fight to be introduced as Mimi Farina, and not as "Joan Baez's sister" or "Wife of the late Richard Farina."

We put more distance between us when I got married, for though David liked Mimi, he was much too involved with our work (and, perhaps, so was I) to do much hanging out, and I was spending a great deal of time being the world's most fastidious housewife. When Gabe was born, I thought Mimi had turned into a shrew.

Looking back, I think Mimi's behavior is not hard to explain. I was infatuated with Gabe, an average spoiled child who could elicit coos and whoopies from me at the utterance of a syllable, and Mimi, feeling jilted, and never having been a mother, was jealous and disgusted. Many years later, she told me of an afternoon at her house when Gabe and I were visiting, and Gabe, in diapers, was twirling around in the middle of her living room rug holding a hard-boiled egg. She was trying to carry on a conversation with me, and I was gazing at my miraculous child, spinning so cleverly in circles, when he let the egg fall onto the rug and stepped on it. He was gleeful, and catching his spirit, I gushed, "Isn't he cute?" Mimi kept quiet at the moment, but later said she didn't know who she wanted to shoot first, him or me.

At that point, also, the imperious habits I'd acquired from my inheritance of "Queen of Folk" and, as David referred to it, "Ms. World Peace," were becoming less and less tolerable to her. Granted, I was known for being a benevolent and good queen, for taking risks, giving away money, caring for the poor, going to jail for my beliefs, and sacrificing my career for more meaningful things. But nonetheless, I had become accustomed to special treatment and had developed some unconscious habits which I still retain and recognize only if someone gently points them out to me.

We didn't have much to say to each other for some time. When we talked, the conversation was stilted, guarded, or simply fake. She seemed to be always angry, and I'm sure I just went on doing what I've been accused of doing more than once—namely, telling stories about myself. Then one day in the late seventies it dawned on us that we had not even a remnant of the close and special relationship we'd had for so many years, and we decided, mutually, to get together for lunch and "talk." We were both late, and later on, confessed that we had both taken a Valium just to be able to face each other.

What I remember most about that lunch was that Mimi had no idea of her own strength and growth. When I suggested that she had often hurt my feelings, she thought I was bluffing or lying. She still saw me as powerful and untouchable, and herself as powerless and insignificant. There were lots of teary moments and righteous assertions as to who was right and who was wrong, and not much was settled, but it was an honest effort, and the beginning of the long road back to a close and honest friendship.

Since then, we've worked hard to stay close. We've had some successes and some near misses. Mimi runs Bread & Roses, a wonderful dreamchild of her own making, an organization which takes entertainment into hospitals, prisons, old people's homes, and other institutions. She and the organization are well known and highly respected in the Bay Area, and other Bread & Roses groups have started up all around the country, largely due to the talent and persistence of Mimi and the hard work of her staff. She still sings for a living, and like all of us, has had to scale everything down because of the lack of demand for our particular kind of music. She still hasn't let go of Dick, and when she goes out on tour, she calls up to say goodbye and usually gets the flu or a cold, or something.

The morning before the day we were to fly east for the Club 47 reunion, she developed a full-fledged head cold. She was beautiful, sad, funny, resigned, and ill. I felt like a mom and wanted to take good care of her so she'd feel as good as possible when she got up on stage at Symphony Hall. We stayed at the Airport Hilton, and I wished that I had no money problems at all so I could just order up special rooms and valet parking and limousines, like the old days. But the bellman recognized us and let us park close to the room, and we had fun sharing accommodations, Mimi stoking up with aspirin and Actifed. Upgraded to ambassador class, we enjoyed a luxurious flight across the country, and were put up at the Copley Plaza in Boston, treated by Tom Rush to the plane fare and two lovely bedrooms and a huge sitting room.

I watched Mimi's body draw swords against her work. The day of her performance, she woke up barely able to speak, head and nose clogged, chest constricted, voice tiny. She had a slight fever. Her eighteen-minute set would consist of two songs alone, one with Maria Muldaur, and one with me. I went off to do my part at the children's concert, a benefit for Ethiopian refugees. (I hate singing for children. Everybody thinks I can be Pete Seeger and amuse any age group for hours, and I can't.) "I Love My Rooster" saved my hide once again. I also had "Whatcha Gonna Do with the Baby-o?" in which you poke out the baby's eyes and throw him against the wall and scrape him off, and kids just love to hear that song.

Back at the hotel, Maria was telling Mimi that there wasn't time to practice their song. I watched Maria standing in Mimi's bathroom doorway, animatedly talking about pasta and weight and how Mimi ought to wear clothes that showed off her tiny waist, and Mimi trying to listen and put her eye shadow on at the same time, but was mainly preoccupied about her songs. Maria went on about Italian food, and I uttered a quick prayer to St. Jude to help us through the evening.

What I didn't notice was that although Mimi was congested and weary and petrified, she was solid as a green tree and outwardly calm. She and Maria did rehearse in the dressing room co-ed lavatory. Maria kept forgetting the words and when someone accused her of being nervous, she said, "But I *never* get nervous! The only time I get Mimi is when I sing with nervous!" We all howled, but I realized that, of course, she was scared, too. At the last minute the order of the program was changed, and Mimi was put after Buskin and Batteau, two young men who make lots of jokes and sing strong lively music, accompanying themselves on piano, guitar, and violin, and who are known for doing a rousing set.

"They're on before me," said Mimi regretfully. "And it's not fair."

I was so nervous I went out onstage to watch them perform while Mimi paced quietly and gracefully back and forth in the excited crowd gathering in the wings as the show neared its finale. She continued going over her songs and plunking the guitar. Buskin and Batteau were playing "The Boy with the Violin," a gorgeous ballad filled with rich violin breaks between each verse, about a lady taking a boy in and sleeping with him and waking in the morning to find the window open and only his footprints left in the dew. There was tumultuous applause when they finished, and my stomach was in knots. Anyone hated to go on after a well received, boisterous set. I ducked out the stage door and took Mimi by the wrist.

"Put it in the hands of God," I said.

"I just did," said Mimi.

She strode out steadily in black silk pants and a brilliant blue-green silk top over a black turtleneck, looking stunningly beautiful. The applause died down and she began to talk. I don't know what I was expecting, but she seemed so fine and commanding. She made a few jokes and the audience responded with light laughter. Then she sang her first song, "Old Woman," which she wrote about old folks: "Oh, Grandmama, is it true what they say? / The river of life keeps on flowing, while time will take us away . . ." Her voice was strong and pure and steady. The next song was a capella, with the audience snapping their fingers in rhythm. It went flawlessly.

Hunkering in the dark, I began to relax and allow myself to feel total admiration for my little sister, when suddenly she was saying, "There is someone missing from this stage tonight," and I didn't know who she was going to name—Tom Jans, her singing partner for years who died as a result of internal injuries from a car wreck? Steve Goodman, the brave little guy who wrote "The City of New Orleans," and who fought leukemia for half of his short lifetime and had recently succumbed? Or one of the sixties souls like Janis Joplin or Geno Foreman?

". . . and that's Richard Farina. He belongs up here with us. And, in fact, the chances are he's not too far away . . ." I found my shoulders shaking softly, with the thousand memories her unexpected mention of Dick conjured up, and with awe that she was saying the name of her sacred person, right there in Symphony Hall, in front of thousands of people. Some of them may have been strangers to Dick, but, by the sound of the applause, many of them were admirers as well. Maria was invited out, and they sang one of the most beautiful duets I've ever heard. It was a capella, and their powerful and true folk voices braided around each other, soaring and plummeting, sustaining words which Dick had written to "The Quiet Joys of Brotherhood." I couldn't get my eyes to dry up through the whole song, and I knew that these ladies were doing something most extraordinary. They were healing wounds. They were telling us something about women survivors.

Surely it was those of us on the inner circle who were the most moved, but who would have expected Geoff Muldaur, Maria's ex-husband, who had always been distant and, I thought, slightly hostile for the many years I'd known him, to say, in the dressing room when we all piled backstage after the finale, "That fucking 'Quiet Joys,' man, just saved me five years of therapy. I mean, I wasn't just spilling a few little tears, I was . . ." and he clutched his throat and mocked a rack of sobs. I had never seen him really smile before, so I went over and said, "Can I have my hug now? I've waited twenty-five years," and he gave me a hug. Goodie was all flushed and going on about the finale and "Amazing Grace" and in the middle of a sentence, said, "And then there was Mimi—Good Christ!" and the tears streamed from his eyes while he turned to hug her. I just kept smiling and marvelling at my sturdy little sister who had knocked us all off our feet. All of us alive are survivors, but how many of us transcend survival?

# 4
# "THALIA'S GHOST"

My sister Pauline says at forty-seven she's lived only one half of her time, and wants the other half to spend in her herb garden. She lives deep in a valley of barking hill dogs and dust-covered crickets. She rarely leaves her sacred hollow, where she is protected from the ravages of TV and newsprint.

What I want to tell you, Pauline, is simple. It is that I love you. You have a special place in my heart, and you just stay there, as you just stay in your valley.

From our childhoods together, we were as different as any two people could be. You don't want anything to do with my world of travel and exposure. And I am mystified by your life of seclusion.

I am in awe of how you build your houses and grow your herbs and sew beautiful clothes. I am in awe of the fact that you've actually *lived* with somebody for twenty years. I love the little girl that you and Peyton had, who is not so little anymore, but is as beautiful as her name, Pearl. And I love your handsome son, who lives on the Lower East Side in New York and wears punk makeup and tartan kilts and is as shy as you. But did you know he held my coat for me, and also walked on the outside when I took him and his girlfriend to dinner in some hip and groovy art deco restaurant in the city?

I know you from the things you have made for me. The quilt from sixteen years ago—royal purple corduroy bordering bright velour patches, a most luxurious gift. It was topped only by the robe. One year I gave you all my unused embroidered Spanish scarves, over-used silk blouses, old velvet jackets, costly pendants, beaded purses, rhinestone belts and tasseled stoles and asked you to make me a robe. You made a glorious, rich, bejewelled, hooded extravaganza which I wear to the opera and to masked balls, where it is coveted by everyone.

The last time I visited you I was in a tizzy over Gabe and had a stomachache, and you made me cup after cup of fresh mint tea, even coming down the ladder from your and Peyton's bedroom at 3:00 a.m. when you heard me up, to chat with me in whispers, and offer comforting hopes about child-rearing. You showed me your sewing nook, filled with mountain knickknacks and lavender sachets. Your eyes filled up at almost everything. Your arms flailed out of soft homemade shirtsleeves. I saw your muscles, big as apples, bobbing, a groove forming at the lower ridge each time you flexed. I noticed your perfect teeth and watched your shining hazel eyes, tearing and drying, tearing and drying. You used to be my white sister. Now I see you are my squaw sister. I hope you have found peace in the valley.

# 5
# "HONEST LULLABY"

The outstanding feeling was utter aloneness—not a self-pitying aloneness, but an acute awareness that today, on parents' weekend, at the St. Mark's varsity football game, I was ridiculously out of place.

David and I had flown back, separately of course, to Gabe's prep school in a tiny town outside of Boston. We were on good enough terms that at my request David had for the most part taken over Gabe's upbringing. Gabe needed a firm male hand upon his twelve-year-old, pre-adolescent shoulder, and perhaps occasionally upon his rump, someone who related to grades and sports. Most of all, Gabe needed a family, and David and his wife, Lacey, could provide that. There was a new baby sister on the way. I had begun, again, to attempt to let go of my son.

I had thought that just being at the game, in the rain, adding my body to the tiny group of parents cheering from the bleachers, was the right thing to do. Someday Gabe will tell me if it was an embarrassment to have his mother standing under her enormous green and white borrowed St. Mark's umbrella trying to shout "Go Blue!" at the right time. Or if it was an embarrassment to have his father, three feet away from me, under his borrowed red and white umbrella, groaning at fumbled passes, mumbling plays to the coach, bellowing "STICK 'EM, GABE!" at predictable intervals, and bustling down to the end zone as St. Mark's struggled to break through the line of a team superior in strength, height, and skill.

I had raced around the campus with Gabe's girlfriend, Lisa, a sweet, elegantly dressed blond upperclassman with milk-white skin and thin ankles, to find an umbrella for David. The most important item on the day's agenda, I thought as an ex-wife, was David's attendance at the game, and the weather was simply dismal.

In the middle of the second quarter I slogged over to the field, wearing my red cowboy boots, two-toned from the wet grass, a neutral corduroy skirt, a white guaranteed-to-wrinkle collar peeping out above a pullover, and an oversize blue jean jacket, hoping I looked an appropriate mixture of a preppy and outdoorsy mother. The umbrella was big enough to protect five people. When I arrived at the game site, St. Mark's had scored one touchdown, but within the last few minutes they had begun to be trounced by the visiting team. The crowd was sparse, with only the most devoted or dogged parents and friends actually out on the bleachers. The others, in their low heels and Burberrys, stood fifty yards from the end zone on the dry library veranda. David was up in the bleachers holding a crumpled blue plastic clothing bag over his head and shouting "GO DEE!" I decided to be patient and it would be revealed to me who "Dee" was. It never was.

"David! Where's your umbrella? Lisa was bringing it to you."

"Oh," he said, his eyes never leaving the pack of muddy bodies thudding and crunching ferociously into each other on the sopping field. Only in retrospect do I realize that he would have preferred I weren't there. I was angry at Lisa, who suddenly wasn't good enough for my son, and tried to share my gigantic umbrella with David. The bleachers were soaking, so everyone had to stand. David is six foot three and made no effort to shrink down and share the umbrella, and holding it must have seemed too cozy, because he never offered.

Out on the field the boys looked like warring earthworms flushed out by the rain, wearing blue and red nose cones.

"Which one's Gabe?" I ventured.

"Number eighty-five. GO BLUE! C'MON, HIT 'EM LOW, HIT 'EM LOW!"

I scanned the sidelines. Number eighty-five was distinguishable by his very white pants and lightly smudged jersey. There was a nice muddy splotch on his graceful-looking rump.

"Does that muddy rear end mean Gabe has played a little?" I asked David.

"No, huh-uh. That's just from warm-ups."

"Oh," I said, and thought, Dear God, let Gabe play just a little. Let him knock the wind out of somebody bigger than him and let him get covered in mud. David was groaning so I assumed that St. Mark's was not performing well. I decided to concentrate and figure out what was happening on the field.

There was an important play going on because everybody on the sidelines was getting louder, and David was beside himself with frustration and excitement, shouting out plays, punching the air with one fist and holding his crumpled blue clothing bag steady with the other. Lisa arrived with the red and white umbrella. David was pleased and dropped the tarp on the soaking bleachers. If I stood nearer than three feet the points of our borrowed St. Mark's umbrellas bumped into each other. I thought that David was using his a little bit like a barbecue fork; I moved away.

Gabe's roommate, Stefan, arrived, bareheaded and dressed in a fashion statement of wrinkled black tie-dyed pants, shirt, and neck scarf. In deference to parents' weekend, he had no snake or cross hanging from his left earlobe, and had shaved off his goatee. He and Lisa and I stood under the green and white umbrella. He found Gabe in the lineup.

"Too clean. His pants are too white," he said.

"Shush. He hasn't played yet."

"I know. Maybe he could throw himself in the mud and roll around while we wait."

I loved Stefan for feeling the way I did about football. He, too, could love Gabe and be his friend and still think football was barbaric.

"There he goes," said Stefan, and I saw Gabe run onto the field.

How can I explain the feelings of this pacifist mother? I love my son more than anything or anyone else on earth. I have no interest in football, and yet was so proud of him that I could have burst. He'd never been aggressive, and now, at fifteen, six feet tall, sweet, bright, languid, hopelessly good-looking, he might decide never to lift a finger again because everything came to him so easily: friends, opportunities, girls by the score, compliments, admiration. Now, for the first time, he was going to war against his own passivity. Football made him move fast, lunge at people, possibly hurt someone, and certainly hurt himself. Gabe had just tackled a guy bigger than himself, and when the big guy wrestled him to his feet and threw Gabe off, Gabe kept ahold of his jersey, clutching it in exasperation, as I would have clutched my sister's blouse during a fight, and he almost brought the boy back down. I wondered if that was fair play or not. I wondered if Gabe would ever get mad enough to really clobber someone on the field. Or off. I remembered a Steig cartoon of a Brooklyn mom hanging out the window witnessing her little boy in a fist fight with a bully. She's shouting, "Get 'em, Johnnie, smash 'em, give him one in the nose!" I understood her now.

Storm was wandering over to our little group. She, like Stefan, was a member of the "artistic community" of St. Mark's. Her feet were plunged into huge, damp men's loafers, and her hands were plunged into the pockets of an oversize, very hip, ugly coat. Her blondish hair was mostly on one side of her head, and all around the ear on the other side the skin was gooseflesh where it had been shaved. She had a black rubber spider hanging from one ear and a pearly bauble from the other. Storm wore her problems on her punked-out sleeve, and many hurts on her big pretty face. She was the daughter of the coach.

"Where's Gabe?" she asked, stepping up to us.

"He's actually been playing," I said, and we all looked out at the warring earthworms and listened to the crunching of helmet and shoulderpad.

"Ooooo, ick, yuck! This is a horrible game! I mean, I don't see the point of it, and all that horrible banging and bone breaking. God, I don't see why anyone bothers!" She saw David look over and said, "Ooooops."

Gabe was out again, this time looking a lot muddier and more banged-up, thank God. The sky was no lighter, but the rain was turning to mist and the benches were drying. Gabe turned around, looking over our heads at the sky. I saw his handsome blue eyes, serious under his broad brows, in a studied frown which said, Fuckin' weather, boy, has it screwed up our game. But what it said to me was, I wonder what my dad thinks of my game, and just as I was about to busy myself talking to Stefan, lest Gabe look down at the bleachers, I saw him catch his dad's eye, and in that instant the ferocious look of agitation and concern was transformed into a resplendent smile. I have just sat at the typewriter for ten minutes trying to think of how to describe all that I saw in that smile which was returned in a mirror image by David. Pride, pleasure, the love that boys find impossible to profess to their fathers.

I had only a three-quarter view of David's face, but I knew his smile, as broad and shameless and proud as his son's. This is it, Gabe, it said. Life is about survival, and you are learning how to survive. It's got nothing much to do with football, but you are doing a fine, fine job today, and you're gonna be all right. And Gabe's said, Look, Dad, I got my uniform muddy, and isn't it all a little foolish, but I am having fun and I know you love me and everything's really quite grand, isn't it, in spite of the rain? When they could no longer contain their glee, the smiles expanded to the bursting point, and at the same exact second they chuckled their identical silent chuckles.

St. Mark's lost miserably, but none of us cared. His dad was first out on the field, camera in hand. He buried Gabe in a hug, and the two of them stood there, shifting from one foot to the other in the mud, going over plays, I imagined. Gabe took off his helmet and posed with his dad and Lisa and then with me and his dad, and when we were through his dad got two more, just of Gabe, close up, wearing the ridiculous giant-size shoulderpads which raised his jersey up so high that it looked as if his head might disappear down the neckhole. Stick 'em, Gabe. You're all right.

# 6

# "A HEARTFELT LINE OR TWO"

Six week concert tour, 1985. Madison, Wisconsin. There is not a great deal of excitement when I pull up in a van with Mary, my tour manager, and Cesar, my accompanist. We have come from Chicago, a three-hour drive. In Chicago, the hotel is the Four Seasons, and courtesy of an assistant manager in the Four Seasons Canada, I've been given a tasteful pale blue suite overlooking lakes and cathedrals, bird's-eye level with a sky full of March clouds. The suite is five hundred dollars a night, and I'm paying one hundred and ten, or I would be down the hall in a modest single room. We have filled the rooms with flowers from last night's concert: pink tulips, a basket of daffodils, bright pink azaleas, and a mixed bouquet next to my stuffed duck on the table at the entrance (and a card from my mother with a blue iris on black painted by Jan Brueghel). I have decided to make these rooms my home, rather than a "stopover." A stopover means no flowers, no view, medium to ugly decor, Styrofoam drinking cups, a tiny bathroom, and not enough floor space to do exercises.

The night we got in to Chicago, I said a little prayer of thanks for the accommodations, and then took a shower and hung up some clothes. Then I put some "space music" on my tiny Sony and settled into the half-lotus position to review the events of the day, and to clear my head for tomorrow. After a few minutes of sitting, my body automatically begins a yoga practice which continues anywhere from fifteen to forty minutes. I go into a state of meditation and prayer, stillness and attentiveness, small thanks and small requests. I re-open negotiations for an attempt to discover my purpose on this earth.

Like any meditation, sometimes it is calm and sometimes rattled. I think about where I have been. I've done two New York concerts and one at Boston Symphony Hall. I've seen my son, gone out dancing till three in the morning, spent the next day in the park throwing Frisbees. I've met my father in Boston, my sweet father who has just returned from India and who has started reading the Bhagavad-Gita. He was moved that I closed the concert with "Let Us Break Bread Together on Our Knees," and said, "That is what you are here for, honey," meaning that spirituality has a great deal to do with my calling. What comes up to the surface of my soul is love and gratitude for my son and father, and tears over the fresh memory of them: Gabe sitting casually in his multi-colored Grateful Dead T-shirt at an after-concert dinner; and my father, two nights later in Boston, with his thick greying hair and dark face, talking about how we are both growing . . .

Concert day in Madison, Wisconsin: Wet snow coming down on a grey, grey day; coffee at ten-thirty with Mary, and an unexpected Jason Robards film on HBO about a dying grandfather and his daughter and her son. Then exercises on the bike, more stretching, a shower, a long vocal practice, a room service hamburger split with Mary, and time to restring the guitar. One of the three false nails I have glued on to play the guitar chips off and the beauty salon in the hotel schedules me in to glue it back on. Mary has ironed my clothes: a black silk skirt, black top and striking Saint Laurent scarf, red cowboy boots. My carry-on bag is full of apples, granola bars, makeup, tape recorder, extra guitar strings, extra socks, a book on Central America, a Guy de Maupassant paperback of short stories in French, and a small French dictionary, earmuffs, and choco-lates.

The van picked us up at one-thirty. Cesar had a cold. The trip to Madison was uneventful. There was no one to greet us when we arrived at the hall at four-thirty, so we followed the signs pointing to "dressing rooms" and ended up in the corridors beneath the old theater. Mary put down the clothing and bags; I put down the guitar and sat on the case and pulled out a copy of *Vogue* to find the Ralph Lauren and Calvin Klein ads. The promoters found us and I was lodged in the same dressing room I had been in eighteen months ago and had no recollection of at all. The stage people were pleasant and helpful, the sound reasonable to good, the atmosphere cozy. There was my stool, the guitar stand, one mike for voice and one for guitar. The piano was also miked. I work with two monitors, Cesar with one. In a good hall with intelligent sound people, sound check takes fifteen minutes. I went into the orchestra pit for a live interview on the local news. They plugged me into remote control, and I had an upbeat interview.

The introduction was quite flattering, all about how I had been around fighting against the war in Vietnam in the sixties, and had always used my music to further political causes. The anchorwoman finished by saying that my latest activity was visiting and bringing to the public eye the plight of the Argentinian mothers whose children had disappeared (a four-year-old story).

It felt fine being a part of the sixties and I'm glad to be out of them and busy trying to find ways to get people to face the realities of the eighties. I have, in fact, been singing a lot over the past seven or eight years, but mostly in Europe.

Why so much time in Europe?

Because I have a broader audience there, and, quite simply, I have gotten spoiled by it, and now it is time to come home and get serious about my work in the U.S.

How does my son feel about my history?

My history is now his history. In fact, he recently told me I was in his history book. I told him I hoped I was portrayed fairly.

Out of all my accomplishments, what one thing could you say you are most proud of?

My son.

I go over to the two people from the student press. The man is deadly serious and takes notes. Madison is a sanctuary town, he tells me. I am delighted. And his newspaper was very outspoken against the war in the seventies. I'd never heard that before. We talk about hope versus optimism, about the swing of the pendulum, about new patriotism, about "the movement." I tell him the word "optimism" is used to distort the facts in a dangerous and volatile world. The word "hope" seems somehow more modest and less myopic. The pendulum, I venture, had swung off the graph and is still swinging, and therefore it is difficult to do anything but adjust to the shock waves and convulsions it is leaving in its wake. It has brought "new patriotism"—a hysterical response to insulted national pride, either created or intensified by the war in Vietnam. I tell him I like the expression "in movement," which describes the people and groups which are continuing to organize against armaments, nuclear and otherwise, and who concern themselves with oppression, hunger, torture, and all wars. And how difficult it is to define "a movement" during a time when there is no cohesive element keeping us together. And that there have to be new and inventive recruiting methods developed in the 1980s to woo kids away from their career-oriented computer-dominated lives into anything that has a social purpose.

The hall was big and old and lovely, and I couldn't help wondering how many of the brown velvet seats would be filled in two and a half hours when the show started. I wandered backstage and munched on the raw vegetables and dips that were requested in the contract. At this juncture, my mood depends almost entirely on whether or not I feel that I have a purpose in life. If the hall is filled and there is excitement in the air, of course, it is easier to feel confident and needed. If the hall is only two-thirds filled, my work is much more difficult.

Tonight is somewhere in between. I have absolutely no anxiety or stage fright. I wonder vaguely who will be out there, and I realize I'd better have a talk with myself. Having a quiet contemplative time before a show is something I started many years ago, only then I did it in order to reduce the size of my ego. To combat the fear that I would lose contact with the order of things, and with the size of me, I would sit quietly by myself and ask for guidance, and ask that the time I spent onstage be spent for the betterment of humankind, in the service of God. Now I go through the same ritual, only the circumstances are reversed. I must remind myself that I *do* count and that there is a reason that I was given these vocal cords. I remind myself that everyone in that hall counts, and that my job is to move them, to treat them with tenderness and extreme care. My job is to sing my heart out, as though it were my last concert on the face of the earth, because it might be, for all I know, and they must leave the hall having laughed, cried, sung, and found out something new or had a timid suspicion confirmed.

So there in Madison, Wisconsin, over a tray of raw broccoli and dip, I come to terms with myself, my audience, and whatever brown velvet seats will be left empty. Mary comes by and offers me a beer which I accept, and we decide that I won't bother changing into my stage clothes. Instead, I'll wear what I have on: a corduroy skirt, plaid shirt, red boots, and bright red leather necktie. I am happy. The audience has more young people in it than usual, and I look forward to informality.

As eight o'clock nears, I am anxious to go out and get started. There is a pleasant buzzing in the hall, and I think the audience will be responsive, which means I will have a good time.

Cesar and I go on at 8:10. The front row is right under my feet, and filled with the refreshing sight of young people. The head usher is in a state because two young women have lost their seats to a group of enthusiasts, two of whom have obviously seated themselves illegally. I love a little distraction, and I horse around with the two front rows hoping things will straighten themselves out. They don't, and I see that the usher is not going to stop pointing and asking to see tickets, and so I invite the two young women up onto the stage. They are thrilled, the usher is speechless, and the audience is delighted. I nod at Cesar, and we start. The first song is "Please Come to Boston," with "Madison" substituted for "Denver" in the second verse.

Who the hell are these kids? I wonder. What a break for me. The house is over eighty percent full, and I have a bunch of lively fans up front. There is an appreciative response to the first song, and then I chat a little, about how this is my twenty-sixth year of giving concerts, and how the next two hours will be traversing those years with some old songs and some new. I tell them that I will spend part of the evening trying to help them forget about the problems of the world, and the other part trying to get them to remember. They laugh. And just when they are wishing I'd quit talking and sing something they came to hear, I do "Farewell, Angelina." This audience is not sophisticated. Their reaction time is not especially fast. But they are not dumb. And I don't hold anything back from them just because they are not New York City. After "Farewell, Angelina" comes a song with words I stole from Emma Lazarus's poem on the Statue of Liberty, and from the Bible. The song became part of the score for the film *Sacco and Vanzetti*. I dedicate it to the refugees from El Salvador and Guatemala, and to the Sanctuary movement, the churches and people who harbor, feed, clothe, and hide the refugees until it is safe for them to return home where most of them want to be.

> Give to me your tired and your poor,
> Your huddled masses longing to breathe free,

The wretched refuse of your teeming shore,
Send these the homeless, tempest tossed to me.

Blessed are the persecuted,
And blessed are the pure in heart,
Blessed are the merciful,
And blessed are the ones who mourn.

The step is hard that tears away the roots,
And says goodbye to friends and family.
The fathers and the mothers weep,
The children cannot comprehend.
But when there is a promised land
The brave will go and others follow.
The beauty of the human spirit
Is the will to try our dreams.
And so the masses teemed across the ocean
To a land of peace and hope,
But no one heard a voice or saw a face
As they were tumbled onto shore,
And no one heard the echo of the phrase,
"I lift my lamp beside the golden door."

I feel the expectation in the audience. There is a great thirst for something that has meaning. So I sing "There But For Fortune," a Phil Ochs song from the sixties about compassion. The response tells me there are old-timers in the audience. With the overwhelming enthusiasm of the front rows, which are the only rows I can really see, it's difficult to tell who is out there. It doesn't matter. I joke around and tell stories and make them laugh and then sing "Children of the Eighties" for the young people:

We're the children of the eighties and haven't we grown?
We're tender as a lotus and tougher than stone,
And the age of our innocence is somewhere in the
garden . . .

We like the music of the sixties
We think that era must have been nifty,
The Rolling Stones, the Beatles, and the Doors,
Flower children, Woodstock, and the war,

Dirty scandals, cover-ups, and more,
Ah, but it's getting harder to deceive us,
We don't care if Dylan's gone to Jesus.
Jimi Hendrix is playing on.
We know Janis Joplin was The Rose,
And we also know that that's the way it goes,
With all the stuff that she put in her arm,
We're not alarmed . . .

We are the children of the eighties . . .

The evening has developed its own rhythm. I am not working. I am just singing and chatting. It passes through my mind that what I will remember of Madison is that the seats are brown velvet and there were two women on the stage and two full rows of young fans.

I am overdosing them on material I've written in the last five years, but they seem eager to be trusted. "Moscow on Hollywood Boulevard," about Natasha and Volodya, two Russian children who have lived their short lives preparing for the Olympics, and what dreams they have when they find out that the Olympics will be held in California. I see Natasha as I am singing. I made her up, of course. She's like Nadia Comaneci, only blond, and not as skinny. Volodya is a little taller than Natasha, and his hair is straight. I always see them in line to get a hot dog, whispering in Russian, pointing out T-shirts and little flags and plaster of paris bric-a-brac. And I think of the great dark mystery that is Russia, and the wealth of brilliance, talent, intellect, humor, satire, that continuously bustles in her underground networks, dodging the shadows of the KGB, and I wonder if the face of that land wouldn't burst into profusions of color and art and gaiety if the politburo crumbled and the tunnels opened into the sun. As I sing tonight, I think of my Russian immigrant friends who are to the right of Reagan, Jeane Kirkpatrick, Nixon, Kissinger, and Attila the Hun. They are the boldest people I've ever met, and I love them, but I despise their patronizing attitude toward me because I think that torture in El Salvador and the circumstances which have brought it about in this decade are as destructive as Soviet expansionism.

There is my stool, with its water glass, and my songs scribbled out on a piece of yellow crumpled paper. How familiar. How very simple. I have a sip of water and introduce "Warriors of the Sun," a song of images which came to my head a few years ago while I was listening to the taped speeches of Martin Luther King. I tell the audience that this song is to encourage people who might have become discouraged in the 1980s—and, by the way, if anyone has not gotten a little discouraged, then they are cuckoo. They listen intently. I try to keep it light. We are dealing with the survival of the planet, and I think the human race is faring badly at the moment. I criticize the current American elixir called "feeling good about myself," which is totally egocentric and shallow. I take a few potshots at the Reagan administration's "myopic optimism," mentioning that the world is in a state of moral and spiritual decay and on the verge of terminating itself, and it does not seem like the appropriate time to encourage a false sense of invulnerability and optimism. And I urge the people not to give up their hopes and dreams; admittedly, I may be off my rocker, but I have held onto mine and it has been worth the effort.

We are the warriors of the sun.
We're fighting post-war battles that somehow never got won.
May be crazy, and it may be the final run,
But, we are the warriors of the sun.

The concert is gliding along, so my daydreams can glide as well. Maybe I *am* crazy, and maybe this *is* the final run. It probably is, in fact. How foolish to think that we can clean up the air and the water and the barrels of waste, and bring back the creatures we have made extinct. In fact, how pompous to think that in this great universe that we would be the only earth! And perhaps one or two of them, or even one or two thousand, are rolling around the heavens doing quite nicely because their form of animal life didn't evolve into our kind of greedy race. I wish I could see farther back into the room.

If it's true 'bout no more water but the fire next time,
Will the children of the eighties be ashes or live to their prime?
If we don't heed the Nobel laureates warning of things to come
We'll all be incinerated warriors of the sun.

I ask for requests. There is a chorus of "Joe Hill"'s, "Diamonds and Rust"'s, "Forever Young"'s; a smattering of old ballads, and few pleas for songs I've long forgotten, or ones impossible to sing without a band. I do "Forever Young." Then I introduce a song I learned off of an Odetta album when I was sixteen years old, telling about the time I sang it to Martin Luther King, and how ten years later, I sang it from the balcony of the Hoa Binh hotel in Hanoi during a bomb raid. I am trying to tell them something about fear and faith, and, in a joking way, about courage. I sing "Oh, Freedom," and it gets the strongest response so far. This song soars, makes real use of the voice, and sometimes, like tonight, my spirit soars with it.

The first half of the concert ends with a silly introduction and "Long Black Veil." In the chorus of "Long Black Veil," my finger misses the string in the same place twice in a row. What a nuisance. The same chord and finger pattern will come up again at the end of the song. If I concentrate, I will make sense of it. I take everyone in the entire room into my heart, and put my tiny problem into God's hands. It seems a very small favor to be making a special request of God. My fingers find their place. The song ends, the crowd applauds vigorously and happily, and I go off the stage for the many hundredth intermission of my life.

Madison was an average concert in the U.S. in 1985. There were other concerts where I had only to fly with the crowd and with the passing minutes. One of them was in Montpelier, Vermont, two weeks earlier on the same tour. A first concert in an area can work either way: like a phantom of the past which doesn't stir up the local population more than a regular visit from the mailman, or like Montpelier. The hall was in the local civic center, with room for only twelve hundred people. The weather was freezing cold outside, and not too warm inside. Mary and I prowled around the building looking for a cozy spot to call a dressing room and found one in the police headquarters, the little room where they book the local drunks, attached to the town's only holding cell. I didn't dress up as the building was too cold.

The crowd was so quick and responsive that I was surprised at first. I started right off telling jokes and stories, saying everything that came to my head, and the public responded with enthusiastic applause and laughter after every other sentence. The songs were the same as they were on other nights, but felt newer. Mary was beaming when I left the stage at the end, and I could only hug her to express my pleasure. When I went back out, we sang "Amazing Grace." Their singing was so strong and beautiful I thought I was in Alabama in 1963 in that tiny packed church. My skin got prickly and I concentrated on the door at the back of the hall so I wouldn't see the soul of little Montpelier on the faces of her people. I remembered the line in "America the Beautiful" about the amber waves of grain.

That's what this gathering of people was like. A marvelous field of waving grain whistling and singing in the wind. Every word of the song was once again alive and vital and meaningful and healing, and nothing mattered except for that moment of song and union.

# 7
# "HAPPY BIRTHDAY, LEONID BREZHNEV"

In Father Jankowski's parish house there was a huge harlequin Great Dane that slept in a sprawl next to the dining room table. At the smell of meat she woke and rose shamelessly to nudge her floppy jowls onto my lap and rest her head, ears perked and eyes cocking back and forth from my face to the meat tray. She is the first thing I remember as I begin to write about Poland.

Then come the grey skies of Gdansk; the leather faces of shipyard workers; the icy road to Lublin lined with children leaning against the cruel wind in their layers of winter coats, faces hidden in fur; a lady slipping in the snow at the foot of the graveyard, recovering herself and her toppled cart with an embarrassed smile; the young priest, Kazimierz, in his robes, blushing scarlet in the doorway as Father Jankowski sweeps me past him from the icy night to the overheated parlor; Father Jankowski's nephew, Maciek (pronounced Machie), freezing at the shipyard monument, earnestly translating every word his uncle speaks, his face so white, his eyes so deep, his dreams so modest. And Lech Walesa.

Why Lech Walesa? Very simple: he is the undisputed leader of the banned Solidarity Union, the guiding light of the third mass nonviolent movement in the history of the world. Perhaps it is merely, or mainly, intelligence that keeps his followers from erupting into violence; or maybe an acute sense of their own history. Perhaps it's just tactical savvy; but I suspect that Lech is like Dr.

King and knows, as King knew about police chief Bull Connor, that General Jaruzelski is his brother in the human family. And I suspect that, partly because of Lech, many Poles actually believe in the moral necessity of nonviolence.

It all started in Ginetta's kitchen on a gusty day in autumn. We were sitting at her small round marble table, sipping tea and speaking French, she with an Italian accent, I with my terrible grammar and limited vocabulary. *"Mais, tu sais que je vais en Pologne?"* Ginetta said. She was going to visit Auschwitz to seek out and face the demons of her youth. Aside from her own experiences as a prisoner of the Nazis, she had lost both her parents in the Holocaust. "But why don't you come?" she said suddenly.

"Do I have to visit Auschwitz?"

"No! Of course not! But you could do some other veesiteeng." Her eyes were twinkling. She knows my dreams.

"O.K." I said, "as long as I çan have dinner with Lech Walesa."

"Yay, wonderful!" she cried, jumping up and throwing her arms in the air. "So many teengs ave been plan at dees leetle table!" And she bent down to hug me and plant a big kiss on each cheek.

Five weeks later—after a concert tour to Australia; a flight from Sydney to Singapore to Bahrein, to London, to Paris; a two-day visit with friends and a flight to Geneva to meet up with Ginetta—I reached Warsaw, cold, cold Warsaw.

Twelve hours later, still jet-lagged, we walked to the forlorn little car which would drive us the six or seven hours to Gdansk and were introduced to the driver, who spoke pidgin German. At my feet was a yellow plastic bag of chocolate bars, M&M's, chewing gum, and Joan Baez T-shirts. In my guitar case was a stack of cassettes of Dire Straits, U2, Paul Young, Hall and Oates, and Joan Baez.

An hour out of the city the car's cassette player ate several tapes, and died, leaving us with a peaceful union of spirits and the rumbling of the rattle trap little car.

Up front, Ginetta was no doubt lost in memories of the underground and her escape to freedom at night in a car with three men disguised as Nazi officials who delivered her into the arms of a waiting nun at the shadowy entrance to a convent.

The Polish countryside was poor, the earth an undernourished grey. Trees lined the roadside, tiny forests streaked with white birches and clotted above with silhouettes of mistletoe. A military compound stretched for miles and miles, fenced in by a thick wall topped with barbed wire. And once we saw, as if a casual reminder, a big ugly Russian tank parked on the roadside. Ginetta and I counted the huge storks' nests which perched solidly at the tips of pointed roofs. The sun was a pale disc floating on a sea of battleship grey. It was not yet dark when we arrived in Gdansk.

The driver placed a telephone call from a pay phone at the train station, and then he and I waited among the milling commuters, under the big clock. I was inescapably visible in my red cowboy boots and matching scarf; even my coat, a sedate navy blue, was ostentatious in its length and style. Seven minutes later a car pulled up to the curbside and three men hopped out. They had workers' hands, drab jackets, and good smile lines. I walked toward them and they welcomed me quickly, kissing my hand and speaking briefly to our driver. We followed them through town, zigzagging around traffic, then zooming toward the suburbs. Giant apartment buildings loomed up to the right and to the left. At last we pulled into a parking lot and everyone disembarked in hushed confusion. Unmarked secret police cars were in evidence all around us.

"Don't panic," I said to Ginetta of the immense eyes and vivid recall, "we are in the hands of friends." I put my arm around her and we followed the men toward the building. Still picturing a cozy family dinner and a good interpreter mingling with the seven children, Lech's wife, Danuta, and a few friends, I began mounting flights of dingy stairs, clutching my plastic bag of American decadence, wondering how old the kids were and if they had any pets. One of the men hustled past me and said something about NBC, and in that second I saw the unsteady glare of a hand-held camera light, plunged my hand too late into my pocket for a tube of lipstick and saw Lech, beaming in the doorway, the TV lights glaring from behind.

Somehow I had not expected him to be so like a schoolboy. Smiling shyly behind his glorious world-renowned moustache, looking not at all fierce, he held out flowers and made a welcoming speech to me and the roomful of people smiling at this wonderful meeting.

"You told Oriana Fallaci that you don't like to be embraced," I said as he smiled quizzically, and when it was translated everyone laughed, Lech put out his arms and we hugged, and I learned that in Poland one kisses three times from cheek to cheek.

The whole scene was bright and warm and animated after the steely horizons of storks' nests and smokeless chimneys. He wore a white shirt and grey jacket with a pin of the Black Madonna on the lapel, and one of *Solidarność* above the breast pocket. He looked proud, pleased, and preoccupied. Co-workers poked their heads out from doorways and halls, but there was no Danuta and there were no children. Lech apologized for being a bad host, but explained that he was confined to his house at the moment, and therefore could not offer me the visit he would like.

In spite of the bad news we were both grinning like fools in between the formalities. We sat down on the couch while the cameras ground away, and he continued to explain his situation. He was detained in his apartment for "medical purposes." "Stress, they are calling it this time." The fact was that he had publicly criticized the recent government elections and had been taken out of circulation. But, he said, "There are so many people awaiting your arrival, at least two hundred this very evening at a small gathering in town, and although you must be exhausted from the journey, could you be imposed upon to meet with them and . . . perhaps . . . sing?" Before I could answer, he was explaining that there would be a mass the next morning, where perhaps I could sing again, and then, if possible, yes, indeed, it was terrible to ask so much, but could I imagine giving a concert for the public in the Brigida church Sunday evening? He sat hunched over, elbows on knees, hands working, his forehead worried in anticipation of the worst. Good God, I thought. Maybe he thinks I'll say I won't appear in public until I have a massage, facial, and coiffure, a dinner of filet mignon and crêpes flambées, some decent wine, and a hot brandy for the throat, a beauty rest, and a guided tour of Gdansk to shop for Polish knick-knacks.

"Listen, Mr. Walesa," I told him when I could finally get a word in edgewise. "I came here for purely selfish motives. I wanted to meet you and spend time with you because I admire you very much. The only thing that can give me more pleasure than dining with you and your family is to be of some use to you and your people. I am not the least bit tired. I am exhilarated, and I would be happy to speak and sing tonight, and sing at mass tomorrow morning, and give a concert tomorrow evening. Now may I please have something to drink? And," I added, "where is Danuta? I want to meet her and get this embarrassing business over with of giving candy and gum to your children."

A half dozen gorgeous children arrived in a pack at the door and tumbled into the room as though bursting from the frame of a beautiful painting. Their cheeks were red and their eyes clear, and they lined up in a row to stare at me. Danuta appeared in the doorway, pregnant in a brown corduroy smock, pretty, weary, but accepting. She leaned in for a hug, and looking bemused, said yes, I could give the candy to the kids. I rummaged around in my bag and then stood there like a great white hunter, handing out plastic-covered Double Bubble balls to one chubby open fist and chocolates to the next, reminding myself that in this very political context children were still children and loved the crackling of cellophane wrappers and the taste of sugar and the blowing of large, disgusting bubbles.

They vanished with their mother. Lech was talking again. He narrowed his eyes and tightened his forehead as though concentrating to make every word be the right one and not wasted. And yet, just behind his eyes and all around his cheeks played a devilishness always at the ready for a wild run. He hinted that he would show up at one of tomorrow's functions, but didn't say which, and then looked around the room and with a small gesture indicated that it was bugged. I knew from articles I'd read that he outwitted the police and showed up on forbidden days at forbidden places, and I was cheered by the confidence that I would see him again.

"Would you like a brief concert? Now? Impromptu?" I asked. Lech was blushing and the room seemed to twitter with excitement. The camera lights came back on as I tuned the guitar, preoccupied with the fact that Danuta was not with us, and simultaneously a complaint was delivered from the kitchen: Danuta was demanding to hear the concert too.

"You should be ashamed of yourself, Lech," I scolded. "If Women's Lib hears about this at home, I'll be shot." I moved over on the couch and indicated for him to make room for Danuta. He moved toward me and held his hand out unconsciously for his wife and launched into a long explanation about how she was really the master of the household. She came in quietly and sat down.

The kids poured back into the room, chewing gum, and arranged themselves on the other side of me, used as they were to family portraits. I sang "Gracias a la Vida." One little one, with a lavishly handsome moon face under uneven bangs, stood in the doorway in overalls, and scowled up at me with a look of fierce concentration. I wanted to laugh at his stern and beautiful expression, but I would have embarrassed him, and besides, Lech was holding Danuta's hand, and a spell hung quietly in the room.

A big, full-featured, clean-shaven man wearing spectacles entered the room and Lech stood up. It was the priest, Father Jankowski. He invited Ginetta and me to stay at the parish house. We accepted, and the priest left.

How I had wanted to talk with Lech! We had only time to begin, to play enough psychic show-and-tell to know we would get along

—a fashion plate gypsy and a union organizer—whose common ground was our adherence to the principles of nonviolence. We were both down-to-earth, both equally and infinitely stubborn, neither to be bought. We spoke briefly about violence and whether there was a qualitative difference between spontaneous fist-fight violence and organized state violence. He said that now when he threatens to swat his kids they remind him that he is the winner of the Nobel Peace Prize. Then he said that the world is divided into two kinds of people: the day-to-day people who must work and run their lives and society, and then those up there—he waved his hand in the air and searched for a word, and all the Poles argued noisily until a word was decided upon—glisten, those up there who glisten, he said. I was someone who glistened. But you also glisten, I thought, and I hope I can come back to Poland sometime when you are free to sit under a tree with a tireless interpreter and talk about glistening, and the taste of fear, and the weight of a stork's nest, and the marvel of laughter.

It was dark when we left the Walesa apartment and drove back into the city, where Father Jankowski greeted us in the courtyard of his parish under the spires of the Brigida church, Lech's place of worship. That's where I met Cora, the dog, and workers and friends and journalists and students.

Ginetta and I were shown to our rooms furnished with white lace curtains, couches, lamps too dim for reading, radiators pumping out air too hot for breathing. But the rooms were only a stopover, because it was already time for dinner and special food had been prepared: fresh ham, fresh pork, salads, eggs, sweets, and wine. As usual, I was too excited to eat. Big Father Jankowski ate plenty, and hosted us and the array of young priests and visitors and parish staff who filled up the big oval dining room table. We were served on fine porcelain. Cora learned that I would always pat her, and slip her a bit of ham. Abruptly after dinner, we put on hats and coats and strode out into the courtyard and beyond, ten of us or so, our voices mingling and echoing about the deserted streets in conspiratorial whispers and bursts of laughter. Here I am in Gdansk, I thought, and in a few minutes, I'll be expected to speak and sing and be generally relevant, and I am delighted. There is no apprehension, no stage fright, only the agreeable feeling of being needed, and the desire to lend my spirit and voice to one more group of people who live in struggle and appreciate me in a special way.

In the faces of two hundred people I saw that the spirit of Solidarity was itself in struggle. These people had a history of unflagging strength and will. I reminded them of that, and I sang to bring them fresh hope and determination.

Two young men were introduced to me and they sang songs in great passions of rage to the strumming of cheap guitars strung with ancient strings. (I will be challenged by the right and by the left for daring to equate their struggles, but no one can challenge the fact that the guitars played by the underground in Chile, El Salvador, and Guatemala are identical to the ones played in Poland and the Soviet Union.) And we ended with "Dona Dona Dona." Father Jankowski led me through the crowd as people came up with flowers, and I walked back into the night air buried in earmuffs, my huge coat, red scarf, and boots, and immense bouquets piled one on top of the other.

A name-day party was being held for one of the parish caretakers, a woman, and thirty or more people were dining at linen-covered tables set one long in the middle and two short at either end. I drank vodka and stuffed on meats, and noticed that some young people were getting up from their end of the table and leaving the room and returning all flushed, and I realized that there was music and dancing just across the hall. Yes, said the man next to me, he would like to dance, and soon everyone was dancing, a kind of Polish two-step, and when I'd practiced it with four or five people, I went and asked Father Jankowski for a dance. He nodded, took my hand, and led me majestically onto the dance floor where he swept me unselfconsciously into his arms and up against his portly tummy. Everyone else stopped while the Father and I danced in a big circle, me laughing and catching glimpses of hands over mouths and fingers pointing, just beyond the dark mass of Father Jankowski's well-sculpted stubborn chin. I was roasting and red as a beet when we were through twirling, and left the Father ambling through the crowd in his skirts, acknowledging compliments.

Maciek, Father Jankowski's nephew, held me gingerly as we high-stepped in the overheated room. He asked me questions: Did I know Dire Straits? What was it like at Woodstock? When did I start to sing? Did I like Poland? Maciek's eyes were sunk deep in his white face, but they shone sparkling blue and were fringed with long and curly lashes. His nose was perfectly straight, his mouth generous and tender, and his white teeth just as straight as his nose. This gaunt but angelic apparition was a fine dancer. I changed partners at the end of "Rose in Spanish Harlem" and danced with everybody, including the cook, who tried to get me drunk on vodka, and in the middle of a polka the room started to spin, and I sat down on a pile of coats and decided it was time for bed.

Kazimierz, the young priest, showed me back to my room and let it be known, in a sentence he'd no doubt been perfecting since I'd arrived, that "if you are needing anything, my room is just next. Right here. Okay?" "Thank you," I said and kissed his burning cheek. "I had a wonderful evening. And you're a good dancer. GOOD DANCER." "Oh, no, yes, well tank you good night," and he flew down the stairs.

Enveloped in white quilts, Ginetta seemed even tinier than usual next to the huge bouquet of accumulated flowers we'd put on her coffee table. I took a picture of her there, smiling in happy exhaustion under a gruesome portrait of the Virgin Mary, who had tears rolling down the flesh-pink valley between her nose and cheek. A bloody heart hung suspended out in front of the baby Jesus.

At six in the dark morning I rose and dressed. At mass, I sat up in front, in the choir pews sideways to the congregation, so I could see the congregation on my left, Father Jankowski at the altar in front of me, and Lech to my right. NBC and BBC were everywhere. The huge church was very cold, but filled with people of all ages and children bundled up in snowsuits, lining the very front rows at the feet of their parents.

Father Jankowski's voice rang out, a reflection of the power and clarity of his spirit and actions. The congregation answered in song. Lech sang, too, a little sheepishly, aware of the proximity of my hand-size tape recorder. I was ecstatic, listening to the ritual and wishing that I shared the Catholic faith. This is what church should be, I thought, the strength of a people, their meeting place, their constant spiritual sustenance and their political home. Lech was nudging me, and Father Jankowski was nodding, so I went forward as planned and stood just in back of the altar and sang, "Gracias a la Vida" without the guitar.

A soprano voice rose from the back of the church, accompanied by an organ, and I sang again as the silver plates were passed. Then there was communion, and at the very end of mass the congregation, most of them already standing as the church was overfull, broke into song, raising their hands in the air with their fingers in the victory sign, and Lech raised his hand as well, and so did I.

We all filed into the courtyard. Snow had begun to fall, and thousands of people drifted toward the parish house. From those rough faces and weary bodies rose a chorus almost fearful in its unity. The interpreter muttered that they wanted me to sing. The air would

paralyze my vocal cords, I explained, so Father Jankowski and Lech
and I went upstairs and stood at a window, me feeling vaguely like
the Pope. A microphone materialized for us, and the crowd struck
up another song as the snow landed on hats and scarves and eyelashes and stuck there like cotton.

"They're singing the Popieluszko song, about the priest—" the
interpreter was saying.

"Yes, I know about him," I said, remembering the hideous details
of his murder. I'd seen the picture of his mother and father in a
magazine, and had wept at the misery and shock in their old wrinkled faces and at the ghastliness and irrevocability of their loss. Father Jankowski handed me the microphone. I told the crowd that I
had not seen such a spirit since the early days of the revolution led
by Martin Luther King and sang, "Ain't Gonna Let Nobody Turn
Me 'Round," and when it was over they started chanting again, but
this time Lech darted into the corner of the room, hidden from the
window, his face crinkled in laughter and flushing once again.

"What is it?" I demanded. "What?!"

"They ask you to take their greetings to your President."

I began to laugh and the interpreter lied and said, "They are only
joking," but they weren't joking, and that only made it funnier.

At that night's concert, I sang the song I'd written for Lech:
"Happy Birthday," it says to a certain very important Russian official, "what a mighty heart must beat in your breast, to hold forty-
nine medals on your chest." The people threw back their heads and
laughed until they were wiping tears from the creases that cut from
their eyes to their cheeks. The words were all sarcastic until the last
verse, which honors Lech and the workers and the Black Madonna.
Referring to the government's silencing of Lech, the very last line
says, "We hear you, Lech Walesa, yes, we hear you, Lech Walesa"
over and over, and when we came to it the people began to sing
along, louder and louder at each repetition. Lech would see it all on
video the next day. In fact, he'd see it three times.

After the performance an ex-political prisoner gave me a black and
red rosary he'd made in prison out of bread, ashes, toothpaste, and
melted plastic. In it were etched tiny, intricately carved symbols of
the Shipyard Movement, the wings of the Polish eagle, and the Black
Madonna. A tiny old woman in a fuzzy hat with grey wisps of hair
poking out from under clutched my arm and handed me something
wrapped in white tissue paper and tied with a blue ribbon. The kid
standing next to me whistled and said, "It's chocolate."

Later at dinner Father Jankowski presented me with a beautiful print of the Black Madonna set in a gold frame. Tired and weepy, I suddenly thought I'd burst into tears if I didn't get some air.

"Maciek," I whispered, "can we take Cora for a walk?"

And so Maciek, Kazimierz, the Great Dane and I set out at midnight to walk to the old section of Gdansk, the ground slick like iced marble under our feet and the wind slicing through us like slivers of metal.

We headed toward Mariacka Street, the old square that before martial law had been full of lights and people. The three of us linked arms, and a police car glided past. My chest tightened and an uncomfortable feeling passed through me. Three weeks before, the police had picked up a nineteen-year-old student. Finding that he was carrying only a student card, and not the proper identification required since martial law, they had taken him off and beat him senseless. Ten days later he died. Forty thousand people came to mourn him, but we didn't hear about it in the West. I pulled my two friends in closer to me: it was unbearable to think of any harm coming to them. Just then Cora ran full tilt toward a silhouette across the square, and the form froze in terror while Kazimierz called out vainly for her to stop. But she was too young and gay and the crystal air too exhilarating, and she charged up to the rigid form and danced around him, licking his hand, or trying to, or so it seemed in the dim street light. Then she came bounding back, ears up and eyes shining, and upon hearing Kazimierz's tone as she drew close, stopped suddenly and slid on the icy pavement that was like marble and sank to the ground at his feet. Kazimierz scolded her softly for a moment and then bent down and patted her reassuringly on the head and neck so that her collar jingled.

Back at the parish house, we three talked in my room about Dire Straits, because I would see them in three days when I left Poland. "You must tell them to come to Poland and there would be," Kazimierz said, "a million young people to see them in one night." I gave the young priest a copy of *The Best of Joan Baez* and he immediately went to his room to put it on the machine. And Maciek—well, Maciek already had a U2 T-shirt, three rock and roll cassettes, and a Joan Baez cassette and a Live Aid T-shirt.

I was a long time awake, lying under my quilt with the radiators turned off and the snow falling silent as paper just two feet from my pillow out in the lonesome courtyard.

Before I returned to Warsaw, Father Jankowski and Maciek took me to visit the shipyard monument. As we passed a big ugly apartment building across from the monument, he looked up.

"One day," he said, "during a march, a man in the crowd looked up at one of deez windows, and he said, 'You know, I have a funny feeling about dat window,' and dere was a man up dere who had a gun, and he shooted him."

I thought for a moment.

"Shot him," I said. "He *shot* him."

"Oh, God! I said shooted? It is an unregular verb?"

"Yes, Maciek. It's unregular."

I thought for another moment.

"Did the man die?"

"Oh, yes, of course, he died."

I sent over a bottle of Nina Ricci eau de cologne for Danuta, and a note which said, "I understand that in order to live with a saint you have to be a martyr"; and for Lech, a crucifix that belonged to my grandfather, a turquoise Joan Baez T-shirt, and a note which said, "Next time maybe we can go fishing. . . ."

The car was puffing white clouds in the courtyard, but Father Jankowski appeared waving his arms and calling that someone from the Catholic University at Lublin was on the phone and wanted me to come and sing a concert for the students the very next day. I sighed and thought about sleeping late on my last day, curled up under the covers in my cold hotel room in Warsaw, in total peace with my broken phone and no schedule, but there was Father Jankowski tilting backward, spreading his arms like a great black eagle, saying that Lublin was the only school of its kind between Japan (waving one hand) and Australia (waving the other). I said yes, I'd come and sing, but they didn't believe me. Father Jankowski took the phone to answer their astonished questions. She charges nothing for you, there is no one with her and she carries no equipment, and you'd better organize things perfectly or I'll shoot you.

I kissed everybody, from the cooks to the Father. Kazimierz was trying to push his blush down below the white collar, but it was no use. Cora came down the stairs with my earmuffs in her mouth, and I took them, sticky and black, and kissed her, and she kissed me back, a huge wet swipe from my nose to my forehead.

On the roads of Poland a Mercedes is a racing car, and it took only five hours, with music all the way, from Gdansk to Warsaw. I gave the driver a tape, and a chocolate bar for his wife. Alone in my hotel room, I sat down on the bed and burst into tears. Ginetta finally wafted in from the snow two hours later, and she chatted with me up and down the hallways, pausing every now and then to hold me away and tell me how tired I looked.

At dinner I asked to take the leftover cauliflower to my room, and they prepared an entire new one, which slid around on the plate like a giant steaming dumpling. Did I want it taken to my room? Oh no, thank you so much, let me, I said, and ten waiters, with nothing to do because of full employment in this socialist society, watched me gather coat and scarf and purse and then, balancing the cauliflower on the porcelain plate, stagger out of the dining room. I woke up in my bed four hours later with the lights on, my clothes in a heap on the floor, and a cold cauliflower on the windowsill. I was still wearing the earphones I must have put on to listen to ah, yes, it was Pink Floyd who had bombed and strafed me to sleep in their war requiem, *The Final Cut.* I shut my eyes and slept six more hours.

Lublin was three hours away and colder as we headed east, the snow slashing across the highway and women walking backward against the wind. The audience had broken the doors down getting in for seats, filled up the little stage, and lined the hallways outside as far as you could see. Teachers abandoned their lectures and whole classes came. I sang newer songs for the kids, and they sang me two songs, and then gave me rosaries and letters for Dire Straits. When I left they said they still couldn't really believe I'd come.

Back in Warsaw, a man was waiting for me in the lobby. He wanted me to meet two political prisoners who were currently out of jail, though I gathered they spent as much time in as out. They were from the intellectual community, a man and wife, aristocratic-looking with beautiful children. The husband listened to me sing and walked around the room quietly while the other guests sat. He had brilliant eyes. He told me of a ninety-eight-year-old man who lives in Warsaw, who when asked about his age, says it's a big nuisance because now, when he does his exercises, he has to stand on his head near a wall so he can lean his feet against it.

Oh, I will miss all of you, your humor and cleverness. I will miss being where the things we say and do make a difference. "What does freedom mean?" a man from the unofficial press asked me. I thought hard and my response was grim. Perhaps there are two kinds of freedom, I said. The kind that is born into and taken for granted, like mine in the States; and the kind measured by the little victories of its acquisition, each one savored and celebrated. At home we have freedom of speech, but fewer and fewer words with any meaning are ever spoken. We have freedom of thought, but nothing pushes us toward creative thinking. We have freedom of choice, and a diminishing quality of moral and spiritual values characterizing our choices. And here, where you have to fight for it, a spirit is created like the one in the courtyard of the parish. The people sing, cherish their children, love their church, and care for their neighbors. This is not a commentary on the East and West, I said, it is a commentary on struggle.

# 8

# "WE ARE THE WORLD"

To pretend that I was less than shamelessly thrilled at the chance to open the USA portion of the biggest rock and roll show in the history of the world would require a sophistication I haven't got. I was given six minutes at the top, which would put me in an unfilled stadium eleven hours from prime time. At the very least, I would be picked up by every international television and radio news and every newspaper and magazine that had a deadline, and many that didn't, just because I was the opener. And though many of my friends in California would sleep through the 6:00 a.m. opening, my friends in France would probably see it at 3:00 p.m. In any event, I had six minutes to make some sense out of yet another "historic moment." I had six weeks to plan my six minutes, and no doubts that the appropriate combination of words and songs would come to me in time. I was ecstatic.

I was on tour when the invitation came. Excitement was building everywhere. TV interviewers were starry-eyed, asking questions about Woodstock versus Live Aid, and whatever happened to all those years in between. The room service maids and people on the street traded rumors about who the latest invitees were and who might make a surprise appearance. One nineteen-year-old girl stood talking to me on a curbside in Andover, Massachusetts, dreamy but determined.

"I'm goin' to Philadelphia."

"You are?" I said, surprised. "Where did you get tickets?"

"Oh, I don't have tickets. I just gotta be there. It's our Woodstock, you know."

There was a growing mystique in the air about the rock and roll world which disturbed me. It was hinted that the people of the world of glitz were suddenly going to live lives of sacrifice and commitment, and change the world by sharing our wealth. More than once I had heard the expression "lifelong commitment to end hunger," and it always made me cringe.

Research from our office told us that Bob Geldof, mastermind of the international fund-raiser, was not going to be duped by dictators, black marketeers, and red tape. And that he was smart enough to know that hunger will not end today or tomorrow or in fifty years unless we restructure everything from our psychologies to our economies. The rhetoric developing in the States, on the other hand, was direct from EST Hunger Project—highly inflated and unrealistic talk about "making a commitment to end world hunger starting today" which gave the misleading impression that by nightfall the very concept of hunger, disquieting to those of us who eat, would have vanished from the face of the earth. We needed only to make this mysterious commitment. And the rock and rollers were now in the forefront of this massive social change.

In fact, there had not been an event since Woodstock approaching the sheer enormity of this one. The current word was "awesome." Live Aid would be awesome. Everybody knew it. We all wanted to be there. I imagined the bloodletting and the IOU-waving going on between managers and Bill Graham, the man who decided who would perform and who would not. So when a reporter treated us entertainers as though we were making a sacrifice, it was embarrassing. Yes, we all paid our own ways to Philadelphia. My rented plane, the only way to get to Philadelphia from Chautauqua, New York, by morning, would cost seventeen hundred dollars. That money was not a sacrifice. It was an investment.

I began to think about my six minutes. "Amazing Grace" was the obvious choice of openers. But most kids don't know it, and they don't sing along except on the hooks and choruses of their favorite rock and roll songs. I started to sing the one song known by all the kids which had a singable chorus and even a hint of social content. I flipped *Private Dancer* out of my Sony and slipped in "We Are the World." Perfect. I could do two verses of "Amazing Grace" for the older generation and the cameras and then break into "We Are the World" for the kids, and with luck, at least forty or fifty thousand people would sing along. I yanked off the earphones and grinned into the wall mirror. I said, "Good morning, Children of the Eighties! This is your Woodstock!," and started to dance. My whole six minutes came to me then, as I stood listening to the tape and scribbling down words and timing little speeches with a stopwatch, looking out at the silly Styrofoam swans on the lake where I was staying in Hyannis, Massachusetts. Amazing Grace: the grace to recognize and appreciate our gifts, and the grace to feel the needs of others. To be moved is to be touched in the spirit of goodness by the spirit of goodness. The Children of the Eighties needed to experience that goodness on a grand and unifying scale. Maybe, just maybe this upcoming mega-media event would move some folks, somehow. I went to sleep at 4:30 in the morning and woke up every half hour. I was excited as a six-year-old child before an Easter egg hunt. And would stay that way until July 13th, and a little bit after.

Nobody is at the airport to pick us up when we arrive in Philadelphia. The East Indian cabbie takes us past the stadium where we peer out at a parking lot full of cars and vans and trailers. Bare-chested young men are sitting on vehicle roofs holding halter-clad young women (the halters are the first visible feature distinguishing Live Aid from Woodstock), drinking good ol' American beer and eating, hollering to each other and trying to hurry the sunup. The cabbie asks if we are here for the concert. We say yes. Do I sing? He is peering in the rearview mirror. He asks my name and when I tell him he nearly runs us into a tree. His wife, he says, has all of my albums, etc. He is very, very happy and turns off the meter, shaking his head. He brings us quietly into the Four Seasons Hotel. I am not recognized by the kids who have lined up to scream at Mick Jagger and Tina Turner and Don Johnson and Duran Duran. I smile to myself, hug the cabbie, and give him an autograph for his wife. The Four Seasons is all pastels and perfection, as always, but tonight the lobby is filled with rock and rollers and newspeople and groupies and hustlers. I am in my room by two o'clock, tired, wired, and thinking about what to wear. I turn my suitcase upside down, littering the floor from wall to wall to get a good look at my entire out-of-date collection of rags and feathers. By three o'clock I have finally ironed a yellow parachute skirt and cobalt blue blouse, dug out the belt with the big silver circles and the necklace made of spoon ladles linked together, and the nineteen-dollar black sandals bedecked with rhinestones. I spend an extra twenty minutes hunting down my half slip, which, after swearing in whole paragraphs and dumping out all the carry-on luggage, I find tucked up in a dress I've already hung in the closet. I fall onto the bed and doze off instantly, my adrenaline suddenly losing the war against Dramamine and exhaustion.

Like a soldier I awake a few minutes before reveille and answer my five-thirty wake-up call cheerfully, trying to sound as if I've been up for hours. I shower quickly and try some vocal exercises and find, to my delight, that my voice has not had time to relax, so instead of being early-morning husky, it is still loose from the concert the evening before. I sing and dress, put on makeup and order coffee and eggs and toast, but only the toast goes down, and there's Mary polishing my spoon necklace. Jeanne and the rest of the troops somehow are in the lobby by seven. I look around me at the first wave of performers. There is something pathetic about rock and rollers in the morning. They are pastier than normal people, even the black ones, like the Four Tops, who are also on the seven-thirty run to the stadium. But there is general hilarity, because if rock and rollers are ambulatory, they wisecrack.

By seven-thirty it is over eighty degrees out. We roll into the stadium, nearly running over a few bodies which look like rejects from the fountain of Lourdes. A long snaking line of ticket holders inches toward the main gate. Most of the people look clean and rosy. We are whisked efficiently into the backstage area, where, in one of the enclaves, I have an air-conditioned van available to me from my arrival till one hour after my performance, at which point the next group will get the van and I am on my own to roam luxuriously about with a backstage pass. The Hooters, Philadelphia's up-and-coming rock band, has the van next to mine. We greet each other, and I hear what will be the general theme of the day from young handsome rock and rollers: "I was raised on your music!" "My mother has all your albums," and "Meeting you is a great honor." It wouldn't be if you knew what I was thinking about your cherubic little mouth, kiddo, is my silent response, but I give each of them a reasonably maternal hug and let them believe what they have to. I retire to my trailer and ask everyone to leave me alone for at least thirty minutes. And I go over and over my set. The greeting, the recognition of the Children of the Eighties, the kind of New Wave prayer, and the songs. I feel suddenly sick to my stomach and dizzy. A doctor friend says to drink liquids and not relax. I drink a soda pop and walk around the room. I'm in there for nearly an hour and a half, but it feels like five minutes.

They come to escort me to the green room. All the saliva in my mouth evaporates on the way. I have to go to the bathroom desperately, but it's too far and won't do any good anyway, so I sit tight, sip water, and ask Mary not to let anyone talk to me.

It's time to leave the green room. We are led down the long tunnel and up the stairs to the stage. I am ushered into a nook to have my picture taken, but it jars my concentration, and I say "Not now, please, maybe afterwards." I sit down again and go back into a trance. Eventually I am led up to the curtain, stage left, with Mary pulling and Jeanne pushing, like parents taking a kid to the dentist. I see the *Cuckoo's Nest's* own Jack Nicholson preparing to step out at nine o'clock sharp and welcome the crowd. I go down on one knee, feeling safer, I guess, close to the ground. I spot Bill Graham also down on one knee, just to my left. He looks terrific, fresh-shaven, and is wearing a clean white shirt. We've been on bad terms since the Dylan/Santana/what's-her-name tour, but today he has already greeted me, and now he is smiling like a nervous kid, and I am smiling too. I go over and hug him and kiss him on the cheek.

Jack is ushered out in front of the gigantic beautiful painted gauze curtains, and the day begins for real. The noise reminds me of the first time I ever saw the Beatles. It was in Denver, Colorado, in 1965, in the Red Rocks Amphitheater. When they trotted out onstage the sky lit up with flashbulbs, and the night was bright as high noon, and the kids screamed at such a pitch that I found myself cupping my hands over my ears and crying. If all the wheelchair people had gotten up and waltzed around in circles, I would not have been the least bit surprised.

Jack is talking, but I can't distinguish the words over the roar of the crowd. My heart knocks recklessly around in my chest. Through the gauze, I can make out thousands of bobbing heads and waving arms. "Lord, God, Father, Mother, I am in your hands," I say to myself, and the curtains are opening and I am hugging Jack, funny, sweet, *Five Easy Pieces* Nicholson, and then I'm on the roller coaster, buckled in, and the switch is pulled, and I turn and face the crowd. My first impression is that the entire scene in front of me is almost exactly as I imagined it would be. The stadium is not yet full, the public is crazed with excitement. The only shock is the uniformity of the rosy, American glow of the crowd. YUMARFs. Young Upwardly Mobile American Rock Fans.

"Good morning, Children of the Eighties! This is your Woodstock, and it's long overdue." There is an enormous roar of what I take to be approval. "And it's nice to know the money out of your pockets will go to food to feed hungry children. I can think of no more glorious way of starting our part of the day than by saying grace together, which means that we thank each of us, his and her own God, for the many blessings that we have in a world in which so many people have nothing. And when we say this grace, we also reach deep in our hearts and our souls and say that we will move a little from the comfort of our lives to understand their hurt, their pain, and their discomfort. And that will make their lives richer and it will make our lives real. 'Amazing Grace, how sweet the sound. . .' "

I am pleased at the response, though the people are so excited they might cheer for anything. Nonetheless, there is a good spirit abroad this morning, a good and generous spirit. I won't know until days later that the things I said and sang touched many people, which is all I ask.

It is ninety degrees when I leave the stage. My troops and I run into the Four Tops, laughing and gulping coffee outside in their trailer while four pretty black women gaze sleepily through their clotted lashes at Ozzy Osbourne, wondering if he actually eats bats' heads and if what he's doing is really making music. I slip into the trailer and eat a cinnamon roll, wondering how my six minutes really went, and then right away it's time for interviews, tons of them— out in the sun, around corners, by potted trees, back in the trailer. Each reporter is looking for a story, trying to figure out what Live Aid really means and what part it will play in history. I get nauseated and dizzy and dream of my cool room in the hotel. Mary Travers (of Peter, Paul and Mary) enters the main gate in a shoulder-padded jacket, with entourage. This is not a good day for them; they have not been invited to sing their own set, only to join Dylan at the finale, and even that won't happen. She pays me a compliment on singing so early in the morning and making the high notes, and I hug her and think, You and I, Mary, will always be printed on the page in history books that tells about the folk boom of the sixties. And there is that Beach Boy, with the good cheekbones. I hug him and we joke about his cheekbones, and then he disappears behind a plant. I hear him answering embarrassing questions about how it feels to be a part of the magnaminous world of rock and roll, now that it is into benefits and sharing. I'm tired and more cynical than usual, and all the est-ian style Hunger Project people drive me nuts. I don't trust anything they say. I flash back to Woodstock:

> It was so real to be rag tag, mud-bound,
> All around,

Brown acid, body paint,
Freaking, streaking,
Bearded and beautiful,
Botticelli maidens,
Virgin hippies,
Bathing naked, they're
Leaning out for love
And they will lean that way forever . . .

I want to take a nap. I'm in the middle of a sentence when I spot Don "Miami Vice" Johnson. This will not be news to his multimillion female viewers, but I find myself suddenly wide awake and having a hot flash. I excuse myself from a conversation and walk around all the tables and chairs, musicians and roadies in the food tent as if I were walking through them, looking at "Miami Vice" Johnson all the way, and I walk right up to him and look him smack in his sparkling eyes. For someone who likes soft skin and peach fuzz, I wasn't slowed down one rpm by his Actor's Guild five-day stubble, not at all. Christ, not since Kris Kristofferson, I think to myself, a man-man, not a boy-man, and I just say right out, to his sparkling eyes and Ralph Lauren hair and not entirely uninterested look of surprise, "Hello, gorgeous. Could we discuss the possibility of rape?" Why, you haven't been a superstar very long, Don Johnson. There's something about you that's fresh as lilac water. And then, fortunately, you laugh. We hang out, just a little, and someone takes our picture, and I don't know what on earth he thinks about me, but I was honest.

Tired and hot and icky, heading for the van back to the hotel, I am cornered by a familiar-looking cockeyed face. The glasses are askew, or perhaps the eyes. I recognize Ken Kragen, mastermind of the USA for Africa record and video benefit bonanza to which I was not invited. He says he must talk to me a minute. "Richie called me from California," he says, hustling me by the elbow, away from the crowd. "He's flyin' in for the finale, and he wants you in it! He saw you this morning, and he thought you were great! I did, too. You *were* great. Anyway, he wants you in the finale. We're gonna end with 'We Are the World,' of course. That's why it's so great, you know, that you opened with it, just perfect! Anyway, we're going to be rehearsing at five o'clock and Lionel will be in and he really wants you to be there, he told me to tell you *PER*sonally." This man is desperate, I think to myself. Oh, yes, I remember, and the light dawns. Stevie and Michael Jackson (black superstar politics, I heard) are boycotting the show, and Bruce Springsteen and Cyndi Lauper couldn't make it. Dylan probably doesn't want to take part. I guess they are looking around for replacements. I'm tired. I honestly don't know if I'm coming back over, I tell him, I'm going to sleep, and then maybe just stay in the hotel and watch it all on TV, but I will certainly let him know, and I thank him very much for the invitation. I feel depressed, just when I suppose I should be feeling "great."

The hotel is like an oasis, my lovely room made-up and waiting, with its big picture window and bathroom full of fine hotel bubble bath and shampoo and body lotion, and a TV control right by my pillow. I lie down and flip on the TV and put three pillows under my head and luxuriate. I can wind down or wind up or doze off or watch the show or just listen. I try to watch, but my eyes are leaden. Shortly after seeing Sally Field for the third time in twenty minutes, I am asleep and don't even hear background music. I wake up and peek at Greg Walker dominating good ol' Santana's set, and I'm happy for him. I am smiling when I doze off again. Somewhere in the afternoon, I am awakened by Paul Young's "Every Time You Go Away." And then I'm out again.

As I begin to come out of the heavy sleep, I see a face I don't recognize on the screen. It must be coming from England because the swaying audience is dotted with union jacks. The singer is dressed in black, and has long, slightly messy brown hair. He is streaming with sweat, and some of his hair is stuck to his cheek, in road map designs, making me want to brush it back. The song is cosmic, heavenly, lilting, and persistent. The singer jumps in the air and stomps around in heavy boots. He doesn't fuck the microphone the way rock stars do when they realize that technology has made it possible for them to extend their egos out over a crowd of thousands. No, this young man is deadly serious about something, and is expressing himself with such tenderness it is enough to break my heart. He calls to the audience. They call back. He sings little bits of songs from the fifties and sixties, all in his utterly unique sound, and they sing back. He is directing a choir. They are the choir, and they are transported. Am I making all of this up? Possibly. The group's name appears next to the Live Aid symbol superimposed over his mystical dance. U2, Live From Wembley Stadium. This is the group my fifteen-year-old advisors have told me to watch. This is the group they say is political, even pacifist. The singer is working his way down toward the crowd, jumping onto a narrow wooden skirt a few feet below the stage. He is gesturing to the crowd, waving someone toward him. He takes the long drop into the orchestra pit, and continues his sign language invitation. Eventually, a young girl is lifted bodily and handed over the fence which separates him from the crowd. She is simply passed over like an offering. She lands on her feet and is in his arms, and he dances with her. She is probably stagestruck and in shock, and her head is sweetly bent down, and for the next few seconds he is cradling her as they dance.

I can't recall ever having seen anything like it in my life. It is an act, but it is not an act. It is a private moment, accepted by seventy thousand people. The dance is short, sensuous, and heartbreakingly tender. He breaks away from her and is helped up to the level just under the stage, and there finds another girl, dances with her the same way. All this while the percussion and hypnotic guitar continue relentlessly, lyrically, with the audience waving their arms back and forth, back and forth, a part of the ritual. The singer moves back onto the stage, and, still pouring with sweat, continues with the song. His voice is nothing special. It is unsteady and cracks. But it is compelling, as he is compelling. There is something about his seriousness which has captivated me.

Rock stars can look and be serious, but it is usually about themselves or their inflated vision of themselves. None of us who stand in front of a hundred thousand people hearing our voice (and band) amplified, tampered with, echoed, and smoothed into cosmic velveteen can escape certain grandiose delusions about ourselves. But this Irish lad is involved with something more than self-aggrandizement. Granted, his ego is well intact, and he is a superb showman, but there is something more going on. And I would like to know what it is. That I would like to be wrapped up in his arms like the little English girl there is no doubt. But if my instincts are correct, there is something which preempts flirtations with him. Something bigger than him or me or us combined, or our music combined. Something to do with politics, kids, freshness, and breakthrough. And love.

Out of the hours of Live Aid that I saw by the end of the day, the high point was witnessing the magic of U2. They moved me as nothing else moved me. They moved me in their newness, their youth, and their tenderness.

I call my folks, who have been watching (well, on and off) all day (monitoring) and are proud of their little girl. I ask my dad if I should take part in the finale. He says, "Well, honey, it's a good cause, and a day worth remembering," and he votes yes, and Mom takes the phone and echoes "Yes! They need more of you, honey." I smile. I know they will always love me. And I would love to sing in the finale. I was just so hurt by those bastards leaving me out of their We Are the World party . . . but that's history.

I take a cold shower, put on a fresh T-shirt. I want to go over to the media event of the decade and hang out. It is not at all cool for superstars to spend the day walking from tent to tent, talking to people. The really hot items, like Tina and Mickey and Madonna, stay hidden. Others just wish they had to stay hidden. I know I can roam around, and besides, I like interviews and chats and meeting people. I will watch the show on TV, have a beer with Bernie in the Hard Rock Cafe, and cruise around watching people.

The lead singer from Judas Priest, wearing dog collar, leathers, chains, and a tiny silver cross dangling from his left ear, tries to shake my hand respectfully and say all the proper things one says to a legend, so I hug him and he asks if I am aware that Judas Priest recorded "Diamonds and Rust." I laugh and say in his ear, yes, I heard it long ago, before my *son* even knew, and his manager is standing two feet away, saying, "I don't believe this. I don't fucking believe this." I float off through the cast of thousands. Even here, in the area set aside for "performers only," there mill friends and family, groupies, and selected hip and groovy nuisances. Surrounded by girls, members of Duran Duran are hovering behind a divan in front of a closed-circuit TV screen. I sit on the floor next to an attractive young man who is falling asleep between questions babbled to him by a pretty little groupie who wants to be in bed with him or anyone. He sits up and is polite to me when he sees who I am, and begins to ask me political questions. We talk about Central America, and we make hash out of the Reagan administration, and it's actually kind of fun. People think they have to talk politics when they meet me. I don't mind, but today I'd just as soon spoof around. I run into Joel Selvin from the *San Francisco Chronicle*. He is wearing an Indiana Jones hat. We shoot the breeze for a while. Am I aware, he asks, that there are only four "acts" on the Live Aid bill which were also on the bill at Woodstock? No kidding, I say, pleased. There was me, the Who, Crosby Stills and Nash, and Santana. Joel laughs at my obvious delight.

I decide to go and check out the rehearsal for the grand finale and run smack into Ken Kragen.

"Fantastic!" he says. "We're just putting the thing together! You'll be singing the first two lines of the chorus with Madonna." He has wheeled around and is walking me to the van. "And then Sheena Easton will take the 'There's a choice we're making . . .' " He prattles on, hoping I won't notice that I'm being bulldozed. Madonna? Why not? Let's treat the world to two madonnas at once, and a good case of culture shock.

The rehearsal van is a movable feast: Mary Travers, Dionne Warwick, Durari Duran, Sheena Easton, to whom I give a big hug because I think she is Madonna, and then I just think she is unhappy. I sit down on the edge of a couch to the right of John Taylor's chair and wisecrack with him.

One of Kragen's people is in charge of getting us organized. I'll give them this much: They seem as if they had all been through est training and know how to assert themselves, and that's the kind of person you need as choral director for a van full of flakey, sunstroked, scatterbrained singers. He shouts out directives. Madonna and I will walk up to the red mike as Harry Belafonte is finishing the intro, and we will sing "We are the world," etc., and then Sheena Easton will sing "There's a choice we're making, we're saving our own lives," and the three of us will finish, "It's true we make a better day, just you and me." Where is Madonna, anyway? Is she exempt from rehearsing? I guess so. Just then, in comes "Miami Vice" Johnson, all smiling and grubby and gorgeous, and I pat the couch next to me for him to sit down, which he does, and I decide to entertain him. His delightfully surprised expression probably means that he never expected me to be fast and funny and a nasty gossip.

I am luxuriating in the company of men. John Taylor is the quintessential Narcissus, his complexion perfect, his pretty alabaster face framed with wavy black hair, his extravagantly lovely eyes direct from the soft cover of a dime store novel, his languid body at ease in draping jackets. He's a sort of New Wave d'Artagnan, though without the fire, and is surprisingly witty. He has returned my attentions to a moderate degree. "Miami Vice" Johnson, whose TV show stands for everything I've spent my entire life fighting against— namely, the glorification and justification of violence—well, he is some charismatic hunk of maleness, with the disarming touch of everlasting youth, the boyish quality of Brando and Dean. He has all of their intensity and sex appeal, and what he may lack in depth, he makes up for in clothing. He is an upwardly mobile undercover agent dressed in thousands of dollars worth of guaranteed-to-wrinkle linen, and, I assume, custom getaway shoes. Even his T-shirts have that wonderful natural-dye, safari stone-ground look that doesn't come for anything less than fifty dollars a shirt. I gaze at his splendid dimple and think it would be nice if he were wearing his gun belt. I love excitement. I realize that I no longer know how to conduct myself around men.

The group disbands as Ken Kragen is telling us that Harry will be flying in between shows in Atlantic City, and Lionel will be here any minute, and we will be joined onstage by a chorus of forty children. What utter chaos, I think, and reluctantly leave my lovely men. I head off to visit the stage, and pass the cute little devil who sings for the Cars. He had sung an excellent set and is now being interviewed by a TV crew. I interrupt his serious responses by giving him a friendly tweek on the cheek and calling him a cute little devil. I don't wait around for the response. Really, I think to myself, I am unmanageable. Who let me out of the cage? And how long have I been in it? Happily, the cute little devil and his wife find me later and tell me they think I'm terrific. I apologize for my behavior.

I pass a TV screen and see a replay of Madonna's performance. What will happen to you, baby child, when the spotlights dim and the morning sunlight finds your eyes red from weeping? Come and see this old madonna, who will tenderly serve you jasmine tea and say quietly in response to the unformed questions struggling up from the ashes of your fiery young life, "I understand, sweetie, I understand." But for now, in the diamond glow of success, dance and sing and bump and grind in your jangling glitz necklaces and skintight mini bun-huggers . . . Someday maybe those handsome *Playboy* tits of yours will find a more earthly purpose and you, a more fulfilling life . . . Trips to the supermarket will not be easy at first.

I walk around and do some interviews and, out of the corner of my eye, spot Udo Lindenberg, German rock star, on the screen. I sit on the ground, pull my knees up under my chin and think about Germany, where I bought my parachute skirt, and I listen to Udo read a strong political statement in his thick accent, and I cheer him on inwardly. Yes, he is saying, it's nice, a concert for the hungry, but the real issues, inseparable from the fact of hunger and famine, are armaments, unfair distribution of wealth, etc.

Though his speech is a little left wing and brash for my taste, I am happy to hear it, and happy to see my friends and compatriots with whom I have something in common. I really live in another world, I think to myself. It doesn't make me unhappy, but it does make me lonely. When Udo finishes the speech, I clap loudly because I can't help it. I am a stranger in my own land, always looking to feel comfortable without selling my soul.

Today, I'm just going to have fun, and one day soon, I will have a record deal, and I will make a beautiful album which is strong and melodic and filled with excitement, and has three of my own songs on it, and there will be a gorgeous picture of me on the cover, grey spikes and all. And when you open it up, there will be a huge picture of me dressed in the black crepe evening gown I bought at Nordstrom's, with its sequined Egyptian profile covering the left breast, and purple ostrich plumes extending at least a foot off the left shoulder, no right shoulder at all—only my tan slender arm, bent at the elbow, back of my hand to the camera, flipping a giant bird to all the major record companies in the United States of America.

It's time to go back to the rehearsal van. Excitement is building. Richie has arrived, and Patti LaBelle, whose presence is electric and dominates the room. Harry and Julie Belafonte blow in from Atlantic City. Harry is as handsome as he was when they wouldn't let him hold hands with Petula Clark on the screen in the fifties. It is announced to me that I will now be singing with Chrissie Hynde. Fine, I think, wondering who Chrissie Hynde is and what happened to Madonna. Chrissie Hynde is nice, but nervous ("Madonna can't make it, so you're stuck with me"), so I chat with her as the van fills up. Duran Duran is back, and Peter Yarrow comes over and takes my hand and just shakes his head, and shakes it and shakes it, I guess because he can't think of anything to say. He is a good soul. I've known Peter since we sang on a TV show together in 1960. He hasn't got a single hair on the top of his head. I smile, thinking of Puff the Magic Dragon, and give him a hug, and I don't think he has said a single word.

Mr. Miami Vice doesn't show. Paul and Mary do. So do a bunch of movie actors and Melissa Manchester. She is buddies with Patti LaBelle. We begin our ragtag rehearsal, which sounds instantly like a tent revival. We are on the wings of high-flying birds, and we do sound superb. Our choir director is panicking and asks everyone who is not performing to please leave the room. Patti LaBelle's flock of children and a few hangers-on shuffle reluctantly to the next room, but remain wide-eyed at the door. Cher pokes her spiked head in the door and makes her way through the party to the couch. She has Indian hands like mine.

That little van is a purse of diamonds, cut and uncut, polished and raw. We can all sing. We sing for the joy of it. We really sing. Patti LaBelle is in a state of wild exhilaration and begins to outsing everybody. Philadelphia is her home, and Live Aid will do no harm to her current comeback. She hits that high G so many times it makes our heads spin, but it's nothing to what she'll do on the stage . . . She is dressed in a white and black gown, and white and black polka-dot pumps, and she has some winged contraption on her head, like a helmet with two corrugated shark fins fanning out in different directions. They are covered with polka-dots, too, and we are supposed to think the whole arrangement is her hair. I almost touch one of the fins, but I'm afraid she'll back up and cut my finger. Her nails are one full inch long and white as paste. But, boy, can she sing. I tell her I'd love to stand next to her onstage, and then realize that Melissa seems to have a franchise on that spot, so I drop the subject, though Patti is gracious and says yes, indeed, she'll give me one whole side, and one whole side of Patti LaBelle is plenty of room.

We have gone over the song at least ten times and are getting nutty, like kids before a football playoff. Ken shouts new instructions. We must all go to the green room NOW for twenty minutes and then up to the stage. We are yakking and gossiping and hanging out and getting cranked up . . . I hear Dylan in the background. He is onstage with two of the Rolling Stones. I don't see their set until two weeks later on a video: they look like three extras playing the undead in an old Vincent Price movie. Melissa and I start to chat and head off for the green room. She is wearing a silver ring on the middle finger of one hand. It has little chains attaching it to a matching bracelet on her wrist. It's the first time I've ever seen a finger in bondage. I admire the whole contraption, and she tells me that her life is different now that she works with street gangs.

We are sitting dutifully in the green room under the bright lights of a television crew, chatting and trying to appear spontaneous on film. Dylan drones on. I realize that his show will end soon, and that Melissa and I must be in the wrong place. We fly out into the milling crowd and look desperately around for anyone from our group. There is no one in view.

I run up to a security guard and ask him if there is another green room somewhere, but he doesn't know. Melissa and I are like two campers who can't find the fireside sing on the farewell night. I take her hand, and we start running to find the entrance to the tunnel to the stage, but it's like a bad dream because neither one of us knows where it is. I am still holding her hand when I grab another security guard by the arm and say, "Please get us to the stage." He can't leave his post, but he points out the tunnel and we run lickety-split, my spoon necklace clanking, her ringlets bouncing; and still clutching hands, we arrive at the top of the stairs in time to see all the stars of the milky way pouring out of a curtained-off area, heading toward downstage, looking like a bunch of kids who got loose and went berserk in the wardrobe room of a circus. I make a last joke to Melissa and look for Chrissie. I am a good little camper at heart, always trying to follow instructions in my own way until I realize the instructions are wrong.

We are gathered in back of the curtain now, in a mad jumble. I look for the "red mike" in the arsenal of equipment which is being set up for us, but I can't find it.

Dylan is nearing the last verse of "Blowin' in the Wind," and I laugh out loud when I think of Ken Kragen saying, "When Bob's finishing up 'Blowin' in the Wind,' Lionel will appear from behind the curtain and put his arm around Bob and say, 'Bob, we've got some of your friends here tonight,' and the curtain will open and there we'll all be!" Dylan will hate it. He can't stand anything going on behind his back.

We are all laughing and hugging and waiting for the big moment. I can't find Chrissie. I dart in and out of the stars looking for my singing partner. Dylan finishes his song. I find Chrissie and grab her hand. The curtains are opening. Dylan looks confused and tiny next to Lionel with his smiling face and easy manner. The familiar chords begin and I look frantically for the "red mike." Lionel begins to sing and the audience is screaming. The stars have fanned out over the whole stage. It's Harry's turn now, but we can't hear him. He must be hoarse from Atlantic City, I think, and I scan the stage one last time for the red mike, but see none, and very suddenly it's almost our turn, and I tug Chrissie, who is quite calm and very sweet through this entire scene. Belafonte's mike is the safest one to use because it is on at last, and we can hear his silken, husky voice and he's on the last line before our grand entrance, so I pull Chrissie up with me behind Harry and nose my way under his arm like a puppy looking for attention, and his fine eyebrows go up ever so slightly in surprise, but there is time only to say "Excuse me" because it is instantly our turn, and I grab the mike with one hand and Chrissie's hand tight with the other, and we give it all we have.

Unfortunately, the engineers have another set of instructions— probably that we will be at the red mike—because for the first few notes there is no sound, but then there *is* sound and it is fantastic. I turn the mike toward Chrissie, knowing my reputation for monopolizing it, and Sheena appears to our left. We are barely finishing up our little contribution when Sheena takes the mike with a quiet ferocity, leans away from us, and in a splendid two lines works out all her frustration at not performing, but only speaking as a hostess.

Well, not *all* her frustration. She hoards the microphone like a newly discovered family heirloom and sings our trio as a solo, leaving me leaning awkwardly toward the unavailable mike and Chrissie completely out of range.

All of this couldn't matter less. We are having a feast of good cheer and song, and the audience is wild.

I think vaguely that I'd like to find Patti LaBelle, just to fly with that voice for a while, but I realize that the aggressive stars are reaching for microphones, and don't feel like competing, so I turn around and head off the front lines and into the crowded stage. I run smack into Peter, Paul and Mary, and Peter asks in a shout over the din if I'd like to link arms with them, but I shake my head no and thank him and slide on through the ranks to the second string, which includes Duran Duran. I go and stand next to John Taylor because he's so gorgeous, and he nestles me nicely in his arms and there we stand, singing our lungs out just in back of forty little kids who have filed onstage.

I am very happy. In fact, I could stay there all night. We can hear Patti and Dionne and Melissa and Lionel, and the rest is a great hodgepodge. Lionel is waving at us to shush and let the audience sing along. Everyone shushes except for Patti and Dionne. I listen to the exhilarated, sunburned, saturated audience, and wonder what the day has meant to them and what it will continue to mean. It's our turn again, and everyone is hugging or kissing or singing or dancing, and eventually the song is over and all the stars are people and all the people are stars, and the day is over.

I hug John Taylor and walk off toward stage left, bumping into everyone and grinning and hugging. The drums start up again and we start the chorus one more time. I run into Mickey Jagger who is dancing his naughty, sexy snake dance by the drums, and I dance with him for a minute. Cameras materialize, and I'm afraid he will think I'm a nuisance, but it is such fun I keep dancing until he snakes off into the crowd. I spot Tina and go up behind her and put my arms around her leather-clad body. She gives a nervous look over her shoulder, sees it's me, and grins a big "Hah!," so I hug her and she puts her head back on my shoulder and we finish out the song, wailing a harmony up to the moon. She laughs her tiger laugh and I let go of her and hold her away from me. She is soaked from head to toe and so hot if you turned a hose on her she'd sizzle. Two hairs from her wig are clinging to her drenched bosom and need to be picked off, but I don't want to embarrass her, and anyway, someone comes to escort her down the stairs from the stage. My concert agent and friend, Peter Grosslight, materializes and sneaks me quietly downstairs and among the wiped-out, grimy, hardworking stage-hands and security people, and past them to the hordes of hotshots, managers, bigwigs, little wigs, groupies, photographers, reporters, and, here and there, performers running for cover.

Peter has saved a seat for me in a bus with Tina, her manager Roger, and their folks. We squeeze in, then Chevy Chase hitches on and then Kenny Loggins. We all sit in the van drinking warm beer, joking and guffawing. Tina is wearing a filmy white ruffled number which seems more like a nightie than a dress. Each time she laughs it falls off her right shoulder and she yanks it just hard enough to get it almost back up, but not quite. I don't think she has a stitch of underwear on. What makes you so pure, Ms. Turner? I mimic her raspy speaking voice, telling stories to make her laugh and watch her marvelous brown face and perfect teeth in the bounce from the backstage security lights.

"Miami Vice" Johnson runs past in front of our van holding his kid in one arm, a string of excited fans trailing him like the tail of a comet. I finish up someone's warm beer and put my head on Rogers's shoulder and shut my eyes. I see the two hairs on Tina's bosom, and the little map of hairs stuck to the youthful Christ-like face of the Irish singer from U2.

At this writing, a month and a half after the concert, I still feel as I did then, that time and the actions of people in the entertainment business will determine if Live Aid, as a day of sharing, was a one shot affair. I hope that the singers and dancers of that glorious July 13th circus are willing to share again and again, and not always wait around for an appearance in the big tent. I ask for the politicization of people, when it should be enough that they are willing to share a little. Perhaps I always ask too much.

# 9
## "GULF WINDS"

My mother is sitting at the far end of the pool, in the shade. My father is perched at the edge of the pool in the sun, and I am facing him with one leg dangling in the water. They separated ten years ago and have had a better relationship (in my opinion) ever since. I listen while he thinks out loud, and I think about his life.

He lives on a marsh, an ecological reserve. He is surrounded by funky little houses all built on water and mud and indestructible pickleweed. The only way to get to his front door is by a long, weather-beaten boardwalk. The people who pass him are all his friends. His other friends are people who fly in from all around the world to visit him: his wife, his daughters, the ducks, the great blue heron, the snowy white egret, the willet, and the grackle. The grackle makes a melancholy sound, he says, which made him sad at first.

A frog leaps off the edge of the pool and swims expertly to the bottom.

My father did some of the earliest work on X-ray microscopy and was one of the pioneers in X-ray holography. He taught at Stanford, Harvard, and The Open University at Buckinghamshire, England. The work with UNESCO in Baghdad began his deep involvement in science education in underdeveloped countries. The list of committees he has chaired and movies he has made in the field of science teaching easily runs a page. He added French to his Spanish and English. As he traveled many parts of the world speaking and heading committees, he developed theories about what he considered to be the most pressing issues of the day: population, poverty, pollution, and proliferation of nuclear weapons. Twenty years later, he expounds on the four C's which he says are needed to understand and cure the four P's: curiosity, creativity, competence, and compassion. Today, by the pool, he says that there may not be time to remedy all the damage that the human race has caused the earth.

He is talking about the fast bang and the slow bang. The fast bang is the holocaust, the final meltdown, World War Three. The slow bang is the steady diminution of the earth's resources due to the greed and ignorance of its inhabitants. He thinks the slow bang is the greater threat, as it is probably already in irreversible progress. The fast bang might still be avoided, but the chances are getting slim. As new thoughts form and shift in his mind, the lines in my father's forehead cut deep and corrugate his skin, and the circles under his eyes become disturbingly prominent. In this moment of disquiet, with his shoulders suddenly too small and rounded, he has a crumpled look. His hands are clasped around his shoulders as he speaks. Seeing his usual bouyancy dampened makes me angry. He will not remember, later on, that he used the word "despair."

The sun continues to dance on my father's face.

Now I am thinking that Ronald Reagan is the same age as my father. They have some things in common. They are both young in spirit, buoyant, well-preserved, and optimistic. Beyond that, I can find only outstanding differences.

The President is either ignorant of, or unconcerned by the ills of the world about which my father and I have been speaking. He is particularly immune to any part America may have in engendering these ills, as he dislikes the inconvenience of thinking beyond his own definitions of good-guys/bad-guys, and also doesn't like to be depressed. His pleasant, bumbling demeanor is preferable to the murderous efficiency of Kissinger and Kirkpatrick, but on the other hand, he is involved in the same dark and bloody deeds, all done under the same vast, all-encompassing and convenient banner of anticommunism. He feels that God is on his side, and that he really can do no wrong.

What piques me is how this man and his followers can write off someone like my father. Because of my father's protestations about the raping of the Amazon forests, the pollution of our rivers, the misuse and depletion of natural energy, and the poisoning of our children's air, people like my father are explained away with the flick of a wrist as a doomsayer, a depressive, a pessimistic liberal.

Looking into my father's intelligent face, I am appalled at where the scholars and men and women of conscience have been relegated in American society. Protesting the four P's does not promote the current trend toward shining new patriotism, whatever that is.

My father doesn't know I am silently comparing them: the short, handsome Mexican scientist who still attends Quaker Meeting, thinks globally, and is preoccupied with the betterment of all people; and the strapping cowboy who reads Louis L'Amour, watches *Rambo* and thinks there is no longer any segregation in Pretoria. Although my father might be flattered by my thoughts, he is much kinder than me and would not revel in them. At the moment he is busy looking for a glow in the ashes of our conversation, and has begun smiling and nodding as he speaks, his perfectly straight row of teeth gleaming bright as those of any Zapata, his eyes shining with an unquashable optimism. He concludes a hopeful thought with an exclamation about the positive forces of nature: "Thank God for the pickleweed!"

You should be in the center of the village, Papa, where all the townspeople go to pay their respects. I would go with them at the close of the day and offer you a bright-colored blanket, a cup of tea, and some of the fine crown jewels you imparted to me at birth. And over tea, I'd tell you how much I have learned from you, and together we'd say a little prayer for the soul of the cowboy.

# EPILOGUE

"And what do you do, Ms. Baez, when you stop traveling and go home, and your life is back to normal?"

Well, there really is no normal, and the things that I do change: study Aikido, take photos, take a dance course, get back into cooking, illustrate a songbook, take on a human rights project—write a book. But there are some friends who have remained constant, who are still living nearby, and whom you should meet.

Old Earl, the convict who befriended David in prison and who finally got out on parole and managed, with our help, to stay out. He drove Gabe to and from school for twelve years, fed the dogs, and did chores around the house and yard. He is now working as a foster grandfather with the severely retarded and handicapped. Earl's twenty-one years in prison left his heart and lungs in bad repair, and I've seen him laid out on the table in the coronary care unit, plugged into a hundred different machines, tubes down his nose, teeth out, cheeks sunken—and two days later, flirting with the nurses in the same unit, improvising songs about how good it is to be alive. He said he'd seen the pearly gates, talked to the angels, shaken his fist at Sister Mary Mathilda, the old nun who whipped him when he was in the orphanage, and told them all he was not ready to join them yet.

Christine, the Catholic British nanny, cook, helper, general facto-tum, was in the Signal Corps in World War II. She helped me raise

Gabe and run the house after Gail left to go to nursing school. I met her in Carmel in 1961 where she was caring for a dying woman in Pebble Beach. I had come to sing for the patient, and the experience had been grueling. Afterward Christine offered me a cup of tea, Constant Comment, to be exact, and we were friends ever after. She worked here at the house until Gabe left for boarding school. When Gabe came home from his first day at a new school as a fifth grader, in his white shorts and T-shirt and a brow of fury, he was clutching a yellow jumprope with red handles and announced that "The fuckers want me to do a *hundred* of these! I can't even do one!" He threw the jumprope in the corner and himself on the rug and proceeded to have a tantrum. Christine breezed past, motioning me not to pay any attention, and later, when Gabe was spent and flopping, scowling, on the couch, she popped into the room and picked up the jumprope. "Oh my! A skipping rope! It's been *yeahs* since I tried one of these. May I have a go?" she said cheerily, letting the rope settle in a nice loop. As Gabe was nodding consent, she proceeded to skip right there in the living room, exclaiming gleefully at every hop. A half-hour later I heard a hesitant but persistent thumping, punctuated with swear words, out on the veranda, and a few minutes later a rosy Gabe appeared for dinner. "I did twenty-five," he announced.

She and I still call each other on Sunday nights to discuss the miserable status of culture in the United States, the glories, in contrast, of Masterpiece Theater, plus any new and brilliant ideas for finding me the "right" man, which we have both conceded is an impossible task.

Jeanne lives fifteen minutes away. Over the last fifteen years she has acted as my personal financial manager, tour manager, director of Humanitas, aide, guide, advisor on just about everything, and compassionate friend. At the moment she is struggling to make some sense out of my financial affairs. In some ways Jeanne knows me, as the expression goes, better than I know myself. We laugh about ending up in wheelchairs on the same front porch, only she doesn't really think it's very funny because she'd rather end up in a wheelchair on a wonderful husband's front porch. We pull each other up out of our mid-life depressions, bolster each others' spirits, go out to dinner, go to the movies, and wonder what it would be like in the world without each other, knowing that we will probably not find out until one of us keels over dead.

Mom lives twenty minutes away. We chat on the phone often

during the week. She brings me ginger ale and pretzels when I'm ill, and calls me when something wonderful is on public television, like a child violinist performing Brahms, or an English mystery unfolding. And she puts a coat over her nightgown and drives over in the night when I need comfort and strength.

Libby is a schoolteacher who helped me find the new school for Gabe. She, too, is always there for a cup of tea, a diet cookie, a morale boost, the 4 a.m. phone call, and some wise words about childrearing.

Ira works at Kepler's Bookstore where I visit him when I need to hear his caustic opinions on world affairs. Ira still gives me the truest perspective of what is *really* going on in the world, and is a constant reminder of what nonviolence is supposed to mean in the face of the terrible inhumanity that surrounds us. He doesn't hold out much hope for the salvation or even survival of the human race, and I tend to agree with him. Unlike Ginetta, he doesn't give a good goddam about leaving diplomatic doors open. He says what he thinks and doesn't worry about being on anybody's popularity list. But somehow, after thirty years, he is still on mine.

Ginetta and I meet frequently. We both miss Europe. Once she admitted to me that she was feeling down. When I asked her what I might bring her, she said sweets. So I took her two almond croissants, a pear popover, and two kiwi and cherry custard tarts. We sat and gorged and laughed and soon she was her old self, hatching up plans for me. "Let's see. Why you don't geeve a fundraiser with Pavarotti at Lincoln Center?" . . .

Gail, after a six-year sojourn with an Indian guru, came to her senses and is continuing her work as a nurse. She is especially talented in working with the dying, the very ill, and ill children. She works all wards, including cystic fibrosis, which she has done for many years. She is also the most talented person at helping me with my lingering phobias. Because of her practical nurses training, her own multitude of neuroses, and her knowledge of me and how I function, she can calm me back to sanity with a combination of compassion, common sense, medical know-how, and hypnosis.

There is Claire, my dancing and joking buddy. She does drug counseling and crisis intervention. We have cappuccinos together when she's taking a break between what she refers to as her "victims." I think her high success rate with her "victims" must come from her ability to get them laughing.

I escape as often as possible to Carmel, to that superb community of people who adopted Michael and me more than twenty-five years ago. There is no more beautiful place on earth, nor more loving and stimulating and appealing friends.

My most important "old people" not thus far mentioned are Francis Heisler's widow, Friedy, now in her eighties (more cups of tea and talk about Europe), and my beloved Mairi Foreman, now eighty-seven. The last time I saw her (she lives in Puerto Rico and has survived her husband by fifteen years), I said, "Why, Mairi! Do you realize we've known each other for *twenty-five years?*" and she replied, her beautiful Irish eyes dancing, "Really, darling? Is that all?"

The tiny but able staff at Humanitas absorbs and carries out every request I make, over and above putting out a newsletter and keeping up projects and programs in human rights, disarmament and nonviolent education. In the last few years I have called upon them to organize a march to protest the United States' bombing of Libya (coordinating with other peace groups we gathered eight hundred people in one city and more than a thousand in another) and to write an open letter with me to South African newspapers in support of Bishop Tutu's nonviolent actions, signed by Lech Walesa, Corazon Aquino, Kim Dae Jung, Mairead Corrigan, Adolfo Perez Esquivel and others. We managed to return Irina Grinina, a Russian dissident in exile, to Moscow for proper health care in time for the birth of her baby. We did so by sending ar appeal from Coretta King, Rosalynn Carter, and myself to the authorities—and to the press. We continue to send off protests against the contra's intervention in Nicaragua and human rights abuses everywhere. In 1986 we received an invitation for me to sing a concent in Reykjavik during "The Summit." I said yes, left the details to the office, and ended up singing a televised concert called "The People's Summit," which showed live on Saturday evening and again on Sunday at the request of the Icelandic public.

I am proud of what Humanitas has accomplished since its inception in 1979; although I cannot always work closely with it on each and every project, it gives me great comfort to know that Humanitas is still constantly at work on the issues that are so important to me.

Today Gabe brought some friends home for lunch. They tumbled in the door, he and his best buddy and two eighties-looking high school girls: beautiful Julie with the extravagant cascading blond hair, winsome blue eyes, Julie Christie nose and perfect teeth, and her black leather jacket over a black T-shirt with heavy metal logo; and a new girl, Michelle, as dark as Julie is light, with short, punkish, moussed hair, brown with a reddish dye, heavy eye makeup, sparkling dangle earrings, shiny bracelets, and a devilish smile; handsome Gabe, with his foot-long hair in a ponytail and a three-week beard, black undershirt beneath his leather jacket; and his friend Arie, short and swift on his feet, a little outlaw who today brings me rare wild mushrooms and some honey from his father's own bees. When I sit and joke with them I feel blessed. I love to be with Children of the Eighties, in all their sweetness, beauty, turmoil, and vulnerability. I hope that, long after Gabe is gone from this house, kids will still visit me.

There are my dancing and drinking buddies from the local Pioneer Saloon, a good ol' bar built in 1880, with stained glass windows and a minuscule dance floor on which I learned the Texas swing. My able dance teachers and partners (whose girlfriends usually share them without a grumble) are: Rick, lean, lanky and blond, who wears a white cowboy hat; Jim, dark-whiskered and dangerous (not really), who wears a black one; Dennis, very short with a huge beard that fans out over his chest like a skirt, wearing no hat; and Big Al, a Vietnam veteran, who sports his black hat covered with sixties buttons, and a frozen logger beard. He was in Okinawa all the way back in 1963, has a front tooth missing, and lives in his truck. You'll find us all there on a night when the California Cowboys are playing, stomping and ya-hooing and twirling each other into a steaming lather to the strains of a fiddle hoedown.

And I dream of my castle in Canisy, Normandy. Cher Ami is married now and lives a few towns away. The count is turning forty and his friends are throwing a grand party for him at the castle.

Two weeks from when I write this last little episode of my book, I am taking Gabe and getting on a plane. We will leave on a Thursday, using up all my bonus flying miles, and fly to Paris. I'm going to take the black velvet dress and the rhinestones (the ones from the fantasy, remember?) and the robe Pauline made me and some fur-lined boots, and Gabe will take a tuxedo. We'll arrive in Canisy on Friday evening. There will be musicians playing in the Rose Room, like the first time I ever saw Canisy. By Saturday afternoon every bedroom will be filled, there will be fires in all the fireplaces, and the champagne and wine and Calvados will flow all night long. The party will not end until sometime Sunday, when Gabe and I will drive back to Paris and board a plane for home. When we stumble into our house fifteen hours later, Mom will have a fire going in the kitchen and perhaps a Brahms trio on the stereo. Gabe will fall into bed, and I will sit in front of the fire, dressed like a Spanish princess, telling Mom how the sun rose, piercing through the mist over the lake as I watched in absolute silence from the immense bedroom window, and how there was peace all around as the castle finally slept.

# Acknowledgments

I wish to thank Nancy Lutzow for her tireless help in researching the many obscure questions put to her by editors, lawyers, and myself; Manny Greenhill for supplying numerous details pertaining to, and photographs taken during 1959-1975; my mother, for emptying her files onto the living room rug and helping choose photographs, childhood drawings, high school papers, and personal letters; my father for the loan of photos from his files; Arthur Samuelson for prodding, encouraging, listening, cutting and pasting; Steve Jobs for forcing me to use a word processor by putting one in my kitchen; and the many friends and relatives who helped refresh my memory or supply information I'd long forgotten.